W9-BHP-434

MODERN FEMINISMS

Political, Literary, Cultural

Gender and Culture
Carolyn G. Heilbrun and
Nancy K. Miller, Editors

GENDER AND CULTURE
A SERIES OF COLUMBIA UNIVERSITY PRESS
Edited by Carolyn G. Heilbrun and Nancy K. Miller

In Dora's Case: Freud, Hysteria, Feminism
Edited by Charles Bernheimer and Claire Kahane

Breaking the Chain: Women, Theory and French Realist Fiction
Naomi Schor

Between Men: English Literature and Male Homosocial Desire
Eve Kosofsky Sedgwick

Romantic Imprisonment: Women and Other Glorified Outcasts
Nina Auerbach

The Poetics of Gender
Edited by Nancy K. Miller

Reading Woman: Essays in Feminist Criticism
Mary Jacobus

Honey-Mad Women: Emancipatory Strategies in Women's Writing
Patricia Yeager

Subject to Change: Reading Feminist Writing
Nancy K. Miller

Thinking Through the Body
Jane Gallop

Gender and the Politics of History
Joan Wallach Scott

Dialogic and Difference: "An/Other Woman" in Virginia Woolf
and Christa Wolf
Anne Hermann

Plotting Women: Gender and Representation in Mexico
Jean Franco

Inspiriting Influences: Tradition, Revision, and
Afro-American Women's Novels
Michael Awkward

Hamlet's Mother and Other Women
Carolyn G. Heilbrun

Rape and Representation
Edited by Lynn A. Higgins and Brenda R. Silver

Shifting Scenes: Interviews on Women, Writing, and Politics
in Post-68 France
Edited by Alice A. Jardine and Anne M. Menke

Tender Geographies: Women and the Origins of
the Novel in France
Joan de Jean

MODERN FEMINISMS
Political, Literary, Cultural

Edited and Introduced by
Maggie Humm

COLUMBIA UNIVERSITY PRESS

NEW YORK

Columbia University Press
New York
Copyright © 1992 Columbia University Press
All rights reserved

Library of Congress Number: 92-12604

ISBN 0–231–08072–7
ISBN 0–231–08073–5 (paperback)

Published in Great Britain under the title *Feminisms: A READER*

Casebound editions of Columbia University Press books
are printed on permanent and durable acid-free paper.

Printed and bound in Great Britain

c 10 9 8 7 6 5 4 3 2 1

Contents

Preface

The basic premise of this anthology is that, in this century, it is feminism which represents *the* major change in social thinking and politics because only feminism *radically* questions our understanding of 'men' and 'women' and the social structures which maintain their differences.

Modern Feminisms is an interdisciplinary reader containing extracts from a wide range of past and present feminist writers, many of which are collected together for the first time. It aims to provide within the covers of a single book a selection of some of the important ideas of Western feminism.

While including writing from well-known feminists such as Adrienne Rich and Kate Millett, *Modern Feminisms* aims to encapsulate the diversity of feminist views – about race, sexuality, language and creativity, politics and class – and the many challenging feminist questions about the continued subordination of women.

The collection does not pretend to be representative of the *whole* spectrum of feminism. Inevitably one effect of the years needed to collect multiple individual author, publisher and translator permissions and clear American, British and French rights, not to mention Japanese and the Phillipine rights, is my inattention to newer developments such as ecofeminism, and feminist writing about theology and about technology. In addition, the collection is theory and not practice orientated; academic and not movement based; first world and not third world directed.

Modern Feminisms is a collection of some aspects of Western feminist thinking. I hope to co-edit a second and larger volume of feminist thinking from outside that diurnity. I have attempted to display the excitement of feminism and the debates which keep it alive by offering a very general map of first and second wave feminisms. In addition the book is organised into some of the major areas in feminist thinking. Before each debate I offer a brief summary of the main issues and before each extract a brief introduction to the ideas of each writer with suggestions for further reading. Editorial comment has been kept deliberately brief in order to give as much space as possible to the source material.

In Britain, Women's Studies proliferates in higher education, non-degree work in further and adult education and schools, thanks to the hard and pioneering work of women teachers and the Women's Studies Network (UK), yet in 1992 the Polytechnic of East London is the first and currently only institution in Britain offering a *full* degree in Women's Studies. The absence of Women's Studies as an undergraduate area of study goes along with the absence in Britain of any full collection of feminist thought. (The very different, and expansive model of American Women's Studies is highlighted in Chapter 17, Feminism and education.)

Some anthologies have already appeared, for example, Sneja Gunew's *A Reader in Feminist Knowledge* (Routledge, 1991) and while welcome and valuable these are often discipline bound, or address only *current* feminist theory and seem pitched at graduates with a high level of feminist knowledge.

What is not absent, of course, in the academy or outside it are women of disparate ages, ethnicities and sexualities who have a high level of interest in other women and are eager to know about the whole spread of feminist knowledge. This book is for them. It is for young women who may never have heard of Kate Millett, for instance, and want a book which clarifies the immense volume and diversity of thought and ideas which have come out of Women's Liberation. It is for black women and women of colour for whom the category of 'black feminism' is itself a challenge to the homogeneity associated with white writing. It is for black lesbian and white lesbian women who know that heterosexual feminists often emphasise the institutions which oppress *them* – glass ceilings – but who often cannot 'see' how they benefit from the institution of 'compulsory heterosexuality'. It is for Marxist and socialist women, black and white, who understand the economics underpinning students' need for cheap, accessible and comprehensive books in a country which allows only 20 per cent of 18-year-olds into higher education and deprives them of the money and the support to keep them there. Therefore, most of all, this *Modern Feminisms* is for my students whose responses to some of this material helped to change my own.

I would like to thank the authors here in this volume and not only to acknowledge them in the conventional way. It was their letters of permission, often adding best wishes and good luck, wanting to know more about British Women's Studies, dialoguing with my ideas, and praising the volume which sustained me through the horrendous task of clearing rights and permissions. I must thank Jackie Jones of Harvester Wheatsheaf for her commitment to this project and for her splendid and professional editing skill, and the careful readers of the manuscript.

The book is dedicated to my students who are my constant source of stimulation but it could not have been edited without the interest and support of my son Dan Humm, my keenest and best critic. *Modern Feminisms* could not have appeared at all without the careful and expert work of Joyce Lock.

List of Abbreviations

CR   Consciousness raising

ERA   Equal Rights Amendment

NAWSA   National American Women's Suffrage Association

NOW   National Organisation of Women

NUWSS   National Union of Women's Suffrage Societies

OWAAD   Organisation of Women of African and Asian Descent

WFL   Women's Freedom League

WILPF   Women's International League for Peace and Freedom

WLM   Women's Liberation Movement

WPU   Women's Political Union

SWPU   Women's Social and Political Union

Chronology of events and texts from 1900 to the present

	Feminist politics	Feminist writing
1903	Women's Social and Political Union, Britain (WSPU) founded by Pankhursts.	
1904	Hubertine Auclert tears up Code Napoleon at Vêndome Column.	
1905–7	Suffrage struggles, Russia.	
1908	Congress of Russian women.	
1910	Feminist demonstrations during Mexican revolution. Second Conference of Socialist Women, Germany when Clara Zetkin names 8 March International Women's day.	
1911	Seitoscha (Blue Stockings) an independent feminist group formed in Japan	Olive Schreiner: *Woman and Labour*
1912	Teresita dei Bonifatti's pacifist campaign Milan, Italy.	
1913		Rebecca West: 'The Life of Emily Davison'; 'Mr Chesterton in Hysterics'.
1914	Congressional Union, later the American Women's Party founded by Alice Paul.	
1917	Muslim Women's Conference, India calls for abolition of polygamy.	
1919	National Union of Societies for Equal Citizenship, Britain formed.	

	Feminist politics	Feminist writing
1921	British Six Point Group founded.	
1923	Egyptian Feminist Union founded by Huda el-Sha'arawi. Equal Rights Amendment proposed to American Congress.	
1926		Winifred Holtby: 'Feminism Divided'.
1927		Vera Brittain: 'Why Feminism Lives'.
1928		Ray Strachey: *The Cause*.
1929		Virginia Woolf: *A Room of One's Own*.
1938		Virginia Woolf: *Three Guineas*.
1942	Death of Franciska Plamnikova founder of Czech feminism in a concentration camp.	
1944	Egyptian Feminist Party founded by Fatma Nimat Rashid and Doria Shafik's Bint-el-Nil Movement.	
1949	Rachel Kagan, first feminist elected to Israeli Knesset.	Simone de Beauvoir: *The Second Sex*.
1951	1,500 women storm Egyptian Parliament.	
1956	Women's hunger strikes cause granting of suffrage, Egypt	
1963		Betty Friedan: *The Feminine Mystique*.
1966	National Women's Organisation (NOW) founded in America.	Juliet Mitchell: *Women: The Longest Revolution*.
1968	First equal pay strike in Britain (Ford sewing machinists). May/June mass student/worker strikes (France). Demonstration at Miss America pageant. Man-Vrouw-Maatschappij (Men-Women-Society) founded in Netherlands.	
1969	Juliet Mitchell teaches Britain's first Women's Studies course at London's Anti-University.	Redstockings' *Manifesto* (New York).

Feminist politics	Feminist writing
1970 Monique Wittig, Rochefort and other women place wreath dedicated to 'Unknown wife of the Soldier' on tomb of Unknown Soldier, Paris. MLF becomes name of French Women's Liberation Movement. Britain's first Women's Liberation Conference, Ruskin College, Oxford. Disruption of Miss World contest, London. Irish Women's Liberation Movement founded. Dolle Mina founded in Netherlands.	Anne Koedt: *The Myth of the Vaginal Orgasm.* Germaine Greer: *The Female Eunuch.* Kate Millett: *Sexual Politics.* Shulamith Firestone: *The Dialectic of Sex.* Mary Sherfey: 'A Theory on Female Sexuality'. 'Personal is Political' coined by Carol Hanisch.
1971 First National Women's conference, Frankfurt Germany.	Adrienne Rich: 'When We Dead Awaken'.
1972 First Women's Refuge opened (Chiswick, London) 41 organisations found Black Women's Federation in South Africa.	Joyce Ladner: *Tomorrow's Tomorrow.* Phyllis Chesler: *Women and Madness.* Sherry Ortner: 'Is Female to Male as Nature is to Culture'.
1973 Indian 'Chipko' movement tie their bodies to trees. First Black British Women's Group founded – Brixton. First British Women's Theatre Festival.	Sheila Rowbotham: *Woman's Consciousness, Man's World.*
1974 Simone de Beauvoir founds Ligue Francoise pour le droit des femmes. First British National Lesbian Conference. Working Women's Charter and TUC Women's Rights Conference.	Adrienne Rich: 'Toward a Woman-Centered University'. Juliet Mitchell: *Psychoanalysis and Feminism.* Luce Irigaray: *Speculum de l'autre femme.* Dorothy Smith: 'Women's Perspective'. Sheila Rowbotham: 'Search and Subject, Threading Circumstance'. Gayle Rubin: 'The Traffic in Women'.
1975 Women's International Year British National Abortion Campaign founded. Virago launched.	Hélène Cixous: 'Le Rire de la Médusa'. Carroll Smith-Rosenberg: 'The Female World of Love and Ritual'.

Feminist politics	Feminist writing
1975 (cont.) Wages for Housework demonstrations. First Women's Liberation Conference Spain.	Susan Brownmiller: *Against Our Will.* Laura Mulvey: 'Visual Pleasure and Narrative Cinema'.
1976 UN Decade for Women (1975–85). Britain's first Rape Crisis Centre. American Women Against Violence in Pornography and Media founded.	Adrienne Rich: *Of Woman Born.* Dorothy Dinnerstein: *The Mermaid and the Minotaur.* Jean Baker Miller: *Toward A New Psychology of Women.* Joan Kelly-Gadol: 'The Social Relation of the Sexes'. Heidi Hartmann: 'Capitalism, Patriarchy and Job Segregation by Sex'.
1977 Northern Ireland Peace Women awarded Nobel Prize. Reclaim the Night first demonstrations. USA National Women's Conference, Houston with 20,000 delegates. Israeli Women's Party founded by Marcia Freedman.	Barbara Smith: *Toward a Black Feminist Criticism.* Julia Kristeva: *Desire in Language.* Luce Irigaray: *Ce sexe qui n'en est pas un.*
1978 Chilean women's *arpilleras* woven, over which women pour blood symbolically. AWAZ first British Asian Women's Group. OWAAD (Organisation of Women of Asian and African descent) formed.	Susan Griffin: *Woman and Nature.* Audre Lorde: 'Uses of the Erotic'. Nancy Chodorow: *The Reproduction of Mothering.* Combahee River Collective: 'A Black Feminist Statement'. Mary Daly: *Gyn/Ecology.*
1979 Canadian Feminist Party founded. 15,000 women seize the Palace of Justice, Teheran. First TUC demonstration in support of feminism – National Abortion Campaign. Leeds Revolutionary Feminist Lesbian declaration. First picket of Armagh Irish Women's Prison. Partido Feminista de España (Feminist Party) formed in Spain.	Elaine Showalter: 'Towards a Feminist Poetics'. Julia Kristeva: 'Le Temps des Femmes'. Carol Gilligan: 'Woman's Place in Man's Life Cycle'. 'Political Lesbianism'. Gerda Lerner: *The Majority Finds Its Past.* Heidi Hartmann: 'The Unhappy Marriage of Marxism and Feminism'.

Feminist politics

Feminist writing

1980

Brazilian women's graffiti campaign against sexual violence.
Women Against Pornography March, New York: 71,000 women. United Nations World Conference on Women. Pentagon encircled by thousands of women.
British Women Against Violence Against Women founded.
Judy Chicago's *The Dinner Party* opens in San Francisco.
National Front for the Liberation and Rights of Women founded, Mexico.

Adrienne Rich: 'Compulsory Heterosexuality and Lesbian Existences'.
Michèle Barrett: *Women's Oppression Today.*
Ros Coward: 'Are Women's Novels Feminist Novels?.
Sarah Kofman: *L'Enigme de la femme.*
Rachel Blau DuPlessis: 'For the Etruscans'.
Audre Lorde: 'An Open Letter to Mary Daly'.

1981

Greenham Common Women's Peace Camp.
National Women's Strike, Holland against Abortion Law.
Australian women anti-rape demonstrations.
Migrant women's strike, Kortex Textiles Australia.

Angela Davis: *Women, Race and Class.*
Andrea Dworkin *Pornography.*
Zillah Eisenstein: *The Radical Future of Liberal Feminism.*
Susan Griffin: *Pornography and Silence.*
Rosario Morales: 'I Am What I Am'.
Gloria Anzaldúa: *'La Prieta'.*
Mitsuye Yamada: 'Asian Pacific American Women and Feminism'.

1982

30,000 women encircle Greenham Common Camp.
Outwrite British Black Women's Paper launched.
GLC establish the first Women's Committee.

Gloria Hull and Barbara Smith: 'The Politics of Black Women's Studies'.
Evelyn Fox Keller: 'Gender and Science'.
Zillah Eisenstein: 'The Sexual Politics of the New Right'.
Carol Gilligan: *In A Different Voice.*
Catharine Mackinnon: 'Feminism, Marxism, Method and the State'.

1983

Women surround missile base Comiso, Italy.
Feminists organise candlelight vigil to protest gang rape, New Bedford, Mass.

Marcia Westkott: 'Women's studies as a strategy for change'.
Charlotte Bunch: *Learning Our Way.*
Alice Walker: *In Search of Our Mothers' Gardens.*

	Feminist politics	Feminist writing
1984	Tens of thousands of Iceland women in 24-hour strike to protest at discrimination. Second Equal Pay Strike by Ford Sewing Machinists. Women Against Pit Closures founded. Argentinian women protest 'the disappeared'. First National Women's Conference, Taiwan. Kadin Cevresi (Women's Circle) founded in Turkey.	Sara Ruddick: 'Preservative Love'. Gayle Rubin: 'Thinking Sex: Notes for a Radical Theory of the Politics of Sexuality'. Teresa de Lauretis: *Alice Doesn't*. Amina Mama: Black Women, the Economic Crisis and the British State'.
1985	South African Women hold National Consumer boycott. 15,000 people tie ribbon 15 miles long around the Pentagon.	Gisela Ecker: *Feminist Aesthetics*. Rosalind Petchesky: *Abortion*.
1986	National Pro-Abortion marches in Washington and Los Angeles. Women Rising in Resistance reclaim the Statue of Liberty. First Conference of Arab feminists, Arab Women's Solidarity Association founded.	
1987	Mass demonstrations by Palestine women in occupied territories. Katya Komisaruk destroyed missile guidance computers at Vandenburg Air Force Base.	Sandra Harding: 'Epistemological Questions'. Griselda Pollock: 'Feminism and Modernism'.
1988	Palestinian women protest with their bodies in occupied territories.	
1989	Women Against Fundamentalism 6 May launched to challenge fundamentalism in all religions. Independent Women's Federation of East Germany founded.	Amina Mama: 'Violence Against Black Women'.
1990	Feminist Network and Szegedi (women's organisations) founded, Hungary. Movement for the Emancipation of Women in Bohemia and Moravia founded.	
1991	Women's Strike 14 June, Swiss TUC Nationwide Women's Strike.	

1 □ History of feminism in Britain and America

Introduction

□ The first idea that is likely to occur in the course of any historical thinking about feminism is that feminism is a *social* force. The emergence of feminist ideas and feminist politics depends on the understanding that, in all societies which divide the sexes into differing cultural, economic or political spheres, women are less valued than men. Feminism also depends on the premise that women can consciously and collectively change their social place. While many languages do not have a noun 'feminism', and 'feminism' as a term for the politics of equal rights for women did not come into English use until the 1890s, the word feminism can stand for a belief in sexual equality combined with a commitment to eradicate sexist domination and to transform society. So that while most writers agree that in Britain feminism, as a group of political and social movements, probably dates from the seventeenth century, feminism as a body of answers to the 'question of woman' has a more diffuse and considerably more long-standing existence.

The *feminisms* that constitute 'feminism' – from social reform and suffrage campaigns through to academic feminist theory – are not indistinct. A broad frame is needed to encompass political activism as well as theory; to enclose feminist grass roots initiatives, the circling of Greenham Common missile base by 30,000 women in 1982, the suffragette banners, the disruption of Miss America pageants, and protests against dowry deaths in India, as well as organised strikes and movements.

With its slogan 'the personal is political', first written by Carol Hanisch (1970), it is contemporary feminism which recognises that politics is too diverse to be contained in the tightly boundaried categories of political parties. It is small collective groups known as consciousness-raising groups (CR), direct action, and radical campaigns which have shaped the political themes of contemporary feminism, not elected politicians. For example, extra-parliamentary tactics include the creation of alternative institutions (Women's Aid), alternative political processes (networking), and alternative political cultures (Greenham pacifism).

1

Yet feminism is shaped too both by the cultural, legal and economic policies of particular societies in which it forms, as well as by the politics of reforming movements which it outgrew.

The first public declarations which describe 'women' as a distinct social category with unequal social status date from before Aphra Behn. A clear example is the eighteenth-century document by Mary Astell, *Some Reflections Upon Marriage* (1700). Organised feminism entered the arena of public politics in America and in Britain in the 1840s with suffrage petitions to Parliament and campaigns for greater legislative equality such as the Married Women's Property Act. Suffragism's success in winning the vote, in 1918 in Britain with a limited franchise and universal suffrage in 1920 in America, narrowed to 'welfare feminism' in the 1930s, 1940s and 1950s with campaigns for family allowances (Britain) and legal equalities (American League of Women). It was in the 1960s that militant feminism, or Women's Liberation, created a new politics out of Marxist and socialist feminisms, radical feminism and other multifarious responses to the question of why women continued to suffer social inequality, exploitation and oppression.

In the short view, if contemporary feminism is marked by its innovatory language ('oppression', 'liberation'), its innovatory practices (CR groups) and its innovatory campaigns around issues of rape, 'battery' and child sexual abuse, including the WSPU Abortion Campaigns started in 1911, it is true that both nineteenth- and twentieth-century feminisms share an urgent desire for equal rights and equal opportunities for women. And in the long view it could be argued that feminist history might stretch from Neolithic matriarchies to contemporary radical feminism, apparent, for example, in Mary Daly's book *Gyn/Ecology* (1978), since the sweep of history gathers myriad forms of 'feminisms'.

America

□ In the 1840s feminism began to grow into a substantial political force in America. The women's rights movement led by Elizabeth Cady Stanton and Susan B. Anthony had its origins in their anti-slavery and temperance campaigns. The exclusion of women delegates, including Stanton, from the World Anti-Slavery Convention held in London in 1840, resulted in the famous Seneca Falls Convention of 1848 and its Declaration of Sentiments which sought to apply the principles of the American Declaration of Independence to women. When the alliance between feminism and the anti-slavery movement began to dissolve, following the nominal enfranchisement of blacks but not women after the American Civil War, Anthony and Stanton founded the National Woman Suffrage Association while Lucy Stone created the more conservative American Woman's Suffrage Association. While Anthony and

Stanton added economic demands such as protective legislation to their suffrage platform in their Working Women's Association and to their 6,000 signature petition to the New York legislature, Stone tackled divorce law reform.

The suffrage movement inspired other organisations such as the International Council of Women, founded in Washington DC in 1888 – the oldest and largest feminist organisation in the world. Both suffrage organisations merged in 1890 to form the National American Woman's Suffrage Association (NAWSA) which gained the support of suffrage activists like Alice Paul who returned from Britain to found the Congressional Union, later the Woman's Party in 1914 and the daughter of Mrs Stanton, Harriet Stanton Blatch who founded the Equality League in 1907. In addition there was a groundswell of socialist feminism perhaps best represented by the settlement movement and by Charlotte Perkins Gilman and her argument, in The Man-Made World (1911), that women should be economically independent from men. When Carrie Chapman Catt took over the leadership of NAWSA (now the League of Women Voters), NAWSA petitions, the state-by-state campaigns and the militant actions of the Woman's Party such as special suffrage trains and anti-Woodrow Wilson demonstrations, resulted in the Nineteenth Amendment of 1920 which gave women the vote.

Legal advances of women in the 1920s and 1930s scattered the possibility of a single suffrage identity of American feminism. The Woman's Party proposed equal rights amendments in order to enforce federal equality which were opposed by the League of Women Voters. While 'welfare feminism' was the aim of New Deal feminist anti-poverty campaigns, pacifist feminists with Jane Addams formed the Woman's Peace Party, later the Women's International League for Peace and Freedom at the 1915 International Congress. But it was the Equal Rights Amendment (ERA), first proposed to Congress in 1923 by the Woman's Party as an amendment to the constitution: 'Men and women shall have equal rights throughout the United States and every place subject to its jurisdiction', which eventually became a focus for the new feminist movements of the late 1960s.

When the Women's Liberation Movement (WLM) emerged in the late 1960s, it was shaped both by its similarity to first wave feminism in the way that both grew out of their limited roles in Black Rights movements (Civil Rights and Anti-Slavery) and also by changes in the political order brought about by that earlier feminism. For example in 1964, the criterion of sex was added to Title 7 of the Civil Rights Act, which prohibited discrimination in employment, and the Act was enforced by an Equal Opportunity Commission.

In other ways Women's Liberation was radically different. Women's Liberation extended the terms 'politics' and 'the economy' to sexuality, the body and emotions, and other areas of social life previously treated as 'personal' only, and the household. The movement also created new political organisations – small anti-hierarchical consciousness-raising groups, organised and acting independently of men with a preference for direct action and alternative living patterns.

The core of WLM, and its socialist and radical heart, grew from: radical groups such as the New York Redstockings whose founding membership included Anne Koedt and Shulamith Firestone; from a concern about reproductive issues (*The Dialectic of Sex*, 1970) and the ubiquity of patriarchy (*Sexual Politics*, 1970); from the first women's studies programmes such as Naomi Weisstein's seminar at the Free University of Chicago in 1967; and from direct actions such as the 1968 Miss America demonstration when bras were trashed (but not burnt).

Another crucial stimulus was the appearance of Betty Friedan's *The Feminine Mystique* (1963), which describes the frustrations of white heterosexual middle-class women without careers, locked into domesticity, and Friedan's founding of the National Organisation of Women (NOW) in 1966. NOW adopted a reformist agenda advocating educational and legal change but, following its 1970 strike for abortion on demand, 24-hour nurseries and equal opportunities, NOW added abortion and gay rights to its platform at the 1977 NOW conference at Houston. The Equal Rights Amendment Campaign, supported by NOW, gathered together a large number of women's organisations to fight for state-by-state ratification until the amendment expired in 1982. This campaign radicalised a wide spectrum of American women. Similarly, by the 1990s campaigns such as Women Against Pornography and Women Against Violence Against Women, Bernice Reagon's 'coalition politics', AIDS activism, Third World Women Against Violence, and the National Coalition of Black Gays, gained support across America so that the women's movement has continued to grow in spite of New Right pro-family campaigns and Republican anti-women budgets.

Britain

□ Although feminist ideas date from before Aphra Behn, the first full political argument for women's rights in Britain is Mary Wollstonecraft's *A Vindication of the Rights of Woman* (1792). Wollstonecraft based her argument on an analysis of the psychological and economic damage done to women from a forced dependence on men and exclusion from the public sphere. Although Chartists and Owenites did hold suffrage discussions it was not until the 1850s that feminism was recognised in public politics in Britain. Josephine Butler's campaigns against the Contagious Diseases Acts of 1864 (which required medical examinations of women suspected to be prostitutes) highlighted women's legal inferiority. In 1856 Barbara Leigh-Smith Bodichon's *A Brief Summary in Plain Language of the Most Important Laws Concerning Women* (1854), initiated the campaign for a Married Women's Property Act; and a national group of women, organised through the Langham Place group of feminists, organised a petition to Parliament to widen the electorate. Further Parliamentary debates on electoral reform inspired the founding of the National Society for Women's Suffrage, supported by J. S. Mill whose *The Subjection of Women* (1869), co-authored with his wife Harriet Taylor, is regarded as a classic liberal argument for equal rights. By the turn of the century Labour women, women in the arts, the Women's Cooperative Guild (1882), with its 18,000 members, and other suffrage groups were combined in the National Union of Women's Suffrage Societies (NUWSS). There were also radical working-class feminists, for example the Women's Protective and Provident League (1874) which opposed protective legislation for women and the exploitation of women workers. But it was the founding of the Women's Social and Political Union (WSPU) in 1903, by Emmeline Pankurst and her daughters, which has become the best known organisation of first wave feminism although equally important were the NUWSS and the Women's Freedom League (WFL). By 1908 a WSPU open-air meeting in Hyde Park attracted between a quarter and half a million people, and NUWSS events similarly engaged large numbers of people. Feminism's continued high public profile, militancy and shrewd political campaigning, together with the combined effects of the WSPU, the WFL and the NUWSS ensured that with the end of the First World War, at least a limited franchise would be considered for women aged over 30 (1918).

First wave feminism, then, was a long-lasting, highly diverse movement stretching from before the liberalism of Mary Wollstonecraft to the militant activism of Edwardian feminism.

The NUWS became the National Union of Societies for Equal Citizenship in 1919 and by the 1920s and 1930s its energy was devoted to the political education of women. It joined the Women's Cooperative Guild, the Women's Labour League and the Six Point Group in 1921. In that group's six objectives: equal pay, widows' pensions, equal rights of guardianship, laws on child assault, equal civil service opportunities, and provision for unmarried mothers. These early decades of the twentieth century saw divisions between 'old' feminists, such as Ray Strachey, who wanted to end protective legislation, and 'new' feminists, such as Eleanor Rathbone, who campaigned for the 'endowment of motherhood' and family allowances. These were the decades of: campaigns for equal pay, for example, the annual resolutions at Labour Women's conferences; pacifist feminism in the Women's International League for Peace and Freedom (WILPF); and the anti-fascist activism of a wide variety of feminist women.

In 1968 the uprise of militant feminism which started in America became visible in Britain. The same involvement in, and the same disenchantment with, New Left causes (in Britain the Campaign for Nuclear Disarmament and the Vietnam Solidarity Campaign) marks the British

Women's Liberation Movement as much as its American sister. What was an additional, and uniquely British, inspiration was the impact of the militancy of women workers in the Ford Strike (1968) for equal pay. The first Women's Liberation Conference at Ruskin College Oxford (1970), had over 600 participants, and funnelled socialist and liberation energies into demands for equal pay, 24-hour child care, free contraception, and abortion on demand. Together with its papers *Shrew* (1969), *Spare Rib* (1972), and *WIRES* (1975), the WLM battled to defend women from sexual and domestic violence by founding the innovative battered women's refuges (Chiswick, 1972) and rape crisis centres. The WLM launched campaigns such as Women Against Violence Against Women and Reclaim the Night, and worked to advance employment rights in a Working Women's Charter (1974) supported by the national Trade Union Council. This pursuit of equal opportunities led to the practical affirmative action programmes of the municipal women's committees of which the largest and most successful was that of the Greater London Council (1982). This far-reaching London programme gave over £4.5 million to women's projects until its disbandment in 1986 by the Conservative government.

The vigour which informs British feminism in the 1980s and 1990s comes from black women's groups who challenge the Eurocentrism of white British feminist theory just as black women challenge white feminism in America and just as the WSPU was anti-colonialist and anti-racist, and included black, Indian and Chinese feminists. The Organisation of Women of African and Asian Descent (OWAAD), founded in 1978, attacked racist immigration laws and focused on Third World issues as well as on issues of black British identity at the National Black Women's Conference in Brixton in 1979. Underlying these campaigns were important issues for all feminists of self-identity and commitment evident in the widening activities of WLM which now include, alongside black activism, the Greenham peace actions (from 1981); socialist feminists' links with the traditional Left ('Beyond the Fragments', 1979); reproductive and abortion rights campaigns and lesbian activism around Clause 28 (banning the public advocacy of homosexuality) consolidating earlier lesbian campaigns.

Summary

□ Internationally the 'question of woman' and the growth of feminism is woven together with the history of nationalist movements which are demanding equality and free government. First wave feminism emerged in many countries in similar ways. For example feminist literature and writing, internationally, drew attention to issues of education and emancipation and women's associations emerged from nationalist parties. The International Woman Suffrage Alliance dedicated itself in 1913 to Asian women's emancipation and by the Second World War there were national women's councils in sixteen Third World countries. In the early decades of the twentieth century there were visits of European feminist campaigners to the Third World, for example Ellen Key, Annie Besant and Margaret Sanger while Third World women made reciprocal journeys. For example, many groups and organisations, including Bhikaiji Cama, were active in India and Paris. The domain of second wave feminism has an even wider sway than first wave feminism. Yet Western concepts must not be applied to Third World countries. For example, Western notions of 'public' and 'private' are inappropriate to describe sexual hierarchies in countries where the sexual division of labour cuts across the public/private divide. Feminist campaigns are inevitably shaped by national priorities and national politics.

Feminism is an historically diverse and culturally varied international movement. Its political aims have been endorsed worldwide: in the United Nations Decade for Women 1975–85; at the International Nairobi conference attended by people from 151 UN countries; by the success of abortion and equal rights reforms and Acts prohibiting sexual discrimination. Yet the value of feminism and its radical implications lie as much in its direct actions and the way in which feminist ideas are now part of everyday thinking. Throughout the world there are now many women's publishers, wide coverage of women's issues on television and an ever-growing number of women's health, rape and crisis centres and women's political committees. Women in the Third World have made radical challenges to the whole fabric of political life with demonstrations against the veil and for women's rights in Egypt in 1923, rural demonstrations against rapists in India in the 1980s and mass demonstrations for peace in Palestine and Cyprus. By the 1990s more than 100 women's peace camps had been established including the pioneer camp at Greenham Common, the Italian Comiso, and Pine Gap in Australia. □

PART I □ FROM OLIVE SCHREINER TO THE 'SECOND WAVE'

2 □ First wave feminism

Introduction

□ Twentieth-century feminism winds its course through progressively new identities of 'women'. Campaigns, such as those of the Six Point Group for family allowances and for women's equal material rights, built the base camp which helped contemporary feminists to that more open expanse criss-crossed by radical and socialist feminisms, and challenged and hopefully changed by the impact of black, lesbian and psychoanalytic theory. Most often twentieth-century feminists speak either about the productive work of women, of women's material rights and the lack of these, or feminists put their faith in women's special and different materiality. The grand shape of twentieth-century American and European feminism has grown from first wave feminism to second wave feminism which lays claim to embodied female differences offering new standards for a future feminist universe.

The movement, from a first wave feminism which is principally concerned with equalities, to a second wave feminism which uses women's difference to oppose the 'legalities' of a patriarchal world, is a radical and visionary formation. In the first moment women are objects, sometime victims of mistaken social knowledge. In the second moment women are challenging that 'knowledge' from the strength of their own experience.

In broad terms, twentieth-century feminists choose one of two positions: largely, first wave feminism (which might be said to end with Simone de Beauvoir's *The Second Sex* (1949)) centres on debates about materialism, about women's individual and collective social and political interests and self-determination. In second wave feminism the arguments are concerned with materiality – moral solidarities created by feminist standpoints and identities based on differences which include women's material, psychic and affiliative strengths.

First wave feminism, at least in Britain and America, had a progressive social vision which encompassed suffragism, 'old' and 'new' feminisms, and 'welfare' feminism. It was represented in Britain by the WSPU, WFL, NUWSS, the Women's Cooperative Guild and by the interwar solidarity of the feminist pacifist organisation, the WILPF. These groups believed that women would become full citizens in a transformed international order when the franchise of 1928, equal entry into the professions and into higher education, the gradual elimination of marriage bars in the 1950s, and full access to public, material space as well as the dismantling of international aggression and warfare, would knock down the hurdles to peaceful and equal existence created by male-dominated institutions and practices.

In order for second wave feminism to give voice to a new and autonomous woman citizen, to assert the legitimacy of her different materiality, feminism came to focus on the specifications of women's differences from men and from each other. Thus, second wave feminism turned to psychoanalytic as well as to social theories about gender difference in order to explain such isues as the increase in sexual violence and in order to create a fresh 'feminist' ethics. The making of a new knowledge from the standpoint of women's embodiment involved the writing of a new language – for example the *écriture féminine* of French feminists Hélène Cixous and Luce Irigaray.

These two phases are not necessarily historically distant one from another and they remain dialectically connected. Many contemporary feminists move from one to the other and return. For example, the American feminists Andrea Dworkin and Catharine MacKinnon have pursued their attack on pornography both through psychoanalytic theories of gender identity and by drafting laws defining pornography as a violation of women's civil rights. And of course the pursuit of social and economic *representation* is dependent on the possession of a feminist *consciousness* which can create new social and economic images of women. This is because, as Catharine MacKinnon suggests, 'feminism is the first theory to emerge from those whose interests it affirms' (MacKinnon, 1989: 93). It embodies our bodies.

In the search for egalitarian social relations and ways to change unequal social conditions, first wave feminism together with labour, working women's and anti-colonial organisations, catalogued women's economic oppressions which necessarily entailed claiming that all women should be equal citizens with men. Second wave feminism, because it focuses on the conditions of many groups and on women's everyday 'difference' from men in the street and in the home, makes visible the powerful realities of gender difference.

First wave feminism resembles other political theories because among other concerns it addresses the State. Second wave feminists challenge this traditional understanding of politics by talking instead to other women – in the resonant belief that 'the personal is political'. Some first wave feminists, for example the Six Point Group, believed that the problem of social inequality could be solved institutionally if 'institutions' such as the family ceased to restrict the potential capacities of women. In the view of most second wave feminists, women's inequality is not simply the result of social restrictions but stems from a controlled and organised androcentric network of meanings not all of which are institutionally visible. The belief that patriarchal power is invisible as well as visibly sexist, that it is a dynamic of our daily lives and not merely a dynamic of electoral politics, informs the demands of current feminism. Thus, the great volume of second wave feminist writing is in the sociocultural field. What second wave feminism terms sexual politics, then, are the links between sexual and social violence and gender difference, which feminists counter, as they did in the 1890s, by creating alternative forms of politics – consciousness-raising groups and Women's Aid houses.

Yet what remains constant throughout both waves of feminism is the idea that women are unequal to men because men create the meanings of equality. It is not that 'difference' is an intrinsic part of our gender identity so much as that difference is an intrinsic *effect* of that identity's construction. The emphasis on multiple identity brings together political thinking across several decades.

Since the idea of what 'a woman' is alters over time, the two waves of feminism are presented in this volume both chronologically and as sets of beliefs incorporating the various themes, categories and terms in twentieth-century feminism. What unites twentieth-century feminists, arguably, is the desire to be united. Twentieth-century feminism has no *Das Kapital*, no *New Testament*, no *Little Red Book*, no originating or primary text from which it derives and to which it constantly defers for guidance. But the feminist questions are consistently similar. Both Olive Schreiner and Audre Lorde ask: is there a specifically female ethics? Both Virginia Woolf and Adrienne Rich ask: do women share a common language? The prosaic but equally demanding question is: do we need a room of our own as well as more space in the boy's locker room?

In 'Women's Time' (*Signs*, (7):1, Autumn 1981) Julia Kristeva describes three phases of feminism not two. She suggests that the first phase – suffragism and existential feminism (in which she includes de Beauvoir) demanded economic and professional equality with men. This phase, which is characterised by a progressive evolutionary model of social change necessarily, Kristeva argues, identifies with masculine time which is linear, the time of history. Phase two, which Kristeva places chronologically after the student revolution of 1968, she defines as radical feminism and this seeks to construct a counter-society whose ethics will be shaped by female identified concerns in 'female time'. Kristeva defines 'female time' as 'monumental' or cyclical time. Finally Kristeva envisages a third phase of feminism where the very notion of a stable identity can be called into question through what she terms a 'demassification' of power. Kristeva's 'demassifications', if they are to occur, will happen only because first wave feminists have already changed the legal and social order with their programmes for women's economic, legal and political enfranchisement. In other words Kristeva's autonomous third phase woman can emerge only because equal rights feminism has become part of women's cultural and political fabric.

Fashions in feminist thought may shift from one decade to another, and clearly women's expectations are shaped by changing economic pressures. But there are also clear continuities. For example, the major theoretical questions posed by Olive Schreiner early in the twentieth century – What is the New Woman and what are the problems of men? – are the major questions of all second wave feminisms. And Schreiner's argument that all women (prostitutes *and* mothers) suffer from the sexual violence of powerful men is the essence of Susan Brownmiller's *Against Our Will* published in 1975. The inventive 'materiality' of second wave feminism, just like Kristeva's 'demassifications', depends on the material gains of first wave feminism.

First wave

☐ It is by no means insignificant that, from Olive Schreiner to Simone de Beauvoir, feminist writers are typically preoccupied with the theme of materialism and specifically with the issue of women's material differences from men. Virginia Woolf consistently argues that women need financial independence (with 'ten shilling notes' as well as with the room of *A Room of One's Own* (1929)), while others, for example Vera Brittain and Winifred Holtby, contemporaries of Virginia Woolf, pressed for women's employment and domestic parity with men. While materialism emerges as the recurrent theme which pulls these particular writers together, I am also struck by how many feminist writers inevitably come around to the question of a woman's special point of view. An urge to relate egalitarian feminism to the different propensities of women seems to motivate each writer.

First wave feminism created a new political identity of women and won for women legal advances and public emancipation. The struggle for the vote, and the later battles for family allowances, contraception, abortion and welfare rights, twists around several axes: women's domestic labour, the endowment of motherhood, protective legislation, and women's legal status.

In *Woman and Labour* (1911), Olive Schreiner described the double exploitation of women in the private as well as in the public sphere and argues that women's candidature for the political sphere depends not only on access to that sphere but also on an alteration in the *meanings* of public and private. Subsequently the campaign for voting rights in the first decades of the twentieth century embraced wider issues. It addressed women's rights as wives and mothers, and divorce and property legislation, and gained the widespread support of working-class women and radical activists. So that while the gains of the post-suffrage period tended to favour middle-class women with educational qualifications, for example with an increase of women into the professions, it is true that access to the public sphere and citizenship brought about major changes in public thinking about women if it did not change the overall economic imbalance between the sexes. Hence while the growing political presence of the Labour Party in Britain in the 1920s attracted some suffragist women many realised that anti-feminism would always be an incipient part of conventional politics, by pointing to the attitudes of British and American trade unions and labour parties to women workers, which were at best highly ambiguous.

If we look closely at some of these debates about women's material inequalities, we can see how the category 'feminism' was deployed. While 'the woman citizen' was the main term of address to women in general by the bulk of women's groups, shaped as they were by the massive involvement of nineteenth-century women in philanthropy, the word 'feminism' was deployed with what has been seen *post hoc* as two different meanings – 'old' and 'new' feminisms. Where 'old' feminists had pressed hard against the notion of separate spheres, arguing that inequalities between the sexes were socially divisive, 'new' feminists agreed that sexual difference shaped the sexual division of labour but argued that women's needs and rights were not identical to those of men.

To some degree the deployment was diluted in practice, in that the notion of 'women as a sex-class' formed a key strand of much feminist thought from the First World War to the Second World War. When Freudian notions became commonplace jargon in the 1920s, this notion of difference received scientific backing. So that while, for example, the recognition that motherhood was a key part of women's identity became a cornerstone of new feminism's campaign for family allowances and birth control information in the 1920s, old, or equality, feminists, like Vera Brittain, supported sex-differentiated campaigns such as paid maternity leave only on the grounds that this would enable women to exercise their *similar* productive rights. Yet *Time and Tide*, the weekly feminist journal founded by Lady Rhondda in 1920, which published Rebecca West, Vera Brittain and Winifred Holtby among many other feminists, also consistently argued that legal and political changes depended on major changes in thinking and in consciousness. A general single category 'feminist' was an impossibility in first wave feminism just as it is today. These writers all attend to the sexual division of labour, to gender roles and inequalities and also to women's radical possibilities. Equipped with full welfare, economic and political rights women, they believed, could transform themselves and the world. □

COMMENTARY: J.W. Scott (1988), *Gender and the Politics of History*, New York: Columbia University Press.

OLIVE SCHREINER 1855–1920

☐ Olive Schreiner began writing *Undine, The Story of an African Farm*, and *From Man to Man* in South Africa before coming to Britain in 1883.

Schreiner was an active feminist and socialist whose impact on British feminism marks the period from the 1880s to the 1920s. Her ideas were shaped in the 1880s by her association with a variety of political groups and individuals in London, including Eleanor Marx, Edith Lees, Dora Montefiore, Stella Brown, Constance Lytton and many others.

Most of the major themes of twentieth-century feminism are systematically argued by Olive Schreiner in *Woman and Labour* (1911), which brings together ideas discussed in her earlier work, which typically combines theorising with imaginative styles of writing. When Olive Schreiner wrote *Woman and Labour* the connection being made was largely between feminism and equal rights. Yet Schreiner's book puts forward a more obdurate account of women's exclusion from productive work, or materialism, and mounts a persuasive argument that marriage is a form of legalised prostitution. It is this double oppression, Schreiner claims, which ensures women's emotional dependence on men. The claim has the ring of later feminist arguments about masculinity in the writings of Simone de Beauvoir, Andrea Dworkin, Monique Wittig and Kate Millett. The 'New Woman' was a term that Olive Schreiner, like other writers, adopted to describe women who had already refused 'sex parasitism' and were beginning to transform their lives productively.

Woman and Labour is an important book in several ways. Not only is it the text most often cited by subsequent feminists, for example Vera Brittain called *Woman and Labour* 'the Bible of the Women's Movement', but Schreiner anticipates contemporary feminism by arguing that the problem for feminism is men and not women, that relationships between women are crucial, and that consciousness raising is as much a part of feminism as the battle for equal rights. Like Virginia Woolf, Schreiner consolidates a progressive new identity for women with her accounts of female psyches and gender differences. In *Woman and Labour*, Olive Schreiner outlines that radical theme of women's essential differences from men and consequent superiority rooted in material differences of experience and consciousness. 'The knowledge of woman, simply as woman, is superior to that of a man; she knows the history of human flesh' (Schreiner, 1911: 173). Technology has contracted the 'sphere of woman's domestic labours' and hence unequal pay for women is 'a wilful "wrong" '. Women's increasing and equal participation in the work-force, Schreiner argues, will change not only economic institutions but also forms of sexuality and femininity.

Pointing out that sexual difference cannot fix 'mental aptitude', Schreiner addresses the issue of essentialism by proposing a women-centred morality based on women's experience of, or psychic aptitude for, nurturing. This linking of feminism with maternity flowers in much later feminist thinking with the mobilisation of maternal iconography by Greenham women. Schreiner draws our attention to the fact that sexual discrimination is not just an issue of economics but that discrimination is encoded in all institutions including the family. *Woman and Labour* is a vision of transcendent womanhood beyond the liberal battle for equal rights.   □

COMMENTARY: L. Stanley (1983), 'Olive Schreiner: New Women, Free Women, All Women', in *Feminist Theorists*, D. Spender (ed.), London: Women's Press. J. Berkman (1989), *The Healing Imagination of Olive Schreiner*, Amherst, MA: University of Massachusetts Press.

EXTRACT

WOMAN AND LABOUR [1911]*

There is, perhaps, no woman, whether she have borne children, or be merely potentially a childbearer, who could look down upon a battlefield covered with slain, but the thought would rise in her, 'So many mothers' sons! So many bodies brought into the world to lie there! So many months of weariness and pain while bones and muscles were shaped within; so many hours of anguish and struggle that breath might be; so many baby mouths drawing life at woman's breasts; – all this, that men might lie with glazed eyeballs, and swollen bodies, and fixed blue, unclosed mouths, and great limbs tossed – this, that an acre of ground might be manured with human flesh, that next year's grass or poppies or karoo bushes may spring up greener and redder, where they have lain, or that the sand of a plain may have a glint of white bones!' And we cry, 'Without an inexorable cause, this should not be!' No woman who is a woman says of a human body, 'It is nothing!'

On that day, when the woman takes her place beside the man in the governance and arrangement of external affairs of her race will also be that day that heralds the death of war as a means of arranging human differences. No tinsel of trumpets and flags will ultimately seduce women into the insanity of recklessly destroying life, or gild the wilful taking of life with any other name than that of murder, whether it be the slaughter of the million or of one by one. And this will be, not because with the sexual function of maternity necessarily goes in the human creature a deeper moral insight, or a loftier type of social instinct than that which accompanies the paternal. Men have in all ages led as nobly as women in many paths of heroic virtue, and toward the higher social sympathies; in certain ages, being freer and more widely cultured, they have led further and better. The

*From: Olive Schreiner (1978), *Woman and Labour*, London: Virago.

fact that woman has no inherent all-round moral superiority over her male companion, or naturally on all points any higher social instinct, is perhaps most clearly exemplified by one curious very small fact: the two terms signifying intimate human relationships which in almost all human languages bear the most sinister and antisocial significance are both terms which have as their root the term 'mother,' and denote feminine relationships – the words 'mother-in-law' and 'step-mother.'

In general humanity, in the sense of social solidarity, and in magnanimity, the male has continually proved himself at least the equal of the female.

Nor will women shrink from war because they lack courage. Earth's women of every generation have faced suffering and death with an equanimity that no soldier on a battlefield has ever surpassed and few have equalled; and where war has been to preserve life, or land, or freedom, unparasitised and labouring women have in all ages known how to bear an active part, and die.

Nor will woman's influence militate against war because in the future woman will not be able physically to bear her part in it. The smaller size of her muscle, which would severely have disadvantaged her when war was conducted with a battle-axe or sword and hand to hand, would now little or at all affect her. If intent on training for war, she might acquire the skill for guiding a Maxim or shooting down a foe with a Lee-Metford at four thousand yards as ably as any male; and undoubtedly, it has not been only the peasant girl of France, who has carried latent and hid within her person the gifts that make the supreme general. If our European nations should continue in their present semi-civilised condition which makes war possible, for a few generations longer, it is highly probable that as financiers, as managers of the commissariat department, as inspectors of provisions and clothing for the army, women will play a very leading part; and that the nation which is the first to employ its women so may be placed at a vast advantage over its fellows in time of war. It is not because of woman's cowardice, incapacity, nor, above all, because of her general superior virtue, that she will end war when her voice is fully, finally, and clearly heard in the governance of states – it is because, on this one point, and on this point almost alone, the knowledge of woman, simply as woman, is superior to that of man; she knows the history of human flesh; she knows its cost; he does not.[1]

Note

1. It is noteworthy that even Catharine of Russia, a ruler and statesman of a virile and uncompromising type, and not usually troubled with moral scruples, yet refused with indignation the offer of Frederick of Prussia to pay her heavily for a small number of Russian recruits in an age when the hiring out of soldiers was common among the sovereigns of Europe.

VIRGINIA WOOLF 1882-1941

☐ Virginia Woolf began her writing career in 1904 at the age of 22. Her first novel, *The Voyage Out*, was published in 1915 and her last, *Between the Acts*, after her death.

Women are Woolf's centre of gravity. *Orlando* (1928), *A Room of One's Own* (1929), *Three Guineas* (1938) and *Moments of Being* (1975) are Woolf's major contributions to feminist theory. *A Room of One's Own* focuses on the history and social context of women's literary production and *Three Guineas* focuses on the relation between male power, and the law, medicine, education and militarism.

Although in *Three Guineas*, Woolf disclaims the label 'feminist', it is only the past history of the term from which Woolf shied. Woolf argues that, while some economic equalities had been achieved, the sexual antagonism of fathers to daughters is an unceasing threat. The experiences of men and women were distinct. Woolf believed that women constituted a sex-class within their social groups and that such a grouping was not simply a sign of victimisation but a means of providing women with the germ of organisation between women and thus a coherent and radical politics. Woolf argues that women should refuse the values of patriarchal society, for example its authoritarianism and militarism, by opposing the traditions of dominant institutions such as higher education, the family and war. Woolf herself was actively involved in the pacifist Women's Cooperative Guild and refused national honours.

Woolf outlines in her writing a huge variety of political propositions all painted with a strong feminist hue. To summarise: Woolf combines a 'new' feminist demand for mothers' allowances and divorce law reform with women's equal rights to education and to the professions. She argues for changes in disciplines such as science, she proposes a women's newspaper, a women's college, the Outsiders Society and a Women's Party and the introduction of a minimum wage and pensions for women.

Woolf's fundamental contribution to feminism is her argument that gender identity is socially constructed and can be challenged and changed, and that gender inequality begins very early in the patriarchal family which in turn leads to, and underpins, fascism. In *A Room of One's Own*, Woolf describes how men socially and psychically dominate women. 'Women as looking glass' is Woolf's resonant phrase describing how women are regarded as the 'Other' by men, and reflect back to men how men want to see themselves. Woolf creates the figure of Judith, Shakespeare's sister who Woolf imagines would be an artist excluded, as all women were, from education and the performing arts. The argument of *A Room of One's Own* is that women are simultaneously victims of themselves as well as victims of men and are upholders of society by acting as mirrors to men. Women's domestic and professional isolation, Woolf believes, is the culmination of their material and ideological domination by men in which women 'collude'.

Woolf's great interest in the social and historical constraints of women's private as well as public lives continues in *Three Guineas*. In this book Woolf has a good deal to say about women's qualities of 'derision' and 'poverty' which women acquire precisely because they are excluded from public life. *Three Guineas* argues that militarism, fascism and legal injustices all derive from patriarchal formations, in part from early sexual divisions in the family. The book is written in three parts as a response to three letters: one from a man asking for money for his pacifist society; one from a woman needing funds for a women's college and the third soliciting money to enable women to enter the professions. Woolf realises that these demands interconnect because a major instigator of pacifism could be a women's college teaching a feminist ethics which would be anti-militaristic with no distinctions of status. In addition a women's college would enable women to enter the professions and change the professions to more feminine and feminist values. Woolf proposes the Outsiders' Society which would be an autonomous women's group 'outside' of patriarchal institutions and formed to preserve women's culture. Woolf's Outsiders's Society presages second wave feminism's consciousness raising groups. In addition, Woolf's belief that women's 'difference' stems from their condition as social outsiders leads directly to Sheila Rowbotham's account of women's thinking in *Woman's Consciousness, Man's World* (1973).   ☐

COMMENTARY: Naomi Black (1983), 'Virginia Woolf: The Life of Natural Happiness' in D. Spender (ed.) *Feminist Theorists*, London: Women's Press; J. Marcus (1986), *Virginia Woolf and the Languages of Patriarchy*, Bloomington, Ind: Indiana University Press.

EXTRACT

A ROOM OF ONE'S OWN [1929]*

But, you may say, we asked you to speak about women and
fiction – what has that got to do with a room of one's own? I
will try to explain.

[. . .]

Professors, schoolmasters, sociologists, clergymen, novel-
ists, essayists, journalists, men who had no qualification
save that they were not women, chased my simple and
single question – Why are women poor? – until it became
fifty questions; until the fifty questions leapt frantically
into mid-stream and were carried away. Every page in my
notebook was scribbled over with notes. To show the state
of mind I was in, I will read you a few of them, explaining
that the page was headed quite simply, WOMEN AND POVER-
TY, in block letters; but what followed was something like
this:

Condition in Middle Ages of,
Habits in the Fiji Islands of,
Worshipped as goddesses by,
Weaker in moral sense than,
Idealism of,

[. . .]

Women have served all these centuries as looking-glasses
possessing the magic and delicious power of reflecting the
figure of man at twice its natural size. Without that power
probably the earth would still be swamp and jungle.

[. . .]

Whatever may be their use in civilised societies, mirrors are
essential to all violent and heroic action. That is why
Napoleon and Mussolini both insist so emphatically upon

*From: Virginia Woolf (1957), *A Room of One's Own*, New York: Harcourt Brace
Jovanovich.

the inferiority of women, for if they were not inferior, they would cease to enlarge. That serves to explain in part the necessity that women so often are to men. And it serves to explain how restless they are under her criticism; how impossible it is for her to say to them this book is bad, this picture is feeble, or whatever it may be, without giving far more pain and rousing far more anger than a man would do who gave the same criticism. For if she begins to tell the truth, the figure in the looking-glass shrinks; his fitness for life is diminished. How is he to go on giving judgement, civilising natives, making laws, writing books, dressing up and speechifying at banquets, unless he can see himself at breakfast and at dinner at least twice the size he really is?

[. . .]

Let me imagine, since facts are so hard to come by, what would have happened had Shakespeare had a wonderfully gifted sister, called Judith, let us say.

[. . .]

Meanwhile his extraordinarily gifted sister, let us suppose, remained at home. She was as adventurous, as imaginative, as agog to see the world as he was. But she was not sent to school. She had no chance of learning grammar and logic, let alone of reading Horace and Virgil. She picked up a book now and then, one of her brother's perhaps, and read a few pages. But then her parents came in and told her to mend the stockings or mind the stew and not moon about with books and papers.

[. . .]

She made up a small parcel of her belongings, let herself down by a rope one summer's night and took the road to London. She was not seventeen.

[. . .]

Men laughed in her face. The manager – a fat, loose-lipped man – guffawed. He bellowed something about poodles dancing and women acting – no woman, he said, could possibly be an actress. He hinted – you can imagine what. She could get no training in her craft. Could she even seek her dinner in a tavern or roam the streets at midnight? Yet her genius was for fiction and lusted to feed abundantly upon the lives of men and women and the study of their ways. At last – for she was very young, oddly like Shakespeare the poet in her face, with the same grey eyes and rounded brows – at last Nick Greene the actor-manager took pity on her; she found herself with child by that gentleman and so – who shall measure the heat and violence of the poet's heart when caught and tangled in a woman's body? – killed herself one winter's night and lies buried at some cross-roads where the omnibuses now stop outside the Elephant and Castle.

[. . .]

The very next words I read were these – 'Chloe liked Olivia . . .' Do not start. Do not blush. Let us admit in the privacy of our own society that these things sometimes happen. Sometimes women do like women.

'Chloe liked Olivia,' I read. And then it struck me how immense a change was there. Chloe liked Olivia perhaps for the first time in literature. Cleopatra did not like Octavia.

[. . .]

Now if Chloe likes Olivia and they share a laboratory, which of itself will make their friendship more varied and lasting because it will be less personal; if Mary Carmichael knows how to write, and I was beginning to enjoy some quality in her style; if she has a room to herself, of which I am not quite sure; if she has five hundred a year of her own – but that remains to be proved – then I think that something of great importance has happened.

[. . .]

The sight was ordinary enough; what was strange was the rhythmical order with which my imagination had invested it; and the fact that the ordinary sight of two people getting into a cab had the power to communicate something of their own seeming satisfaction. The sight of two people coming down the street and meeting at the corner seems to ease the mind of some strain, I thought, watching the taxi turn and make off. Perhaps to think, as I had been thinking these two days, of one sex as distinct from the other is an effort. It interferes with the unity of the mind.

[...]

I have said that a woman writing thinks back through her mothers. Again if one is a woman one is often surprised by a sudden splitting off of consciousness, say in walking down Whitehall, when from being the natural inheritor of that civilisation, she becomes, on the contrary, outside of it, alien and critical.

EXTRACT

THREE GUINEAS [1938]*

Obviously, then, it must be an experimental college, an adventurous college. Let it be built on lines of its own. It must be built not of carved stone and stained glass, but of some cheap, easily combustible material which does not hoard dust and perpetrate traditions. Do not have chapels.[1] Do not have museums and libraries with chained books and first editions under glass cases. Let the pictures and the books be new and always changing. Let it be decorated afresh by each generation with their own hands cheaply. The work of the living is cheap; often they will give it for the sake of being allowed to do it. Next, what should be taught in the new college, the poor college? Not the arts of dominating other people; not the arts of ruling, of killing, of acquiring land and capital. They require too many overhead expenses; salaries and uniforms and ceremonies. The poor college must teach only the arts that can be taught cheaply and practised by poor people; such as medicine, mathematics, music, painting and literature. It should teach the arts of human intercourse; the art of understanding other people's lives and minds, and the little arts of talk, of dress, of cookery that are allied with them. The aim of the new college, the cheap college, should be not to segregate and specialize, but to combine. It should explore the ways in which mind and body can be made to cooperate; discover what new combinations make good wholes in human life.

[. . .]

It would be easy to define in greater number and more exactly the duties of those who belong to the Society of Outsiders, but not profitable. Elasticity is essential; and some degree of secrecy, as will be shown later, is at present even more essential. But the description thus loosely and

*From: Virginia Woolf (1977), *Three Guineas*, Harmondsworth: Penguin.

imperfectly given is enough to show you, Sir, that the Society of Outsiders has the same ends as your society – freedom, equality, peace; but that it seeks to achieve them by the means that a different sex, a different tradition, a different education, and the different values which result from those differences have placed within our reach. Broadly speaking, the main distinction between us who are outside society and you who are inside society must be that whereas you will make use of the means provided by your position – leagues, conferences, campaigns, great names, and all such public measures as your wealth and political influence place within your reach – we, remaining outside, will experiment not with public means in public but with private means in private. Those experiments will not be merely critical but creative. To take two obvious instances: – the outsiders will dispense with pageantry not from any puritanical dislike of beauty. On the contrary, it will be one of their aims to increase private beauty; the beauty of spring, summer, autumn; the beauty of flowers, silks, clothes; the beauty which brims not only every field and wood but every barrow in Oxford Street; the scattered beauty which needs only to be combined by artists in order to become visible to all. But they will dispense with the dictated, regimented, official pageantry, in which only one sex takes an active part – those ceremonies, for example, which depend upon the deaths of kings, or their coronations to inspire them. Again, they will dispense with personal distinctions – medals, ribbons, badges, hoods, gowns – not from any dislike of personal adornment, but because of the obvious effect of such distinctions to constrict, to stereotype and to destroy.

And if, Sir, pausing in England now, we turn on the wireless of the daily press we shall hear what answer the fathers who are infected with infantile fixation now are making to those questions now. 'Homes are the real places of the women . . . Let them go back to their homes . . . The Government should give work to men. . . . A strong protest is to be made by the Ministry of Labour. . . . Women must not rule over men. . . . There are two worlds, one for women,

the other for men. . . . Let them learn to cook our din-
ners . . . Women have failed . . . They have failed . . . They
have failed . . .'

Even now the clamour, the uproar that infantile fixation
is making even here is such that we can hardly hear ourselves speak; it takes the words out of our mouths; it makes
us say what we have not said.

[. . .]

'They must be women, and not range at large. Servants,
take them within.' That is the voice of Creon, the dictator.
To whom Antigone, who was to have been his daughter,
answered, 'Not such are the laws set among men by the
justice who dwells with the gods below.' But she had neither capital nor force behind her. And Creon said: 'I will
take her where the path is loneliest, and hide her, living, in
a rocky vault.' And he shut her not in Holloway or in a
concentration camp, but in a tomb.

Note

1. Until the death of Lady Stanley of Alderley, there was no chapel at Girton.
   'When it was proposed to build a chapel, she objected, on the ground that
   all the available funds should be spent on education. "So long as I live,
   there shall be no chapel at Girton." I heard her say. The present chapel was
   built immediately after her death.' (*The Amberley Papers*, Patricia and
   Bertrand Russell, vol. I, p. 17.) Would that her ghost had possessed the
   same influence as her body! But ghosts, it is said, have no cheque books.

REBECCA WEST 1892–1983

☐ Cicily Isabel Fairfield adopted the pen name Rebecca West from the character in Ibsen's *Rosmersholm* in which she once acted. Beginning with her contributions to the feminist journal *The Freewoman* in 1911, and continuing in her essays *The Strange Necessity* (1928), and *Ending in Earnest* (1931) and in her novels, such as *The Fountain Overflows* (1957), West continually analysed features of male power and devised new tactics for the feminist women whose hour was yet to come. Although West, with irony, claims not to be able to define 'feminism', the concept flags all her writing. West supported the main feminist demands of her time with her articles about the economic exploitation of working-class women, the role of the Labour Party in relation to the WSPU, and with her plans for women's communal organisations.

Two of West's feminist qualities deserve special mention. One is her choice of a writing style perfectly consonant with feminist theory because West chose to speak in a very personal, autobiographical voice about issues of sexual difference and patriarchy. Another quality was her ability to relate the lives of ordinary women to extraordinary women or 'heretics' as West calls them in a term redolent of Mary Daly. West wrote best, because she wrote most convincingly, about women. In her essay about Mrs Pankhurst, West links the private moments of Mrs Pankhurst's childhood in France with the public events of her political life in order to explain Mrs Pankhurst's nationalism. West's most dramatic essay is her account of the suffragette Emily Davison who 'led a very ordinary life for a woman of her type and times. She was imprisoned eight times; she hunger-struck seven times; she was forcibly fed forty-nine times' (Marcus, 1983: 179).

Rebecca West passionately believed in women's creativity, which she felt springs from an imaginative feminine unconscious. West vividly captured this 'unconscious' in her fiction. For example in the short story 'An Indissoluble Matrimony' West depicts a male/female battle won by Evadne, the heroine with her skills of passive resistance and intuitive power. ☐

COMMENTARY: J. Marcus (ed.) (1983), *The Young Rebecca: Writings of Rebecca West 1911–1917*, London: Virago.

EXTRACT

THE LIFE OF EMILY DAVISON [1913]*

I never dreamed how terrible the life of Emily Davison must have been. Yet she was to me quite a familiar personality ever since I first met her just after her first imprisonment four years ago. She was a wonderful talker. Her talk was an expression of that generosity which was her master-passion, which she has followed till today she is beggared even of her body; it was as though, delighted by the world, which her fine wits and her moral passion had revealed to her, she could not rest till you had seen it too. So I knew her, though I never spoke to her again. I saw her once more; last summer I saw her standing in some London street collecting for the wives and children of the dockers, her cheerfulness and her pyrotechnic intelligence blazing the brighter through a body worn thin by pain and the exactions of good deeds.

But for her last triumph, when in one moment she, by leaving us, became the governor of our thoughts, she led a very ordinary life for a woman of her type and times. She was imprisoned eight times; she hunger-struck seven times; she was forcibly fed forty-nine times. That is the kind of life to which we dedicate our best and kindest and wittiest women; we take it for granted that they shall spend their kindness and their wits in ugly scuffles in dark cells. And now in the constant contemplation of their pain we have become insensible. When enlightened by her violent death, we try to reckon up the price that Emily Davison paid for wearing a fine character in a mean world, we realise that her whole life since she joined the Women's Social and Political Union in 1906 was a tragedy which we ought not to have permitted. For if, when we walked behind her bier on Saturday, we thought of ourselves as doing a dead

*From: J. Marcus (ed.) (1983), *The Young Rebecca: Writings, of Rebecca West 1911–1917*, London: Virago.

comrade honour, we were wrong. We were making a march of penitence behind a victim we allowed the Government to do to death.

Emily Davison was a woman of learning: she had taken honours in both the English schools of Oxford and classics and mathematics in London University. When she became a militant suffragist she turned her back on opportunities of distinction as a journalist and teacher. More than that, she entered into a time of financial insecurity; no comfortable background offered her ease between her battles. And eight times she went to prison. So many women have been brave enough to pass through prison unconsumed that, doubting if our race could furnish so much courage at one time, we have come to wonder whether prison is such a place of horror after all. But it was a hell through which she passed eight times. Once, indeed, the law of the land pursued those who maltreated her in gaol. A more than common ruffianly gang of visiting magistrates, who turned a hose of icy water on to her as she barricaded herself in her cell against forcible feeding, had to answer for their offence in the law courts.

[...]

If we subjected the most infamous woman, expert in murder, to such mental and physical torture, we should make ourselves criminals. And this woman was guiltless of any crime. Such torture, so unprovoked, would have turned most of us to the devising of more bitter violence against the Government; but there was a generous twist even to her rebellion. She longed not for a satisfying revenge, but for the quickest end to the tormenting of her friends.

[...]

For twelve months she was brooding over this plan to close a bloody war by giving her body to death. We belittle her if we think that her great decision can have made that decision to die an easy one; her last months before death must have been a time of great agony. To a woman of such quick senses life must have been very dear, and the abandonment of it a horror which we, who are still alive and mean to remain so, who have not even had the pluck to unseat the Government and shake it into sense, cannot conceive.

[. . .]

When I came out of the memorial service where, in our desire to testify that the way of high passion which she had trodden was the only way, we had said and sung rather inadequate things over her coffin, I heard that Mrs Pankhurst had been re-arrested. And for a moment I was choked with rage at the ill-manners of it. Imagine a government arresting an opponent simply and solely to prevent her doing honour to the body of another opponent! But then I realised what it meant. Mrs Pankhurst was very ill, so ill that her nurse had tried to dissuade her from rising for the funeral, lest she should die on the way. And now she was taken back to Holloway and the hunger-strike. I felt a feeling that is worse than grief. It was the feeling that one has when one is very ill and has not slept all night. There comes an hour in the early morning when one realises that one will not sleep again for a long, long time; perhaps never. So now it was not only that England had passed through a hot restless night of delirious deeds. But England has murdered sleep. Before us stretch the long, intolerable weeks during which they are going to murder Mrs Pankhurst. During that time we shall know no innocent rest, and surely some plague should fall upon us afterwards.

They have released her since. It must be for the last time.

EXTRACT

MR CHESTERTON IN HYSTERICS: A STUDY IN PREJUDICE [1913]*

I myself have never been able to find out precisely what feminism is: I only know that people call me a feminist whenever I express sentiments that differentiate me from a doormat or a prostitute. But it is obviously as imbecile to say that the feminist movement shows a 'priggish imperviousness to the instincts of the sexes and the institution of the family' as it would be to say that it shows 'a priggish imperviousness' to the greenness of grass and the shrinkage of the ancestral caecum to the appendix.

[. . .]

*From: J. Marcus (ed.) (1983), *The Young Rebecca: Writings of Rebecca West 1911–1917*, London: Virago.

RAY STRACHEY 1887–1940

☐ Ray Strachey was a 'party' political activist who stood for Parliament as an Independent three times, in 1918, 1922 and 1923. As an equality feminist, Strachey dedicated her career to promoting the economic and political rights of women in the years immediately following the First World War. She was involved in the London and National Society for Women's Services, Parliamentary Secretary for the National Union of Women's Suffrage Societies, and her last feminist initiative was to found the Women's Employment Federation in the 1920s.

Strachey's *The Cause* (1928) is regarded as the classic history of the women's movement in Britain although it is implacably hostile to the WSPU. Strachey's politics stem from nineteenth-century liberal feminism and she makes a social-democratic address to feminist issues.

The message of *The Cause* is that feminism is defined by its campaigns for women's entry into the public sphere and for women's productive unity with men. *The Cause* is a detailed history of women's achievements in education, the law and the professions as seen by a liberal rather than a radical feminist of her time. Strachey believed that arguments about woman's radical difference from man were clearly invalid; she associates the emancipation of women with the achievement of citizenship and a more democratic society and her particular concern, her subtext, is to mobilise the younger generation of women to feminism.

Strachey characterises feminist politics by the actions of exceptional, individual liberal women such as Millicent Garrett Fawcett, a life-long friend of Strachey, and the doctor Elizabeth Garrett Anderson. Therefore a large part of the book describes women's battle for access into higher education. *The Cause* ignores the contribution of working-class women to suffragism but does give a significant account of liberal feminist views and feminist campaigns.

If a general solidarity of feminists was not feasible between the wars given divisions between 'new' and 'old' feminists and between middle-class and working-class women, certainly it was possible, after reading *The Cause*, to be convinced that women *had* made real legal gains. ☐

COMMENTARY: Kathryn Dood (1990), 'Cultural Politics and Women's Historical Writing: The Case of Ray Strachey's *The Cause*', *Women's Studies International Forum*, 13(n. 1 and 2).

EXTRACT

THE CAUSE [1928]*

The first to be affected, of course, were those who had already come into direct touch with some part of the Women's Movement – the girls at college, the women who had shared in Mrs Butler's crusade, and those who were following the developments of the old Humanitarian impulse. Almost all these women would at any time have signed petitions for Women's Suffrage, but, like Florence Nightingale and Harriet Martineau, they would have let it rest at that. They had believed in, but had not cared for suffrage. Politics had seemed to them a remote and comparatively useless matter, important no doubt in the long run, and clearly a thing which should be open to women; but for practical purposes their own work in a settlement, a school, or a philanthropic society appeared more immediate and urgent. In the early years of the century, however, women of this sort found themselves suddenly called upon to defend their belief in Women's Suffrage. All about them people were beginning to discuss the matter, disapproving, jeering, making fun; and as they defended, protested, and argued, their eyes were opened. They saw that this thing in which they had passively believed was after all the key to the whole position. Driven by their own arguments they realised that philanthropy without political power was but a patching up of old abuses; that education without enfranchisement was but selfishness. They began to look at themselves and their mission in the world in a new light, and poured into the suffrage societies all the enthusiasm which they had thought to devote to other ends. These women, the backbone of the new Suffrage Movement, did not see the struggle as the militants did. To them it was not primarily a fight between men and women, hardly even a matter of 'rights' at all. What they saw in it, and what they

*From: Ray Strachey (1978), *The Cause*, London: Virago.

wanted from it, was an extended power to do good in the world. Just as, a generation before, the desire for cottage visiting had driven young ladies to seek a small measure of personal freedom, so now the longing to do a reformer's work in the world sent young ladies to street corners to demand the vote. The development was natural and inevitable; it was the consequence of what had gone before; and the startling advocacy and flaming challenge of the militants did not create it; but they did, undoubtedly, hasten and quicken what was already coming to birth.

With the militant advertisement on the one hand, and the growing enthusiasm of the constitutional forces on the other, women who had never before given a thought to public questions began to be roused, and when once they had accepted the main doctrine they quickly became enthusiastic. They read into the Cause not only what lay upon the surface, but all the discontents which they, as women, were suffering; their economic dependence, their conventional limitations, and all the multitude of trifles which made them hate being women and long to have been men; and they saw in the Suffrage Movement a symbol of their release from all these evils.

The years which followed were the great years of the Women's Movement, when organised societies were expanding with incredible rapidity, when agitation was becoming an exact science, and when the ever-recurring crises seemed to have a glamour greater than the light of common day. The meetings which multiplied in halls and drawing-rooms, in schools and chapels, at street corners, and on village greens, did not seem like the dull and solemn stuff of politics; they were missionary meetings, filled with the fervour of a gospel, and each one brought new enthusiasts to the ranks. It was the flowering time of the Women's Movement; the long years of preparation and slow growth were forgotten, and the Cause seemed to be springing new born from the enthusiasm of the time.

VERA BRITTAIN 1893–1970 and WINIFRED HOLTBY 1898–1935

☐ In 1914 Vera Brittain won an exhibition to Somerville College, Oxford which she left a year later to enlist as a VAD nurse in the First World War. She describes her wartime experiences and her ensuing pacifism in *Testament of Youth* (1933). Winifred Holtby met Brittain when she returned to Somerville and Holtby later became a journalist for the *Manchester Guardian*, the *News Chronicle* and *Time and Tide*. Holtby's first novel was published in 1923 and she later lectured for the League of Nations Union.

By the 1930s with the achievement of suffrage, the feminist agenda was to be, not that of Woolf's Outsiders' Society, but one of welfare feminism. Both in print and in their public activities, Vera Brittain and Winifred Holtby identified wholeheartedly with equal rights feminism and vigorously argued the case for equal pay for equal work and equal opportunities for women in education and the professions.

Throughout their journalism, autobiographies and fiction, both writers carefully questioned the implications for women of living in a society where women *had* a legitimate claim to equal treatment but were facing contradictions about motherhood and the sexual division of labour which legislative change did not touch. In a 'A Generation of Women's Progress', Winifred Holtby wrote in 1935 that women's influence 'on public affairs is only one indication of the transformed position of women in the world at large . . . the profoundest change of all, perhaps, is that which has affected individual minds' (Berry and Bishop, 1985: 95). Encouraged by that transformation Holtby wrote *Women* (1934), which describes a full history of women culminating in the politics of suffragism. The book is imbued with Holtby's belief in evolutionary change and in the upward progress of women.

Vera Brittain claimed that Olive Schreiner had 'supplied the theory' which could link these public and private experiences of women and Winifred Holtby points to Schreiner's originating argument that if half of humanity 'whether of "inferior" sex or "inferior" race is deprived of the opportunity for development, it endangers the whole progress of civilisation' (Berry and Bishop, 1985: 147). The subordination of women continued to occupy a shifting terrain since marriage and motherhood made equal opportunity for many women 'an insubstantial myth' (Berry and Bishop, 1985: 145). The Six Point Group was the focus of much of Brittain's activity, so named from its six goals: pensions for widows, equal pay for teachers and equal opportunities in the Civil Service, equal rights of guardianship for parents, improvement of the laws dealing with child assault and with unmarried mothers. The Group campaigned continually for a 'fair field and no favour' for women entering the public sphere. After the First World War an ideology of separate spheres was substantially reinforced by the imposition of a 'marriage bar' on women pursuing many professional and manual careers. For educated, political women like Holtby and Brittain the choice they might have to make between marriage and work was obviously an agonising one. Vera Brittain claimed that an ideal marriage should be one of 'free, generous and intelligent comradeship' in an 'elastic arrangement of semi-detachment' (Berry and Bishop, 1985: 132), an arrangement very like her own domestic ménage with her husband George Catlin and Winifred Holtby. As Holtby pointed out, 'whenever society has tried to curtail the opportunities and powers of women, it has done so in the sacred names of marriage and maternity' (Berry and Bishop, 1985: 132).

The final thread in Brittain's feminism is her commitment to pacifism. Like Schreiner and later contemporary feminists as well as the important WILPF, Brittain believed that women's reproductive functions predispose them to preserve life and to acquire the values of peaceful cooperation. Brittain's goal – that there should be a radical shift in the relation of public and private – makes her theories seem far in advance of her time just as Holtby's championing of rights for black South Africans marks her as a liberal humanist forerunner of contemporary black feminism. □

COMMENTARY: Muriel Mellown (1983), 'Vera Brittain: Feminist In A New Age', in D. Spender (ed.), *Feminist Theorists*, London: Women's Press. J. Lewis (1984), *Women in England 1870–1950: Sexual Divisions and Social Change*, Brighton: Harvester.

WHY FEMINISM LIVES [1927]*

This sense that the dignity of woman's work has never been wholly acknowledged inspires such remarks as that of Miss Margery Fry during the discussions on the Oxford statute which limited the number of women undergraduates: 'Women do their best work when they are allowed to do it, not as women, but as human beings.' It is the urge behind woman's growing demand for employment unhandicapped by inadequate pay or unnecessary restrictions as whether she is married or whether her husband has an income. The right to separate her public and private affairs as every man is allowed to separate his is no 'minor grievance', but the test of a fundamental distinction – the distinction between a social chattel and an independent, responsible individual.

Thus the issue behind the suffrage movement and behind the subsequent agitations over 'equal rights' is, and always has been, the same; it is not so much a demand for the vote, which in itself might well be described as a 'minor grievance' rather than as a 'grand old cause', but a demand for a satisfactory answer to the fundamental question: 'Should a woman be treated as a human being, and if not, why not?'

Woman herself, long conscious of complete humanity, today desires only that others shall recognize it and honestly accept the implications of such recognition. The fight for acknowledgement now bores rather than enthralls her; its postponement seems illogical, an anachronism, a waste of precious time. Her goal is the work of citizenship which awaits her as soon as she is allowed to play her full part in the making of civilization; she continues to agitate, often a little wearily, only because she desires to abolish the need for agitation.

*From: P. Berry and A. Bishop (eds) (1985), *Testament of a Generation: The Journalism of Vera Brittain and Winifred Holtby*, London: Virago.

The word 'feminism' – a much maligned word, which has come to stand for many irrelevancies, such as dowdiness and physical abnormality – still adequately expresses her true desire, a desire that might well be summed up in one sentence addressed to mankind: 'Recognize our full humanity, and we will trouble you no more.'

EXTRACT

FEMINISM DIVIDED [1926]*

On returning this week from South Africa, my attention was directed to several significant signs of a reawakening of Feminism from the six years' lassitude which followed the partial success of 1919. Among other things, I was shown Mrs Hubback's interesting article on 'Feminism Divided,' in the *Yorkshire Post* of 12 July. Mrs Hubback sees among feminists two schools of thought – the Old Feminists, who view with misgiving any 'decline from the pure milk of the word' of 'equality of liberties, status and opportunities between men and women,' and the New Feminists, who believe that 'the satisfactory solution of these points is undoubtedly in sight,' and that 'the time has come to look beyond them.' They have, therefore, included in their programme reforms such as family allowances, birth control, and similar policies affecting the lives of 'women who are doing work that only women can do,' together in some cases with causes of more general interest such as peace by arbitration.

The division concerns both the aims and policy of the feminist movement, and superficially the New Feminism appears more tolerant, sane and far-sighted. Old Feminism, with its motto, 'Equality First', and its concentration upon those parts of national life where sex differentiation still prevails, may seem conservative, hysterical, or blindly loyal to old catchwords. This is not the real truth. The New Feminism emphasizes the importance of the 'women's point of view', the Old Feminism believes in the primary importance of the human being.

Of course, sex differentiation is important; but its influence on human life is unlikely to be underestimated, and the Old Feminists believe that hitherto it has been allowed

*From: P. Berry and A. Bishop (eds) (1985), *Testament of a Generation: The Journalism of Vera Brittain and Winifred Holtby*, London: Virago.

too wide a lordship. It belongs to the irrational, physical, and emotional part of a man's nature, where it holds almost undivided sway; but the experience of the past six years alone has taught us that in politics and economics, W.S. Gilbert was as good a psychologist as Freud. Politically, every child born into the world alive appears to be a little Liberal or a little Conservative, irrespective of sex. Educationists have proved that their inclinations are towards science, arts, sport, and manual work. The economic history of the war proved the same disrespect of persons, male and female, for industrial efficiency. Hitherto, society has drawn one prime division horizontally between two sections of people, the line of sex differentiation, with men above and women below. The Old Feminists believe that the conception of this line, and the attempt to preserve it by political and economic laws and social traditions, not only checks the development of the woman's personality, but prevents her from making that contribution to the common good which is the privilege and the obligation of every human being.

Personally, I am a feminist, and an Old Feminist, because I dislike everything that feminism implies. I desire an end of the whole business, the demands for equality, the suggestions of sex warfare, the very name of feminist. I want to be about the work in which my real interests lie, the study of inter-race relationships, the writing of novels and so forth. But while the inequality exists, while injustice is done and opportunity denied to the great majority of women, I shall have to be a feminist, and an Old Feminist, with the motto Equality First. And I shan't be happy till I get it.

SIMONE DE BEAUVOIR 1908–1986

☐ Simone de Beauvoir graduated in philosophy at the Sorbonne coming second in the class to Jean-Paul Sartre, her life-long companion. Her first novel, *L'Invitée*, was published in 1943 but it is with *The Second Sex* (*Le Deuxième Sexe*, 1949) that second wave feminism is associated. The book sold 22,000 copies in the first few weeks and many contemporary feminists acknowledge their debt to de Beauvoir's pioneering critique. Shulamith Firestone dedicated *The Dialectic of Sex* (1970) to de Beauvoir, Betty Friedan adopted de Beauvoir's idea that woman is the 'Other' of man for her book *The Feminine Mystique* (1963).

De Beauvoir's careful distinctions between sex and gender and her claim that women's social functions are interdependent with our maternal and natural functions but not dependent on biological givens, had an enormous impact on later writers, Nancy Chodorow, Dorothy Dinnerstein and Susan Griffin.

The title *The Second Sex* sums up de Beauvoir's argument: that society sets up the male as a positive norm and 'woman' as the negative, second sex, or 'Other'. This insight is in some ways analogous to Virginia Woolf's notion of 'woman as mirror'. *The Second Sex* works through biological, Marxist, and psychoanalytic theories to show how all aspects of social life and thinking are dominated by this assumption of woman as 'Other' which, de Beauvoir argues, is further internalised by women themselves. 'One is not born but rather becomes, a woman.' Feminists today, as well, cannot resist the power in this insight from Book 2 of *The Second Sex*. Here de Beauvoir speculates that woman's role as Other dates from prehistory and derives from her relegation to the reproductive sphere, which leads to the sexual division of labour. Presaging the arguments of contemporary feminist anthropologists, for example Sherry Ortner, de Beauvoir claims that society sets up oppositions such as culture/nature; production/reproduction all of which combine to place woman in an inferior position. By starting with biology de Beauvoir creates a metaphor for her understanding that women are victims of menstruation and of maternity. De Beauvoir argues that reproduction only gains significance through systems of interpretation such as biology, psychology and Marxism.

De Beauvoir's starting point is perhaps determined by the then current scientific interest in situationism. Yet it is a starting point which enables de Beauvoir to outline a general theory of women's situation throughout history. She is able to identify strategies for women's liberation based on the kind of economic transformations which can help women to affirm productive capacities.

Attacking Engels for his ahistoricism and Freud for his biological determinism, de Beauvoir concludes that being female is not the same thing as being constructed as 'woman'. If women break out of objectification then patriarchy will end. *The Second Sex* itself provided a rationale for that explosive radical charge. De Beauvoir gave her readers a grand sweep of women's history by including the autobiographies, letters and life histories of fifty leading French women – artists, soldiers and feminists. Sadly the book's original translator, Pashley, omitted these 300 pages and their dramatic feminist history.

Some contemporary feminists, for example Cora Kaplan and Toril Moi, argue that de Beauvoir does not sufficiently acknowledge the power of the unconscious as a source of women's alienation and also as a source of our diversity. Others criticise de Beauvoir's assumption that women's economic freedom is gained only at the expense of her body and her neglect of race and ethnicity, yet de Beauvoir is one of the first, presumably, non-lesbians, in Western feminism to claim that since women are naturally homosexual then lesbianism might escape the social and reproductive determinants society seeks to impose on women.

De Beauvoir believed that women's revolutionary goals could be achieved only with our liberation from biological differences and with the civic enfranchisement of our rational abilities. In this belief she follows Mary Wollstonecraft and many first wave feminists in a shared distrust of femininity. It also must be remembered that *The Second Sex* is very much part of its moment. French Left critiques of the 1940s said little about women's oppression and any disparagement of woman's biology and maternity is comprehensible in a climate of illegal abortions and illegal contraception.

In the 1970s de Beauvoir organised pro-abortion demonstrations with the organisation MLF (Mouvement de la libération des femmes). She was president of the 'Ligue Francaise pour le droit des femmes' (League of Women's Rights) and founded a feminist newspaper *Nouvelles feminism* (1974) and later a journal of feminist theory *Questions féministes* (1977) which published the writers Monique Wittig and Christine Delphy, among others.

Although de Beauvoir's argument that women can achieve independence only through production, not reproduction, places *The Second Sex* firmly at the cusp of first wave feminism, de Beauvoir's major contributions to contemporary second wave feminism include her view that a huge dichotomy exists between the interests of men and of women, and her attack on men's biological, *psychological* and economic discriminations against women.   □

COMMENTARY: Mary Evans (1985), *Simone de Beauvoir*, London: Tavistock.

EXTRACT

THE SECOND SEX [1949]*

If her functioning as a female is not enough to define woman, if we decline also to explain her through 'the eternal feminine', and if nevertheless we admit, provisionally, that women do exist, then we must face the question: what is a woman?

To state the question is, to me, to suggest, at once, a preliminary answer. The fact that I ask it is in itself significant. A man would never set out to write a book on the peculiar situation of the human male. But if I wish to define myself, I must first of all say: 'I am a woman'; on this truth must be based all further discussion. A man never begins by presenting himself as an individual of a certain sex; it goes without saying that he is a man. The terms *masculine* and *feminine* are used symmetrically only as a matter of form, as on legal papers. In actuality the relation of the two sexes is not quite like that of two electrical poles, for man represents both the positive and the neutral, as is indicated by the common use of *man* to designate human beings in general; whereas woman represents only the negative, defined by limiting criteria, without reciprocity. In the midst of an abstract discussion it is vexing to hear a man say: 'You think thus and so because you are a woman'; but I know that my only defence is to reply: 'I think thus and so because it is true,' thereby removing my subjective self from the argument. It would be out of the question to reply: 'And you think the contrary because you are a man', for it is understood that the fact of being a man is no peculiarity. A man is in the right in being a man; it is the woman who is in the wrong. It amounts to this: just as for the ancients there was an absolute vertical with reference to which the oblique was defined, so there is an absolute human type,

*From: Simone de Beauvoir (1972), *The Second Sex*, (ed.) H.M. Parshlay, Harmondsworth: Penguin.

the masculine. Woman has ovaries, a uterus: these peculiarities imprison her in her subjectivity, circumscribe her within the limits of her own nature. It is often said that she thinks with her glands. Man superbly ignores the fact that his anatomy also includes glands, such as the testicles, and that they secrete hormones. He thinks of his body as a direct and normal connection with the world, which he believes he apprehends objectively, whereas he regards the body of woman as a hindrance, a prison, weighed down by everything peculiar to it. 'The female is a female by virtue of a certain *lack* of qualities,' said Aristotle; 'we should regard the female nature as afflicted with a natural defectiveness.' And St Thomas for his part pronounced woman to be an 'imperfect man', an 'incidental' being. This is symbolized in Genesis where Eve is depicted as made from what Bossuet called 'a supernumerary bone' of Adam.

Thus humanity is male and man defines woman not in herself but as relative to him; she is not regarded as an autonomous being. Michelet writes: 'Woman, the relative being . . .' And Benda is most positive in his *Rapport d'Uriel*: 'The body of man makes sense in itself quite apart from that of woman, whereas the latter seems wanting in significance by itself . . . Man can think of himself without woman. She cannot think of herself without man.' And she is simply what man decrees; thus she is called 'the sex', by which is meant that she appears essentially to the male as a sexual being. For him she is sex – absolute sex, no less. She is defined and differentiated with reference to man and not he with reference to her; she is the incidental, the inessential as opposed to the essential. He is the Subject, he is the Absolute – she is the Other.[1]

The category of the *Other* is as primordial as consciousness itself. In the most primitive societies, in the most ancient mythologies, one finds the expression of a duality – that of the Self and the Other. This duality was not originally attached to the division of the sexes; it was not dependent upon any empirical facts. It is revealed in such works as that of Granet on Chinese thought and those of Dumézil on the East Indies and Rome. The feminine element was at first no more involved in such pairs as Varuna-Mitra, Uranus-Zeus, Sun-Moon, and Day-Night than it was in the contrasts between Good and Evil, lucky and unlucky auspices, right and left, God and Lucifer. Otherness is a fundamental category of human thought.

Thus it it that no group ever sets itself up as the One without at once setting up the Other over against itself. If three travellers chance to occupy the same compartment, that is enough to make vaguely hostile 'others' out of all the rest of the passengers on the train. In small-town eyes all persons not belonging to the village are 'strangers' and suspect; to the native of a country all who inhabit other countries are 'foreigners'; Jews are 'different' for the anti-Semite, Negroes are 'inferior' for American racists, aborigines are 'natives' for colonists, proletarians are the 'lower class' for the privileged.

[. . .]

One is not born, but rather becomes, a woman. No biological, psychological, or economic fate determines the figure that the human female presents in society; it is civilization as a whole that produces this creature, intermediate between male and eunuch, which is described as feminine. Only the intervention of someone else can establish an individual as an *Other*.

[. . .]

New relations of flesh and sentiment of which we have no conception will arise between the sexes; already, indeed, there have appeared between men and women friendships, rivalries, complicities, comradeships – chaste or sensual – which past centuries could not have conceived. To mention one point, nothing could seem more debatable than the opinion that dooms the new world to uniformity and hence to boredom. I fail to see that this present world is free from boredom or that liberty ever creates uniformity.

To begin with, there will always be certain differences between man and woman; her eroticism, and therefore her sexual world, have a special form of their own and therefore cannot fail to engender a sensuality, a sensitivity, of a special nature. This means that her relations to her own body, to that of the male, to the child, will never be identical with those the male bears to his own body, to that of the female, and to the child; those who make much of 'equality in difference' could not with good grace refuse to grant me the possible existence of differences in equality. Then again, it is institutions that create uniformity. Young and pretty, the slaves of the harem are always the same in the sultan's embrace; Christianity gave eroticism its savour of sin and legend when it endowed the human female with a soul; if society restores her sovereign individuality to woman, it will not thereby destroy the power of love's embrace to move the heart.

It is nonsense to assert that revelry, vice, ecstasy, passion, would become impossible if man and woman were equal in concrete matters; the contradictions that put the flesh in opposition to the spirit, the instant to time, the swoon of immanence to the challenge of transcendence, the absolute of pleasure to the nothingness of forgetting, will never be resolved; in sexuality will always be materialized the tension, the anguish, the joy, the frustration, and the triumph of existence. To emancipate woman is to refuse to confine her to the relations she bears to man, not to deny them to her; let her have her independent existence and she will continue none the less to exist for him *also*: mutually recognizing each other as subject, each will yet remain for the other an *other*. The reciprocity of their relations will not do away with the miracles – desire, possession, love, dream, adventure – worked by the division of human beings into two separate categories; and the words that move us – giving, conquering, uniting – will not lose their meaning. On the contrary, when we abolish the slavery of half of humanity, together with the whole system of hypocrisy that it implies, then the 'division' of humanity will reveal its genuine significance and the human couple will find its true form. 'The direct, natural, necessary relation of human creatures is the *relation of man to woman*,' Marx has said.[2] The nature of this relation determines to what point man himself is to be considered as a *generic being*, as mankind; the relation of man to woman is the most natural relation of human being to human being. By it is shown, therefore, to what point the *natural* behaviour of man has become *human* or to what point the *human* being has become his *natural* being, to what point his *human nature* has become his *nature*.'

The case could not be better stated. It is for man to establish the reign of liberty in the midst of the world of the given. To gain the supreme victory, it is necessary, for one thing, that by and through their natural differentiation men and women unequivocally affirm their brotherhood.

Notes

1. E. Lévinas expresses his idea most explicitly in his essay *Temps et l'Autre*. 'Is there not a case in which otherness, alterity [*altérité*], unquestionably marks the nature of a being, as its essence, an instance of otherness not consisting purely and simply in the opposition of two species of the same genus? I think that the feminine represents the contrary in its absolute sense, this contrariness being in no wise affected by any relation between it and its correlative and thus remaining absolutely other. Sex is not a certain specific difference . . . no more is the sexual difference a mere contradiction . . . Nor does this difference lie in the duality of two complementary terms, for two complementary terms imply a pre-existing whole . . . Otherness reaches its full flowering in the feminine, a term of the same rank as consciousness but of opposite meaning.'

   I suppose that Lévinas does not forget that woman, too, is aware of her own consciousness, or ego. But it is striking that he deliberately takes a man's point of view, disregarding the reciprocity of subject and other. When he writes that woman is mystery, he implies that she is mystery for man. Thus his description, which is intended to be objective, is in fact an assertion of masculine privilege.
2. *Philosophical Works*, vol. VI (Marx's italics).

PART II □ THEORIES, POLITICS, DOCUMENTS AND DEBATES

3 □ Second wave feminism

Themes

□ 'Reproduction', 'experience', 'difference' – second wave feminism has developed these issues into a new body of feminism, one which is deeply political and infinitely expansive. The contemporary focus on 'reproduction' is the sum of radical campaigns, of theories of gender difference, of sexual preferences, of social representations, of family identities, oentific paradigms, of environmental and pacifist issues and, crucially, of differences of race. Reproductive rights are to second wave feminism what productive rights were to first wave feminism. First wave feminists, even women as politically diverse as Mrs Pankhurst and Vera Brittain, describe the conditions of women's freedom in terms of a 'release' from our 'biological fate'. In first wave feminism it is women's bodies which make possible the domination of women by men.

Second wave feminism takes as its starting point the politics of reproduction, while sharing first wave feminism's politics of legal, educational and economic equal rights for women. But first and second wave feminisms share the recognition that woman's oppression is tied to her sexuality. In the 1920s and 1930s the popularisation of Freud's theories endorsed the annexation of women's bodies to the heterosexual family and second wave feminists, for example Kate Millett and Andrea Dworkin, fight against the successive heterosexist and anti-woman designations visible in pornography, advertising and New Right anti-abortion campaigns and in feminism itself. So that while feminist theory and politics has different historical and national characteristics, the goal is constant – a full understanding of the effects of living the category 'woman'.

It is the institutionalisation of reproduction among other effects by patriarchy which bears down hard on women's opportunity to enter into the sphere of production. This is why the analysis of reproductive power and reproductive technology, by second wave feminism, is of crucial importance because the notion of 'biological fate' still determines many young women's responses to their future roles and encourages their entry into part-time and low-paid work. Theory proves necessary when common sense designations are at stake.

As contemporary feminist theory evolves, the word 'reproduction' shifts its meaning. Among feminists who came from a socialist/Marxist background in the late 1960s 'reproduction' means 'political and ideological work' (Barrett, 1979: 74). In the essays of Audre Lorde, 'reproduction' means reproducing the erotic power of each others' differences. Feminist theory has changed from the 1970s when it minimised differences between women to celebrating in the 1990s the electric charge of racial and sexual 'difference' and women-centred perspectives. That change liberates women from the conviction of a single, universal experience into a world of multiple and mobile racial, class and sexual preferences.

The core of second wave feminism is reproductive rights. As Mary O'Brien suggests 'Where does feminist theory start? I answer within the process of women's reproduction (O'Brien, 1981: 9). The fight for reproductive rights entails a fight against sexual and domestic violence, and has profound repercussions for gender identity.

Feminist theory questions sexual stereotypes and the orthodoxies of sociopsychological theories. For example, in Britain the National Abortion Campaign (1975) and the publicity surrounding the Yorkshire Ripper murders of thirteen women in 1980 made clear that women's lack of legal rights to their bodies was tied to the sexual objectification of women by men and to women's vulnerability to male violence. By the late 1980s, women's reproductive issues became a crucial area of feminist research, theory and campaigns. Feminist theories about the causes of rape and violence connected the development of gender identity to gender power. 'Reclaim the Night', pro-abortion campaigns and the establishing of women's refuges were supported by a questioning of gender identities in relation to race and to class and the growth of feminist health care, for example the Boston Health Collective and the Women's Therapy Centre in Islington, London. By the 1990s the issue of 'reproduction' had grown to include feminist campaigns for safe environmental reproduction, and peace campaigns for major changes in the reproduction of world politics, including the well-known Greenham and Svevo peace camps.

Historical overview

□ When Betty Friedan's *The Feminine Mystique* appeared in 1963 feminism, like the American women's angst which she uncovered, was invisible in the media. Second wave feminism gained its impetus in America from the assertiveness of the New Left, the Civil Rights and the antipsychiatry movements, and in Britain from socialist and Marxist anti-Vietnam campaigns and from CND. Pre-dating the growth of feminism, came a growth in women's employment, in women's entry into higher education and an increase in rates of divorce.

In Britain the increase in women's participation in paid employment changed the nature of employment more generally, for example, the move from full-time to part-time jobs and women's trade union membership rose from 25 per cent in 1971 to 35 per cent in 1985 in a period when male trade union support was declining. The idea of full citizenship was helped by the founding of new municipal women's committees and major self-help endeavours, for example battered women's refuges. The Inner London Education Authority, inspired by the Women's Liberation Movement, like many other authorities introduced a major anti-sexist programme to eradicate the reproduction of sexual stereotypes in London's education. In America the state-by-state ratification of ERA showed to many women the connection between economic inequality and lack of representation. And in Britain dramatic evidence of the connection between reproductive rights and the economy came in 1979 when the TUC officially supported women's campaigns against government abortion restrictions.

One characteristic distinguishing the British from the American women's movement is its closer ties to the organised Left. Another difference is a greater American commitment to women's studies as a distinct discipline and to national organisations. By the end of the 1970s most American colleges and universities had courses on women or women's studies while the first *full* degree in Women's Studies in Britain was not validated until 1991, and in the 1980s NOW membership had grown to 220,000. New theories and a new language were needed by this new politics and terms such as 'consciousness raising', 'sisterhood is powerful', 'sexism', and 'the personal is political' were invented. This was the language of the first British national Women's Liberation conference in 1970 in Oxford which demanded free contraception and abortion on demand, 24-hour child care, equal pay and education. The same aims shaped NOW's seven task forces – in education, employment, religion, poor women, women's image in the mass media, women's political rights and the family.

The recognition that public policies could be crafted from private experience is unique to feminism. Indeed the single most important feature of second wave feminism is its challenge to traditional political concepts. By connecting issues of reproduction with issues of production, the personal with the political, second wave feminism has changed contemporary political thinking. The narrative of second wave feminism weaves its way from the widely read and popular books of Betty Friedan and Germaine Greer, whose *The Female Eunuch* (1970) explored the destructive emasculation of women by patriarchy; through the reassessments of socialism and psychoanalysis undertaken by Sheila Rowbotham and Juliet Mitchell; and through the radical feminism of Kate Millett, Adrienne Rich and others. Feminist theory underpinned the activism of groups like the New York Radicalesbians and the British Wages for Housework Campaign. Such theory and activism has been followed by the major categories of response collected in this book. The dissemination of feminist ideas through women's publishing presses worldwide, for example Manushi, Kitchen Table Press and Virago, gave women's issues public visibility. But it was the development of radical women-centred activism, for example the women's refuges, which highlighted the connections between reproduction, sexuality and violence and other forms of women's oppression such as the patriarchal family and the sexual division of labour.

Feminist theory and the academic disciplines

☐ The fundamental claim of contemporary feminism is that in order to speak about the condition of women we need to speak in a new way about women's lives. The precise specifying of women's experiences as well as of our needs, is the major contribution to knowledge made by second wave feminism. Only feminist writers place women at the centre of knowledge as 'knowers' of inquiry, and not objects, and thus as newly recognised creators of ideas. From its inception feminism has attacked the masculinist organisation of traditional knowledge, for example its polarised categories of subjective and objective. But it is second wave feminism which most dramatically reconceptualises knowledge itself, which academic feminism reflects in new institutional practices (women's studies). Altered understandings about gender have emerged in a number of disciplines.

Anthropology

Because the favoured subject matter of anthropology is kinship and the cultural dimensions of gender relations, feminist theory has taken a prominent place in the contemporary history of the discipline. From Margaret Mead's account of Samoan sexuality in Coming of Age in Samoa (1928) through to Sherry Ortner, Michelle Rosaldo and Sally Slocum's significant evidence that women are cross-culturally devalued as a gender because of our reproductive activities, it has been anthropology that links questions about social authority with questions about gender across cultures. Anthropology insists that the actual lived reality of gender and the meanings of male and female are culturally constructed. Anthropology questions the presumed ahistoricity of sexed identities. For example Sally Slocum demolished the theory that 'man-as-hunter' was the main contributor to evolutionary success and replaced this theory with a counter image of woman-the-gatherer.

Economics

With the publication of Ester Boserup's Woman's Role in Economic Development (1970), feminist economists were able to show how conventional development economics not only ignores the particular experiences and contributions of women but it sees women only as blocks to, or helpers of, greater agricultural or industrial productivity, which in turn often decreased women's economic power. The book had a major impact on the work of international agencies such as Oxfam. Feminist economists have gone on to make visible women's hitherto invisible economic activity throughout the world in reproduction, in domestic labour and as farmers, for example the household economy of the Dawn Movement.

History

Feminism attacks the false neutrality of history with its consistent attention to masculine endeavours such as war. For example, Joan Kelly-Gadol attacked history's dependence on periods arguing that terms such as 'Renaissance' cannot describe a time when women's power was not reborn but actually declined. Contesting the historical division between public and private life, Carroll Smith-Rosenberg coined the term 'domestic feminism' to describe a nineteenth-century middle-class woman's private but 'political' control of reproduction. Similarly, Patricia Branca argues that women's domestic skills contributed technological innovation, for example with the development of the sewing machine. Whether they are writing Afro-American, lesbian, Hispanic or Native American histories all feminist historians place a premium on women-as-actors. For example Angela Davis suggests that the official history of slavery, with its images of victimised Black women, needs revising with attention to Black slave women's power over production and reproduction. Similarly, deconstructionist historians such as Joan Scott refuse to freeze feminist history into equality-versus-difference debates.

Law

In America feminist challenges to sex-biased classifications in legislation have been instrumental in showing how the law helps male heads of households to exercise power. According to English law, feminists argue, agreements between spouses are unenforceable in the courts because such agreements are private, which makes women less than full citizens. Feminist critiques of state legislation addressed additional legal institutions by showing how the law functions to reinforce sex-biased social policies. Feminist anti-pornographers, for example Andrea Dworkin and Catharine MacKinnon, created new civil ordinances which could be used to defend women's rights but have not, as yet, been legislated and cannot be practised.

Literature

It was during the 1970s that feminist critics, for example Kate Millett and Maud Ellman, began to expose the misogyny of the literary establishment and its adherance to a literary tradition which had 'canonised' only the texts written by male authors. Feminist writers such as Sandra Gilbert and Susan Gubar, Ellen Moers and Elaine Showalter, went on to make visible an extensive history of women's writing and constituted women's literature as a specific field. Subsequently many branches of feminist criticism, including Marxist, black, lesbian, myth, psychoanalysis and linguistics, developed sophisticated analyses of cultural and linguistic forms and the links between these. For example in her language studies sociologist Dale Spender acutely notes that the sexual division of labour structures the representation of gender in language just as much as it controls women's representation in society.

Media

Film and television are powerful media. In them women are, for the most part, represented negatively or stereotypically or are not represented at all.

Analysis of women's roles in mainstream media and the creation of feminist alternatives to these representations has therefore been an important project in feminist theory. Feminist criticism first centred on a content analysis of sexual stereotypes in magazines, advertising and in films, but feminists soon became convinced that it was the medium itself as much as its content which enabled or created sexist meanings. Drawing on psychoanalytic critiques, feminists are able to think about how media's address to specific spectators (usually male) shapes film form. For example Laura Mulvey argues that women are controlled in films by having to act *for* men as sexual spectacles and through the assumed 'gaze' of a male hero and male director.

Medicine

Medicine is a strategic target of feminist criticism because it is such a powerful source of sexist ideology in our culture. Feminist theory suggests that, in the historical relationship between women and medicine, women's bodies have often been damaged and our health issues marginalised. A sexist objectification of women is most explicit in the way in which medicine controls women's reproduction. Reproductive technology and its medical practices rely on machine metaphors, on invasive technological intervention, and on an inappropriate biomedical model, all of which are hostile to women and to men, indeed. The feminist health movement has created new health agendas for women, overcome women's ignorance of and fears about our bodies and created new medical knowledge about environmental hazards and women's physiology.

Psychoanalysis

Phyllis Chesler's pathbreaking work with women patients in New York in the early 1970s argued that psychoanalysis regards sickness as a normative characteristic of femininity. Men's fear of women, Dorothy Dinnerstein went on to argue, is determined psychoanalytically by women's domination of child care. While initially second wave feminists, such as Kate Millett claimed that the definitions and practices of psychoanalysis were sexist, Juliet Mitchell, Sarah Kofman and others re-evaluated Freud's work to argue that his account of the instability of the 'feminine' has a radical potential. Feminist object relations theorists, for example Nancy Chodorow, have transferred attention from Freud's Oedipal moment by studying women's and men's early sex-role socialisation in relation to mothers. The French feminists Julia Kristeva, Hélène Cixous and Luce Irigaray call these psychical components of pre-Oedipal existence 'the semiotic' because they relate to language.

The sciences

Feminist theorists in science have undertaken two tasks: the examination of ways in which scientific methods, scientific theories and the institution of 'science' itself are sexist; and the task of devising new nonsexist scientific methods. They argue that the Cartesian dualisms of subject/object and culture/nature categorise women and men in terms of their differences from one another with emotion/nature/body symbolising woman and femininity and science/mind/reason being reserved for masculinity. Women are marginalised in science as workers and science gives little attention to women's health concerns. Inevitably all of these issues inhibit the full progress of science itself.

Sociology

Many feminist sociologists argue that although sociological investigations now include gender as a variable (alongside other factors such as education and income) sociology is unreflective about the *nature* of gender as a social category. Gender is assumed to be a property of individuals rather than a principle of social organisation. Black theorists argue that the specificities of racial difference are not often described, while other critics point to sociology's antagonism to recognising feeling and emotion as part of sociology's concerns. Some feminists, for example, Dorothy Smith, Liz Stanley and Sue Wise have helped to develop a feminist epistemology within sociology.

Summary

□ Over the past twenty years, certain themes have dominated feminist theory: the notion that patriarchy is ubiquitous; that the public and private divisions of traditional politics devalue women's experiences and that the celebration of women's experiences and diversity are a necessary part of liberation.

Feminist politics and feminist theories of the 1990s have a fresh set of priorities including those of the black women's movement, of women from non-Western countries, the Peace movement, and by a renaissance of feminist culture in the media and in teaching. For example, black feminists have attacked the implicit racism in many texts written by white Anglo-American women. The Combahee River Collective, one of the first contemporary black groups in America, was formed in 1974 to create a more adequate feminist theory of racial difference. Black American and British Asian and Afro-Caribbean women share some similar experiences – lower wages and longer working hours than white women, a more discriminatory education system as well as domestic violence. In Britain the formation of OWAADC, the Organisation of Women of Asian and African Descent (1978), and the new women's municipal committees were examples of changes in feminist priorities. These changes represent a challenge to feminist theory to articulate how institutional, economic and cultural oppressions differentially affect black women and white women, lesbian women and heterosexual women, and women with or without disabilities. These new invocations of feminism alter conventional views of 'politics'. For example a major focus of feminist attention in environmental and peace activism has been on non-hierarchical forms of organisation and on feminist spirituality. The aim of all feminist theory and praxis is the creation of equal rights shared by non-alienated beings of women and of men free to attend to personal and collective reproduction and autonomy.   □

COMMENTARY: M. O'Brien (1981), *The Politics of Reproduction*, London: Routledge & Kegan Paul. Barrett, M. *et al.* (eds) (1989) *Ideology and Cultural Production*, London: Croom Helm.

KATE MILLETT 1934–

☐ Kate Millett's radical feminism dates from her early involvement in the civil rights movement of the 1960s, and *Sexual Politics* (1970) is one of the first and most influential texts of second wave feminism. Indeed it was the *cause célèbre* following the book's publication – the media baiting of NOW's Chair of the New York education committee, Kate Millett – which forced feminists in 1970 to add the specific oppression of lesbian women to feminist agendas. Millett's argument in *Sexual Politics* is that ideological indoctrination, as much as economic inequality, is the cause of women's oppression. This idea opened the way for second wave feminism to think afresh about reproduction and sexuality. The title *Sexual Politics* sums up Millett's theory of patriarchy. She argues that patriarchal power is ubiquitous. There is a deeply entrenched politics of sexuality, beginning with the reproduction of patriarchy through psychosocial conditioning in the family which operates in all economic and social structures. Patriarchy is a fundamental part of individual heterosexual relationships because these are permeated by male power. The book is a pioneering synthesis of literary, social and historical images of masculinity. This overarching explanation of male dominance was taken up by other second wave feminists, for example Shulamith Firestone, and Millett's attack on psychoanalysis for colluding in women's socialisation parallels the work of Phyllis Chesler. Millett's analysis of the way sexist ideologies work in literature paved the way for feminist literary criticism.

Millett's fundamental conviction is that women's oppression derives, not from biology (except in the patriarchal association of women with 'impure' nature) but from the social construction of femininity. Sexual politics is a paradigm of social power, and like all social power, sexual power controls individuals both through indoctrination and through violence.

Millett's expansive understanding of politics – that the personal, sexual life was political – became the fundamental premise of second wave feminism, just as Millett's interdisciplinary, interrogative, autobiographical and moral style gave second wave feminism a new way of writing theory. ☐

COMMENTARY: A. Carter (1988), *The Politics of Women's Rights*, London and New York: Longman. C. Kaplan (1979), 'Radical Feminism and Literature: Rethinking Millett's *Sexual Politics*', *Red Letters*, no. 9, reprinted in *Sea Changes: Culture and Feminism*, London: Verso, 1986.

EXTRACT

SEXUAL POLITICS [1970]*

In introducing the term 'sexual politics,' one must first answer the inevitable question 'Can the relationship between
the sexes be viewed in a political light at all?' The answer
depends on how one defines politics.[1] This essay does not
define the political as that relatively narrow and exclusive
world of meetings, chairmen, and parties. The term 'politics' shall refer to power-structured relationships, arrangements whereby one group of persons is controlled by
another. By way of parenthesis one might add that although
an ideal politics might simply be conceived of as the arrangement of human life on agreeable and rational principles from whence the entire notion of power *over* others
should be banished, one must confess that this is not what
constitutes the political as we know it, and it is to this that
we must address ourselves.

The following sketch, which might be described as 'notes
toward a theory of patriarchy,' will attempt to prove that
sex is a status category with political implications. Something of a pioneering effort, it must perforce be both tentative and imperfect. Because the intention is to provide an
overall description, statements must be generalized, exceptions neglected, and subheadings overlapping and, to some
degree, arbitrary as well.

The word 'politics' is enlisted here when speaking of the
sexes primarily because such a word is eminently useful in
outlining the real nature of their relative status, historically
and at the present. It is opportune, perhaps today even man-
datory, that we develop a more relevant psychology and
philosophy of power relationships beyond the simple conceptual framework provided by our traditional formal politics. Indeed, it may be imperative that we give some
attention to defining a theory of politics which treats of

*From: Kate Millett (1977), *Sexual Politics*, London: Virago.

power relationships on grounds less conventional than those to which we are accustomed.[2] I have therefore found it pertinent to define them on grounds of personal contact and interaction between members of well-defined and coherent groups: races, castes, classes, and sexes. For it is precisely because certain groups have no representation in a number of recognized political structures that their position tends to be so stable, their oppression so continuous.

In America, recent events have forced us to acknowledge at last that the relationship between the races is indeed a political one which involves the general control of one collectivity, defined by birth, over another collectivity, also defined by birth. Groups who rule by birthright are fast disappearing, yet there remains one ancient and universal scheme for the domination of one birth group by another – the scheme that prevails in the area of sex. The study of racism has convinced us that a truly political state of affairs operates between the races to perpetuate a series of oppressive circumstances. The subordinated group has inadequate redress through existing political institutions, and is deterred thereby from organizing into conventional political struggle and opposition.

Quite in the same manner, a disinterested examination of our system of sexual relationship must point out that the situation between the sexes now, and throughout history, is a case of that phenomenon Max Weber defined as *herrschaft*, a relationship of dominance and subordinance.[3] What goes largely unexamined, often even unacknowledged (yet is institutionalized nonetheless) in our social order, is the birthright priority whereby males rule females. Through this system a most ingenious form of 'interior colonization' has been achieved. It is one which tends moreover to be sturdier than any form of segregation, and more rigorous than class stratification, more uniform, certainly more enduring. However muted its present appearance may be, sexual domination obtains nevertheless as perhaps the most pervasive ideology of our culture and provides its most fundamental concept of power.

This is so because our society, like all other historical

civilizations, is a patriarchy.[4] The fact is evident at once if one recalls that the military, industry, technology, universities, science, political office, and finance – in short, every avenue of power within the society, including the coercive force of the police, is entirely in male hands. As the essence of politics is power, such realization cannot fail to carry impact. What lingers of supernatural authority, the Deity, 'His' ministry, together with the ethics and values, the philosophy and art of our culture – its very civilization – as T.S. Eliot once observed, is of male manufacture.

If one takes patriarchal government to be the institution whereby that half of the populace which is female is controlled by that half which is male, the principles of patriarchy appear to be two fold: male shall dominate female, elder male shall dominate younger. However, just as with any human institution, there is frequently a distance between the real and the ideal; contradictions and exceptions do exist within the system. While patriarchy as an institution is a social constant so deeply entrenched as to run through all other political, social, or economic forms, whether of caste or class, feudality or bureaucracy, just as it pervades all major religions, it also exhibits great variety in history and locale.

Notes

1. The American Heritage Dictionary's fourth definition is fairly approximate: 'methods or tactics involved in managing a state or government.' *American Heritage Dictionary* (New York: American Heritage and Houghton Mifflin, 1969). One might expand this to a set of strategems designed to maintain a system. If one understands patriarchy to be an institution perpetuated by such techniques of control, one has a working definition of how politics is conceived in this essay.
2. I am indebted here to Ronald V. Samson's *The Psychology of Power* (New York: Random House, 1968) for his intelligent investigation of the connection between formal power structures and the family and for his analysis of how power corrupts basic human relationships.
3. 'Domination in the quite general sense of power, i.e. the possibility of imposing one's will upon the behavior of other persons, can emerge in the most diverse forms.' In this central passage of *Wirtschaft und Gesellschaft* Weber is particularly interested in two such forms: control through social authority ('patriarchal, magisterial, or princely') and control through economic force. In patriarchy as in other forms of domination 'that control

over economic goods, i.e. economic power, is a frequent, often purposively willed, consequence of domination as well as one of its most important instruments.' Quoted from Max Rheinstein's and Edward Shil's translation of portions of *Wirtschaft und Gesellschaft* entitled *Max Weber on Law in Economy and Society* (New York: Simon and Schuster, 1967), pp. 323–24.

4. No matriarchal societies are known to exist at present. Matrilineality, which may be, as some anthropologists have held, a residue or a transitional stage of matriarchy, does not constitute an exception to patriarchal rule, it simply channels the power held by males through female descent –, e.g. the Avunculate.

SHULAMITH FIRESTONE 1945–

☐ Shulamith Firestone helped found one of the pioneering groups of American women's liberation, the New York Redstockings. Together with Anne Koedt, Firestone wrote its first liberation Manifesto, and her subsequent work *The Dialectic of Sex* (1970) became a major text of second wave feminism. The book's popularity stems from its ironic insistence that there is a universal answer to the question of why it is that women are dominated universally by men. It is reproduction, Firestone argues, which is the basis of female subjection. Biological mothering and its concomitant features of menstruation and the tyranny of heterosexual reproductive practices are the material base of women's oppression. Reappraising Marx's concepts of class and production, Firestone argued that the 'material' of woman's body is the source of her enslavement but that technological change would give women the chance to seize control of reproduction just as Marx had argued that changes in capitalist production would enable the working class to break their chains.

Firestone's book pointed feminism towards its major understanding that women's reproductive and productive roles are not distinct. The physical realities of reproduction encourage the association of woman with the domestic sphere and hence determine her social inferiority and lack of economic status. Firestone's call for women's control over reproduction became the key demand of the 1970 Women's Liberation Conference in Britain. Firestone has been criticised, by Michèle Barrett and others, for her universalism and her utopian hope that freedom could be gained *through*, rather than in spite of, technology. Yet *The Dialectic of Sex* is a powerful book, first because it recognised women's oppression in a grand way, second because it traces a causal relationship between reproduction and the sexual division of labour and also because Firestone does discuss the contradictions of racism and sexism. ☐

COMMENTARY: H. Eisenstein (1984), *Contemporary Feminist Thought*, London: Unwin; J. Donovan (1985), *Feminist Theory*, New York: Ungar.

EXTRACT

THE DIALECTIC OF SEX: THE CASE FOR FEMINIST REVOLUTION [1970]*

The problem becomes political, demanding more than a comprehensive historical analysis, when one realizes that, though man is increasingly capable of freeing himself from the biological conditions that created his tyranny over women and children, he has little reason to want to give this tyranny up. As Engels said, in the context of economic revolution:

> It is the law of division of labour that lies at the basis of the division into classes. [Note that this division itself grew out of a fundamental biological division.] But this does not prevent the ruling class, once having the upper hand, from consolidating its power at the expense of the working class, from turning its social leadership into an intensified exploitation of the masses.

Though the sex class system may have originated in fundamental biological conditions, this does not guarantee once the biological basis of their oppression has been swept away that women and children will be freed. On the contrary, the new technology, especially fertility control, may be used against them to reinforce the entrenched system of exploitation.

So that just as to assure elimination of economic classes requires the revolt of the underclass (the proletariat) and, in a temporary dictatorship, their seizure of the means of *production*, so to assure the elimination of sexual classes requires the revolt of the underclass (women) and the seizure of control of *reproduction*: not only the full restoration to women of ownership of their own bodies, but also their (temporary) seizure of control of human fertility – the new population biology as well as all the social institutions of

*From: Shulamith Firestone (1979), *The Dialectic of Sex: The Case for Feminist Revolution*, London: The Women's Press.

child-bearing and child-rearing. And just as the end goal of socialist revolution was not only the elimination of the economic class *privilege* but of the economic class *distinction* itself, so the end goal of feminist revolution must be, unlike that of the first feminist movement, not just the elimination of male *privilege* but of the sex *distinction* itself: genital differences between human beings would no longer matter culturally. (A reversion to an unobstructed *pansexuality* – Freud's 'polymorphous perversity' – would probably supersede hetero/homo/bi-sexuality.) The reproduction of the species by one sex for the benefit of both would be replaced by (at least the option of) artificial reproduction: children would be born to both sexes equally, or independently of either, however one chooses to look at it; the dependence of the child on the mother (and vice versa) would give way to a greatly shortened dependence on a small group of others in general, and any remaining inferiority to adults in physical strength could be compensated for culturally. The division of labour would be ended by the elimination of labour altogether (through cybernetics). The tyranny of the biological family would be broken.

And with it the psychology of power. As Engels claimed for strictly socialist revolution: 'The existence of not simply this or that ruling class but of any ruling class at all [will have] become an obsolete anachronism.' That socialism has never come near achieving this predicated goal is not only the result of unfulfilled or misfired economic preconditions, but also because the Marxian analysis itself was insufficient: it did not dig deep enough to the psychosexual roots of class. Marx was on to something more profound than he knew when he observed that the family contained within itself in embryo all the antagonisms that later develop on a wide scale within the society and the state. For unless revolution uproots the basic social organization, the biological family – the vinculum through which the psychology of power can always be smuggled – the tapeworm of exploitation will never be annihilated. We shall need a sexual revolution much larger than – inclusive of – a socialist one to truly eradicate all class systems.

I have attempted to take the class analysis one step further to its roots in the biological division of the sexes. We have not thrown out the insights of the socialists; on the contrary, radical feminism can enlarge their analysis, granting it an even deeper basis in objective conditions and thereby explaining many of its insolubles. As a first step in this direction, and as the groundwork for our own analysis we shall expand Engels's definition of historical materialism.

[. . .]

Just as we have assumed the biological division of the sexes for procreation to be the fundamental 'natural' duality from which grows all further division into classes, so we now assume the sex division to be the root of this basic cultural division as well. The interplay between these two cultural responses, the 'male' Technological Mode and the 'female' Aesthetic Mode, recreates at yet another level the dialectic of the sexes – as well as its superstructure, the caste, and the economic–class dialectic. And just as the merging of the divided sexual, racial, and economic classes is a precondition for sexual, racial, or economic revolution respectively, so the merging of the aesthetic with the technological culture is the precondition of a cultural revolution. And just as the revolutionary goal of the sexual, racial, and economic revolutions is, rather than a mere levelling of imbalances, of class, an elimination of class categories altogether, so the end result of a cultural revolution must be, not merely the integration of the two streams of culture, but the elimination of cultural categories altogether, the end of culture itself as we know it.

SUSAN BROWNMILLER 1935–

☐ Susan Brownmiller, like Firestone and Millett, helped to found pioneering women's liberation groups such as the New York Radical Feminists and she made a major contribution to feminist theory with her book *Against Our Will: Men, Women and Rape* (1975).

A key aim of second wave feminism is to understand the relationship between women's reproductive roles and our physical and psychological oppressions. Where Firestone claims that women's lack of collective control over our own reproductive functions is the source of our social subordination, Brownmiller argues that it is sexual violence, specifically rape and the threat of rape, which enables men to control women.

Brownmiller's meshing of rape with women's subordination consolidates several issues. First, Brownmiller is able to claim that *all* women are afflicted by rape because the *threat* of rape subordinates women and therefore benefits all men implicitly. Second, Brownmiller argues that since the convicted rapist is not defined as an abnormal type in criminal terms, rape is therefore a masculine activity given general legal and social status. Third, and related, Brownmiller attacks everyday assumptions about rape. In her view rape stems, not from a momentary loss of individual control, but is the act which links biological male-constructed aggression and patriarchy. Using examples from early history, anthropology, military warfare and criminology, Brownmiller systematically reduces the confusion between biological necessity and masculinity and rejects biological explanations in favour of social construction theory.

As a result, Brownmiller is able to put forward a radical, historical critique of rape which highlights the extent to which rape is created by masculine social power. Criticised by black feminists, for example Alison Edwards and Angela Davis, for failing to put the white myth of the black rapist into an adequate historical context, Brownmiller's linking of violent pornography, male aggression, rape and militarism leads to the work of Cynthia Enloe and peace activists.   ☐

COMMENTARY: C. MacKinnon (1989), *Toward a Feminist Theory of the State*, Harvard, MA.: Harvard University Press.

EXTRACT

AGAINST OUR WILL: MEN, WOMEN AND RAPE [1975]*

The case against pornography and the case against tolera-
tion of prostitution are central to the fight against rape, and
if it angers a large part of the liberal population to be so
informed, then I would question in turn the political understanding of such liberals and their true concern for the
rights of women. Or to put it more gently, a feminist analysis approaches all prior assumptions, including those of the
great, unquestioned liberal tradition, with a certain open-
minded suspicion, for all prior traditions have worked
against the cause of women and no set of values, including
that of tolerant liberals, is above review or challenge. After
all, the liberal *politik* has had less input from the feminist
perspective than from any other modern source; it does not
by its own considerable virtue embody a perfection of
ideals, it has no special claim on goodness, rather, it is most
receptive to those values to which it has been made sensitive by others.

The defense lawyer mentality had such a hold over the
liberal tradition that when we in the women's movement
first began to politicize rape back in 1971, and found ourselves on the side of the prosecutor's office in demanding
that New York State's rape laws be changed to eliminate
the requirement of corroborative proof, the liberal
establishment as represented by the American Civil Liberties Union was up in arms. Two years later the ACLU had
become sensitized to the plight of rape victims under the
rules of law, thanks to the lobbying efforts of feminist law-
yers, and once this new concern for rape victims was balanced against the ACLU's longstanding and just concern for
the rights of all defendants, the civil-liberties organization

*From: Susan Brownmiller (1975), *Against Our Will: Men, Women and Rape*, London:
Secker and Warburg.

withdrew its opposition to corroboration repeal. This, I believe, was a philosophic change of significant proportions, and perhaps it heralds major changes to come. In any event, those of us who know our history recall that when the women's liberation movement was birthed by the radical left the first serious struggle we faced was to free ourselves from the structures, thought processes and priorities of what we came to call the male left – and so if we now find ourselves in philosophic disagreement with the thought processes and priorities of what has been no less of a male liberation tradition, we should not find it surprising.

Once we accept as basic truth that rape is not a crime of irrational, impulsive, uncontrollable lust, but is a deliberate, hostile, violent act of degradation and possession on the part of a would-be conqueror, designed to intimidate and inspire fear, we must look toward those elements in our culture that promote and propagandize these attitudes, which offer men, and in particular, impressionable, adolescent males, who form the potential raping population, the ideology and psychologic encouragement to commit their acts of aggression *without awareness, for the most part, that they have committed a punishable crime,* let alone a moral wrong. The myth of the heroic rapist that permeates false notions of masculinity, from the successful seducer to the man who 'takes what he wants when he wants it,' is inculcated in young boys from the time they first become aware that being a male means access to certain mysterious rites and privileges, including the right to buy a woman's body. When young men learn that females may be bought for a price, and the acts of sex command set prices, then how should they not also conclude that that which may be bought may also be taken without the civility of a monetary exchange?

[. . .]

I am of the opinion that the most perfect rape laws in the land, strictly enforced by the best concerned citizens, will not be enough to stop rape. Obvious offenders will be punished, and that in itself will be a significant change, but the huge gray area of sexual exploitation, of women who are psychologically coerced into acts of intercourse they do not desire because they do not have the wherewithal to physically, or even psychologically, resist, will remain a problem beyond any possible solution of criminal justice. It would be deceitful to claim that the murky gray area of male sexual aggression and female passivity and submission can ever be made amenable to legal divination – nor should it be, in the final analysis. Nor should a feminist advocate to her sisters that the best option in a threatening, unpleasant situation is to endure the insult and later take her case to the courts.

Unfortunately for strict constructionists and those with neat, orderly minds, the male–female sexual dynamic at this stage in our human development lends itself poorly to objective arbitration. A case of rape and a case of unpleasant but not quite criminal sexual extortion in which a passive, egoless woman succumbs because it never occurred to her that she might, with effort, repel the advance (and afterward quite justifiably feels 'had') flow from the same oppressive male ideology, and the demarcation line between the two is far from clear. But these latter cases, of which there are many, reflect not only the male ideology of rape but a female paralysis of will, the result of a deliberate, powerful and destructive 'feminine' conditioning.

[. . .]

Is it possible that there is some sort of metaphysical justice in the anatomical fact that the male sex organ, which has been misused from time immemorial as a weapon of terror against women, should have at its root an awkward place of painful vulnerability? Acutely conscious of their susceptibility to damage, men have protected their testicles throughout history with armor, supports and forbidding codes of 'clean' above-the-belt fighting. A gentleman's agreement is understandable – among gentlemen. When women are threatened, as I learned in my self-defense class, 'Kick him in the balls, it's your best maneuver.' How strange it was to hear for the first time in my life that women could fight back, *should* fight back and make full use of natural advantage; that it is *in our interest* to know how to do it. How strange it was to understand with the full force of unexpected revelation that male allusions to psychological defeat, particularly at the hands of a woman, were couched in phrases like emasculation, castration and ball-breaking because of that very special physical vulnerability.

Fighting back. On a multiplicity of levels, that is the activity we must engage in, together, if we – women – are to redress the imbalance and rid ourselves and men of the ideology of rape.

Rape can be eradicated, not merely controlled or avoided on an individual basis, but the approach must be long-range and cooperative, and must have the understanding and good will of many men as well as women.

My purpose in this book has been to give rape its history. Now we must deny it a future.

SUSAN GRIFFIN 1943–

□ Like Adrienne Rich, Susan Griffin is both a poet (her first collection of poetry *Dear Sky* was published in 1971) and a feminist theorist.

A persistent theme of radical feminism is the socially constructed or innate aggression of male psyches and men's propensity to be driven by hatred of women. In *Woman and Nature* (1978), *Rape: and the Power of Consciousness* (1979) and *Pornography and Silence* (1981) Susan Griffin argues that, in part, global violence has to do with men's fear of rejection by women. Griffin is seized by the similar ways in which what she calls the 'pornographic imagination' and the Western Christian tradition share a profound contempt for, and fear of, women – specifically a fear of women's bodies.

Like Brownmiller, Griffin argues that rape is the 'all-American crime' and she traces the metaphors and actual practices of rape in an archaeology of masculine violence. Griffin claims that Western science works to control and dominate nature, which it characterises as female. Griffin claims that a greater sensual understanding of nature is given to women, and has been denied to men by our differential gender development. She conveys a real sense both of the ferocity of society's attack on nature and our need to be reunited with our reproductive powers as full sentient beings. By linking the regeneration of life with fresh thinking about women's gender identity, Griffin prepares the way for contemporary arguments about gender and ecology by Greenham women and theorists of vegetarianism and animal rights. □

COMMENTARY: N. Hartsock (1983), *Money, Sex and Power*, London: Longman.

EXTRACT

WOMAN AND NATURE: THE ROARING INSIDE HER [1978]*

He says that woman speaks with nature. That she hears voices from under the earth. That wind blows in her ears and trees whisper to her. That the dead sing through her mouth and the cries of infants are clear to her. But for him this dialogue is over. He says he is not part of this world, that he was set on this world as a stranger. He sets himself apart from woman and nature.

And so it is Goldilocks who goes to the home of the three bears, Little Red Riding Hood who converses with the wolf, Dorothy who befriends a lion, Snow White who talks to the birds, Cinderella with mice as her allies, the Mermaid who is half fish, Thumbelina courted by a mole. *(And when we hear in the Navaho chant of the mountain that a grown man sits and smokes with bears and follows directions given to him by squirrels, we are surprised. We had thought only little girls spoke with animals.)*

We are the bird's eggs. Bird's eggs, flowers, butterflies, rabbits, cows, sheep; we are caterpillars; we are leaves of ivy and sprigs of wallflower. We are women. We rise from the wave. We are gazelle and doe, elephant and whale, lilies and roses and peach, we are air, we are flame, we are oyster and pearl, we are girls. We are woman and nature. And he says he cannot hear us speak.

But we hear.

the body go cold and hard, we may tear the wings apart and cut open the body and remove what we want to see, but still this blackbird will not be ours and we will have nothing. And even if we keep her alive. Train her to stay

*From: Susan Griffin (1984), *Woman and Nature: The Roaring Inside Her*, London: The Women's Press.

indoors. Clip her wings. Train her to sit on our fingers, though we feed her, and give her water, still this is not the blackbird we have captured, for the blackbird, which flies now over our heads, whose song reminds us of a flute, who migrates with the stars, who lives among reeds and rushes, threading a nest like a hammock, who lives in flocks, chattering in the grasses, this creature is free of our hands, we cannot control her, and for the creature we have tamed, the creature we keep in our house, we must make a new word. For we did not invent the blackbird, we say, we only invented her name. And we never invented ourselves, we admit. And my grandmother's body is now part of the soil, she said. *Only now, we name ourselves. Only now, as we think of ourselves as passing, do we utter the syllables. Do we list all that we are. That we know in ourselves. We know ourselves to be made from this earth. We know this earth is made from our bodies. For we see ourselves. And we are nature. We are nature seeing nature. We are nature with a concept of nature. Nature weeping. Nature speaking of nature to nature. The red-winged blackbird flies in us, in our inner sight. We see the arc of her flight. We measure the ellipse. We predict its climax. We are amazed. We are moved. We fly. We watch her wings negotiate the wind, the substance of the air, its elements and the elements of those elements, and count those elements found in other beings, the sea urchin's sting, ink, this paper, our bones, the flesh of our tongues with which we make the sound 'blackbird' the ears with which we hear, the eye which travels the arc of her flight. And yet the blackbird does not fly in us but is somewhere else free of our minds, and now even free of our sight, flying in the path of her own will,* she wrote, the ink from her pen flowing on this paper, her words, she thought, having nothing to do with this bird, except, she thought, as she breathes in the air this bird flies through, except, she thought, as the grass needs the body of the bird to pass its seeds, as the earth needs the grass, as we are made from this earth, she said, and the sunlight in the grass enters the body of the bird, *enters us,* she wrote on this paper, and the sunlight is pouring into my eyes from your eyes. Your eyes.

Your eyes. The sun is in your eyes. I have made you smile.
Your lips part. The sunlight in your mouth. Have I made
the sun come into your mouth? I put my mouth on yours.
To cover that light. To breathe it in. My tongue inside your
mouth, your lips on my tongue, my body filled with light,
filled with light, with light, shuddering, you make me shud-
der, you make the movement of the earth come into me,
you fill me, you fill me with sound, is that my voice crying
out? The sunlight in you is making my breath sing, sing
your name, your name to you, beautiful one, I could kiss
your bones, put my teeth in you, white gleam, whiteness, I
chew, beautiful one, I am in you, I am filled with light
inside you, I have no boundary, the light has extinguished
my skin, I am perished in light, light filling you, shining
through you, carrying you out, through the roofs of our
mouths, the sky, the clouds, bursting, raining, raining free,
falling piece by piece, dispersed over this earth, into the
soil, deep, deeper into you, into the least hair on the deepest
root in this earth, into the green heart flowing, into the
green leaves and they grow, they grow into a profusion,
moss, fern, and they bloom, cosmos, and they bloom, cycla-
men, in your ears, in your ears, calling their names, this
sound from my throat echoing, my breath in your ears, your
eyes, your eyes continuing to see, continuing, your eyes
telling, telling the light, the light. And she wrote, when I let
this bird fly to her own purpose, when this bird flies in the
path of his own will, the light from this bird enters my
body, and when I see the beautiful arc of her flight, I love
this bird, when I see, the arc of her flight, I fly with her,
enter her with my mind, leave myself, die for an instant,
live in the body of this bird whom I cannot live without, as
part of the body of the bird will enter my daughter's body,
because I know I am made from this earth, as my mother's
hands were made from this earth, as her dreams came from
this earth and all that I know, I know in this earth, the body
of the bird, this pen, this paper, these hands, this tongue
speaking, all that I know speaks to me through this earth
and I long to tell you, you who are earth too, and listen *as
we speak to each other of what we know: the light is in us.*

EXTRACT

PORNOGRAPHY AND SILENCE: CULTURE'S REVENGE AGAINST NATURE [1981]*

These pages will argue that pornography is an expression not of human erotic feeling and desire, and not of a love of the life of the body, but of a fear of bodily knowledge, and a desire to silence eros. This is a notion foreign to a mind trained in this culture. We have even been used to calling pornographic art 'erotic.' Yet in order to see our lives more clearly within this culture, we must question the meaning we give to certain words and phrases, and to the images we accept as part of the life of our minds. We must, for example, look again at the idea of 'human' liberation. For when we do, we will see two histories of the meaning of this word, one which includes the lives of women, and even embodies itself in a struggle for female emancipation, and another, which opposes itself to women, and to 'the other' (men and women of other 'races,' 'the Jew'), and imagines that liberation means the mastery of these others.

Above all, we must look into the mind that I will call 'the chauvinist mind,' which has defined this second use of the word 'human' to exclude women, and decipher what the image of woman, or 'the black,' or 'the Jew,' means in that mind. But this is why I write of pornography. For pornography is the mythology of this mind; it is, to use a phrase of the poet Judy Grahn, 'the poetry of oppression.' Through its images we can draw a geography of this mind, and predict, even, where the paths of this mind will lead us.

[. . .]

We begin to see pornography more as if it were a modern building, built on the site of the old cathedrals, sharing the

*From: Susan Griffin (1981), *Pornography and Silence: Culture's Revenge Against Women*, London: The Women's Press.

same foundation. And if one were to dig beneath this foundation, we imagine, one might see how much the old structure and the new resemble one another. For all the old shapes of religious asceticism are echoed in obscenity. And every theme, every attitude, every shade of pornographic feeling has its origin in the church.

[. . .]

But now we are beginning to know why a woman's body is so hated and feared. And why this body must be humiliated. For a woman's body, by inspiring desire in a man, must recall him to his own body. When he wants a woman, his body and his natural existence begin to take control of his mind. The pornographer protests that he is compelled by desire. That he cannot control himself. And this lack of control must recall him to all that is in nature and in his own nature that he has chosen to forget.

For nature can make him want. Nature can cause him to cry in loneliness, to feel a terrible hunger, or a thirst. Nature can even cause him to die.

[. . .]

One sees this image over and over in pornography – a woman driven to a point of madness out of the desire to put a man's penis in her mouth. So that finally, by this image, we are called back: this image reminds the mind of another scene, a scene in which this avidity to put a part of the body into the mouth is not a mystery. Here is a reversal again. For it is the infant who so overwhelmingly needs the mother's breast in his mouth. The infant who thought he might die without this, who became frantic and maddened with desire, and it was his mother who had the power to withhold.

[. . .]

For the pornographic mind and the racist mind are really identical, both in the symbolic content and in the psychological purposes of the delusionary systems they express. And now, if we undertake to study this mind, we shall begin to see precisely how a cultural delusion gradually shapes itself into such devastating social events as the mass murder of European Jewry, which we have come to know as the Holocaust.

Finally one comes to recognize that the contents of the racist mind are fundamentally pornographic. And with this recognition, it can be seen how the pornographic images of racism provide social forms through which private disturbances may be expressed as public conflicts. In this way, the pornographic sensibility affects history even more deeply than one would have suspected. And when one examines the dynamic shape of racist propaganda, one can see that it, too, has the same shape as the movement of the pornographic mind. Indeed, here is a classic mental pattern by which images must accelerate in their violence until they become actual events, events which devastate countless human lives.

ANDREA DWORKIN 1946–

☐ Andrea Dworkin is a leading radical feminist best known for her theories about pornography. Particularly in *Pornography* (1981) Dworkin tackles the relationship between masculine power, sexual aggression and pornography, and demonstrates how historically pornography has guaranteed and justified men's need to objectify women with specifically racist intent in the sense that pornography creates sexual antagonism which itself is heightened by a 'racist male hierarchy' (Dworkin, 1981: 160).

It is imperative, Dworkin argues, to hang onto the connection between masculine identity formation, pornography and violence towards women, while conceding as little as possible to the notion of biological givens. One example of these links Dworkin identifies as a genre called the 'pornography of pregnancy' where pregnant women are portrayed as 'malevolent'. This grouping of women, by the sexual industry, as unequal cultural objects fixed by a profoundly violent sexual imagery, can be overcome Dworkin hopes, if the 'unequal' is distinguished and rethought.

Andrea Dworkin and Catharine MacKinnon argue that if pornography is designated as a civil offence (which their MacKinnon–Dworkin Ordinance in Minneapolis aimed to do) then the chance for alterations in the legal reproductive/sexual objectification of women could occur. By distinguishing between a masculine and illegal abuse of women's sexuality and the entity 'woman' and her sexual variants and reproductive capacities, Dworkin put a progressive identity of 'woman' at the service of second wave feminism. ☐

COMMENTARY: R. Tong (1989), *Feminist Thought*, London and Sydney: Unwin Hyman.

EXTRACT

PORNOGRAPHY: MEN POSSESSING WOMEN [1981]*

The major theme of pornography as a genre is male power, its nature, its magnitude, its use, its meaning. Male power, as expressed in and through pornography, is discernible in discrete but interwoven, reinforcing strains: the power of self, physical power over and against others, the power of terror, the power of naming, the power of owning, the power of money, and the power of sex. These strains of male power are intrinsic to both the substance and production of pornography; and the ways and means of pornography are the ways and means of male power. The harmony and coherence of hateful values, perceived by men as normal and neutral values when applied to women, distinguish pornography as message, thing, and experience. The strains of male power are embodied in pornography's form and content, in economic control of and distribution of wealth within the industry, in the picture or story as thing, in the photographer or writer as aggressor, in the critic or intellectual who through naming assigns value, in the actual use of models, in the application of the material in what is called real life (which women are commanded to regard as distinct from fantasy). A saber penetrating a vagina is a weapon; so is the camera or pen that renders it; so is the penis for which it substitutes (*vagina* literally means 'sheath'). The persons who produce the image are also weapons as men deployed in war become in their persons weapons. Those who defend or protect the image are, in this same sense, weapons. The values in the pornographic work are also manifest in everything surrounding the work. The valuation of women in pornography is a secondary theme in that the degradation of women exists in order to postulate, exercise, and celebrate

*From: Andrea Dworkin (1981), *Pornography: Men Possessing Women*, London: The Women's Press.

male power. Male power, in degrading women, is first concerned with itself, its perpetuation, expansion, intensifica-
tion, and elevation. In her essay on the Marquis de Sade,
Simone de Beauvoir describes Sade's sexuality as autistic.
Her use of the word is figurative, since an autistic child
does not require an object of violence outside of himself
(most autistic children are male). Male power expressed in
pornography is autistic as de Beauvoir uses the word in
reference to Sade: it is violent and self-obsessed; no perception of another being ever modifies its behavior or per-
suades it to abandon violence as a form of self-pleasuring.
Male power is the raison d'être of pornography; the degradation of the female is the means of achieving this power.

[...]

Which comes first, the fetish or the philosophy, is an un-
solvable riddle: but every fetish, expressed on whatever
level, manifests the power of the erect penis, especially its
power in determining the sensibility of the male himself,
his ethical as well as his sexual nature. Since men never
judge ethical capacity on the basis of justice toward women,
the sexual meaning of the fetish remains subterranean,
while on the cultural level the fetish is expanded into myth,
religion, idea, aesthetics, all necessarily and intrinsically
male-supremacist. The uniting theme is the hatred expressed toward women.

[...]

Male sexual domination is a material system with an ideology and a metaphysics. The sexual colonialization of
women's bodies is a material reality: men control the sexual and reproductive uses of women's bodies. The institutions of control include law, marriage, prostitution,
pornography, health care, the economy, organized religion,
and systematized physical aggression against women (for
instance, in rape and battery). Male domination of the
female body is the basic material reality of women's lives;
and all struggle for dignity and self-determination is rooted
in the struggle for actual control of one's own body,

especially control over physical access to one's own body. The ideology of male sexual domination posits that men are superior to women by virtue of their penises; that physical possession of the female is a natural right of the male; that sex is, in fact, conquest and possession of the female, especially but not exclusively phallic conquest and phallic possession; that the use of the female body for sexual or reproductive purposes is a natural right of men; that the sexual will of men properly and naturally defines the parameters of a woman's sexual being, which is her whole identity. The metaphysics of male sexual domination is that women are whores. The basic truth transcends all lesser truths in the male system. One does not violate something by using it for what it is: neither rape nor prostitution is an abuse of the female because in both the female is fulfilling her natural function; that is why rape is absurd and incomprehensible as an abusive phenomenon in the male system, and so is prostitution, which is held to be voluntary even when the prostitute is hit, threatened, drugged, or locked in. The woman's effort to stay innocent, her effort to prove innocence, her effort to prove in any instance of sexual use that she was used against her will, is always and unequivocably an effort to prove that she is not a whore. The presumption that she is a whore is a metaphysical presumption: a presumption that underlies the system of reality in which she lives. A whore cannot be raped, only used. A whore by nature cannot be forced to whore – only revealed through circumstance to be the whore she is. The point is her nature, which is a whore's nature. The word *whore* can be construed to mean that she is a cunt with enough gross intelligence to manipulate, barter, or sell. The cunt wants it; the whore knows enough to use it. *Cunt* is the most reductive word; *whore* adds the dimension of character – greedy, manipulative, not nice. The word *whore* reveals her sensual nature (cunt) and her natural character.

[. . .]

On the Left, the sexually liberated woman is a woman of pornography. Free male sexuality wants, has a right to, produces, and consumes pornography because pornography is pleasure. Leftist sensibility promotes and protects pornography because pornography is freedom. The pornography glut is bread and roses for the masses. Freedom is the mass-marketing of woman as whore. Free sexuality for the woman is in being massively consumed, denied an individual nature, denied any sexual sensibility other than that which serves the male. Capitalism is not wicked or cruel when the commodity is the whore; profit is not wicked or cruel when the alienated worker is a female piece of meat; corporate bloodsucking is not wicked or cruel when the corporations in question, organized crime syndicates, sell cunt; racism is not wicked or cruel when the black cunt or yellow cunt or red cunt or Hispanic cunt or Jewish cunt has her legs splayed for any man's pleasure; poverty is not wicked or cruel when it is the poverty of dispossessed women who have only themselves to sell; violence by the powerful against the powerless is not wicked or cruel when it is called sex; slavery is not wicked or cruel when it is sexual slavery; torture is not wicked or cruel when the tormented are women, whores, cunts. The new pornography is leftwing; and the new pornography is a vast graveyard where the Left has gone to die. The Left cannot have its whores and its politics too.

4 □ Socialist/Marxist feminism

Introduction

□ While Firestone, Brownmiller, Griffin and Dworkin were creating a material history of the exploitation of women's bodies, socialist and Marxist feminists were extending the critique of class developed by Marx and Engels into a feminist history of the material and economic subordination of women.

A Marxist distinguishes societies by their forms of productivity and characterises the history of any society in terms of *changes* in production. A Marxist answer to the question of 'woman' would point to the sexual division of labour and the implications of this division for power differentials between women and men. A central concern of socialist and Marxist feminism therefore has been to determine the ways in which the institution of the family and women's domestic labour are structured by, and 'reproduce', the sexual division of labour.

Where American second wave feminism is marked more by liberalism and radicalism, many sections of the British Women's Liberation Movement took for granted Britain's long-term socialist traditions and in the 1970s actively engaged with Marxism because Marxism offered a familiar and comprehensive explanation for capitalism's subordination of women.

In Britain the first important assessments of Marxist theory were undertaken by Juliet Mitchell, Sheila Rowbotham and Michèle Barrett. The key questions in their writing centre on whether Marxist concepts can be applied specifically to women's situation, for example whether women did form a distinct sex-class, and how far patriarchy continues to reproduce itself in a similar way over time. By widening the Marxist concept of reproduction to include household labour and childcare, feminists made a major contribution to our understanding of the interaction of gender and the economy. Classic Marxist theory ignores many kinds of activities traditionally undertaken by women, for example housework and child rearing. In addition because reproducing and sustaining capitalism in the home did not reproduce surplus value, women's work did not count as productive labour. But reproduction does constrain women workers. For example women often take part-time and less skilled employment in order to care for their children.

Rethinking the relation between paid work and domestic labour meant that socialist feminists could highlight the full impact of the sexual division of labour, for example by pointing out that women in the home do more of the work. The 'domestic labour' debate discussed the economic and cultural significance of women's unpaid domestic work. Another crucial socialist feminist debate concerned 'the reserve army of labour', a term used to explain gender inequality in work. This debate discussed the ways in which women (and ethnic minorities of both sexes) were a 'reserve' work-force, one which could be used or discarded at will by capitalism. The ideas and issues discussed in these debates contributed a great deal to American feminist activists working in campaigns for comparable worth and in Britain to grassroots campaigns in community education and Wages for Housework. ☐

COMMENTARY: S. Walby, (1990), *Theorizing Patriarchy*, Cambridge: Polity.

JULIET MITCHELL 1940–

☐ Juliet Mitchell has taught English at the Universities of Leeds and Reading and has been actively involved in feminist politics from the late 1960s. The first steps towards a comprehensive socialist feminist theory were taken by Mitchell in her essay 'Women: the Longest Revolution', which appeared in *New Left Review* in 1966 more than two years before any women's liberation groups were founded in Britain.

Mitchell's overall focus in the essay is on the relation of production to reproduction whose recent changes, due to modern contraception, Mitchell called a 'world-historic event'. Mitchell gives a grander account of reproduction than Firestone's description of biological materialism (which Mitchell later attacked as ahistoric). Like Firestone, Mitchell argued that women's reproductive functions had escaped the attention of classic Marxism but, unlike Firestone, Mitchell claims that women's subordination comes as a result more of *historical* changes in production and specifically from changes in four structures: reproduction, production, the socialisation of children and sexuality. These structures are interdependent and they combine in the family. Hence the overthrow of patriarchy would not necessarily follow the overthrow of capitalism. There could be no single solution to women's subordination because capitalist relations were primarily economic while patriarchy controlled through culture and the unconscious. Women's liberation would be achieved only if *all* four structures were radically transformed. This transformation would need a psychic as well as a material revolution and the search for signs of psychic change took Mitchell in the direction of psychoanalytic theory. ☐

COMMENTARY: S. Walby (1990), *Theorizing Patriarchy*, Cambridge: Polity.

EXTRACT

WOMEN: THE LONGEST REVOLUTION [1966]*

The classical literature on the problem of woman's condition is predominantly economist in emphasis, stressing her simple subordination to the institutions of private property. Her biological status underpins both her weakness as a producer, in work relations, and her importance as a possession, in reproductive relations. The fullest and most recent interpretation gives both factors a psychological cast. The framework of discussion is an evolutionist one which nevertheless fails noticeably to project a convincing image of the future, beyond asserting that socialism will involve the liberation of women as one of its constituent 'moments'.

What is the solution to this impasse? It must lie in differentiating woman's condition, much more radically than in the past, into its separate structures; which together form a complex – not a simple – unity. This will mean rejecting the idea that woman's condition can be deduced derivatively from the economy or equated symbolically with society. Rather, it must be seen as a *specific* structure, which is a unity of different elements. The variations of woman's condition throughout history will be the result of different combinations of these elements – much as Marx's analysis of the economy in *Precapitalist Economic Formations* is an account of the different combinations of the factors of production, not a linear narrative of economic development. Because the unity of woman's condition at any one time is the product of several structures, it is always 'overdetermined'.[1] The key structures can be listed as follows: Production, Reproduction, Sex and Socialisation of Children. The concrete combination of these produces the 'complex unity' of her position; but each separate structure

*From: Juliet Mitchell (1984), *Women: The Longest Revolution: Essays in Feminism, Literature and Psychoanalysis*, London: Virago.

may have reached a different 'moment' at any given historical time. Each then must be examined separately in order to see what the present unity is and how it might be changed.

Note

1. See Louis Althusser, *Contradiction et Surdétermination* in *Pour Marx* (1965). Althusser advances the notion of a complex totality in which each independent sector has its own autonomous reality but each of which is ultimately, but only ultimately, determined by the economic. This complex totality means that no contradiction in society is ever simple. As each sector can move at a different pace, the synthesis of the different time-scales in the total social structure means that sometimes contradictions cancel each other out and sometimes they reinforce one another. To describe this complexity, Althusser uses the Freudian term 'overdetermination'.

SHEILA ROWBOTHAM 1943–

☐ When Rowbotham wrote *Woman's Consciousness, Man's World* (1973), the Women's Liberation Movement in Britain had scarcely begun. Sheila Rowbotham is one of its pioneering activists and created much of its theory. Her book is one of the first feminist attempts to integrate working women's conscious understanding into socialist theories about the economy and politics.

Rowbotham argued that the emergence of socialist feminism depended on a movement of working-class women because only working-class women fully experience the double oppression of the sexual division of labour in work and in the home. Rowbotham realised that Marxism had traditionally ignored the realm of personal experience and she examined aspects of women's language and culture in terms of feminist politics. Rowbotham pointed out that because women as a class group were harmed by the psychological consequences of their subordination at work and in the family, women collectively had a special and unique relationship to economic production in most societies although this varied historically. Rowbotham later went on to attack the use of the term 'patriarchy' because she felt that the term failed to account for the historically specific, complex and diverse relationships between women and economic production, a charge rejected by proponents of its use.   ☐

COMMENTARY: S. Basnett (1986), *Feminist Experiences: The Women's Movement in Four Cultures*, London: Allen & Unwin.

EXTRACT

WOMAN'S CONSCIOUSNESS, MAN'S WORLD [1973]*

Mirrors

When I was a little girl I was fascinated by the kind of dressing-table mirror which was in three parts. You could move the outer folding mirrors inwards and if you pressed your nose to the glass you saw reflections of yourself with a squashed nose repeated over and over again. I used to wonder which bit was really me. Where was I in all these broken bits of reflection? The more I tried to grasp the totality, the more I concentrated on capturing myself in my own image, the less I felt I knew who I was. The mirror held a certain magic. The picture started to assume its own reality. My sense of self-ness came back through the shape of my nose. I defined my own possibility in relation to the face I saw in front of me. But impatient with the inability of the image to act independently I used to want to walk through the mirror. I had a nagging and irreconcilable notion that if I could only get through the mirror a separate self would emerge who would confirm the existence of the first self by recognizing it. Without this recognition I felt invisible inside myself although my appearance was clearly visible in the glass. Sometimes in the effort to relate my internal bewilderment to the external phenomena of my self I would even peer round the back to see if anything changed round there. Of course it was always frustratingly the same. Just old brown unpolished wood which slightly grazed the tips of your fingers when you touched it. I thought I had finally found the secret in my mother's hand mirror which had

*From: Sheila Rowbotham (1973), *Woman's Consciousness, Man's World*, Harmondsworth: Penguin.

glass on both sides. But that was no good either, just another illusion.

The vast mass of human beings have always been mainly invisible to themselves while a tiny minority have exhausted themselves in the isolation of observing their own reflections. Every mass political movement of the oppressed necessarily brings its own vision of itself into sight. At first this consciousness is fragmented and particular. The prevailing social order stands as a great and resplendent hall of mirrors. It owns and occupies the world as it is and the world as it is seen and heard. But the first glimpse of revolutionary possibility leaves a small but indestructible chink in its magnificent self-confidence. Capitalism now carries not chinks but great slits and gashes. It bears the mark of revolution.

In order to create an alternative an oppressed group must at once shatter the self-reflecting world which encircles it and, at the same time, project its own image onto history. In order to discover its own identity as distinct from that of the oppressor it has to become visible to itself. All revolutionary movements create their own ways of seeing. But this is a result of great labour. People who are without names, who do not know themselves, who have no culture, experience a kind of paralysis of consciousness. The first step is to connect and learn to trust one another.

[...]

The oppressed without hope are mysteriously quiet. When the conception of change is beyond the limits of the possible, there are no words to articulate discontent so it is sometimes held not to exist. This mistaken belief arises because we can only grasp silence in the moment in which it is breaking. The sound of silence breaking makes us understand what we could not hear before. But the fact that we could not hear does not prove that no pain existed. The revolutionary must listen very carefully to the language of silence. This is particularly important for women because we come from such a long silence.

We perceived ourselves through anecdote, through immediate experience. The world simply was and we were in it. We could only touch and act upon its outer shapes while seeing through the lens men made for us. We had no means of relating our inner selves to an outer movement of things. All theory, all connecting language and ideas which could make us see ourselves in relation to a continuum or as part of a whole were external to us. We had no part in their making. We lumbered around ungainly-like in borrowed concepts which did not fit the shape we felt ourselves to be. Clumsily we stumbled over our own toes, lost in boots which were completely the wrong size. We struggled to do our/their flies up for us/them. We clowned, mimicked, aped our own absurdity. Nobody else took us seriously, we did not even believe in ourselves. We were dolly, chick, broad. We were 'the ladies', 'the girls'. Step forward now dears, let's see you perform. Every time we mounted the steps of their platforms we wanted to run away and hide at home. We had a sense of not belonging. It was evident we were intruders. Those of us who ventured into their territory were most subtly taught our place.

[. . .]

There is also the question of language. As soon as we learn words we find ourselves outside them. To some extent this is a shared exclusion. The word carries a sense of going beyond one's self, theory carries the possibility of connecting and transforming in the realm beyond self. Language conveys a certain power. It is one of the instruments of domination. It is carefully guarded by the superior people because it is one of the means through which they conserve their supremacy.

[. . .]

The underground language of people who have no power to define and determine themselves in the world develops its own density and precision. It enables them to sniff the wind, sense the atmosphere, defend themselves in a hostile terrain. But it restricts them by affirming their own dependence upon the words of the powerful. It reflects their inability to break out of the imposed reality through to a reality they can define and control for themselves. It keeps them locked against themselves.

[...]

We have to start off where we came in. The predicament of being born a woman in capitalism is specific. The social situation of women and the way in which we learn to be feminine is peculiar to us. Men do not share it, consequently we cannot be simply included under the general heading of 'mankind'. The only claim that this word has to be general comes from the dominance of men in society. As the rulers they presume to define others by their own criteria.

Women are not the same as other oppressed groups. Unlike the working class, who have no need for the capitalist under socialism, the liberation of women does not mean that men will be eliminated. Sex and class are not the same. Similarly people from oppressed races have a memory of a cultural alternative somewhere in the past. Women have only myths made by men.

We have to recognize our biological distinctness but this does not mean that we should become involved in an illusory hunt for our lost 'nature'. There are so many social accretions round our biology. All conceptions of female 'nature' are formed in cultures dominated by men, and like all abstract ideas of human nature are invariably used to deter the oppressed from organizing effectively against that most unnatural of systems, capitalism.

The oppression of women differs too from class and race because it has not come out of capitalism and imperialism. The sexual division of labour and the possession of women by men predates capitalism. Patriarchal authority is based on male control over the woman's productive capacity, and over her person. This control existed before the development of capitalist commodity production. It belonged to a society in which the persons of human beings were owned by others. Patriarchy, however, is contradicted by the dominant mode of production in capitalism because in capitalism the owner of capital owns and controls the labour power but not the persons of his labourers.

What form female oppression took in the distant past is impossible to verify and the search for it rapidly becomes a chimerical pursuit of origins. We can only guess that the physical weakness of women and the need of protection during pregnancy enabled men to gain domination.

More relevant to us are the consequences of opposing a form of oppression which has taken a specific shape in capitalism, but which nevertheless existed in precapitalist society. In order to act effectively we have to try to work out the precise relationship between the patriarchal dominance of men over women, and the property relations which come from this, to class exploitation and racism.

HEIDI HARTMANN

☐ Now Director of the Institute for Women's Policy Research, Washington DC, Heidi Hartmann has, since the early 1970s strategically linked feminist economic theory with policy making. *Capitalist Patriarchy and the Case for Socialist Feminism* (1979), which contains Hartmann's influential essay 'The Unhappy Marriage of Marxism and Feminism: Towards a More Progressive Union', was the first collection of American socialist feminist writing.

Hartmann describes the ways in which capitalism reproduces economically the patriarchal segregation of women and men. The 'unhappy marriage' was Hartmann's term for the necessary but tense relationship of Marxism and feminism. Only a combination of both critiques could explain how women reproduce capitalist relations in a double way – in the home and at work. Like Michèle Barrett, Heidi Hartmann believes that patriarchy predates capitalism and she believes that it is the sexual division of labour, or job segregation by sex, which is a crucial factor in women's subordination throughout the world. Hartmann developed a 'dual-systems' theory of economics. This argues that the two systems of patriarchy and capitalism are distinct but that these are interacting forms of oppression because both help men to maintain power by wage differentials, by segregation at work, by the concept of a family wage (capitalism) and by assigning women to the domestic sphere and appropriating her domestic labour (patriarchy). ☐

COMMENTARY: S. Walby (1990), *Theorizing Patriarchy*, Cambridge: Polity.

EXTRACT

CAPITALISM, PATRIARCHY, AND JOB SEGREGATION BY SEX [1976]*

The division of labor by sex appears to have been universal throughout human history. In our society the sexual division of labor is hierarchical, with men on top and women on the bottom. Anthropology and history suggest, however, that this division was not always a hierarchical one. The development and importance of a sex-ordered division of labor is the subject of this paper. It is my contention that the roots of women's present social status lie in this sex-ordered division of labor. It is my belief that not only must the hierarchical nature of the division of labor between the sexes be eliminated, but the very division of labor between the sexes itself must be eliminated if women are to attain equal social status with men and if women and men are to attain the full development of their human potentials.

The primary questions for investigation would seem to be, then, first, how a more sexually egalitarian division became a less egalitarian one, and second, how this hierarchical division of labor became extended to wage labor in the modern period. Many anthropological studies suggest that the first process, sexual stratification, occurred together with the increasing productiveness, specialization, and complexity of society; for example, through the establishment of settled agriculture, private property, or the state. It occurred as human society emerged from the primitive and became 'civilized.' In this perspective capitalism is a relative latecomer, whereas patriarchy,[1] the hierarchical relation between men and women in which men are dominant and women are subordinate, was an early arrival.

I want to argue that, before capitalism, a patriarchal system was established in which men controlled the labor of

*From: Heidi Hartmann (1983), 'Capitalism, Patriarchy, and Job Segregation by Sex', in E. Abel and E.K. Abel (eds), The Signs Reader: Women, Gender and Scholarship, Chicago: University of Chicago Press.

women and children in the family, and that in so doing men learned the techniques of hierarchical organization and control. With the advent of public–private separations such as those created by the emergence of state apparatus and economic systems based on wider exchange and larger production units, the problem for men became one of maintaining their control over the labor power of women. In other words, a direct personal system of control was translated into an indirect, impersonal system of control, mediated by society-wide institutions. The mechanisms available to men were (1) the traditional division of labor between the sexes, and (2) techniques of hierarchical organization and control. These mechanisms were crucial in the second process, the extension of a sex-ordered division of labor to the wage-labor system, during the period of the emergence of capitalism in Western Europe and the United States.

The emergence of capitalism in the fifteenth to eighteenth centuries threatened patriarchal control based on institutional authority as it destroyed many old institutions and created new ones, such as a 'free' market in labor. It threatened to bring all women and children into the labor force and hence to destroy the family and the basis of the power of men over women (i.e., the control over their labor power in the family).[2] If the theoretical tendency of pure capitalism would have been to eradicate all arbitrary differences of status among laborers, to make all laborers equal in the marketplace, why are women still in an inferior position to men in the labor market? The possible answers are legion; they range from neoclassical views that the process is not complete or is hampered by market imperfections to the radical view that production requires hierarchy even if the market nominally requires 'equality.'[3] All of these explanations, it seems to me, ignore the role of men – ordinary men, men as men, men as workers – in maintaining women's inferiority in the labor market. The radical view, in particular, emphasizes the role of men as capitalists in creating hierarchies in the production process in order to maintain their power. Capitalists do this by segmenting the labor market (along race, sex, and ethnic lines among others) and playing workers off against each other. In this paper I argue that male workers have played and continue to play a crucial role in maintaining sexual divisions in the labor process.

[. . .]

Conclusion

The present status of women in the labor market and the current arrangement of sex-segregated jobs is the result of a long process of interaction between patriarchy and capitalism. I have emphasized the actions of male workers throughout this process because I believe that emphasis to be correct. Men will have to be forced to give up their favored positions in the division of labor – in the labor market and at home – both if women's subordination is to end and if men are to begin to escape class oppression and exploitation.[4] Capitalists have indeed used women as unskilled, underpaid labor to undercut male workers, yet this is only a case of the chickens coming home to roost – a case of men's co-optation by and support for patriarchal society, with its hierarchy among men, being turned back on themselves with a vengeance. Capitalism grew on top of patriarchy; patriarchal capitalism is stratified society par excellence. If non-ruling-class men are to be free they will have to recognize their co-optation by patriarchal capitalism and relinquish their patriarchal benefits. If women are to be free, they must fight against both patriarchal power and capitalist organization of society.

Because both the sexual division of labor and male domination are so long standing, it will be very difficult to eradicate them and impossible to eradicate the latter without the former. The two are now so inextricably intertwined that it is necessary to eradicate the sexual division of labor itself in order to end male domination.[5] Very basic changes at all levels of society and culture are required to liberate women. In this paper, I have argued that the maintenance of job segregation by sex is a key root of women's status, and I have relied on the operation of society-wide institutions to explain the maintenance of job segregation by sex. But the consequences of that division of labor go very deep, down to the level of the subconscious. The subconscious influences behavior patterns, which form the micro underpinnings (or complements) of social institutions and are in turn reinforced by those social institutions.

I believe we need to investigate these micro phenomena as well as the macro ones I have discussed in this paper. For example, it appears to be a very deeply ingrained behavioral rule that men cannot be subordinate to women of a similar social class. Manifestations of this rule have been noted in restaurants, where waitresses experience difficulty in giving orders to bartenders, unless the bartender can reorganize the situation to allow himself autonomy; among executives, where women executives are seen to be most successful if they have little contact with others at their level and manage small staffs; and among industrial workers, where female factory inspectors cannot successfully correct the work of male production workers.[6] There is also a deeply ingrained fear of being identified with the other sex. As a general rule, men and women must never do anything which is not masculine or feminine (respectively).[7] Male executives, for example, often exchange handshakes with male secretaries, a show of respect which probably works to help preserve their masculinity.

At the next deeper level, we must study the subconscious – both how these behavioral rules are internalized and how they grow out of personality structure.[8] At this level, the formation of personality, there have been several attempts to study the production of gender, the *socially* imposed differentiation of humans based on biological sex differences.[9] A materialist interpretation of reality, of course, suggests that gender production grows out of the extant division of labor between the sexes,[10] and, in a dialectical process, reinforces that very division of labor itself. In my view, because of these deep ramifications of the sexual division of labor we will not eradicate sex-ordered task division until we eradicate the socially imposed gender differences between us and, therefore, the very sexual division of labor itself.

In attacking both patriarchy and capitalism we will have to find ways to change both society-wide institutions and our most deeply ingrained habits. It will be a long, hard struggle.

Notes

1. I define patriarchy as a set of social relations which has a material base and in which there are hierarchical relations between men, and solidarity among them, which enable them to control women. Patriarchy is thus the system of male oppression of women. Rubin argues that we should use the term 'sex-gender system' to refer to that realm outside the economic system (and not always coordinate with it) where gender stratification based on sex differences is produced and reproduced. Patriarchy is thus only one form, a male dominant one, of a sex-gender system. Rubin argues further that patriarchy should be reserved for pastoral nomadic societies as described in the Old Testament where male power was synonymous with fatherhood. While I agree with Rubin's first point, I think her second point makes the usage of patriarchy too restrictive. it is a good label for most male-dominant societies (see Gayle Rubin, 'The Traffic in Women,' in *Toward an Anthropology of Women*, ed. Rayna Reiter [New York: Monthly Review Press, 1975]). Muller offers a broader definition of patriarchy 'as a social system in which the status of women is defined primarily as wards of their husbands, fathers, and brothers,' where wardship has economic and political dimensions (see Viana Muller, 'The Formation of the State and the Oppression of Women: A Case Study in England and Wales,' mimeographed [New York: New School for Social Research, 1975], p. 4, n. 2). Muller relies on Karen Sacks, 'Engels Revisited: Women, the Organization of Production, and Private Property,' in *Woman, Culture and Society*, ed. Michelle Z. Rosaldo and Louise Lamphere (Stanford, Calif.: Stanford University Press, 1974). Patriarchy as a system between and among men as well as between men and women is further explained in a draft paper, 'The Unhappy Marriage of Marxism and Feminism: Towards a New Union,' by Amy Bridges and Heidi Hartmann.

2. Marx and Engels perceived the progress of capitalism in this way, that it would bring women and children into the labor market and thus erode the family. Yet despite Engels's acknowledgement in *The Origin of the Family, Private Property, and the State* (New York: International Publishers, 1972), that men oppress women in the family, he did not see that oppression as based on the control of women's labor, and, if anything, he seems to lament the passing of the male-controlled family (see his *The Condition of the Working Class in England* [Stanford, Calif.: Stanford University Press, 1968], esp. pp. 161–64).

3. See Richard C. Edwards, David M. Gordon, and Michael Reich, 'Labor market Segmentation in American Capitalism,' draft essay, and the book

they edited, *Labor Market Segmentation* (Lexington, Mass.: Lexington Books, 1975) for an explication of this view.

4. Most Marxist–feminist attempts to deal with the problems in Marxist analysis raised by the social position of women seem to ignore these basic conflicts between the sexes, apparently in the interest of stressing the underlying class solidarity that should obtain among women and men workers. Bridges and Hartmann's draft paper (n. 1 above) reviews this literature. A few months ago a friend (female) said, 'We are much more likely to be able to get Thieu out of Vietnam than we are to get men to do the dishes.' She was right.

5. In our society, women's jobs are synonymous with low-status, low-paying jobs: '. . . we may replace the familiar statement that women earn less because they are in low paying occupations with the statement that women earn less because they are in *women's jobs*. . . . As long as the labor market is divided on the basis of sex, it is likely that the tasks allocated to women will be ranked as less prestigious or important, reflecting women's lower social status in the society at large' (Francine Blau [Weisskoff], 'Women's Place in the Labor Market,' *American Economic Review* 62, no. 4 [May 1972]: 161).

6. Theodore Caplow, *The Sociology of Work* (New York: McGraw-Hill Book Co., 1964), pp. 237 ff., discusses several behavioral rules and their impact. Harold Willensky, 'Women's Work: Economic Growth, Ideology, Structure,' *Industrial Relations* 7, no. 3 (May 1968): 235–48, also discusses the implication for labor-market phenomena of several behavioral rules.

7. 'The use of tabooed words, the fostering of sports and other interests which women do not share, and participation in activities which women are intended to disapprove of – hard drinking, gambling, practical jokes, and sexual essays of various kinds – all suggest that the adult male group is to a large extent engaged in a reaction *against* feminine influence, and therefore cannot tolerate the presence of women without changing its character entirely' (Caplow, p. 239). Of course, the lines of division between masculine and feminine are constantly shifting. At various times in the nineteenth century, teaching, selling in retail stores, and office work were each thought to be totally unsuitable for women. This variability of the boundaries between men's jobs and women's jobs is one reason why an effort to locate basic behavioral principles would seem to make sense – though, ultimately, of course, these rules are shaped by the division of labor itself.

8. Caplow based his rules on the Freudian view that men identify freedom from female dominance with maturity, i.e., they seek to escape their mothers.

9. See Rubin (n. 1 above), and Juliet Mitchell, *Feminism and Psychoanalysis* (New York: Pantheon Books, 1974), who seek to re-create Freud from a feminist perspective. So does Shulamith Firestone, *The Dialectic of Sex* (New York: Bantam Books, 1971).

10. For example, the current domestic division of labor in which women nurture children profoundly affects (differentially) the personality structures of girls and boys. For a non-Freudian interpretation of this phenomenon, see N. Chodorow (1978), *The Reproduction of Mothering: Psychoanalysis and the Sociology of Gender*, Berkeley, CA: University of California Press.

EXTRACT

THE UNHAPPY MARRIAGE OF MARXISM AND FEMINISM: TOWARDS A MORE PROGRESSIVE UNION [1979]*

The 'marriage' of marxism and feminism has been like the marriage of husband and wife depicted in English common law: marxism and feminism are one, and that one is marxism.[1] Recent attempts to integrate marxism and feminism are unsatisfactory to us as feminists because they subsume the feminist struggle into the 'larger' struggle against capital. To continue our simile further, either we need a healthier marriage or we need a divorce.

The inequalities in this marriage, like most social phenomena, are no accident. Many marxists typically argue that feminism is at best less important than class conflict and at worst divisive of the working class. This political stance produces an analysis that absorbs feminism into the class struggle. Moreover, the analytic power of marxism with respect to capital has obscured its limitations with respect to sexism. We will argue here that while marxist analysis provides essential insight into the laws of historical development, and those of capital in particular, the categories of marxism are sex-blind. Only a specifically feminist analysis reveals the systemic character of relations between men and women. Yet feminist analysis by itself is inadequate because it has been blind to history and insufficiently materialist. Both marxist analysis, particularly its historical and materialist method, and feminist analysis, especially the identification of patriarchy as a social and historical structure, must be drawn upon if we are to understand the development of western capitalist societies and

*From: Heidi Hartmann (1981), 'The Unhappy Marriage of Marxism and Feminism: Towards a More Progressive Union', in L. Sargent (ed.), *Women and Revolution: A Discussion of the Unhappy Marriage of Marxism and Feminism*, London: Pluto Press.

the predicament of women within them. In this essay we suggest a new direction for marxist feminist analysis.

[...]

Towards a more progressive union

Many problems remain for us to explore. Patriarchy as we have used it here remains more a descriptive term than an analytic one. If we think marxism alone inadequate, and radical feminism itself insufficient, then we need to develop new categories. What makes our task a difficult one is that the same features, such as the division of labor, often reinforce both patriarchy and capitalism, and in a thoroughly patriarchal capitalist society, it is hard to isolate the mechanisms of patriarchy. Nevertheless, this is what we must do. We have pointed to some starting places: looking at who benefits from women's labor power, uncovering the material base of patriarchy, investigating the mechanisms of hierarchy and solidarity among men. The questions we must ask are endless.

Can we speak of the laws of motion of a patriarchal system? How does patriarchy generate feminist struggle? What kinds of sexual politics and struggle between the sexes can we see in societies other than advanced capitalist ones? What are the contradictions of the patriarchal system and what is their relation to the contradictions of capitalism? We know that patriarchal relations gave rise to the feminist movement, and that capital generates class struggle – but how has the relation of feminism to class struggle been played out in historical contexts? In this section we attempt to provide an answer to this last question.

Feminism and class struggle

Historically and in the present, the relation of feminism and class struggle has been either that of fully separate paths ('bourgeois' feminism on one hand, class struggle on the other), or, within the left, the dominance of feminism by marxism. With respect to the latter, this has been a consequence both of the analytic power of marxism, and of the power of men within the left. These have produced both open struggles on the left, and a contradictory position for marxist feminists.

Most feminists who also see themselves as radicals (anti-system, anti-capitalist, anti-imperialist, socialist, communist, marxist, whatever) agree that the radical wing of the women's movement has lost momentum while the liberal sector seems to have seized the time and forged ahead. Our movement is no longer in that exciting, energetic period when no matter what we did, it worked – to raise consciousness, to bring more women (more even than could be easily incorporated) into the movement, to increase the visibility of women's issues in the society, often in ways fundamentally challenging to both the capitalist and patriarchal relations in society. Now we sense parts of the movement are being coopted and 'feminism' is being used against women – for example, in court cases when judges argue that women coming out of long-term marriages in which they were housewives don't need alimony because we all know women are liberated now. The failure to date to secure the passage of the Equal Rights Amendment in the United States indicates the presence of legitimate fears among many women that feminism will continue to be used against women, and it indicates a real need for us to reassess our movement, to analyze why it has been coopted in this way. It is logical for us to turn to marxism for help in that reassessment because it is a developed theory of social change. Marxist theory is well developed compared to feminist theory, and in our attempt to use it, we have sometimes been sidetracked from feminist objectives.

The left has always been ambivalent about the women's movement, often viewing it as dangerous to the cause of socialist revolution. When left women espouse feminism, it may be personally threatening to left men. And of course many left organizations benefit from the labor of women. Therefore, many left analyses (both in progressive and traditional forms) are self-serving, both theoretically and politically. They seek to influence women to abandon attempts to develop an independent understanding of women's situation and to adopt the 'left's' analyses of the situation. As for our response to this pressure, it is natural that, as we ourselves have turned to marxist analysis, we would try to join the 'fraternity' using this paradigm, and we may end up trying to justify our struggle to the fraternity rather than trying to analyze the situation of women to improve our political practice. Finally, many marxists are satisfied with the traditional marxist analysis of the women question. They see class as the correct framework with which to understand women's position. Women should be understood as part of the working class; the working class's struggle against capitalism should take precedence over any conflict between men and women. Sex conflict must not be allowed to interfere with class solidarity.

As the economic situation in the United States has worsened in the last few years, traditional marxist analysis has reasserted itself. In the sixties the civil rights movement, the student free speech movement, the antiwar movement, the women's movement, the environmental movement, and the increased militancy of professional and white collar groups all raised new questions for marxists. But now the return of obvious economic problems such as inflation and unemployment had eclipsed the importance of these demands and the left has returned to the 'fundamentals' – working class (narrowly defined) politics. The growing 'marxist–leninist preparty' sects are committed antifeminists, in both doctrine and practice. And there are signs that the presence of feminist issues in the academic left is declining as well. Day care is disappearing from left conferences. As marxism or political economy become intellectually acceptable, the 'old boys' network of liberal academia is replicated in a sidekick 'young boys' network of marxists and radicals, nonetheless male in membership and outlook despite its youth and radicalism.

The pressures on radical women to abandon this silly stuff and become 'serious' revolutionaries have increased.

Our work seems a waste of time compared to inflation and unemployment. It is symptomatic of male dominance that *our* unemployment was never considered in a crisis. In the last major economic crisis, the 1930s, the vast unemployment was partially dealt with by excluding women from many kinds of jobs – one wage job per family, and that job was the man's. Capitalism and patriarchy recovered – strengthened from the crisis. Just as economic crises serve a restorative function for capitalism by correcting imbalances, so they might serve patriarchy. The thirties put women back in their place.

The struggle against capital and patriarchy cannot be successful if the study and practice of the issues of feminism is abandoned. A struggle aimed only at capitalist relations of oppression will fail, since their underlying supports in patriarchal relations of oppression will be overlooked. And the analysis of patriarchy is essential to a definition of the kind of socialism useful to women. While men and women share a need to overthrow capitalism they retain interests particular to their gender group. It is not clear – from our sketch, from history, or from male socialists – that the socialism being struggled for is the same for both men and women. For a human socialism would require not only consensus on what the new society should look like and what a healthy person should look like, but more concretely, it would require that men relinquish their privilege.

As women we must not allow ourselves to be talked out of the urgency and importance of our tasks, as we have so many times in the past. We must fight the attempted coercion, both subtle and not so subtle, to abandon feminist objectives.

This suggests two strategic considerations. First, a struggle to establish socialism must be a struggle in which groups with different interests form an alliance. Women should not trust men to liberate them after the revolution, in part, because there is no reason to think they would know how; in part, because there is no necessity for them to do so. In fact their immediate self-interest lies in our continued oppression. Instead we must have our own organizations and our own power base. Second, we think the sexual division of labor within capitalism has given women a practice in which we have learned to understand what human interdependence and needs are. While men have long struggled *against* capital, women know what to struggle *for*.[2] As a general rule, men's position in patriarchy and capitalism prevents them from recognizing both human needs for nurturance, sharing, and growth, and the potential for meeting those needs in a nonhierarchical, nonpatriarchal society. But even if we raise their consciousness, men might assess the potential gains against the potential losses and choose the status quo. Men have more to lose than their chains.

As feminist socialists, we must organize a practice which addresses both the struggle against patriarchy and the struggle against capitalism. We must insist that the society we want to create is a society in which recognition of interdependence is liberation rather than shame, nurturance is a universal, not an oppressive practice, and in which women do not continue to support the false as well as the concrete freedoms of men.

Notes

1. Often paraphrased as 'the husband and wife are one and that one is the husband,' English law held the 'by marriage, the husband and wife are one person in law: that is, the very being or legal existence of the women is suspended during the marriage, or at least is incorporated and consolidated into that of the Husband,' I. Blackstone, *Commentaries*, 1965, pp. 442–445, cited in Kenneth M. Davidson, Ruth B. Ginsburg, and Herma H. Kay, *Sex Based Discrimination* (St. Paul, Minn.: West Publishing Co., 1974), p. 117.
2. Lise Vogel, 'The Earthly Family,' *Radical America*, Vol. 7, no. 4–5 (July–October 1973), pp. 9–50.

MICHÈLE BARRETT 1949–

☐ Michèle Barrett is a Professor of Sociology at the City University, London, and like other British Marxist and socialist feminists she is critical of reductionist biological arguments which do not account for historical differences. Beginning with her Ph.D. research on Virginia Woolf, as a member of the *Feminist Review* collective and continuing in *Women's Oppression Today: Problems in Marxist Feminist Analysis* (1980) and later books, Barrett points out that historically, the sexual division of labour predates capitalism and that there are differences in this division over time, for example an increasing specialisation.

Women's Oppression Today attempts a comprehensive account of processes of production and reproduction in relation to women's inequality. Barrett argues that it is specifically the institution of the nuclear family (a married couple with children) which enables men to dominate women not simply men's greater economic power over women. This is because the family, or what Barrett terms the 'family-household system', controls woman's access to paid labour by handicapping her as a reproducer and pleaser of men. The institution of the family creates and constructs a sexist gender ideology making inevitable the sexual division of labour because women's roles at work and in the home reinforce each other. ☐

COMMENTARY: J. Brenner and M. Ramas (1984), 'Rethinking Women's Oppression', *New Left Review*, 144: 31–71.

EXTRACT

WOMEN'S OPPRESSION TODAY: PROBLEMS IN MARXIST FEMINIST ANALYSIS [1980]*

It is relatively easy to demonstrate that women are oppressed in Britain, as in other contemporary capitalist societies, but more contentious to speak of a 'Marxist
feminist' analysis of their oppression. In recent years attempts have been made to develop a theoretical perspective
that might confidently be termed 'Marxist feminist', yet
the work so generated remains fragmentary and contradictory, lacking a conceptual framework adequate to its project. This, perhaps, is only to be expected, given the
magnitude of the task and the obstacles that any synthesis
must overcome.

The problem faced by any such analysis can be put
simply in terms of the different objects of the two perspectives. Marxism, constituted as it is around relations of appropriation and exploitation, is grounded in concepts that
do not and could not address directly the gender of the
exploiters and those whose labour is appropriated. A Marxist analysis of capitalism is therefore conceived around a
primary contradiction between labour and capital and operates with categories that, as has recently been argued, can
be termed 'sex-blind'.[1] Feminism, however, points in a different direction, emphasizing precisely the relations of gender – largely speaking, of the oppression of women by men –
that Marxism has tended to pass over in silence. Of course,
just as there are many varieties of 'Marxism' so there are
many 'feminisms' and indeed one task of any 'Marxist feminism' must be to identify which version of the one is being
bracketed with which version of the other. But what is clear
is that any feminism must insist on the specific character of

*From: Michèle Barrett (1980), *Women's Oppression Today: Problems in Marxist Feminist Analysis*, London: New Left Books.

gender relations. Some forms of feminism may pose these relations as the primary contradiction of social organization, just as Marxism poses the labour/capital contradiction as primary in the analysis of capitalism, but all must surely pose them as distinct.

What then might be the object of Marxist feminism? In the most general terms it must be to identify the operation of gender relations as and where they may be distinct from, or connected with, the processes of production and reproduction understood by historical materialism. Thus it falls to Marxist feminism to explore the relations between the organization of sexuality, domestic production, the household and so on, and historical changes in the mode of production and systems of appropriation and exploitation. Such questions are now being addressed by Marxist feminists working in anthropology, the sociology of development, and political economy.[2] This book, however, deals with the relations of gender and the oppression of women in a contemporary capitalist society. In this context a Marxist feminist approach will involve an emphasis on the relations between capitalism and the oppression of women. It will require an awareness of the specific oppression of women in capitalist relations of production, but this must be seen in the light of gender divisions which preceded the transition to capitalism and which, as far as we can tell, a socialist revolution would not of itself abolish.

[. . .]

The discussion throughout this book has emphasized the importance of ideology in the construction and reproduction of women's oppression. A particular household organization and an ideology of familialism are central dimensions of women's oppression in capitalism and it is only through an analysis of ideology that we can grasp the oppressive myth of an idealized natural 'family' to which all women must conform. It is only through an analysis of ideology and its role in the construction of gendered subjectivity that we can account for the desires of women as well as men to reproduce the very familial structures by which we are oppressed. To argue this is not to suggest that needs for intimacy, sexual relations, emotional fulfilment, parenthood and so on are in themselves oppressive. What is oppressive is the assumption that the present form of such needs is the only possible form, and that the manner in which they should be met is through the family as it is today. We can have little knowledge of the form such personal needs have taken in the past, and still less of what form they might take in a future society. What feminism requires, however, in order to reach out to a wider group of women, is a more perceptive and sympathetic account not only of how or why a dominant meaning of femininity has been constructed, but how or why women have sought, consciously and unconsciously, to embrace and desire it. This requires not simply an analysis of collusion or false consciousness, but a much deeper analysis of subjectivity and identity, which presents us with the task of carrying on where earlier feminists such as Simone de Beauvoir have begun.

[. . .]

It is, perhaps, possible to resolve this problem without recourse to the analytically paralysing thesis of 'absolute autonomy', or to a form of materialism that displaces the labour/capital contradiction from its centrality in the analysis of capitalist society. First, we can note that the ideology of gender – the meaning of masculinity and femininity – has varied historically and should not be treated as static or unified, but should be examined in the different historical and class contexts in which it occurs. Second, we can note that the meaning of gender in capitalism today is tied to a household structure and division of labour that occupy a particular place in the relations of production, and that, therefore, this ideology does, concretely and historically, have some material basis. Third, we can recognize the difficulty of posing economic and ideological categories as exclusive and distinct. The relations of production and reproduction of contemporary capitalism may operate in general according to exploitative capital accumulation processes that are technically 'sex-blind', but they take the form of a division of labour in which ideology is deeply embedded.

[. . .]

Feminism seeks to change not simply men or women, or both, as they exist at present, but seeks to change the relations between them. Although the basis for this will be provided by an autonomous women's liberation movement the strategy must involve political engagement with men rather than a policy of absolute separatism. Socialist men, like other men, stand to lose political power and social privilege from the liberation of women but, more than other men, they have shown now and in the past some political intention to support feminist struggle. This is not a question of benevolence on their part. For if women's oppression is entrenched in the structure of capitalism then the struggle for women's liberation and the struggle for socialism cannot wholly be disengaged. Just as we cannot conceive of women's liberation under the oppression of capitalism so we cannot conceive of a socialism whose principles of equality, freedom and dignity are vitiated by the familiar iniquities of gender.

Notes

1. See Heidi Hartmann, 'The Unhappy Marriage of Marxism and Feminism: Towards a More Progressive Union', *Capital and Class*, no. 8, 1979, and Mark Cousins, 'Material Arguments and Feminism', *m/f*, no. 2, 1978.
2. See, for instance, the special issue of *Critique of Anthropology*, vol. 3, nos. 9/10, 1977.

CATHARINE MACKINNON

☐ Catharine MacKinnon is one of the foremost American critics putting Marxist theories about production and reproduction to the service of feminism. With its resonating opening phrase 'sexuality is to feminism what work is to marxism: that which is most one's own, yet most taken away' MacKinnon's essay ('Feminism, Marxism, Method, and the State: An Agenda for Theory', 1982) brings us to the limits of socialist feminism with her persuasive argument that the central organising categories of Marxism and feminism – production and sexuality (or reproduction) – will always be distinct. This is because, MacKinnon argues, women's experiences of sexual objectification – of rape, pornography, and violence – are the true core of women's oppression.

Marxism's insistence on the primacy of production, and Marxist feminism's choice of the family as a site of oppression cannot adequately explain male aggression, MacKinnon claims, although they may account for some of its features. MacKinnon places her theory on the cusp between socialist feminism and radical feminism. MacKinnon's ideas support second wave feminism's startling and original discovery of the extent of male sexual violence by arguing that it is the sexual objectification of women, not simply the sexual division of labour, which shapes our roles at work (through sexual harassment) and in the home (through domestic violence). Framing a feminist jurisprudence in the Minneapolis Anti-Pornography Ordinance, MacKinnon and Dworkin sought to connect in law women's unequal civil rights with our unequal sexual rights. It is sexual violence or the threat of violence, not only economic inequality which is the material reality of women's lives.   ☐

COMMENTARY: W.B. Warner (1989), 'Treating Me Like an Object: Reading Catharine MacKinnon's "Feminism" and D. Landry's response "Treating Him Like an Object" ', in L. Kauffman, *Feminism and Institutions*, Oxford: Blackwell, 1989.

EXTRACT

FEMINISM, MARXISM, METHOD, AND THE STATE: AN AGENDA FOR THEORY [1982]*

Sexuality is to feminism what work is to marxism: that which is most one's own, yet most taken away. Marxist theory argues that society is fundamentally constructed of the relations people form as they do and make things needed to survive humanly. Work is the social process of shaping and transforming the material and social worlds, creating people as social beings as they create value. It is that activity by which people become who they are. Class is its structure, production its consequence, capital its congealed form, and control its issue.

Implicit in feminist theory is a parallel argument: the molding, direction, and expression of sexuality organizes society into two sexes – women and men – which division underlies the totality of social relations. Sexuality is that social process which creates, organizes, expresses, and directs desire,[1] creating the social beings we know as women and men, as their relations create society. As work is to marxism, sexuality to feminism is socially constructed yet constructing, universal as activity yet historically specific, jointly comprised of matter and mind. As the organized expropriation of the work of some for the benefit of others defines a class – workers – the organized expropriation of the sexuality of some for the use of others defines the sex, woman. Heterosexuality is its structure, gender and family its congealed forms, sex roles its qualities generalized to social persona, reproduction a consequence, and control its issue.

Marxism and feminism are theories of power and its distribution: inequality. They provide accounts of how social

*From: Catharine MacKinnon (1982), 'Feminism, Marxism, Method, and the State: An Agenda for Theory', in N.O. Keohane et al. (eds), Feminist Theory: A Critique of Ideology, Brighton: Harvester.

arrangements of patterned disparity can be internally rational yet unjust. But their specificity is not incidental. In marxism to be deprived of one's work, in feminism of one's sexuality, defines each one's conception of lack of power per se. They do not mean to exist side by side to insure that two separate spheres of social life are not overlooked, the interests of two groups are not obscured, or the contributions of two sets of variables are not ignored. They exist to argue, respectively, that the relations in which many work and few gain, in which some fuck and others get fucked,[2] are the prime moment of politics.

[...]

In order to account for women's consciousness (much less propagate it) feminism must grasp that male power produces the world before it distorts it. Women's acceptance of their condition does not contradict its fundamental unacceptability if women have little choice but to *become* persons who freely choose women's roles. For this reason, the reality of women's oppression is, finally, neither demonstrable nor refutable empirically. Until this is confronted on the level of method, criticism of what exists can be undercut by pointing to the reality to be criticized. Women's bondage, degradation, damage, complicity, and inferiority – together with the possibility of resistance, movement, or exceptions – will operate as barriers to consciousness rather than as means of access to what women need to become conscious of in order to change.

Male power is real; it is just not what it claims to be, namely, the only reality. Male power is a myth that makes itself true. What it is to raise consciousness is to confront male power in this duality: as total on one side and a delusion on the other. In consciousness raising, women learn they have *learned* that men are everything, women their negation, but that the sexes are equal. The content of the message is revealed true and false at the same time; in fact, each part reflects the other transvalued. If 'men are all, women their negation' is taken as social criticism rather than simple description, it becomes clear for the first time that women *are* men's equals, everywhere in chains. Their chains become visible, their inferiority – their inequality – a product of subjection and a mode of its enforcement. Reciprocally, the moment it is seen that this – life as we know it – is not equality, that the sexes are not socially equal, womanhood can no longer be defined in terms of lack of maleness, as negativity. For the first time, the question of what a woman *is* seeks its ground in and of a world understood as neither of its making nor in its image, and finds, within a critical embrace of woman's fractured and alien image, that world women have made and a vision of its wholeness. Feminism has unmasked maleness as a form of power that is both omnipotent and nonexistent, an unreal thing with very real consequences. Zora Neale Hurston captured its two-sidedness: 'The town has a basketfull of feelings good and bad about Joe's positions and possessions, but none had the temerity to challenge him. They bowed down to him rather, because he was all of these things, and then again he was all of these things because the town bowed down.'[3] If 'positions and possessions' and rulership create each other, in relation, the question becomes one of form and inevitability. This challenges feminism to apply its theory of women's standpoint to the regime.[4]

Feminism is the first theory to emerge from those whose interest it affirms. Its method recapitulates as theory the reality it seeks to capture. As marxist method is dialectical materialism, feminist method is consciousness raising: the collective critical reconstitution of the meaning of women's social experience, as women live through it. Marxism and feminism on this level posit a different relation between thought and thing, both in terms of the relationship of the analysis itself to the social life it captures and in terms of the participation of thought in the social life it analyzes. To the extent that materialism is scientific it posits and refers to a reality outside thought which it considers to have an objective – that is, truly nonsocially perspectival – content. Consciousness raising, by contrast, inquires into an intrinsically social situation, into that mixture of thought and materiality which is women's sexuality in the most generic sense. It approaches its world through a process that shares its determination: women's consciousness, not as individual or subjective ideas, but as collective social being. This method stands inside its own determinations in order to uncover them, just as it criticizes them in order to value them on its own terms – in order to *have* its own terms at all. Feminism turns theory itself – the pursuit of a true analysis of social life – into the pursuit of consciousness and turns an analysis of inequality into a critical embrace of its own determinants. The process is transformative as well as perceptive, since thought and thing are inextricable and reciprocally constituting of women's oppression, just as the state as coercion and the state as legitimizing ideology are indistinguishable, and for the same reasons. The pursuit of consciousness becomes a form of political practice. Consciousness raising has revealed gender relations to be a collective fact, no more simply personal than class relations. This implies that class relations may also be personal, no less so for being at the same time collective. The failure of marxism to realize this may connect the failure of workers in advanced capitalist nations to organize in the socialist sense with the failure of left revolutions to liberate women in the feminist sense.

Feminism stands in relation to marxism as marxism does to classical political economy: its final conclusion and ultimate critique. Compared with marxism, the place of thought and things in method and reality are reversed in a seizure of power that penetrates subject with object and theory with practice. In a dual motion, feminism turns marxism inside out and on its head.

To answer an old question – how is value created and distributed? – Marx needed to create an entirely new account of the social world. To answer an equally old question, or to question an equally old reality – what explains the inequality of women to men? or, how does desire become domination? or, what is male power? – feminism revolutionizes politics.

Notes

1. 'Desire' is selected as a term parallel to 'value' in marxist theory to refer to that substance felt to be primordial or aboriginal but posited by the theory as social and contingent. The sense in which I mean it is consonant with its development in contemporary French feminist theories, e.g., in Hélène Cixous, 'The Laugh of Medusa: Viewpoint,' trans. Keith Cohen and Paula Cohen, *Signs: Journal of Women in Culture and Society* 1, no. 4 (Summer 1976): 875–93; and in works by Gauthier, Irigaray, LeClerc, Duras, and Kristeva in *New French Feminisms: An Anthology,* ed. Elaine Marks and Isabelle de Courtivron (Amherst: University of Massachusetts Press, 1980). My use of the term is to be distinguished from that of Gilles Deleuze and Felix Guattari, *Anti-Oedipus: Capitalism and Schizophrenia* (New York: Viking Press, 1977); and Guy Hocquenghem, *Homosexual Desire* (London: Allison & Busby, 1978), for example.
2. I know no nondegraded English verb for the activity of sexual expression that would allow a construction parallel to, for example, 'I am working,' a phrase that could apply to nearly any activity. This fact of language may reflect and contribute to the process of obscuring sexuality's pervasiveness in social life. Nor is there *any* active verb meaning 'to act sexually' that specifically envisions a woman's action. If language constructs as well as expresses the social world, these words support heterosexual values.
3. Zora Neale Hurston, *Their Eyes Were Watching God* (Urbana: University of Illinois Press, 1978), pp. 79–80.
4. In the second part of this article, 'Feminism, Marxism, Method, and the State: Toward Feminist Jurisprudence' (forthcoming in *Signs*), I argue that the state is male in that objectivity is its norm.

5 □ Asian, black, and women of colour lesbianisms/ feminisms

Introduction

□ For black, Asian and women of colour the feminist issue is also a race issue. Black feminists alert us to the ethnocentricity which informs feminist work which depicts black women as victims but not as wise women. Racism haunts sexism and their interrelations should not be ignored. But it is all too easy to argue, as do white feminists, that reproductive controls, and the family and legal inequalities are major features of patriarchy. Black feminism has a different relationship to dominating social policies than does white feminism. For example a black woman's family and labour market experience might shape her economic inequality but also, and often, the family might be a source of succour and collective support. Therefore the strident feminist calls in the 1970s for abortion on demand could not adequately address these black understandings of the family and of sexuality. Race cannot be added to other aspects of social institutions as an additional variable, for black feminists argue that race, class and gender are *interlocking* systems of oppression not additive systems. From this perspective there are continuities between Asian and black British and black American writing and writing by women of colour.

Most take feminism to involve a recognition of 'multiple identities'. The basic components of Asian and black feminist thought – its themes and methods – are shaped by a black woman's or a woman of colour's position as an insider/outsider and by her imbeddedness in Afro-American or Asian culture. So that, for example, while the theme of the journey also appears in the work of black men, black feminists explore journeys to freedom in ways that are characteristically female for their journeys are less often geographic than personal and psychological and thus political movements.

The core themes of black and other feminisms, both in America and in Britain, are: a shared history of struggle, the gaining of theory from everyday actions and experience, and the sense that 'community' is not a fragile concept but a source of care and emotional strength. Reproducing the views of ordinary black women is an essential ingredient of black feminist theory. For example Alice Walker, in *In Search of Our Mothers' Gardens* (1984), draws on the alternative Afro-American standpoints of her family and friends. Dialogue and call and response are a crucial means of knowledge creation in Afro-American culture. The sound and forms of Asian and black expression are an important part of its meaning. Asian and black feminists intensively explore the emotional and material bonds between mothers and daughters and women of different generations, sharing a responsibility to Asian and black women far beyond their immediate historical moment or national place.

A poetics of Asian and black feminism searches for racial meanings as historically constituted in the traditions, history and culture of mothers, for example in the spiritual energy of oral history, of songs, cooking and gardens. From a black standpoint, literature is integral with other social activities; it is not 'high art'. Writing as well as music often provide aafe spaces in which these standpoints can be defined. For example many heroines of black literature, as Gwendolyn Brook's *Maud Martha* (1953) shows, can transform their lives through anger. Education has long served black feminism as the source of important connections between self, change and empowerment. From Sojourner Truth, the black abolitionist and freed slave who spoke out at the women's Akron convention in 1851 onwards, black women wanted education to secure community development as much as self development or individual entry into the white middle class. There are specific issues, however, which cannot be added to a general theory of black women's oppression, for example other minority women in Britain point to the absence of ethnic, *non*-black identity in any single image of ethnic minorities, for example the experiences of Greek-Cypriot women.

The body of writing which has come from Asian African and Afro-Caribbean women in Britain and from Afro-Americans, women of colour and Asian Pacific women and others in America offers new categories of thought, for example Alice Walker's term 'familiars' for her spiritual foremothers. Black feminism's multilayered and multi-tissued approach to feminist thought has changed feminism. For example *Yours in Struggle* describes the work of principled coalitions of Jewish and black women. Attending to black women's long history of political action and community experience helps to ensure the integrity and survival of feminist praxis. □

COMMENTARY: P.H. Collins (1990), *Black Feminist Thought*, London: Unwin Hyman; E.V. Spelman (1990), *Inessential Women*, London: The Women's Press; E. Bulkin *et al.* (1984) *Yours in Struggle*, Brooklyn, NY: Long Haul Press.

JOYCE LADNER

☐ Joyce Ladner's work made a major contribution to the new black feminist scholarship of the 1970s which attacked the misnomers and stereotypes of black women and black families which had shaped government and state reports in the mid-1960s. Ladner was one of the first American sociologists to promote a black perspective and she deliberately subverted traditional methods of the social sciences by refusing a false objectivity. For example, Ladner pointed to the connection between her own experience of growing up as a black woman in the South and her social consciousness and the disparity between these two in traditional sociology. Ladner's work highlights a crucial theme of feminist theory: 'double consciousness'.

Ladner argued that black adolescent girls had an autonomous image of black womanhood, one in which reproduction and child rearing was a positive not a negative activity. These girls chose models of black womanhood from a variety of sources, including their mothers' histories, Afro-American culture and their own specific economic and community environments.

Although in her replication study in 1984, Ladner found that the futures of teenagers and their mothers were harsher and bleaker than a decade before, she argues convincingly that black girls' concepts of work, women and the meaning of their lives were not only at odds with the values of white society but created images of strong and positive black women not of women as victims of white racism. ☐

COMMENTARY: La Frances Rodgers (ed.) (1989), *The Black Woman*, Beverly Hills: Sage.

EXTRACT

TOMORROW'S TOMORROW: THE BLACK WOMAN [1972]*

Many books have been written about the Black community[1] but very few have really dealt with the intricate lives of the people who live there. By and large, they have attempted to analyze and describe the pathology which allegedly characterizes the lives of its inhabitants while at the same time making its residents responsible for its creation. The unhealthy conditions of the community such as drug addiction, poverty, crime, dilapidated housing, unemployment, and the multitude of problems which characterize it have caused social analysts to see the conditions as producing millions of 'sick' people, many of whom are given few chances ever to overcome the wretchedness which clouds their existence. Few authorities on the Black community have written about the vast amount of strength and adaptability of the people. They have ignored the fact that this community is a force which not only acts upon its residents but which is also acted upon. Black people are involved in a dynamic relationship with their physical and cultural environment in that they both influence and are influenced by it. This reciprocal relationship allows them to exercise a considerable amount of power over their environs. This also means that they are able to exercise control over their futures, whereas writers have tended to view the low-income Black community as an all-pervasive force which is so devastating as to compel its powerless residents to succumb to its pressures. Their power to cope and adapt to a set of unhealthy conditions – not as stereotyped sick people but as normal ones – is a factor which few people seem to accept or even realize. The ways Blacks have adapted to

*From: Joyce Ladner (1987), 'Introduction' to Tomorrow's Tomorrow: The Black Woman in S. Harding (ed.) Feminism and Methodology: Social Science Issues, Milton Keynes: Open University Press.

poverty and racism, and yet emerged relatively unscarred, are a peculiar quality which Americans should commend.

The concept of social deviance is quite frequently applied to the values and behavior of Blacks because they represent a departure from the traditional white middle-class norm, along with criminals, homosexuals and prostitutes.

But these middle-class standards should not have been imposed because of the distinctiveness that characterizes the Black life-style, particularly that of the masses.

Most scholars have taken a dim view of any set of distinct life-styles shared by Blacks, and where they were acknowledged to exist, have of course maintained that these forces were negative adaptations to the large society. There has never been an admission that the Black community is a product of American social policy, *not* the cause of it – the structure of the American social system, through its practices of institutional racism, is designed to create the alleged 'pathology' of the community, to perpetuate 'the social disorganization' model of Black life. Recently, the Black culture thesis has been granted some legitimization as an explanatory variable for much of the distinctiveness of Black life. As a result of this more positive attitude toward understanding the strengths of life in the Black community, many scholars, policy makers et al. are refocusing their attention and reinterpreting the many aspects of life that comprise the complex existence of American blacks.

There must be a strong concern with redefining the problem. Instead of future studies being conducted on *problems* of the Black community as represented by the *deviant perspective,* there must be a redefinition of the *problem as being that of institutional racism.* If the social system is viewed as the *source* of the deviant perspective, then future research must begin to analyze the nature of oppression and the mechanisms by which institutionalized forms of subjugation are initiated and act to maintain the system intact. Thus, studies which have as their focal point the alleged deviant *attitudes* and *behavior* of Blacks are grounded within the racist assumptions and principles that only render Blacks open to further exploitation.

The challenge to social scientists for a redefinition of the basic *problem* has been raised in terms of the 'colonial analogy.' It has been argued that the relationship between the *researcher* and his *subjects*, by definition, resembles that of the oppressor and the oppressed, because it is the oppressor who defines the problem, the nature of the research, and, to some extent, the quality of interaction between him and his subjects. This inability to understand and research the fundamental problem – *neo-colonialism* – prevents most social researchers from being able accurately to observe and analyze Black life and culture and the impacts racism and oppression have upon Blacks. Their inability to understand the nature and effects of neo-colonialism in the same manner as Black people is rooted in the inherent bias of the social sciences. The basic concepts and tools of white Western society are permeated by this partiality to the conceptual framework of the oppressor. It is simple enough to say that the difference between the two groups – the oppressor and the oppressed – prevents the former from adequately comprehending the essence of Black life and culture because of a fundamental difference in perceptions, based upon separate histories, life-styles, and purposes for being. Simply put, the slave and his master do not view and respond to the world in the same way.

Note

1. I am using the term 'Black community' to refer to what is traditionally called the 'ghetto.' I am speaking largely of the low-income and working-class masses, who comprise the majority of the Black population in this country.

ANGELA DAVIS 1944–

☐ Angela Davis was a member of black liberation movements in the 1960s and 1970s (Civil Rights and the Black Panthers) and it is their ideas, combined with her subsequent disaffection with black sexism and white racism which shape her thinking. For example in her critiques of Shulamith Firestone and Susan Brownmiller, Davis argues that black feminists must contest social misnomers such as 'black matriarchy' as well as fight economic oppression.

In *Women, Race and Class* (1981), Davis points out that black women suffer a double jeopardy in economic production when racism and sexism combine to relegate black women to low-paid jobs, but that a black woman's awareness of oppression and her activism challenges white feminist theory. Often the strength a black woman gains from her family community and reproductive roles cushions her in her harsh public labour. Criticising the stock concept of a culturally homogeneous black woman, Davis undertook extensive historical research into black women's slave roles to discover the ways in which black women have always actively resisted white incursions. Davis argues that contemporary black feminism is in debt to these generational militancies. Davis contests both white *and* black male histories of slavery which describe only active *male* slave rebellions and she counterposes to this picture an alternative narrative about the educative and procreative power of black women slaves.

Davis created a more accurate history of black women not only to bring to attention and to preserve a tradition of black women's activism, but also to question conventional accounts of reproduction. For example, Davis shows that child rearing was not an oppressive experience in slavery but often a way for black women slaves to anchor themselves in a community. In *Women, Culture and Politics* (1989), Davis went on to argue that black women's empowerment must come from an activism which connects middle-class and working-class black women together with their history. ☐

COMMENTARY: P. Giddings (1984), *When and Where I Enter: The Impact of Black Women on Race and Sex in America*, New York: Wm Morrow.

EXTRACT

WOMEN, RACE AND CLASS [1981]*

If and when a historian sets the record straight on the experiences of enslaved Black women, she (or he) will have performed an inestimable service. It is not for the sake of
historical accuracy alone that such a study should be conducted, for lessons can be gleaned from the slave era which
will shed light upon Black women's and all women's current battle for emancipation. As a layperson, I can only
propose some tentative ideas which might possibly guide a
reexamination of the history of Black women during
slavery.

Proportionately, more Black women have always worked
outside their homes than have their white sisters.[1] The
enormous space that work occupies in Black women's lives
today follows a pattern established during the very earliest
days of slavery. As slaves, compulsory labor overshadowed
every other aspect of women's existence. It would seem,
therefore, that the starting point for any exploration of
Black women's lives under slavery would be an appraisal of
their role as workers.

The slave system defined Black people as chattel. Since
women, no less than men, were viewed as profitable labor-
units, they might as well have been genderless as far as the
slaveholders were concerned. In the words of one s holar,
'the slave woman was first a full-time worker for her owner,
and only incidentally a wife, mother and homemaker.'[2]
Judged by the evolving nineteenth-century ideology of femininity, which emphasized women's roles as nurturing
mothers and gentle companions and housekeepers for their
husbands, Black women were practically anomalies.

Though Black women enjoyed few of the dubious benefits of the ideology of womanhood, it is sometimes assumed

*From: Angela Davis (1982), *Women, Race and Class*, London: The Women's Press.

that the typical female slave was a houseservant – either a cook, maid, or mammy for the children in the 'big house.' Uncle Tom and Sambo have always found faithful companions in Aunt Jemima and the Black Mammy – stereotypes which presume to capture the essence of the Black woman's role during slavery. As is so often the case, the reality is actually the diametrical opposite of the myth. Like the majority of slave men, slave women, for the most part, were field workers. While a significant proportion of border-state slaves may have been houseservants, slaves in the Deep South – the real home of the slaveocracy – were predominantly agricultural workers. Around the middle of the nineteenth century, seven out of eight slaves, men and women alike, were field workers.[3]

[. . .]

It would be a mistake to regard the institutionalized pattern of rape during slavery as an expression of white men's sexual urges, otherwise stifled by the specter of white womanhood's chastity. That would be far too simplistic an explanation. Rape was a weapon of domination, a weapon of repression, whose covert goal was to extinguish slave women's will to resist, and in the process, to demoralize their men. These observations on the role of rape during the Vietnam War could also apply to slavery: 'In Vietnam, the U.S. Military Command made rape "socially acceptable"; in fact, it was unwritten, but clear, policy.'[4] When GIs were encouraged to rape Vietnamese women and girls (and they were sometimes advised to 'search' women 'with their penises'[5]) a weapon of mass political terrorism was forged. Since the Vietnamese women were distinguished by their heroic contributions to their people's liberation struggle, the military retaliation specifically suited for them was rape. While women were hardly immune to the violence inflicted on men, they were especially singled out as victims of terrorism by a sexist military force governed by the principle that war was exclusively a man's affair. 'I saw one case where a woman was shot by a sniper, one of our snipers,' a GI said.

When we got up to her she was asking for water. And the lieutenant said to kill her. So he ripped off her clothes, they stabbed her in both breasts, they spread her eagle and shoved an E tool (entrenching) up her vagina. And then they took that out and used a tree limb and then she was shot.[6]

In the same way that rape was an institutionalized ingredient of the aggression carried out against the Vietnamese people, designed to intimidate and terrorize the women, slaveowners encouraged the terroristic use of rape in order to put Black women in their place. If Black women had achieved a sense of their own strength and a strong urge to resist, then violent sexual assaults – so the slaveholders might have reasoned – would remind the women of their essential and inalterable femaleness. In the male supremacist vision of the period, this means passivity, acquiescence and weakness.

[. . .]

In the history of the United States, the fraudulent rape charge stands out as one of the most formidable artifices invented by racism. The myth of the Black rapist has been methodically conjured up whenever recurrent waves of violence and terror against the Black community have required convincing justifications. If Black women have been conspicuously absent from the ranks of the contemporary anti-rape movement, it may be due, in part, to that movement's indifferent posture toward the frame-up rape charge as an incitement to racist aggression. Too many innocents have been offered sacrificially to gas chambers and lifer's cells for Black women to join those who often seek relief from policemen and judges. Moreover, as rape victims themselves, they have found little if any sympathy from these men in uniforms and robes. And stories about police assaults on Black women – rape victims sometimes suffering a second rape – are heard too frequently to be dismissed as aberrations. 'Even at the strongest time of the civil rights movement in Birmingham,' for example, young activists often stated that nothing could protect Black women from being raped by Birmingham police. As recently as December, 1974, in Chicago, a 17-year old Black woman reported that she was gang-raped by 10 policemen. Some of the men were suspended, but ultimately the whole thing was swept under the rug.[7]

During the early stages of the contemporary anti-rape movement, few feminist theorists seriously analyzed the special circumstances surrounding the Black woman as rape victim. The historical knot binding Black women – systematically abused and violated by white men – to Black men – maimed and murdered because of the racist manipulation of the rape charge – has just begun to be acknowledged to any significant extent.

Notes

1. See W.E.B. DuBois, 'The Damnation of Women,' Chapter VII of *Darkwater* (New York: Harcourt, Brace and Howe, 1920).
2. Kenneth M. Stampp, *The Peculiar Institution: Slavery in the Antebellum South* (New York: Vintage Books, 1956), p. 343.
3. *Ibid.*, pp. 31, 49, 50, 60.
4. Arlene Eisen-Bergman, *Women in Vietnam* (San Francisco: People's Press, 1975), p. 63.
5. *Ibid.*, p. 62. 'When we went through the villages and searched people, the women would have all their clothes taken off and the men would use their penises to probe them to make sure they didn't have anything hidden anywhere; and this was raping, but it was done as searching.' Quoted from Sgt. Scott Camil, First Marine Division, in VVAW, *Winter Soldier Investigation* (Boston: Beacon Press, 1972), p. 13.
6. *Ibid.*, p. 71. Quoted from *Winter Soldier Investigation*, p. 14.
7. 'The Racist Use of Rape and the Rape Charge.' A Statement to the Women's Movement From a Group of Socialist Women (Louisville, Ky: Socialist Women's Caucus, 1974), pp. 5–6.

COMBAHEE RIVER COLLECTIVE 1974

☐ A black feminist group was founded in 1974 explicitly to contest the presumptive power of white feminists to speak for universal women. The group named itself after Harriet Tubman's battle, in June 1863 in South Carolina, which freed more than 750 slaves. The Combahee River Collective has declared itself to be socialist/lesbian and committed to developing socialist and Marxist theories about black women's work, although many contemporary lesbians are dismayed by their politics. The Combahee statement, part of which is reprinted here, openly speculates about the precise meaning of racism, about definitions of the 'Black experience', and about what constitutes the 'known facts' of black history.

The central theme of the group's work and of this pioneering and influential statement, is the simultaneity of black oppressions. Combahee argue that no one 'had ever examined' the multilayered texture of black women's lives. Like Audre Lorde and other black feminists, Combahee insists on the pressure of racism within white feminism, for example by suggesting that only Afro-Americans can be black feminists. But it is capitalism, they argue, which is the major source of black women's oppression. A crucial feature of black feminism, they claim, must be political activism. Hence Combahee argues against black women separating from black male anti-racist work.   ☐

COMMENTARY: P.H. Collins (1990), *Black Feminist Thought*, London: Unwin Hyman.

A BLACK FEMINIST STATEMENT [1978]*

Above all else, our politics initially sprang from the shared belief that Black women are inherently valuable, that our liberation is a necessity not as an adjunct to somebody else's but because of our needs as human persons for auto- nomy. This may seem so obvious as to sound simplistic, but it is apparent that no other ostensibly progressive movement has ever considered our specific oppression as a priority or worked seriously for the ending of that oppres- sion. Merely naming the pejorative stereotypes attributed to Black women (e.g. mammy, matriarch, Sapphire, whore, bulldagger), let alone cataloging the cruel, often murderous, treatment we receive, indicates how little value has been placed upon our lives during four centuries of bondage in the Western hemisphere. We realize that the only people who care enough about us to work consistently for our lib- eration is us. Our politics evolve from a healthy love for ourselves, our sisters and our community which allows us to continue our struggle and work.

This focusing upon our own oppression is embodied in the concept of identity politics. We believe that the most profound and potentially the most radical politics come dir- ectly out of our own identity, as opposed to working to end somebody else's oppression. In the case of Black women this is a particularly repugnant, dangerous, threatening and therefore revolutionary concept because it is obvious from looking at all the political movements that have preceded us that anyone is more worthy of liberation than ourselves. We reject pedestals, queenhood, and walking ten paces be- hind. To be recognized as human, levelly human, is enough.

We believe that sexual politics under patriarchy is as per- vasive in Black women's lives as are the politics of class and

*From: The Combahee River Collective (1982), 'A Black Feminist Statement', in G.T. Hull et al. (eds), *All the Women Are White, All the Blacks Are Men, But Some of Us Are Brave: Black Women's Studies*, New York: The Feminist Press.

race. We also often find it difficult to separate race from class from sex oppression because in our lives they are most often experienced simultaneously. We know that there is such a thing as racial-sexual oppression which is neither solely racial nor solely sexual, e.g., the history of rape of Black women by white men as a weapon of political repression.

Although we are feminists and lesbians, we feel solidarity with progressive Black men and do not advocate the fractionalization that white women who are separatists demand. Our situation as Black people necessitates that we have solidarity around the fact of race, which white women of course do not need to have with white men, unless it is their negative solidarity as racial oppressors. We struggle together with Black men against racism, while we also struggle with Black men about sexism.

We realize that the liberation of all oppressed peoples necessitates the destruction of the political-economic systems of capitalism and imperialism as well as patriarchy. We are socialists because we believe the work must be organized for the collective benefit of those who do the work and create the products, and not for the profit of the bosses. Material resources must be equally distributed among those who create these resources. We are not convinced, however, that a socialist revolution that is not also a feminist and antiracist revolution will guarantee our liberation. We have arrived at the necessity for developing an understanding of class relationships, that takes into account the specific class position of Black women who are generally marginal in the labor force, while at this particular time some of us are temporarily viewed as doubly desirable tokens at white-collar and professional levels. We need to articulate the real class situation of persons who are not merely raceless, sexless workers, but for whom racial and sexual oppression are significant determinants in their working/economic lives. Although we are in essential agreement with Marx's theory as it applied to the very specific economic relationships he analyzed, we know that his analysis must be extended further in order for us to understand our specific economic situation as Black women.

A political contribution which we feel we have already made is the expansion of the feminist principle that the personal is political. In our consciousness-raising sessions, for example, we have in many ways gone beyond white women's revelations because we are dealing with the implications of race and class as well as sex. Even our Black women's style of talking/testifying in Black language about what we have experienced has a resonance that is both cultural and political. We have spent a great deal of energy delving into the cultural and experiential nature of our oppression out of necessity because none of these matters has ever been looked at before. No one before has ever examined the multilayered texture of Black women's lives.

AUDRE LORDE 1934–

☐ Audre Lorde is an Afro-American lesbian poet and philosopher who describes the year 1968, when her first book was published (*The First Cities*) and she made her first trip to the deep South, as 'pivotal' because it inspired Lorde's intense concern with issues of repression and violence.

The central themes and motifs of Lorde's life and writing are: issues of male power and violence; the cultural history of Africa and her belief that 'I cannot be simply a Black person and not be a woman too, nor can I be a woman without being a lesbian.' Lorde makes a prolonged effort in her writing to reach into a spiritual tradition (the ancient myths of Dahomey) combined with a militant opposition to sexual violence, her experiences with cancer and the strengths which she learned from illness.

Lorde frees the concept of 'difference' from a hierarchical binary image of 'superior' and 'inferior'. When Lorde calls herself Sister Outsider (the title of her major collection of essays) she is claiming a tension *between* identities and creating a connection between two apparently contradictory positions. Believing that sexual preference and race have interlocking features, Lorde argues that a black feminist standpoint must be an integrated, holistic knowledge. Both capitalism and the white feminist academy have silenced women of colour, symbolised for Lorde in the term 'minority discourse'. The 'Open Letter to Mary Daly' exactly illustrates this point. In it Lorde argues that Daly's *Gyn/Ecology* (1978) distorts black women's history by presenting black women only as victims, for example of genital mutilation, and not as warriors and goddesses. As Lorde points out, black women have continually created positive cultural images although for the most part in proverbs, stories and black activism.

The strength of Lorde's feminism lies in her belief that women must combine an African understanding of emotion together with the rationality of the European enlightenment in order to challenge racism and sexism. Affirming that women have cultural differences but that we all share a need to survive, Lorde makes an extensive mapping of matrilineal diasporas in her meshings of history, myth and poetry. ☐

COMMENTARY: B. Christian (1985), *Black Feminist Criticism*, Oxford: Pergamon.

EXTRACT

AN OPEN LETTER TO MARY DALY [1980]*

To dismiss our Black foremothers may well be to dismiss where european women learned to love. As an African-american woman in white patriarchy, I am used to having my archetypal experience distorted and trivialized, but it is terribly painful to feel it being done by a woman whose knowledge so much touches my own.

When I speak of knowledge, as you know, I am speaking of that dark and true depth which understanding serves, waits upon, and makes accessible through language to ourselves and others. It is this depth within each of us that nurtures vision.

What you excluded from *Gyn/Ecology* dismissed my heritage and the heritage of all other noneuropean women, and denied the real connections that exist between all of us.

[...]

We remember the old traditions of power and strength and nurturance found in the female bonding of African women. It is there to be tapped by all women who do not fear the revelation of connection to themselves.

Have you read my work, and the work of other Black women, for what it could give you? Or did you hunt through only to find words that would legitimize your chapter on African genital mutilation in the eyes of the other Black women? And if so, then why not use our words to legitimize or illustrate the other places where we connect in our being and becoming? If, on the other hand, it was not Black women you were attempting to reach, in what way did our words illustrate your point for white women?

*From: Audre Lorde (1984), *Sister Outsider*, Trumansburg, New York: The Crossing Press.

[. . .]

Mary, I ask that you re-member what is dark and ancient and divine within yourself that aids your speaking. As outsiders, we need each other for support and connection and all the other necessities of living on the borders. But in order to come together we must recognize each other. Yet I feel that since you have so completely un-recognized me, perhaps I have been in error concerning you and no longer recognize you.

I feel you do celebrate differences between white women as a creative force toward change, rather than a reason for misunderstanding and separation. But you fail to recognize that, as women, those differences expose all women to various forms and degrees of patriarchal oppression, some of which we share and some of which we do not. For instance, surely you know that for nonwhite women in this country, there is an 80 percent fatality rate from breast cancer; three times the number of unnecessary eventrations, hysterectomies and sterilizations as for white women; three times as many chances of being raped, murdered, or assaulted as exist for white women. These are statistical facts, not coincidences nor paranoid fantasies.

[. . .]

The oppression of women knows no ethnic nor racial boundaries, true, but that does not mean it is identical within those differences. Nor do the reservoirs of our ancient power know these boundaries. To deal with one without even alluding to the other is to distort our commonality as well as our difference.

For then beyond sisterhood is still racism.

ALICE WALKER 1944–

☐ Alice Walker claims that she was 'called to life' by the Civil Rights movement of the 1960s. It was in 1972, at Wellesley College, that Walker taught the first American course about black women writers, so that for more than twenty years Walker has been asking feminist questions about racism, sexual violence, reproductive rights and the relation of these issues to black women's culture.

Alice Walker's writing exemplifies the main features and varieties of black feminism. The most obvious is Walker's re-evaluation of women's traditional and domestic arts and her recognition of anonymous artists in her own and other black families. Reclaiming a non-literate intellectual tradition has involved Walker in 'writing all the things I should have been able to read'. Another feature is her historical accounts of the violation of black women by black and by white men. In her landmark essay 'In Search of Our Mothers' Gardens' (1984), Walker describes an Afro-American aesthetic which is composed of music, dance and quiltmaking and which relies on colour contrasts and everyday 'stuff' rather than on the abstraction favoured in white Euro-American aesthetics. Walker reveals how the racist economy of slavery (captured in racist contemporary histories) devalues traditional black female activities such as herbal medicine and midwifery.

Although Walker does not exclude coalitions with white feminists, since she suggests that all feminists are writing one huge story with different perspectives, she argues that black feminist terms and definitions must be self generated. Examples of this process include Walker's own extensive dialogues with black women writers she admires such as Zora Neale Hurston, and also the way in which she assesses the value of such writing by listening to the responses of her family to collective readings rather than through traditional literary criticism. For this reason Walker prefers to call black women who love other women 'womanists' to put black terms into feminist theory. Currently Walker makes strong connections between political thinking and spiritual transformation and in *The Temple of My Familiar* (1989) describes pansophic spirits which create redemptive images of black women.   ☐

COMMENTARY: M. Evans (1985), *Black Women Writers*, London: Pluto.

EXTRACT

IN SEARCH OF OUR MOTHERS' GARDENS [1983]*

somanist 1. From *womanish*. (Opp. of 'girlish,' i.e., frivo-
lous, irresponsible, not serious.) A black feminist or feminist of color. From the black folk expression of mothers
to female children, 'You acting womanish,' i.e., like a
woman. Usually referring to outrageous, audacious, courageous or *willful* behavior. Wanting to know more and
in greater depth than is considered 'good' for one. Interested in grown-up doings. Acting grown up. Being grown
up. Interchangeable with another black folk expression:
'You trying to be grown.' Responsible. In charge. *Serious.*

[. . .]

2. *Also*: A woman who loves other women, sexually and/or
nonsexually. Appreciates and prefers women's culture,
women's emotional flexibility (values tears as natural
counterbalance of laughter), and women's strength.
Sometimes loves individual men, sexually and/or nonsexually. Committed to survival and wholeness of entire
people, male *and* female. Not a separatist, except
periodically, for health. Traditionally universalist, as in:
'Mama, why are we brown, pink, and yellow, and our
cousins are white, beige, and black?' Ans.: 'Well, you
know the colored race is just like a flower garden, with
every color flower represented.' Traditionally capable, as
in: 'Mama, I'm walking to Canada and I'm taking you
and a bunch of other slaves with me.' Reply: 'It wouldn't
be the first time.'

3. Loves music. Loves dance. Loves the moon. *Loves* the
Spirit. Loves love and food and roundness. Loves struggle. *Loves* the Folk. Loves herself. *Regardless.*

[. . .]

4. Womanist is to feminist as purple to lavender.

*From: Alice Walker (1984), *In Search of Our Mothers' Gardens*, London: The Women's Press.

GLORIA ANZALDÚA

☐ As a mestiza woman from the TexMex border, Gloria Anzaldúa claims that her Chicana identity is grounded in a long history of resistance to racism. She has been active in the migrant farm workers' movement and now teaches Chicano studies. *This Bridge Called My Back* (1981) which she co-edited, was a pathbreaking collection of essays by women of colour which broke the silence about Chicana lesbianism. In the collection women of colour effected two simultaneous moves. They diversified ideas about difference and in so doing they threw into question the entire notion of ethnic taxonomies.

Anzaldúa's own writing is a model of diversity. *Borderlands/La Frontera* (1987) is an impressive account of matrilineal descent in Hispanic Toltec culture: of the goddess Coatlalopeuh; of the psychic experience, 'la facultad' which Anzaldúa claims, is stronger for marginal people; and of how Chicana Spanish 'tribal cultures' do not hide the arts away in museums but 'bathe, feed and clothe them' in their homes. Anzaldúa summarises the future envisaged by Chicana feminist theory as a 'left handed world' where others can feel at home in international feminism. ☐

COMMENTARY: D. Fisher (1980), *The Third Woman: Minority Women Writers of the United States*, Boston: Houghton Mifflin.

EXTRACT

LA PRIETA [1981]*

The mixture of bloods and affinities, rather than confusing or unbalancing me, has forced me to achieve a kind of equilibrium. Both cultures deny me a place in *their* universe. Between them and among others, I build my own universe, *El Mundo Zurdo*. I belong to myself and not to any one people.

I walk the tightrope with ease and grace. I span abysses. Blindfolded in the blue air. The sword between my thighs, the blade warm with my flesh. I walk the rope – an acrobat in equipoise, expert at the Balancing Act.

The rational, the patriarchal, and the heterosexual have held sway and legal tender for too long. Third World women, lesbians, feminists, and feminist-oriented men of all colors are banding and bonding together to right that balance. Only *together* can we be a force. I see us as a network of kindred spirits, a kind of family.

We are the queer groups, the people that don't belong anywhere, not in the dominant world nor completely within our own respective cultures. Combined we cover so many oppressions. But the overwhelming oppression is the collective fact that we do not fit, and because we do not fit *we are a threat*. Not all of us have the same oppressions, but we empathize and identify with each other's oppressions. We do not have the same ideology, nor do we derive similar solutions. Some of us are leftists, some of us practitioners of magic. Some of us are both. But these different affinities are not opposed to each other. In El Mundo Zurdo I with my own affinities and my people with theirs can live together and transform the planet.

*From: Gloria Anzaldúa (1983), 'La Prieta', in C. Moraga and G. Anzaldúa (eds), *This Bridge Called My Back: Writings by Radical Women of Color*, New York: Kitchen Table.

ROSARIO MORALES 1930–

☐ Puerto Ricans suffer the highest poverty rates in New York City, the centre of Puerto Rican immigration, and a uniquely harsh economic and social exclusion because upward mobility has not been a major feature of Puerto Rican lives. The false universalism in much of feminist theory is therefore particularly damaging to these women of colour. Rosario Morales is a Puerto Rican activist who calls herself a working class Marxist anti-imperialist. She has been a communist since 1949 and writes to create a feminist theory which does not deny the realities of race and class differences and which refuses the view that women are unilaterally defined by colour or by class.

Morales's major areas of concern are: the different rites of passage experienced by women of colour in their histories of immigration; changes in communities, and the role of mothering in minority cultures. In addition she sets these themes into a radically new form of feminist writing. Morales foregrounds contradictions to such an extent that contradictions become the very texture of her writing. She deliberately challenges the autonomy of theory and its separation from daily experience and from daily languages like conversations, by creating a huge diversity of linguistic styles – poems, conversations, consciousness journals.

Morales argues that women of colour best reveal historical and cultural differences in autobiography and create a distinctive approach to feminist culture, an approach often called the logic of neither/nor. Life history writing can aid self preservation because life histories can give an historical perspective to the everyday political struggles of Puerto Rican women. ☐

COMMENTARY: E. Acosta-Belen (1979), *The Puerto Rican Woman*, New York: Praeger.

EXTRACT

I AM WHAT I AM [1981]*

I am what I am and I am U.S. American   I haven't
wanted to say it because if I did you'd take away the Puerto
Rican but now I say go to hell   I am what I am and you
can't take it away with all the words and sneers at your
command   I am what I am   I am Puerto Rican   I
am U.S. American   I am New York Manhattan and the
Bronx   I am what I am I'm not hiding under no stoop
    behind no curtain   I am what I am   I am Boricua
as boricuas come from the isle of Manhattan and I croon
Carlos Gardel tangoes in my sleep and Afro-Cuban beats in
my blood and Xavier Cugat's lukewarm latin is so familiar
and dear   sneer dear but he's familiar and dear   but
not Carmen Miranda   who's a joke because I never was a
joke   I was a bit of a sensation   See! here's a real true
honest-to-god Puerto Rican girl and she's in college   Hey! Mary   come here and look she's from right
here   a South Bronx girl and she's honest-to-god in college now   Ain't that something   who would believed
it Ain't science wonderful or some such thing a wonder a
wonder
    And someone who did languages for a living stopped me
in the subway because how I spoke was a linguist's
treat   I mean there it was yiddish and spanish and fine
refined college educated english and irish which I mainly
keep in my prayers   It's dusty now   I haven't said my
prayers in decades but try my Hail Marrrry full of grrrace
with the nun's burr with the nun's disdain   its all true
and its all me   do you know I got an English accent from
the BBC I always say   For years in the mountains of
Puerto Rico when I was 22 and 24 and 26   all those
young years   I listened to the BBC and Radio Moscow's

*From: Rosario Morales (1983), 'I Am What I Am', in C. Moraga and G. Anzaldúa
(eds), *This Bridge Called My Back: Writings by Radical Women of Color*, New York:
Kitchen Table.

English   english announcers announce and denounce
and then I read Dickens all the way thru three or four times
at least and then later I read Dickens aloud in voices and
when I came back to the U.S. I spoke mockdickens and
mockBritish especially when I want to be crisp efficient I
know   what   I   am   doing   and   you   can't   scare
me   tough   that's why I am what I am and I'm a bit of
a snob too   Shit! why am I calling myself names   I
really really dig the funny way the British speak   and it's
real it's true   and I love too the singing of yiddish sentences that go with shrugs and hands and arms doing mel-
ancholy or lively dances   I love the sound and look of
yiddish in the air   in the body   in the streets   in
the English language   nooo   so what's new   so go
by the grocer and buy some fruit   oye vey   gevalt
gefilte fish   raisele   oh and those words   hundreds
of them dotting the english language like raisins in the
bread   shnook   and   schlemiel   suftik   tush
schmata   all those soft sweet sounds saying sharp sharp
things   I am what I am and I'm naturalized Jewish-
American   wasp is foreign and new but Jewish-
American is old show familiar   schmata familiar and its
me dears its me   bagels blintzes and all   I am what I
am   Take it or leave me alone.

MITSUYE YAMADA

☐ Mitsuye Yamada was born in Japan and interned in Idaho during the Second World War. *Camp Notes and Other Poems* (1976) and her other writing deals with these experiences together with issues of cultural identity and the diversifications of racial interaction.

The writing of feminist theory is an urgent task for Asian and non-black minority women because by creating stories of personal struggle such theory can provide an ideological climate in which Asian women have a place. Theory can also help to consolidate Asian and non-black history by making visible more diverse traditions and communities. While most ethnic groups have been able to develop their own cultural myths, often *unilateral* models of 'minority' have been the lot of Asian women. For example Mitsuye Yamada argues firmly that an ethnic woman's identity must be integral with the history of her mother's culture as much as with other ethnic American women because there are fundamental differences in Asian women's experiences. Yamada's goal, in all her poems and short stories, is to affirm matrilineal relations and to disclose Asian Americans' organic links with the landscape of Japanese American history and with feminism. ☐

COMMENTARY: *Echoes from Gold Mountain: An Asian American Journal* (1978), Asian American Studies, Long Beach, CA: California State University.

EXTRACT

ASIAN PACIFIC AMERICAN WOMEN AND FEMINISM [1981]*

Earlier this year, when a group of Asian Pacific American women gathered together in San Francisco poet Nellie Wong's home to talk about feminism, I was struck by our general agreement on the subject of feminism *as an ideal*. We all believed in equality for women. We agreed that it is important for each of us to know what it means to be a woman in our society, to know the historical and psychological forces that have shaped and are shaping our thoughts which in turn determine the directions of our lives. We agreed that feminism means a commitment to making changes in our own lives and a conviction that as women we have the equipment to do so. One by one, as we sat around the table and talked (we women of all ages ranging from our early twenties to the mid-fifties, single and married, mothers and lovers, straight women and lesbians), we knew what it was we wanted out of feminism, and what it was supposed to mean to us. For women to achieve equality in our society, we agreed, we must continue to work for a common goal.

But there was a feeling of disappointment in that living room toward the women's movement as it stands today. One young woman said she had made an effort to join some women's groups with high expectations but came away disillusioned because these groups were not receptive to the issues that were important to her as an Asian woman. Women in these groups, were, she said 'into pushing their own issues' and were no different from the other organizations that imposed opinions and goals on their members rather than having them shaped by the needs of the members in the organizations. Some of the other women present

*From: Mitsuye Yamada (1983), 'Asian Pacific American Women and Feminism', in C. Moraga and G. Anzaldúa (eds), *This Bridge Called My Back: Writings by Radical Women of Color*, New York: Kitchen Table.

said that they felt the women's organizations with feminist goals are still 'a middle-class women's thing.' This pervasive feeling of mistrust toward the women in the movement is fairly representative of a large group of women who live in the psychological place we now call Asian Pacific America. A movement that fights sexism in the social structure must deal with racism, and we had hoped the leaders in the women's movement would be able to see the parallels in the lives of the women of color and themselves, and would 'join' *us* in our struggle and give *us* 'input'.

It should not be difficult to see that Asian Pacific women need to affirm our own culture while working within it to change it. Many of the leaders in the women's organizations today had moved naturally from the civil rights politics of the 60's to sexual politics, while very few of the Asian Pacific women who were involved in radical politics during the same period have emerged as leaders in these same women's organizations. Instead they have become active in groups promoting ethnic identity, most notably ethnic studies in universities, ethnic theater groups or ethnic community agencies. This doesn't mean that we have placed our loyalties on the side of ethnicity over womanhood. The two are not at war with one another; we shouldn't have to sign a 'loyalty oath' favoring one over the other. However, women of color are often made to feel that we must make a choice between the two.

AMINA MAMA 1958–

☐ Amina Mama grew up in Nigeria and worked with a range of black women's organisations in Britain and the African Women's Movement, so that necessarily she points to the diverse ethnic, cultural and political histories of black women. In Britain, as elsewhere in Europe and in America, black women disproportionately occupy low-paid jobs and have been pushed back from the higher rungs of the education ladder. In British black thinking 'reproduction' operates as a challenge to white feminist theory. Black feminists point to the way in which a white model of the family is underpinned by a drive toward totalisation and closed knowledge.

In a precise elaboration of certain key themes in black feminism, Mama argues that black kinship, extended or otherwise, and black struggles for reproductive controls need the support of other feminists but not if black women are painted as victims. In her essays Mama addresses the history and institutionalisation of British racism. She argues that British public services are an example of racism because they entirely depend on the labour of black women who often occupy the least skilled and worst paid occupational levels while black women, as consumers, have the poorest access to health and welfare services. Mama describes the past and emerging features of State oppression, for example its criminalisation of black people, and its differential effect on black women and Asian women. She makes clear the connections between class, race and gender oppression in Britain today, and black and Asian women's need for autonomous organisations. ☐

COMMENTARY: B. Bryan, S. Dadzie and S. Scafe (1985), *The Heart of the Race: Black Women's Lives in Britain*, London: Virago.

BLACK WOMEN, THE ECONOMIC CRISIS AND THE BRITISH STATE [1984]*

Clarifying terms and identifying communities

The historical and political origins of the term 'Black' require particular attention in the light of the prevalent attempts to group all who are not white *and* English ('non-whites') together as 'ethnic minorities' or 'third world' persons, thereby reducing us to an amorphous, homogeneously underdeveloped and oppressed mass. This negation of the validity of 'Black' traditionally comes from the political right, which fails to recognize racism. It has also come from 'marxists', the most recent example being Anthias and Yuval-Davies (1983), ostensibly because they feel that:

> The notion of 'Black women' as delineating the boundaries of the alternative feminist movements to white feminism leaves non-British, non-black women (like us – a Greek-Cypriot and an Israeli Jew) unaccounted for politically.

It is interesting that we now have white women responding to Black women's historically-rooted tradition of autonomous organization in this manner: first by seeing it as 'an alternative movement' and secondly 'that this somehow makes them feel 'left out' of things. We have also witnessed the extension of the term 'Black' to include all those subject to imperialist domination, so that 'Black' sometimes refers to 'white' people. Despite the glaring historical inaccuracy and political foolishness of the exercise, time has been wasted arguing whether or not to include Iranians, Palestinians, Phillipinos, even Irish, as 'Black'. In the U S some American feminists have attempted to resolve the issue raised there by Hispanics, Native Americans and others, by

---

*From: Amina Mama (1984), 'Black Women, the Economic Crisis and the British State', *Feminist Review*, 17.

adopting the phrase 'women of colour', thus reserving 'Black' for Africans.

In Britain it is clear that Black refers to Africans (continental and of the diaspora), and Asians (primarily of Indian subcontinent descent). All have a shared history of oppression by British colonialism and racism. Only the Carribean African (Afro-Caribbean) community have the specific history of enslavement. They share with fellow Africans elements of a Pan-Africanist consciousness ('Black consciousness'). Amongst the Asian communities, which include those from the Asian diaspora (the Caribbean, east and southern Africa, (cf Tinker 1974)), the political consciousness that includes self-definition as 'Black' is more recent. It has come from the superimposition of the experience of white racism on the experiences of indentured labour and colonial domination.

Historically, Black consciousness (Pan-Africanism) has its origins in two related sources. First on the African continent it was manifest in movements against settler colonialism in the south and east. These date back to the Khoisan attacks on the white settlers invading the Cape in the 1600's (Marks and Atmore 1971), through to the 1906 Zulu rebellion in Natal (Marks (1970) and Chilembwe's revolt in Nyasaland, 1915. Today we have a political movement and continuing liberation war against the scourge of apartheid (for example the Black Consciousness Movement of Azania).

In East Africa there was the Nyabingi protest movement (referred to as a 'Cult'), which immobilized the administrative efforts of three colonial powers for nearly two decades in South-Western Uganda, up until 1928. One of the most powerful and feared warrior leaders was a woman known as Muhumusa. Indeed Nyabingi was also female, as were most of her 'bagwira' (mediums or representatives). Male bagwira maintained their influence in part by adopting female patterns of dress. East Africa was also the site of the famous Mau Mau rebellion.

West African political consciousness developed somewhat differently. The Indirect Rule system employed in

Northern Nigeria for example, did not facilitate the polarization of class interests along the specific dimension of skin colour in quite the same way (for example see Azikwe in Langley 1979). However, it took numerous military campaigns to conquer each of the people and empires: Benn, Ashanti, Kebbi and Sokoto. Even after formal assumption of sovereignty over Northern Nigeria, for example, Lord Lugard had to wage successive campaigns to take over lands whose armies were supplied with arms by the Nupe kingdom (Bida and Kontagora 1900, Yola 1901, Bauchi 1902, Kano 1903, Sokoto 1903 and Burmi 1903).

The diasporean source of Black consciousness must be traced back to the earliest slave rebellions; for example the Maroon wars in Jamaica, the Haitian rebellions; and in post slavery resistance. The reader is referred to the writings and practices of Blyden, Garvey, Padmore, Cesaire, DuBois, CLR James.

'Black' therefore has a particular significance for African peoples. Those from the Indian subcontinent come out of their own history of struggle.

Amongst Asians, two subgroups are additionally of interest. East African Asians had a particular relationship both with colonials (for whom they performed petit-bourgeois functions) and with the Africans (who rejected this role with the departure of the colonial masters). This is relevant to the status of this group today, who like the African elites enjoy a class position here which is often facilitated by links with capital 'back home'.

Amongst Indo-Caribbeans, the relation to Black consciousness varies between the different nations, depending on numbers, and the consequent extent of 'creolization'. In Guyana (where Asians are the majority) and Trinidad (where they are the largest single group) communities have remained largely distinct, and thus been less exposed to Africanist Black consciousness.

From this we can see that Black women in Britain are historically rooted in three different continents. It would be foolish even to attempt to summarize the diverse cultural, religious and socio-political histories out of which we have evolved. African women, for example, may come from any part of a continent so diverse that a single nation may have 250 languages reflecting cultural differences which include extremely diverse gender and status relations. To try to isolate the 'position of women' from any such cultural context is difficult yet necessary. To generalize for a whole continent borders on the foolish, and in respect of three continents must be the height of folly. Furthermore, Black women's experiences and struggles, apart from being rooted in so many different contexts are further complicated by the varying penetrations by and relations with British society. Black women here constantly identify with and politically support a range of movements, and accord varying priority to African national liberation struggles, African and Caribbean movements and events in Asia. There is also general political support for other anti-imperialist struggles such as the Latin American fight against Euro-American domination and the Irish liberation struggle against British imperialism.

From another angle we can be viewed as three 'generations'. First there are those who have inhabited Liverpool, Cardiff and London since the seventeenth century, who arrived either as slaves, or as the daughters of Black ex-slaves, or of unions between Black sailors and native white women. The middle 'generation' of Black women came as migrants from the tropical reaches of the British empire. Most recent is the growing generation born and/or predominantly raised here, by migrant parents. This last group is influenced to varying degrees by parental cultures. It is noteworthy here that a substantial proportion of the 'non-white' population is of mixed origin – this ranges from 6% in the West Midlands to 40% in Merseyside (1981 Labour force survey). Most of us are urban: 40% of the 'New Commonwealth and Pakistani origin' community lives in the GLC area (59% of West Indians), 20% in eight large cities and the remaining 40% in smaller cities. 50% of the Black community are Asian, 30% West Indian, with the remaining 20% from 'Africa, the Far East and the Mediterranean' (Population Trends 28, 1982).

In addition to the various 'parent cultures', there are new cultural and political forms evolving out of the Black British woman's unique experience, textured as this is by contemporary forms of racial, class and sexual oppression, and the corresponding patterns of rebellion and resistance (see Black Women Organizing, this issue).

Black feminism in this country reflects the diversity of origin and variation in geographical, historical and cultural reference points. The unity of Black women as Black feminists is a political phenomenon that seeks a coherent and coordinated rebellion against the varied manifestations of opprecan and Asian women's organizations such as OWAAD, is a fundamental aspect of the growing awareness of the need for a united front at a time when the British State is intensifying its discriminatory practices in ways detrimental to us all.

References

Anthias, F. and Yuval-Davies, N. (1983) 'Contextualizing Feminism; Gender, Ethnic and Class Divisions' Feminist Review number 15.

Centre for Contemporary Cultural Studies, Race and Politics Group (1982) The Empire Strikes Back London: Hutchinson.

Langley, A. (1979) Ideologies of Liberation in Black Africa 1856–1970.

Marks, S. (1970) 'The Zulu Disturbances in Natal's in Rotberg and Mazrui (1970).

Marks, S. and Atmore, A. (1971) 'Firearms in Southern Africa' Journal of African History, vol. 12 no. 2.

Population Trends, 28 (1982).

Tinker, H. (1974) A New System of Slavery: The Export of Indian Labour Overseas 1830–1920 Oxford: Oxford University Press.

EXTRACT

VIOLENCE AGAINST BLACK WOMEN: GENDER, RACE AND STATE RESPONSES [1989]*

Conceptual inadequacies in recent feminist theory

In recent years there has been an increased sophistication in European feminist and socialist analyses of the state. Partly through the resurgent appreciation of Gramsci's work there has been a move away from structuralist schema in which the state is a monolithic apparatus with various arms. Recent work advocates a reappraisal of some of the prevalent hypotheses about the articulation between gender and the state: Dahlerup (1987), for example, argues that the private/public dichotomy is no longer an adequate way of conceptualizing women/men's lives and relations to the power structure. Women in late capitalist countries are now highly involved in public life, both as clients/citizens of public services, and as workers in local government institutions and the welfare state. Private has a double semantic in the context of privatization, and can mean returning certain services to the private companies as well as the privacy of the nuclear domestic sphere. Privatization carries this logic through; it is merely that wealth becomes the currency of 'respectability' in a more overt manner.

Hernes (1987), amongst others, has noted that there has been a shift of women's dependency from the individual man to the welfare state, both for sustenance and for employment. This shift represents the development of new types of patriarchal power, which demand a more careful analytic and political scrutiny of the state (Borchorst and Siim 1987).

The lack of organized feminist or socialist opposition to the major attack on public services has led some to

*From: Amina Mama (1989), 'Violence Against Black Women: Gender, Race and State Responses, *Feminist Review*, 32.

conclude that such apathy 'stems from changing needs, changing desires, and changing material circumstances' (Showstack Sassoon, 1987:41). While this may be true, it is not a full picture. I would argue that inaction also suggests that the advantages of having a welfare state have been easily subverted, and that the alternative path of improving and developing existing services to meet existing and changing needs is not being paved in the eighties. The dominant regime will permit and encourage market forces to be the custodians of welfare. Recent years have seen a steady running down and depletion of health and welfare services that has undermined resistance to more radically Conservative plans by nourishing disaffection. The British left appears to be in a state of frozen shock, reacting to each new batch of legislation with increasing incredulity. Given this longer-term depletion of housing and welfare services, combined with the unrectified inegalitarian character of the large, alienating and unaccountable bureaucracies of modern welfare, it is not surprising that their defence has not been more positive. The regulatory and coercive aspects of the welfare state, the manner in which sections of the public deemed to be suspicious or undeserving are policed,[1] the popular dislike for the red-tape and intrusiveness of the bureaucracies and their power, have all contributed to the lack of resistance to the Thatcherite assault on welfare. So has the resurgent popular ethos that 'you get what you pay for' – as if the welfare state was not in fact already being paid for through taxation.

If a race/class/gender approach is taken to these issues, however, then the ease with which gains won by the long hard battles of class and interracial conflict during British history are being lost ceases to be surprising. My analysis suggests that this ease makes sense if it is understood in terms of the contradictory and socially divisive discourses out of which the modern welfare state was born. 'Second wave' socialist and feminist thinkers are having difficulties in meeting the challenge of contemporary reaction at least partly because their approaches have still not incorporated the fundamental contradictions that a race/gender/class analysis yields. For example, if they had taken in what Black women have been saying about the discrimination they have faced and still face in all forms of service delivery, they would have been able to consider the argument raised here: that public services were never intended to reach particular groups of the public. The 'deserving' and 'reputable' groups earmarked for good welfare services and provisions exclude women who are not in traditional nuclear families and Black people. There have always been degrees of eligibility for so-called public resources.

In, for example, Showstack Sassoon's 1987 compilation of Western European and American women's work on the state, class is not central to the analyses, and the racial machinations of the state are neglected entirely. In some cases (Borchorst and Siim, Hernes, Waerness, Dahlerup) this could be due to the fact that several authors are discussing Scandinavian countries where antiracism is not on the political agenda, but the American (Smith), and British (Showstack Sassoon) contributors exhibit the same ethnocentrism. This means that their analyses are of limited value to those of us struggling to come to grips with advanced capitalist states like Britain, whose development has been forged out of the contradictions of imperialism and who owe much of their success to the successful exploitation of race and class, as well as gender divisions. While such works do discuss new forms of patriarchal power creatively, because they do not simultaneously engage race as a tool, they cannot aid an understanding of the ways in which race and gender can be played off in service delivery in multicultural contexts. For example, Black women with British-born children are threatened with deportation when they leave violent husbands. Or Black women rehoused under the domestic violence policies fought for by feminists in some Local Authorities can find themselves housed in accommodation which had to be abandoned by the previous Black family because of racial harassment. They are thus forced to become homeless all over again as a result of racist violence. Similarly, police responding to feminist critiques of their non-action in cases of domestic violence can set up domestic violence response units, but locate them in Black communities, and be uncritically commended in a way that condones the identification of domestic violence as a 'Black crime' (see below).

To reiterate: we are dealing with a state which is not only patriarchal, but also imperialist and racist. Critical social analysts need to take this multiply divisive character of the late capitalist state on board. The current situation demands a rallying of forces around more holistic analyses of the situation, the necessity for these analyses having been demonstrated by Black feminist critiques of the welfare state (e.g., Mama, 1984).

[. . .]

Conclusion

More can be done by feminists than reacting with paper equal opportunities policies. Full support could be offered to specialist refuges to meet the needs of different groups of women, as well as the taking of immediate steps to purge racism from the women's movement. In this way it may be possible to build a spirit of co-operation which can work towards sisterhood, although the difficulties of achieving this in a non-centralized network structure present particular challenges. The National Office of the Women's Aid Federation have expressed a policy commitment to Equal Opportunities and it remains to be seen how this will be implemented in identifying and challenging racism in refuges both in terms of their employment policy and in their service delivery. It means doing more, for example, than employing Black women, mainly as part-time workers and child workers.

It also means understanding that racism involves a great deal more than the overt abuse and physical attack which the term evokes. Racism rarely takes such crude forms in women's organizations. The problem is more likely to be that racism is made into a taboo subject, with open discussion blocked by fear and guilt on the part of white women who feel threatened or irritated by the subject, and righteous

anger on the part of Black women. The recent reconvening of
the Black Women's Group within Women's Aid is a hopeful
step in the right direction, for women's organizations are in a
position to recognize the importance of separate forums in
challenging racism. Black women must be empowered to
articulate our experience of racial oppression within the organization before it can be overcome. Overall, it is clear that
both separate and integrated strategies need to be adopted in
any racially mixed national organization in Britain. The example of Women's Aid, and the development of Black re-
fugees have much that can be drawn on when it comes to
devising broader survival strategies for the coming period.

More generally, the situation is one which urgently demands a broader housing strategy for women. Refuges were
set up only as an emergency response to a particular problem which many women face. They are intended to provide
temporary emergency accommodation, and to offer the specialized support which traumatized women and their children may require. Currently, the wider problem of women's
access to housing threatens to overwhelm even this limited
provision. Many refuges are unwillingly becoming longstay
hostels. Refuges are in danger of being unable to meet the
needs of battered women needing somewhere to go: the
shortfall in places is becoming acute. This is particularly so
in Black refuges – where fewer houses, workers and resources can mean that Black women have no option other
than to stay for as long as three years, or face the isolation
and stress of other forms of temporary accommodation (bed
and breakfast hotels, mixed hostels and reception centres
lacking security). What is needed is for women to have control of housing that can offer permanent homes to women,
both to meet wider needs and to support the refuge movement, possibly through a nationwide network of women's
co-operatives or housing associations.

When collective survival strategies like the refuge movement emerge spontaneously, they open up and expose fundamental contradictions in the relations between women
and the state. The often contradictory responses of the various organs of the state should then be monitored and analyzed. I have noted that central government has responded

to women's needs very narrowly and coercively, by equip-
ping and instructing the police and other arms of the repressive apparatuses to intervene and prosecute men. For Black
women this has particular implications because of the
broader criminalization of Black people that occurs. Our
problem is too much police intervention of particular
kinds, and we do not experience the police force as protec-
tors in the same way that white women may do. It is this
type of differential experience and location in relation to
state agencies which requires urgent acknowledgement and
action through the refuge movement.

[. . .]

Finally, I would conclude that the struggle against the
Thatcherite state may well in future be conducted outside
the remaining, residual corridors of the local state, that is,
in the voluntary sector and through autonomous community organizations and initiatives. Particularly in the case of
housing, Local Authorities have so far proved unable to
resist central government with the result that power is becoming increasingly centralized and handed over to the
corporate financial interests. National resources and public
services in key areas like health, social security and housing are being handed over to the private sector for manipulation in the interests of profit for the few rather than out
of any consideration of the human needs or the rights of the
majority. The increased complexity of the state process can
mask the general direction towards increased totalitaria-
nism covered by a veneer of contradictory but consensual
discourses. The use of class, race and gender analyses when
developed will prove central in meeting these challenges.

Note

1. Policing is used here after Donzelot (1977) *The Policing of Families.*

References

Amin, K. (1987) 'Black Women and Racist Attacks' *Foundation* No. 2, July.
Austerberry, H. and Watson, S. (1986) *Housing and Homelessness: A Femi-
nist Perspective* London: Routledge & Kegan Paul.
Balbo, L. (1987) 'Crazy Quilts: Rethinking the Welfare State from a Woman's
Point of View' in Showstack Sassoon (1987).

Bhatt, C. (1987) 'Racial Violence and the Local State' *Foundation* No. 2, July.

Binney, V., Harkell, G., and Nixon, J. (1981) *Leaving Violent Men – A Study of Refuges and Housing for Battered Women* London Women's Aid Federation.

Borchorst, A. and Siim, B. (1987) Women and the Advanced Welfare State: A New Kind of Patriarchal Power? in Showstack Sassoon (1987).

Brion, M. and Tinker, A. (1980) *Women in Housing: Access and Influence* Housing Centre Trust.

Commission for Racial Equality (1984) *Race and Council Housing in Hackney; Report of a Formal Investigation.*

Dahlerup, D. (1987) 'Confusing Concepts – Confusing Reality: A Theoretical Discussion of the Patriarchal State' in Showstack Sassoon (1987).

Donnison, D. (1985) 'Why the Cohabitation Rule Makes Sense' in Ungerson (1985).

Donzelot, J. (1977) *The Policing of Families: Welfare vs the State* translated from French 1980, London: Hutchinson.

Edwards, S. (1986) *The Police Response to Domestic Violence in London* Polytechnic of Central London.

Greater London Council (1986) *Women and Housing* Committee Reports.

Gilroy, P. (1987) *There Ain't No Black in the Union Jack* London: Hutchinson.

Henderson, J. and Karn, V. (1987) *Race, Class and State Housing: Inequality and the Allocation of Public Housing in Britain* Aldershot: Gower.

Hernes, H. (1987) 'Women and the Welfare State: the Transition from Private to Public Dependence' in Showstack Sassoon (1987).

Karn, V. (1983) *Race and Housing in Britain: The Role of the Major Institutions* London: Heinemann.

Lawrence, E. and Mama, A. (1988) *The Reproduction of Inequality in Housing* Public Lecture delivered to The Runnymeade Trust, London, 22.11.88.

Mama, A. (1984) 'Black Women, the Economic Crisis and the British State' *Feminist Review* No. 17.

Mama, A. (1989) 'The Silent Struggle'. London Race and Housing Research Report.

McGuire, S. (1988) ' "Sorry Love" – Violence Against Women in the Home and the State Response' (unpub. manuscript).

Pahl, J. editor (1985) *Private Violence and Public Policy: the Needs of Battered Women and the Response of Public Services* London: Routledge & Kegan Paul.

Phizacklea, A. editor (1983) *One Way Ticket: Migration and Female Labour* London: Routledge & Kegan Paul.

Report of the Select Committee on Violence in Marriage (1975) London: HMSO.

Showstack Sassoon, A. editor (1987) *Women and the State* London: Hutchinson.

Smith, V. (1987) The Circular Trap: Women and Part-Time Work in Showstack Sassoon.

Ungerson, C. editor (1985) *Women and Social Policy: A Reader* London: Macmillan.

Waerness, K. (1987) *On the Rationalisation of Caring* in Showstack Sassoon (1987).

Women's Equality Group (1987) 'Tenancy Implications for Women of Relationship Breakdowns – A Review of Borough Practice' London Strategic Policy Unit.

6 □ Lesbian feminism

Introduction

□ The pioneering essay 'The Woman Identified Woman' (1970), by the New York Radicalesbians, showed that contemporary lesbian feminism was a definable cultural phenomenon with an articulate theory. Their term 'woman identified woman' became a rallying call of second wave feminism and gave 'lesbianism' a broad definition characterised by desires, experiences and self perceptions rather than social categories. Radicalesbians argue that 'lesbianism' is shaped by ideological and political preferences as much as by explicit sexual practices. In this sense lesbian desire could be said to be a general feminist condition. The Radicalesbians gave second wave feminism a reconstructed 'lesbian' free from pejorative connotations. 'Lesbianism' was no longer to be limited to one form of sexual activity. It could contain many meanings, for example a sociopolitical conception of community and a recognition that it was heterosexuality not simply male economic power that was, as Charlotte Bunch argued, a 'cornerstone of male supremacy'.

In 1979 the British pamphlet 'Political Lesbianism: The Case Against Heterosexuality', published by the Leeds Revolutionary Feminists, confronted feminism with a further startling model the idea that heterosexuality was reactionary, even that heterosexual women were collaborators with patriarchy. The link between sexual preference, language and power was explicit in the slogan 'feminism is the theory and lesbianism the practice', used by these separatist women.

Since contemporary lesbianism had grown out of a conjuncture between personal and political resistance feminists were inspired in the 1970s to examine similar resistances in women's histories. The feminist historians Martha Vicinus and Carroll Smith-Rosenberg identified a tradition of women identified 'resistances' which, they suggest, for nineteenth-century middle-class women became a form of 'domestic feminism'. While lesbian history has been a major focus of lesbian scholarship, lesbian life narratives also contest homogeneous and universal images of women. Jill Johnstone's *Lesbian Nation* (1974) and the collection *This Bridge Called My Back* (1981), challenged the homophobia and the racism of the academy.

By the late 1970s Adrienne Rich, Mary Daly and Charlotte Bunch were celebrating the creative and affiliative aspects of women's difference. These writers contributed to making lesbian feminism a recognisable entity by describing a huge range of emotional and liberating identifications women might make with each other. ☐

COMMENTARY: E.B. Freedman *et al.* (1985), *The Lesbian Issue*, Chicago: University of Chicago.

MARY DALY 1928–

☐ Mary Daly is an American theologist who has pioneered radical feminist philosophy. A concern for women's collective strengths, and a polemical attack on the dominant centres of heterosexuality are systematically pursued in her major book *Gyn/Ecology* (1978). The book builds on Daly's account of ec-centric spirituality started in *Beyond God The Father* (1973), to argue, like Rich, that male dominance relies on sexual violence throughout history and in all cultures. Patriarchy, Daly claims, governs all institutions including religion, medicine and science and it erupts in sado-rituals such as footbinding and cliterodectomy. To contest phallic culture women must work together reversing male myths and renouncing male language and beliefs. Daly therefore includes in her book an index of new words in order to create a 'gynomorphic' vocabulary which women can use instead of conventional language.

Gyn/Ecology invites women identified women to make a metaphorical journey – a territorial examination of the space and architecture of women's prehistory and myths hypothesised as women's future – by means of 'spooking' and 'sparking' and 'spinning' (women's cultural activities). The erotic power of 'spooking' informs Daly's subsequent book *Pure Lust* (1984), which is a detailed account of the rich cultures women can make when released from 'potted passions'. ☐

COMMENTARY: C. Ramazanoglu (1989), *Feminism and the Contradictions of Oppression*, London: Routledge.

EXTRACT

GYN/ECOLOGY: THE METAETHICS OF RADICAL FEMINISM [1978]*

The Journey of this book, therefore, is (to borrow an expression from the journal *Sinister Wisdom*) 'for the Lesbian Imagination in All Women.'[1] It is for the Hag/Crone/Spinster in every *living* woman.[2] It is for each individual Journeyer to decide/expand the scope of this imagination within her. It is she, and she alone, who can determine how far, and in what way, she will/can travel. She, and she alone, can dis-cover the mystery of her own history, and find how it is interwoven with the lives of other women.

Yes-saying by the Female Self and her Sisters involves intense work – playful cerebration. The Amazon Voyager can be anti-academic. Only at her greatest peril can she be anti-intellectual. Thus this book/Voyage can rightly be called anti-academic because it celebrates cerebral Spinning. If this book/Voyage could be placed neatly in a 'field' it would not be this book. I have considered naming its 'field' Un-theology or Un-philosophy. Certainly, in the house of mirrors which is the universe/university of reversals, it can be called Un-ethical.

Since Gyn/Ecology is the Un-field/Ourfield/Outfield of Journeyers, rather than a game in an 'in' field, the pedantic can be expected to perceive it as 'unscholarly.' Since it *confronts* old molds/models of question-asking by being itself an Other way of thinking/speaking, it will be invisible to those who fetishize old questions – who drone that it does not 'deal with' *their* questions.

Since Gyn/Ecology Spins around, past, and through the established fields, opening the coffers/coffins in which 'knowledge' has been stored, re-stored, re-covered, its meaning will be hidden from the Grave Keepers of

*From: Mary Daly (1979), *Gyn/Ecology: The Metaethics of Radical Feminism*, London: The Women's Press.

tradition. Since it seeks out the *threads of connectedness* within artificially separated/segmented reality, striving 'to put the severed parts together,' specious specialists will decry its 'negativity' and 'failure to present the whole picture.' Since it Spins among fields, leaping over the walls that separate the halls in which academics have incarcerated the 'bodies of knowledge,' it will be accused of 'lumping things together'.

[. . .]

This book is about the journey of women becoming, that is, radical feminism. The voyage is described and roughly charted here. I say 'roughly' by way of understatement and pun. We do not know exactly what is on the Other Side until we arrive there – and the journey *is rough*. The charting done here is based on some knowledge from the past, upon present experience, and upon hopes for the future. These three sources are inseparable, intertwined. Radical feminist consciousness spirals in all directions, discovering the past, creating/dis-closing the present/future.

[. . .]

The purpose, the method, the style of this book

Writing this book is participating in feminist process. This is problematic. For isn't a book by its definition a 'thing,' an objectification of thinking/imagining/speaking? Here is a book in my hands: fixed, solid. Perhaps – hopefully – its author no longer wholly agrees with it. It is, at least partially, her past. The dilemma of the living/verbing writer is real, but much of the problem resides in the way books are perceived. If they are perceived/used/idolized as Sacred Texts (like the bible or the writings of chairman Mao), then of course the idolators are caught on a wheel that turns but does not move. They 'spin' like wheels on ice – a 'spinning' that in no way resembles feminist process.

We cannot avoid this static kind of 'spinning wheel' by becoming anti-literate, anti-cerebral. 'Feminist' anti-intellectualism is a mere reaction against moronizing masculinist education and scholarship, and it is a trap. We need creative crystallizing in the sense of producing works – such as books. Like crystal balls, Glowing Globes, these help us to foretell the future and to dis-cover the past, for they further the process itself by transforming the previously unknown into that which we explicitly know, and therefore can reflect upon, criticize. Thus they spark new visions. This creative crystallizing is a translation of feminist journeying, of our encounters with the unknown, into a chrysalis.[4] This writing/metamorphosing/spinning is itself part of the journey, and the chrysalis – the incarnation of experience in words – is a living, changing reality. It is the transmission of our transitions. Feminist process must become sensible (in actions, speech, works of all kinds) in order to become. The journey requires the courage to create, that we may learn from lucid criticism, that we may remember the dismembered body of our heritage, that we may stop repeating the same mistakes. Patriarchal erasure of our tradition forces us to relearn what our foresisters knew and to repeat their blunders.

[...]

The fact is that we live in a profoundly anti-female society, a misogynistic 'civilization' in which men collectively victimize women, attacking us as personifications of their own paranoid fears, as The Enemy. Within this society it is men who rape, who sap women's energy, who deny women economic and political power. To allow oneself to know and name these facts is to commit anti-gynocidal acts. Acting in this way, moving through the mazes of the anti-female society, requires naming and overcoming the obstacles constructed by its male agents and token female instruments. As a creative crystallizing of the movement beyond the State of Patriarchal Paralysis, this book is an act of Dispossession; and hence, in a sense beyond the limitations of the label *anti-male*, it is absolutely Anti-androcrat, A-mazingly Anti-male, Furiously and Finally Female.

Notes

1. *Sinister Wisdom* is available at feminist bookstores, and by writing to P.O. Box 30541, Lincoln, Neb. 68503.
2. See Simone de Beauvoir, *The Ethics of Ambiguity*, trans. by Bernard Frechtman (Secaucus, N.J.: The Citadel Press, 1972), pp. 82–3. She points out that 'if all it [life] does is maintain itself, then living is only not dying.'
3. Virginia Woolf writes of the delight and rapture she experienced in putting the severed parts together. See her *Moments of Being: Unpublished Autobiographical Writings*, ed. by Jeanne Schulking (New York: Harcourt Brace Jovanovich, 1976), p. 72. I owe the idea of 'threads of connectedness' to Fran Chelland, who has developed many threads in her thinking and writing, particularly in an unpublished paper entitled 'Mind over/versus Matter: The Spiritual Reversal.'
4. This name, appropriately, is the title of a feminist journal – *Chrysalis: A Magazine of Women's Culture*.

CHARLOTTE BUNCH 1944–

□ Since the late 1960s, both as editor of *Quest* magazine and as a feminist activist, Charlotte Bunch has consistently argued that lesbian feminism is a major part of feminism because lesbians have a *'materially'* different sense of reality and can reveal the extremes of heterosexual privilege. Feminist theory will inevitably benefit from the critical force of lesbian thinking.

Bunch puts the radical politics of lesbian feminism together with socialist feminism in order to attack the economic and political power of patriarchy as well as its sexual violence. It is Bunch's unflagging conviction that heterosexual assumptions underpin the organisation of labour, for example in the notion of a family wage and in sexual harassment at work, and that these assumptions shape militarism and patriarchy's rape of the environment. Bunch does not limit lesbian feminism only to a matter of sexual choice, but argues that lesbian feminism recognises domination in all its manifestations. The most striking feature of all three lesbian writers represented in this chapter is their vision of a global feminism with a base in independent lesbian thinking. □

COMMENTARY: J. Donovan (1985), *Feminist Theory*, New York: Ungar.

EXTRACT

NOT BY DEGREES: FEMINIST THEORY AND EDUCATION [1983]*

While my growing sense of the importance of theory applied to all my feminist work, the urgency that I felt about it became clearest during my involvement with lesbian-feminism. When the lesbian issue became a major controversy in the women's movement in the early 1970s, I realized that in order for lesbians to function openly, we would have to understand *why* there was so much resistance to this issue. It was not enough to document discrimination against homosexuals or to appeal to fairness. We had to figure out why lesbianism was taboo, why it was a threat to feminists, and then devise strategies accordingly. I saw that my life as a lesbian in the movement depended on, among other things, the development of a theory that would explain our immediate conflicts in the context of a long-term view of feminism. This theoretical perspective developed along with our activism, but it required us to consciously ask certain questions, to look at our experiences in and out of the movement, and to consider existing feminist theory in new ways. Through this process, new interpretations of the relationship between lesbianism and feminism, and new strategies for ending lesbian oppression emerged.

For example, as we examined feminists' fear of being called lesbians, we were able to confront directly the role that such name calling played in the oppression of all women. Having a theory about lesbian oppression did not tell us what to do tactically, but it did provide a framework for understanding situations, for placing them in a broader context, and for evaluating possible courses of action. This experience showed me that theory was not simply intellectually interesting, but was crucial to the survival of feminism.

*From: Charlotte Bunch (1983), 'Not By Degrees: Feminist Theory and Education', in C. Bunch and S. Pollock (eds), *Learning Our Way: Essays in Feminist Education*, New York: The Crossing Press.

The functions of feminist theory

Theory enables us to see immediate needs in terms of long-range goals and an overall perspective on the world.[1] It thus gives us a framework for evaluating various strategies in both the long and the short run, and for seeing the types of changes that they are likely to produce. Theory is not just a body of facts or a set of personal opinions. It involves explanations and hypotheses that are based on available knowledge and experience. It is also dependent on conjecture and insight about how to interpret those facts and experiences and their significance.

No theory is totally 'objective,' since it reflects the interests, values, and assumptions of those who created it. Feminist theory relies on the underlying assumption that it will aid the liberation of women. Feminist theory, therefore, is not an unengaged study of women. It is an effort to bring insights from the movement and from various female experiences together with research and data gathering to produce new approaches to understanding and ending female oppression.

While feminist theory begins with the immediate need to end women's oppression, it is also a way of viewing the world. Feminism is an entire world view or *gestalt*, not just a laundry list of 'women's issues.' Feminist theory provides a basis for understanding every area of our lives, and a feminist perspective can affect the world politically, culturally, economically, and spiritually. The initial tenets of feminism have already been established – the idea that power is based on gender differences and that men's illegitimate power over women taints all aspects of society, for instance. But now we face the arduous task of systematically working through these ideas, fleshing them out and discovering new ones.

When the development of feminist theory seems too slow for the changes that we seek, feminists are tempted to submerge our insights into one of the century's two dominant progressive theories of reality and change: democratic liberalism or Marxist socialism.[2] However, the limitations of both of these systems are increasingly obvious. While feminism can learn from both of them, it must not be tied to either because its greatest strength lies in providing an alternative view of the world.

The full implications of feminism will evolve over time, as we organize, experiment, think, analyze, and revise our ideas and strategies in light of our experiences. No theory emerges in full detail overnight; the dominant theories of our day have expanded and changed over many decades. That it will take time should not discourage us. That we might fail to pursue our ideas – given the enormous need for them in society today – is unconscionable.

Because feminist theory is still emerging and does not have agreed upon answers (or even approaches to many questions), it is difficult to work out strategies based on that theory. This difficulty can lead feminists to rely on the other theories of change or to fall into the 'any action/no action' bind. When caught in this bind, one may go ahead with action – any action – for its own sake, or be paralyzed, taking no action for lack of a sense of what is 'right.' To escape this bind, we must remember that we do not need, and indeed never will have, all the answers before we act, and that it is often only through taking action that we can discover some of them. The purpose of theory, then, is not to provide a pat set of answers about what to do, but to guide us in sorting out options, and to keep us out of the 'any action/no action' bind. Theory also keeps us aware of the questions that need to be asked, so that what we learn in each activity will lead to more effective strategies in the future. Theory thus both grows out of and guides activism in a continuous, spiraling process.

In pursing feminist theory as an activist, I have become increasingly aware of the need to demystify it. Theory is not something set apart from our lives. Our assumptions about reality and change influence our actions constantly. The question is not whether we have a theory, but how aware we are of the assumptions behind our actions, and how conscious we are of the choices we make – daily – among different theories. For example, when we decide whether to put our energies into a rape crisis center or into efforts to change rape laws, we are acting according to certain theories about how service projects and legislation affect change. These theories may be implicit or explicit, but they are always there.

Notes

1. There are many approaches to theory, and those interested in exploring more about how theory is constructed should look at the literature of political philosophy. Another model for feminist theory similar to the one that I discuss in this paper was developed by Judy Smith of the Women's Resource Center, in Missoula, Montana.
2. For more discussion of this problem and of nonaligned feminism as a response to it, see 'Beyond Either/Or: Feminist Options,' pp. 46–60.

ADRIENNE RICH 1929–

☐ Adrienne Rich is an American lesbian feminist poet and philosopher who transformed feminist thinking with her hugely influential article 'Compulsory Heterosexuality and Lesbian Existence' (1980). Rich begins with the resonating question: Why do women redirect to men given the overwhelming centrality of the mother–daughter bond in the development of female gender identity? Building on de Beauvoir's premise that women are originally homosexual, Rich pushed further than de Beauvoir to argue that women's experience, history, culture and values are distinct from the dominant patriarchal, heterosexual culture. 'Compulsory heterosexuality' is Rich's term for the social power of heterosexuality and its visible devices of romance and rape. Heterosexuality is a construct, a system imposed on women by societies throughout history which makes lesbian experience invisible or seem 'abnormal'.

Rich coins the two terms 'lesbian existence' and 'lesbian continuum' to describe how lesbianism can be a part of every woman's emotional, if not necessarily physical, experience in the same way as motherhood. 'Lesbian continuum' is the exploration of lesbian history and culture, in which every feminist should engage.

'Lesbian experience' includes the specifically sexual component of lesbian identity. Although the essay generated criticism and a great deal of debate, Rich's account forcefully illustrates the multilayered possibilities of lesbian feminism by inviting all women to join a rich history of women identified culture. ☐

COMMENTARY: J. Donovan (1985), *Feminist Theory*, New York: Ungar.

EXTRACT

COMPULSORY HETEROSEXUALITY AND LESBIAN EXISTENCE [1980]*

If women are the earliest sources of emotional caring and physical nurture for both female and male children, it would seem logical, from a feminist perspective at least, to pose the following questions: whether the search for love and tenderness in both sexes does not originally lead toward women; *why in fact women would ever re-direct that search*; why species-survival, the means of impregnation, and emotional/erotic relationships should ever have become so rigidly identified with each other; and why such violent structures should be found necessary to enforce women's total emotional, erotic loyalty and subservience to men. I doubt that enough feminist scholars and theorists have taken the pains to acknowledge the societal forces which wrench women's emotional and erotic energies away from themselves and other women and from woman-identified values. These forces, as I shall try to show, range from literal physical enslavement to the disguising and distorting of possible options.

[. . .]

But whatever its origins, when we look hard and clearly at the extent and elaboration of measures designed to keep women within a male sexual purlieu, it becomes an inescapable question whether the issue we have to address as feminists is, not simple 'gender inequality,' nor the domination of culture by males, not mere 'taboos against homosexuality,' but the enforcement of heterosexuality for women as a means of assuring male right of physical,

*From: Adrienne Rich (1983), 'Compulsory Heterosexuality and Lesbian Existence', in E. Abel and E.K. Abel (eds), *The Signs Reader: Women, Gender and Scholarship*, Chicago: University of Chicago Press.

economical, and emotional access.[1] One of many means of enforcement is, of course, the rendering invisible of the lesbian possibility, an engulfed continent which rises fragmentedly to view from time to time only to become submerged again. Feminist research and theory that contributes to lesbian invisibility or marginality is actually working against the liberation and empowerment of woman as a group.[2]

The assumption that 'most women are innately heterosexual' stands as a theoretical and political stumbling block for many women. It remains a tenable assumption, partly because lesbian existence has been written out of history or catalogued under disease; partly because it has been treated as exceptional rather than intrinsic; partly because to acknowledge that for women heterosexuality may not be a 'preference' at all but something that has had to be imposed, managed, organized, propagandized, and maintained by force, is an immense step to take if you consider yourself freely and 'innately' heterosexual. Yet the failure to examine heterosexuality as an institution is like failing to admit that the economic system called capitalism or the caste system of racism is maintained by a variety of forces, including both physical violence and false consciousness. To take the step of questioning heterosexuality as a 'preference' to 'choice' for women – and to do the intellectual and emotional work that follows – will call for a special quality of courage in heterosexually identified feminists but I think the rewards will be great: a freeing-up of thinking, the exploring of new paths, the shattering of another great silence, new clarity in personal relationships.

I have chosen to use the terms *lesbian existence* and *lesbian continuum* because the word *lesbianism* has a clinical and limiting ring. *Lesbian existence* suggests both the fact of the historical presence of lesbians and our continuing creation of the meaning of that existence. I mean the term *lesbian continuum* to include a range – through each woman's life and throughout history – of woman-identified experience; not simply the fact that a woman has had or consciously desired genital sexual experience with another woman. If we expand it to embrace many more forms of primary intensity between and among women, including the sharing of a rich inner life, the bonding against male tyranny, the giving and receiving of practical and political support; if we can also hear in it such associations as *marriage resistance* and the 'haggard' behavior identified by Mary Daly (obsolete meanings: 'intractable,' 'willful,' 'wanton,' and 'unchaste' . . . 'a woman reluctant to yield to wooing')[3] we begin to grasp breadths of female history and psychology which have lain out of reach as a consequence of limited, mostly clinical, definitions of 'lesbianism.'

Lesbian existence comprises both the breaking of a taboo and the rejection of a compulsory way of life. It is also a direct or indirect attack on male right of access to women. But it is more than these, although we may first begin to perceive it as a form of nay-saying to patriaochy, an act of resistance. It has of course included role playing, self-hatred, breakdown, alcoholism, suicide, and intrawoman violence; we romanticize at our peril what it means to love and act against the grain, and under heavy penalties; and lesbian existence has been lived (unlike, say, Jewish or Catholic existence) without access to any knowledge of a tradition, a continuity, a social underpinning. The destruction of records and memorabilia and letters documenting the realities of lesbian existence must be taken very seriously as a means of keeping heterosexuality compulsory for women, since what has been kept from our knowledge is joy, sensuality, courage, and community, as well as guilt, self-betrayal, and pain.[4]

[. . .]

The work that lies ahead, of unearthing and describing what I call here 'lesbian existence' is potentially liberating for all women. It is work that must assuredly move beyond the limits of white and middle-class Western women's studies to examine women's lives, work, and groupings within every racial, ethnic, and political structure. There are differences, moreover, between 'lesbian existence' and the 'lesbian continuum' – differences we can discern even in the movement of our own lives. The lesbian continuum, I suggest, needs delineation in light of the 'double-life' of women, not only women self-described as heterosexual but also of self-described lesbians. We need a far more exhaustive account of the forms the double-life has assumed. Historians need to ask at every point how heterosexuality as institution has been organized and maintained through the female wage scale, the enforcement of middle-class women's 'leisure,' the glamorization of so-called sexual liberation, the withholding of education from women, the imagery of 'high art' and popular culture, the mystification of the 'personal' sphere, and much else. We need an economics which comprehends the institution of heterosexuality, with its doubled workload for women and its sexual divisions of labor, as the most idealized of economic relations.

The question inevitably will arise: Are we then to condemn all heterosexual relationships, including those which are least oppressive? I believe this question, though often heartfelt, is the wrong question here. We have been stalled in a maze of false dichotomies which prevents our apprehending the institution as a whole: 'good' versus 'bad' marriages; 'marriage for love' versus arranged marriage; 'liberated' sex versus prostitution; heterosexual intercourse versus rape; Liebeschmerz versus humiliation and dependency. Within the institution exist, of course, qualitative differences of experience; but the absence of choice remains the great unacknowledged reality, and in the absence of choice, women will remain dependent upon the chance or luck of particular relationships and will have no collective power to determine the meaning and place of sexuality in their lives. As we address the institution itself, moreover, we begin to perceive a history of female resistance which has never fully understood itself because it has been so fragmented, miscalled, erased. It will require a courageous grasp of the politics and economics, as well as the cultural propaganda, of heterosexuality to carry us beyond individual cases or diversified group situations into the complex kind of overview needed to undo the power men everywhere wield over women, power which has become a model for every other form of exploitation and illegitimate control.

Notes

1. For my perception of heterosexuality as an economic institution I am indebted to Lisa Leghorn and Katherine Parker, who allowed me to read the unpublished manuscript of their book, *Woman's Worth: Sexual Economics and the World of Women* (London and Boston: Routledge & Kegan Paul, 1981).

2. I would suggest that lesbian existence has been most recognized and tolerated where it has resembled a 'deviant' version of heterosexuality; e.g., where lesbians have, like Stein and Toklas, played heterosexual roles (or seemed to in public) and have been chiefly identified with male culture. See also Claude E. Schaeffer, 'The Kuterai Female Berdache: Courier, Guide, Prophetess and Warrior,' *Ethnohistory* 12, no. 3 (Summer 1965): 193–236. (Berdache: 'an individual of a definite physiological sex [m. or f.] who assumes the role and status of the opposite sex and who is viewed by the community as being of one sex physiologically but as having assumed the role and status of the opposite sex' [Schaeffer, p. 231].) Lesbian existence has also been relegated to an upper-class phenomenon, an elite decadence (as in the fascination with Paris salon lesbians such as Renée Vivien and Natalie Clifford Barney), to the obscuring of such 'common women' as Judy Grahn depicts in her *The Work of a Common Woman* (Oakland, Calif.: Diana Press, 1978) and *True to Life Adventure Stories* (Oakland, Calif.: Diana Press, 1978).

3. Daly, *Gyn/Ecology*, p. 15.

4. 'In a hostile world in which women are not supposed to survive except in relation with and in service to men, entire communities of women were simply erased. History tends to bury what it seeks to reject' (Blanche W. Cook, ' "Women Alone Stir My Imagination": Lesbianism and the Cultural Tradition,' *Signs: Journal of Women in Culture and Society* 4, no. 4 [Summer 1979]: 719–20). The Lesbian Herstory Archives in New York City is one attempt to preserve contemporary documents on lesbian existence – a project of enormous value and meaning, still pitted against the continuing censorship and obliteration of relationships, networks, communities, in other archives and elsewhere in the culture.

7 □ Liberal feminism

Introduction

□ Liberal feminism aims to achieve equal legal, political and social rights for women. It wishes to bring women equally into all public institutions and to extend the creation of knowledge so that women's issues can no longer be ignored.

Liberal feminism has a long and familiar history dating at least from Mary Wollstonecraft's classic feminist text *A Vindication of the Rights of Woman* (1792). Wollstonecraft's main argument is that women should have the same civil liberties as, and educational parity with, men. In America it is generally agreed that the Seneca Falls Resolution (1848) which called for women's equal rights to suffrage set an overshadowing agenda for liberal feminism. In the 1960s and early 1970s, liberal feminism shaped many of the major political programmes of the American women's movement. When Betty Friedan founded the National Organisation of Women (NOW) in 1966 a contemporary model of liberal feminism was created. NOW campaigned for equal civil rights, equal access to education, to health and welfare and equal pay for women. Contemporary liberal feminists, for example FACT (Feminist Anti Censorship Taskforce), campaign to eradicate gender stereotyping but do not campaign for alternatives to traditional forms of gender relations such as heterosexual marriage. Liberal feminism has always informed American feminism much more than British feminism, perhaps because programmes of positive discrimination (the selection of women over men if equally qualified) accord with American democratic values.

Challenges to liberal feminism come from those, for example Alison Jagger, who claim that liberalism is often ethnocentric and individualistic although all feminists would agree with liberals that the single most important goal of women's liberation is equality of opportunity.   □

COMMENTARY: A. Phillips (1987), *Feminism and Equality*, Oxford: Blackwell.

BETTY FRIEDAN 1921–

☐ As the founder and first president of NOW, Betty Friedan is acknowledged to be one of the pioneers of the American Women's Movement. *The Feminine Mystique* (1963) reveals the private angst which many middle-class white American women were experiencing in the 1950s as unwaged housewives and consumers. The 'mystique' was Friedan's term for the 'problem with no name' – the psychic distress experienced by women who had no public careers and were immured in domestic concerns.

Friedan pragmatically reworked de Beauvoir's *The Second Sex* to advocate women's equal entry into the professions and into higher education. The book is based in part on a survey of Smith College graduates which repeats Catherine Beecher Stowe's 1846 survey of 200 friends' psychosomatic illnesses. The book led to the setting up of NOW in 1966, which has since become America's largest women's organisation. NOW campaigns for women's equal rights in education, in the family and in law. Like other feminists of the early 1970s, Friedan rejects the biological determinism of Freudian theory. Her view that women are a weaker *social* group led her to argue for a massive self-help programme which would enable women to re-enter the labour market through increased educational opportunities. However Friedan's solution to economic discrimination fails to address the sexual division of labour in the home and in the work place, and the structural changes needed by society if women *are* to have choices about careers and about motherhood.

The second stage of feminism (the title of Friedan's subsequent book) would find ways of enabling women to be creative mothers with fulfilling careers. *The Second Stage* (1981) paints a wildly optimistic picture of equality within the family. Yet, together with NOW's current stand on reproductive rights (for example the Women's Bill of Rights which demanded nationwide childcare facilities), *The Feminine Mystique* is a pioneering attempt to turn women's personal experiences into political issues. ☐

COMMENTARY: J. Stacey (1986), 'Are Feminists Afraid to Leave Home? The Challenge of Conservative Pro-Family Feminism', in J. Mitchell and A. Oakley, *What Is Feminism*, Oxford: Blackwell.

EXTRACT

THE FEMININE MYSTIQUE [1963]*

Gradually, without seeing it clearly for quite a while, I came to realize that something is very wrong with the way American women are trying to live their lives today. I sensed it first as a question mark in my own life, as a wife and mother of three small children, half-guiltily, and therefore half-heartedly, almost in spite of myself using my abilities and education in work that took me away from home. It was this personal question mark that led me, in 1957, to spend a great deal of time doing an intensive questionnaire of my college classmates, fifteen years after our graduation from Smith. The answers given by 200 women to those intimate open-ended questions made me realize that what was wrong could not be related to education in the way it was then believed to be. The problems and satisfaction of their lives, and mine, and the way our education had contributed to them, simply did not fit the image of the modern American woman as she was written about in women's magazines, studied and analysed in classrooms and clinics, praised and damned in a ceaseless barrage of words even since the end of the Second World War. There was a strange discrepancy between the reality of our lives as women and the image to which we were trying to conform, the image that I came to call the feminine mystique. I wondered if other women faced this schizophrenic split, and what is meant.

And so I began to hunt down the origins of the feminine mystique, and its effect on women who lived by it, or grew up under it.

*From: Betty Friedan (1983), *The Feminine Mystique*, Harmondsworth: Penguin.

ZILLAH EISENSTEIN 1948–

☐ Zillah Eisenstein is an American political writer who has made an extensive critique of liberal feminism. In *The Radical Future of Liberal Feminism* (1981) she argues that capitalism did not supersede patriarchy but extended male power to further limit women's options in the family and in employment. Eisenstein points out that while the Equal Rights Amendment (ERA) dissolved many American prejudices against feminism, legal reform can only be a first stage in a feminist agenda. What equal rights campaigns demonstrate to women in the work-force is the power of patriarchy. Patriarchy denies capitalism its economic potential by denying women full access to labour (for example by curtailing adequate childcare) and in New Right campaigns against ERA.

Eisenstein broadens the scope of liberal feminism by predicting its 'radical' potential which, she suggests, stems from the connections it makes between capitalism and patriarchy. While patriarchy controls ideology and capitalism dominates the economy, it is developments in capitalism caused by women's massive entry into the workforce, Eisenstein claims, which will change patriarchal ideology. One example is the radical platform at the liberal Houston Conference on Women's Rights in 1977, where reproductive rights and freedom of sexual preference were demanded along with a policy of full employment. The visible paradoxes of liberal feminism, Eisenstein suggests, may be its greatest strength. ☐

COMMENTARY: S. Walby (1990), *Theorizing Patriarchy*, Cambridge: Polity.

EXTRACT

THE RADICAL FUTURE OF LIBERAL FEMINISM [1981]*

A progressive feminist politics will have to be guided by the concerns of the 'working mother' and her exploitation in the sexual ghetto in the market. By doing so, feminist politics, rooted in a firm understanding of woman's sexual-class oppression within marriage and the market, will cut through the liberal blinders that dichotomize life into male and female, public and private, state and family, home and work spheres. This perspective undermines the ideology of liberal individualism in feminism because it reveals that woman is part of sexual class and that this class definition is part of her individual identity. This recognition of the sexual-class character of woman's oppression focuses on the patriarchal roots of liberalism. It is because of this aspect of liberal feminism – that it demands equality on behalf of women as a sexual class and in order to achieve this must dismantle the patriarchal oppression on which the state is founded – that the state seeks to inhibit the class consciousness of women as women. The point, however, is that the contradiction which exists between liberal individualism and patriarchy or liberalism and feminism cannot be mediated successfully. Even the state's embrace of the narrow version of liberal feminism recognizes and therefore undermines the system of patriarchal privilege. This self-contradictory nature of liberal feminism, its critique of patriarchy, recognizes women as an excluded or oppressed group, against liberal individualism, which makes it potentially subversive to the state. I argue that the crisis of liberalism today is rooted in this crisis of patriarchal control as women have come to question the separate sexual sphere doctrine and as a result have inadvertently questioned the

*From: Zillah Eisenstein (1981), *The Radical Future of Liberal Feminism*, London: Longman.

basis of the state (i.e., the formal institutionalization of the separateness of male and female life). Therefore, the state is at present looking for new forms of patriarchal control.

Once one recognizes the state's dual role in trying to mediate and therefore coopt the subversive potential of feminism and its incapacity to do so fully, one must rethink the important role of political reform in this context. Feminists need to reconceptualize the relationship between reform and revolution to better understand how they can use liberal feminist reforms to challenge their oppression while the state's concern is to use the reform process to sustain woman's subordination. Part of understanding this is realizing that many of the demands made by liberal feminists today, like those of the 1978 government-funded Houston conference, require revolutionary upheaval of the society. Further examination is needed about the seemingly contradictory nature of 'requesting' revolutionary 'demands' from the state. Patriarchy will not 'wither away,' nor will it be destroyed through liberal reforms alone. But how these assessments are connected to a meaningful revolutionary analysis remains for feminists to articulate.

The contradictory nature of legal reform for feminists lies in this fact that it can deradicalize the potentially subversive nature of feminism by instituting limited gains, and at the same time it challenges woman's oppression by affecting woman's consciousness of herself as a person with certain rights. Only by recognizing that both these aspects exist as consequences of feminist legal reform can women begin to define a politics in their full interests. Women can then know that while they fight for the greatest equality possible in the United States, they will not achieve equality from reform alone; that these fights lay the basis for a revolutionary consciousness and revolutionary action. Reform cannot replace revolution; it is rather an assessment of how feminists must build a revolution from the existing political context.[1]

[. . .]

Toward a feminist theory of the state

The government is an arena of state power that is institutionalized, visible, overt, and legitimated. Liberals think government is equivalent to the state and the multiple relations of power it represents. It sits above the conflicts of society and is not seen as a part of them. It rather regulates society, the family, the economy, and so on, from the outside. The state is separate and apart; it regulates public life and is separate from private life.

Instead of viewing the state from this liberal vantage point, feminists need to understand that the state is a part of the struggles within society. The activity of the state actually grows out of the irreconcilability of conflicts[2] within society. its commitment is to the creation of order and political cohesion by mediating these conflicts. Nicos Poulantzas has defined the state as 'not a theory but a relation, more exactly the condensation of a balance of forces.'[3] But this Marxist and neo-Marxist conception of the state has yet to define patriarchy as one of the major forces the state must reinforce and mediate. It is to this question that feminists must turn in order to understand how the state represents not only capitalist class interest but patriarchal class interests as well.

The state deals with the arising conflicts between the needs of capital and the needs of patriarchy in terms of the political relations and purposes that define the state in the first place: the hierarchical relations that structure both the relations of capital and patriarchy. The (a) governmental apparatus with its relatively autonomous[4] relation to (b) the economic class structure, (c) the sexual class structure, and (d the racist division of labor, protect the capitalist patriarchal system as a whole. However, the choice of how to go about creating political cohesion, while conflicts arise between the needs of capital and the needs of patriarchy, reflects the relative autonomy of the state. Within this limited realm of choice (i.e., the protection of capitalist patriarchy), conflicts internal to the state appear. In other words, the state does not merely reflect the interests of the capitalist class or patriarchy. Because there are conflicts within the capitalist class and between the actual needs of capitalism and patriarchy, the state cannot merely be an instrument of one or the other. This is because there are conflicting and unresolvable conflicts that the state first has to attempt to mediate, within capitalism, within patriarchy, and between the two systems.

Notes

1. See Rosa Luxemburg, 'Reform or Revolution,' in Selected Political Writings, ed. Dick Howard (New York: Monthly Review Press, 1971), for her discussion of the relationship between reform and revolution. Her concern with the economic class relations of society and the particular historical-political context in which she wrote allowed her to make a simple and clear distinction between the two activities. I argue that a feminist theory of the state, as well as an assessment of the present political situation in the United States, reveals the inadequacy of this model for our present purposes.

2. Lenin's theory of the state recognized the irreconcilable conflicts generated by the economic class structure. Patriarchy had no identity on the state level for him, nor did it play a part in creating irresolvable conflict for the state. However, I intend to use the conception of irreconcilable state conflict to better understand the relationship between patriarchy and capitalism on the political level.

3. Nicos Poulantzas, Classes in Contemporary Capitalism (London: Verso Editions, 1974), p. 161.

4. See Ralph Miliband, Marxism and Politics (Oxford, England: Oxford University Press, 1977), for a clear discussion of how the conception of the relative autonomy of the state is distinguished from the instrumentalist view, which sees the state as a mere instrument of the capitalist class. His view elaborates the way the state mediates conflicts within the capitalist ruling class, rather than merely being an instrument of the dominant class. For further clarification of the noninstrumentalist, noneconomistic theory of the state, see Louis Althusser, Lenin and Philosophy and Other Essays (New York: Monthly Review Press, 1971); Sally Hibbin et al., Politics, Ideology and the State (London: Lawrence and Wishart, 1978); Annette Kuhn and Ann Marie Wolpe, eds., Feminism and Materialism (London: Routledge and Kegan Paul, 1978); Gary Littlejohn et al., Power and the State (London: Croom Helm, 1978); Ralph Miliband, 'The Capitalist State: Reply to Nicos Poulantzas,' New Left Review 59 (January–February 1970): 53–60; idem, 'Poulantzas and the Capitalist State,' New Left Review 82 (November–December 1973): 83–92; Poulantzas, State, Power, Socialism; idem, 'The Problem of the Capitalist State,' New Left Review 58 (November–December 1969): 67–78; and idem, 'The Capitalist State: A Reply to Miliband and Laclau,' New Left Review 95 (January–February 1976).

EXTRACT

THE SEXUAL POLITICS OF THE NEW RIGHT: UNDERSTANDING THE 'CRISIS OF LIBERALISM' FOR THE 1980S [1982]*

The New Right's attack is directed so forcefully against married wage-earning women and 'working mothers'[1] because, so I argue in *The Radical Future of Liberal Feminism*, it is these women who have the potential to transform society. The New Right correctly understands this. The reality of the wage-earning wife's double day of work uncovers the patriarchal bias of liberalism and capitalist society.[2] As these women begin to understand the sexual bias in the marketplace (where a woman earns 58 cents to the male worker's $1.00) and continue to bear the responsibilities of housework and child care as well, they begin to voice feminist demands for affirmative action programs, equal pay, pregnancy disability payments, and abortion rights. They press for the equal rights promised by liberal ideology. The New Right focuses its attack on both liberalism *and* feminism precisely because mainstream feminist demands derive from the promises of liberalism as an ideology – individual autonomy and independence, freedom of choice, equality of opportunity, and equality before the law – and because they threaten to transform patriarchy, and with it capitalism, by uncovering the 'crisis of liberalism.' Feminist demands uncover the truth that capitalist patriarchal society cannot deliver on its 'liberal' promises of equality or even equal rights for women without destabilizing itself.

[. . .]

Changes in the structure of the economy and in the family both reflect and create changes in the system of capitalist

*From: Zillah Eisenstein (1982), 'The Sexual Politics of the New Right: Understanding the "Crisis of Liberalism" for the 1980s', from N.O. Keohane *et al.* (eds), *Feminist Theory: A Critique of Ideology*, Brighton: Harvester.

patriarchy. Although the state seeks to develop policy that protects the totality of capitalist patriarchy, I am arguing that present conflicts have developed between capitalism and patriarchy that will ultimately undermine the future of liberalism and the welfare state. The question is whether the New Right and the neoconservatives can use these conflicts to indict liberalism and create a 'friendly fascism'[3] or whether feminists and leftists can develop a politics out of these conflicts that will lead to a more democratic and feminist state. In order for feminists and leftists to achieve this end, mainstream feminism will have to deal more self-consciously with the capitalist expression of patriarchy, and left-liberals and leftists will have to recognize the patriarchal structure of capitalism.

Although capitalism and patriarchy function as a mutually dependent totality,[4] they also operate as differentiated and conflictual systems. As such they remain two systems that are *relatively* autonomous from each other,[5] never totally separate today and yet always differentiated in purpose. Sexual life, which is what patriarchy ultimately must regulate, and economic life, which capitalism must ultimately regulate, cannot be conflated into one system; yet at present they are not separate, dual systems.[6] They are differentiated, relatively autonomous, and dialectically related. If they were not separate *and* connected to each other, one would not face the irreconcilable conflict of the married wage-earning woman today.

[. . .]

This contradiction in New Right policy between a noninterventionist state (cutting social services) and an interventionist state (legislating family morality) poses serious problems for its profamily program[7] and has slowed enactment of much of its legislation. First of all, 72 percent of the American public reject the idea of a human life bill that would consider the fetus a person and make abortion and some forms of birth control illegal.[8] A majority of the American public does not believe that this issue should be regulated by government or that anyone but the woman and her doctor should decide whether she should have an abortion or not. Second, to the extent that a majority of Americans do not live in the family form that will benefit from the New Right's profamily policies, the New Right will have difficulty enacting its legislation, if a politics rooted in the other family forms can be articulated and politically mobilized.

The welfare state has its problems, given its own contradictory nature. Irving Howe has defined at least two functions of the welfare state: 'It steps in to modulate the excesses of the economy, helping to create rationality and order, and thereby to save capitalism from its own tendency to destruction. And it steps in to provide humanizing reforms, as a response to insurgent groups and communities.'⁹ The problem, however, is not the welfare state, although that is a problem. The problem is rather the kind of society we live in, which is both patriarchal and capitalist, which would return individuals to self-reliance while maintaining structural barriers related to economic, racial, and sexual class that limit and curtail the individual. It is up to feminists of all political persuasions, left-liberals, and leftists to shift the critique from the welfare state to the patriarchal society that creates it. As feminists we need to marshal the liberal demands for individual self-determination, freedom of choice, individual autonomy, and equality before the law to indict capitalist patriarchal society. This use of liberal ideology by feminists will permit us to direct the public's consciousness to a critique of capitalist patriarchy, not merely of the welfare state.

The New Right assault is aimed against feminism precisely because it is women's liberal feminist consciousness about their rights to equality that is the major radicalizing force of the 1980s. Liberalism is in crisis today not merely because the welfare state is in crisis as the New Right believes, or because liberalism contains cultural contradictions as the neoconservatives argue, or because capitalism itself is in crisis, as Marxists and left-liberals contend. The 'crisis of liberalism' is a result of the conflict between the traditional white patriarchal family, advanced capitalism, and the ideology of liberalism. The married wage-earning woman, black and white, and the potential of her feminist consciousness demonstrates this reality. Hence the New Right assault against her and the feminist movement in general.

Notes

1. The New Right's attack on the married woman wage-earner is at one and the same time a criticism of what it terms the 'working mother.'
2. See Zillah R. Eisenstein, *The Radical Future of Liberal Feminism* (New York: Longman, Inc., 1981), for a fuller accounting of this point.
3. Bertram Gross, *Friendly Fascism* (New York: M. Evans & Co., 1980).
4. See my 'Developing a Theory of Capitalist Patriarchy and Socialist Feminism,' in *Capitalist Patriarchy and the Case for Socialist Feminism*, ed. Zillah Eisenstein (New York: Monthly Review Press, 1979), pp. 5–40, for a discussion of the mutual dependence of capitalism and patriarchy.
5. See my *Radical Future of Liberal Feminism*, esp. chaps. 9 and 10.
6. See Iris Young, 'Socialist Feminism and the Limits of Dual Systems Theory,' *Socialist Review* 10, no. 2–3 (March–June 1980): 169–88, for what I think is an incorrect assessment of my concept of capitalist patriarchy as reflecting a 'dual system'.
7. See Allen Hunter, 'In the Wings: New Right Organization and Ideology,' *Radical America* 15, nos. 1–2 (Spring 1981): 113–40, for a similar discussion which he terms selective antistatism.
8. Documented in a February 1981 *Newsday* poll that was conducted nationwide and reported in *The National NOW Times* (April 1981), p. 2. See also Frederick Jaffe, Barbara Lindheim, and Philip Lee, *Abortion Politics, Private Morality and Public Policy* (New York: McGraw-Hill Book Co., 1981), for a full discussion of public opinion about abortion.
9. Irving Howe, 'The Right Menace,' published in *Dissent* pamphlet no. 1, *The Threat of Conservatism*, p. 29 (available from *Dissent*, 505 Fifth Avenue, New York, New York 10017).

8 □ Difference

Introduction

□ Sexuality, along with race and class is used as a category to identify differences between groups. These differences are then manipulated by society to encourage one social group to dominate another. The existence of sexual differences is common in all societies although, of course, the forms in which this occurs alter historically and culturally.

From the beginning feminism has fought against the systematic social stereotypes of sexual difference. Where in the nineteenth century feminist campaigns for social reform and suffrage often minimised sexual differences, currently feminism attacks universalism and describes and celebrates the experiences and identities of many 'different' women. This concern, by and large, divides into three broad schools of thought. There are those writers, for example Hélène Cixous and Luce Irigaray, who focus on sexual differences in language and there are those, for example Carol Gilligan and Nancy Chodorow, who describe sexual differences in gender identity. In addition, the women-centred perspectives of the late 1970s and the 1980s, for example those of Adrienne Rich and Mary Daly, define difference(s) in terms of sexual preferences not simply in terms of gender difference.

What marks all feminist accounts of sexual difference is their interest in history and their sensitivity to women's language. The writing of Julia Kristeva, and Hélène Cixous among others, follows on from Simone de Beauvoir's description of 'woman as Other to man' and examines the opposites (or binaries) – man/woman, mind/nature – which are the dominant version of sexual difference. Feminists believe that differences between men and women are products of our gender identities rather than products of our biologies, and many of these critics, in particular Kristeva and Cixous, consider that art and literature offer important evidence of the ways in which differences of thought are structured. Perhaps the most crucial development in feminist thinking about difference since the 1970s has been in the writing of Barbara Smith and other black feminists who describe the specific contours of black women's objectification and the ways in which Afro-American women are always subordinated by dichotomies of difference and the proliferation of lesbian identities transnationally.   □

COMMENTARY: E. Gelfland and V. Thorndike Hules (1984), *French Feminist Criticism: Women, Language and Literature*, New York: Garland; K. King (1990), 'Producing Sex, Theory and Culture', in M. Hirsch and E. Fox Keller (eds), *Conflicts in Feminism*, London: Routledge.

HÉLÈNE CIXOUS 1937–

☐ Hélène Cixous is a creative writer and philosopher who teaches at the Centre d'Etude Féminines at the University of Paris, Vincennes. The author of many novels, plays, short stories and essays, Hélène Cixous believes that woman's difference from man is both a sexual and a linguistic difference. Cixous's aim is to speak and write about a positive representation of femininity in a discourse which she calls *écriture féminine*, or women's writing. The social script, Cixous argues, depends upon gendered binary oppositions and these operate in syntax, on sources of knowledge, and in our perceptions. Related to these formal differences there are differences between a 'masculine' language and women's desires. The 'feminine' is always the 'Other' or the negative in any hierarchies which society constructs. Cixous argues that if women's writing 'working on the difference' becomes *écriture féminine* then it can subvert 'masculine' symbolic language.

Cixous makes that radical break in her novels and essays, particularly in 'The Laugh of the Medusa' (1975). This has been an influential text. The essay celebrates women's differences which, Cixous argues, have been historically repressed. Cixous writes with an erotic, fluid syntax and new images, puns and absences in order to release women's bodies from existing representations. In many ways Cixous's writing resembles psychotherapy. Cixous claims that the language, the rhetoric of difference that women will learn from praising our bodies will create new identities for women and eventually new social institutions.   ☐

COMMENTARY: S. Sellers (ed.) (1988), *Writing Differences: Readings from the Seminar of Hélène Cixous*, Milton Keynes: Open University.

EXTRACT

THE LAUGH OF THE MEDUSA [1975]*

I shall speak about women's writing: about *what it will do*. Woman must write her self: must write about women and bring women to writing, from which they have been driven away as violently as from their bodies – for the same reasons, by the same law, with the same fatal goal. Woman must put herself into the text – as into the world and into history – by her own movement.

The future must no longer be determined by the past. I do not deny that the effects of the past are still with us. But I refuse to strengthen them by repeating them, to confer upon them an irremovability the equivalent of destiny, to confuse the biological and the cultural. Anticipation is imperative.

Since these reflections are taking shape in an area just on the point of being discovered, they necessarily bear the mark of our time – a time during which the new breaks away from the old, and, more precisely, the (feminine) new from the old (*la nouvelle de l'ancien*). Thus, as there are no grounds for establishing a discourse, but rather an arid millennial ground to break, what I say has at least two sides and two aims: to break up, to destroy; and to foresee the unforeseeable, to project.

I write this as a woman, toward women. When I say 'woman,' I'm speaking of woman in her inevitable struggle against conventional man; and of a universal woman subject who must bring women to their senses and to their meaning in history. But first it must be said that in spite of the enormity of the repression that has kept them in the 'dark' – that dark which people have been trying to make them accept as their attribute – there is, at this time, no general woman, no one typical woman. What they have

*From: Hélène Cixous (1983), 'The Laugh of the Medusa', in E. Abel and E.K. Abel (eds), *The Signs Reader: Women, Gender and Scholarship*, Chicago: University of Chicago Press.

in common I will say. But what strikes me is the infinite richness of their individual constitutions: you can't talk about *a* female sexuality, uniform, homogeneous, classifiable into codes – any more than you can talk about one unconscious resembling another. Women's imaginary is inexhaustible, like music, painting, writing: their stream of phantasms is incredible.

I have been amazed more than once by a description a woman gave me of a world all her own which she had been secretly haunting since early childhood. A world of searching, the elaboration of a knowledge, on the basis of a systematic experimentation with the bodily functions, a passionate and precise interrogation of her erotogeneity. This practice, extraordinarily rich and inventive, in particular as concerns masturbation, is prolonged or accompanied by a production of forms, a veritable aesthetic activity, each stage of rapture inscribing a resonant vision, a composition, something beautiful. Beauty will no longer be forbidden.

I wished that that woman would write and proclaim this unique empire so that other women, other unacknowledged sovereigns, might exclaim: I, too, overflow; my desires have invented new desires, my body knows unheard-of songs. Time and again I, too, have felt so full of luminous torrents that I could burst – burst with forms much more beautiful than those which are put up in frames and sold for a stinking fortune. And I, too, said nothing, showed nothing; I didn't open my mouth, I didn't repaint my half of the world. I was ashamed. I was afraid, and I swallowed my shame and my fear. I said to myself: You are mad! What's the meaning of these waves, these floods, these outbursts? Where is the ebullient, infinite woman who, immersed as she was in her naiveté, kept in the dark about herself, led into self-disdain by the great arm of parental-conjugal phallocentrism, hasn't been ashamed of her strength? Who, surprised and horrified by the fantastic tumult of her drives (for she was made to believe that a well-adjusted normal woman has a . . . divine composure), hasn't accused herself of being a monster? Who, feeling a funny desire stirring inside her (to sing, to write, to dare to speak, in short, to bring out something new), hasn't thought she was sick? Well, her shameful sickness is that she resists death, that she makes trouble.

And why don't you write? Write! Writing is for you, you are for you; your body is yours, take it. I know why you haven't written. (And why I didn't write before the age of twenty-seven.) Because writing is at once too high, too great for you, it's reserved for the great – that is, for 'great men'; and it's 'silly.' Besides, you've written a little, but in secret. And it wasn't good, because it was in secret, and because you punished yourself for writing, because you didn't go all the way; or because you wrote, irresistibly, as when we would masturbate in secret, not to go further, but to attenuate the tension a bit, just enough to take the edge off. And then as soon as we come, we go and make ourselves feel guilty – so as to be forgiven; or to forget, to bury it until the next time.

Write, let no one hold you back, let nothing stop you: not man; not the imbecilic capitalist machinery, in which publishing houses are the crafty, obsequious relayers of imperatives handed down by an economy that works against us and off our backs; and not *yourself*. Smug-faced readers, managing editors, and big bosses don't like the true texts of women – female-sexed texts. That kind scares them.

I write woman: woman must write woman. And man, man. So only an oblique consideration will be found here of man; it's up to him to say where his masculinity and femininity are at: this will concern us once men have opened their eyes and seen themselves clearly.[1]

Now women return from afar, from always: from 'without,' from the heath where witches are kept alive; from below, from beyond 'culture'; from their childhood which men have been trying desperately to make them forget, condemning it to 'eternal rest.' The little girls and their 'ill-mannered' bodies immured, well-preserved, intact unto themselves, in the mirror. Frigidified. But are they ever seething underneath! What an effort it takes – there's no end to it – for the sex cops to bar their threatening return. Such a display of forces on both sides that the struggle has for centuries been immobilized in the trembling equilibrium of a deadlock.

[. . .]

It is by writing, from and toward women, and by taking up the challenge of speech which has been governed by the phallus, that women will confirm women in a place other than that which is reserved in and by the symbolic, that is, in a place other than silence. Women should break out of the snare of silence. They shouldn't be conned into accepting a domain which is the margin or the harem.

Listen to a woman speak at a public gathering (if she hasn't painfully lost her wind). She doesn't 'speak,' she throws her trembling body forward; she lets go of herself, she flies; all of her passes into her voice, and it's with her body that she vitally supports the 'logic' of her speech. Her flesh speaks true. She lays herself bare. In fact, she physically materializes what she's thinking; she signifies it with her body. In a certain way she *inscribes* what she's saying, because she doesn't deny her drives the intractable and impassioned part they have in speaking. Her speech, even when 'theoretical' or political, is never simple or linear or 'objectified,' generalized: she draws her story into history.

There is not that scission, that division made by the common man between the logic of oral speech and the logic of the text, bound as he is by his antiquated relation – servile, calculating – to mastery. From which proceeds the niggardly lip serice which engages only the tiniest part of the body, plus the mask.

In women's speech, as in their writing, that element which never stops resonating, which, once we've been permeated by it, profoundly and imperceptibly touched by it, retains the power of moving us – that element is the song: first music from the first voice of love which is alive in every woman. Why this privileged relationship with the voice? Because no woman stockpiles as many defenses for countering the drives as does a man. You don't build walls around yourself, you don't forgo pleasure as 'wisely' as he. Even if phallic mystification has generally contaminated good relationships, a woman is never far from 'mother' (I mean outside her role functions: the 'mother' as nonname and as source of goods). There is always within her at least a little of that good mother's milk. She writes in white ink.

Woman for women – There always remains in woman that force which produces/is produced by the other – in particular, the other woman. *In* her, matrix, cradler; herself giver as her mother and child; she is her own sister-daughter. You might object, 'What about she who is the hysterical offspring of a bad mother?' Everything will be changed once woman gives woman to the other woman. There is hidden and always ready in woman the source; the locus for the other. The mother, too, is a metaphor. It is necessary and sufficient that the best of herself be given to woman by another woman for her to be able to love herself and return in love the body that was 'born' to her.

[. . .]

It is impossible to *define* a feminine practice of writing, and this is an impossibility that will remain, for this practice can never be theorized, enclosed, coded – which doesn't mean that it doesn't exist. But it will always surpass the discourse that regulates the phallocentric system; it does and will take place in areas other than those subordinated to philosophico-theoretical domination. It will be conceived of only by subjects who are breakers of automatisms, by peripheral figures that no authority can ever subjugate.

[. . .]

To this self-effacing, merger-type bisexuality, which would conjure away castration (the writer who puts up his sign: 'bisexual written here, come and see,' when the odds are good that it's neither one nor the other), I oppose the *other bisexuality* on which every subject not enclosed in the false theater of phallocentric representationalism has founded his/her erotic universe. Bisexuality: that is, each one's location in self (*repérage en soi*) of the presence – variously manifest and insistent according to each person, male or female – of both sexes, nonexclusion either of the difference or of one sex, and, from this 'self-permission,' multiplication of the effects of the inscription of desire, over all parts of my body and the other body.

Now it happens that at present, for historico-cultural reasons, it is women who are opening up to and benefiting from this vatic bisexuality which doesn't annul differences but stirs them up, pursues them, increases their number. In a certain way, 'woman is bisexual'; man – it's a secret to no one – being poised to keep glorious phallic monosexuality in view. By virtue of affirming the primacy of the phallus and of bringing it into play, phallocratic ideology has claimed more than one victim. As a woman, I've been clouded over by the great shadow of the scepter and been told: idolize it, that which you cannot brandish. But at the same time, man has been handed that grotesque and scarcely enviable destiny (just imagine) of being reduced to a single idol with clay balls. And consumed, as Freud and his followers note, by a fear of being a woman! For, if psychoanalysis was constituted from woman, to repress femininity (and not so successful a repression at that – men have made it clear), its account of masculine sexuality is now hardly refutable; as with all the 'human' sciences, it reproduces the masculine view, of which it is one of the effects.

[. . .]

Let the priests tremble, we're going to show them our sexts!

Too bad for them if they fall apart upon discovering that women aren't men, or that the mother doesn't have one. But isn't this fear convenient for them? Wouldn't the worst be, isn't the worst, in truth, that women aren't castrated, that they have only to stop listening to the Sirens (for the Sirens were men) for history to change its meaning? You only have to look at the Medusa straight on to see her. And she's not deadly. She's beautiful and she's laughing.

[. . .]

This doesn't mean that she's an undifferentiated magma, but that she doesn't lord it over her body or her desire. Though masculine sexuality gravitates around the penis, engendering that centralized body (in political anatomy) under the dictatorship of its parts, woman does not bring about the same regionalization which serves the couple head/genitals and which is inscribed only within boundaries. Her libido is cosmic, just as her unconscious is worldwide. Her writing can only keep going, without ever inscribing or discerning contours, daring to make these vertiginous crossings of the other(s) ephemeral and passionate sojourns in him, her, them, whom she inhabits long enough to look at from the point closest to their unconscious from the moment they awaken, to love them at the point closest to their drives; and then further, impregnated through and through with these brief, identificatory embraces, she goes and passes into infinity. She alone dares and wishes to know from within, where she, the outcast, has never ceased to hear the resonance of fore-language. She lets the other language speak – the language of 1,000 tongues which knows neither enclosure nor death. To life she refuses nothing. Her language does not contain, it carries; it does not hold back, it makes possible. When id is ambiguously uttered – the wonder of being several – she doesn't defend herself against these unknown women whom she's surprised at becoming, but derives pleasure from this gift of alterability. I am spacious, singing flesh, on which is grafted no one knows which I, more or less human, but alive because of transformation.

Note

1. Men still have everything to say about their sexuality, and everything to write. For what they have said so far, for the most part, stems from the opposition activity/passivity, from the power relation between a fantasized obligatory virility meant to invade, to colonize, and the consequential phantasm of woman as a 'dark continent' to penetrate and to 'pacify.' (We know what 'pacify' means in terms of scotomizing the other and misrecognizing the self.) Conquering her, they've made haste to depart from her borders, to get out of sight, out of body. The way man has of getting out of himself and into her whom he takes not for the other but for his own, deprives him, he knows, of his own bodily territory. One can understand how man, confusing himself with his penis and rushing in for the attack, might feel resentment and fear of being 'taken' by the woman, of being lost in her, absorbed, or alone.

LUCE IRIGARAY 1939–

☐ Luce Irigaray trained with the psychoanalyst Jacques Lacan but was expelled from his 'school' for her outspoken critiques. Irigaray addresses a key feminist question: What is the difference and therefore the politics of women's writing? Like Cixous and Julia Kristeva, Irigaray links language and sexuality, but by contrast Irigaray praises the radical otherness of women's eroticism. *Speculum de l'Autre Femme* (1974), which Irigaray presented as her thesis in philosophy, and *Ce Sexe qui n'en est pas un* (1977) which ends with 'When Our Lips Speak Together', lay out the connections between women's bodies and women's meaning making in language. Irigaray examines the ways in which women speak to each other (*'parler-entre-elles'*) and can disrupt symbolic or social language.

Irigaray shows how a more adequate representation of a woman's difference, particularly physical aspects of her sexuality, can reveal how a woman's identity is a continuous fluidity. For example Irigaray symbolizes the mother–daughter relationship in her essays in order to assert the importance of female affiliation. In addition she incorporates images of touch, menstruation and the semiotic mother, or memories of the mother from early childhood. Irigaray finds that in the writings of Freud in particular, and throughout the entire Western philosophical tradition from Plato to Hegel, women are the 'sex' which is not 'one'. Women's true sexuality is not represented and the feminine is suppressed. Only the celebration of women's difference – of their fluidity and multiplicity – can escape conventional Western representations of women. ☐

COMMENTARY: A. Nye (1988), *Feminist Theory and the Philosophies of Man,* London: Croom Helm.

THIS SEX WHICH IS NOT ONE [1977]*

But *woman has sex organs just about everywhere.* She experiences pleasure almost everywhere. Even without speaking of the hysterization of her entire body, one can say that the geography of her pleasure is much more diversified, more multiple in its differences, more complex, more subtle, than is imagined – in an imaginary centered a bit too much on one and the same.

'She' is indefinitely other in herself. That is undoubtedly the reason she is called temperamental, incomprehensible, perturbed, capricious – not to mention her language in which 'she' goes off in all directions and in which 'he' is unable to discern the coherence of any meaning. Contradictory words seem a little crazy to the logic of reason, and inaudible for him who listens with ready-made grids, a code prepared in advance. In her statements – at least when she dares to speak out – woman retouches herself constantly. She just barely separates from herself some chatter, an exclamation, a half-secret, a sentence left in suspense – When she returns to it, it is only to set out again from another point of pleasure or pain. One must listen to her differently in order to hear an *'other meaning' which is constantly in the process of weaving itself, at the same time ceaselessly embracing words and yet casting them off to avoid becoming fixed, immobilized.* For when 'she' says something, it is already no longer identical to what she means. Moreover, her statements are never identical to anything. Their distinguishing feature is one of contiguity. They touch (*upon*). And when they wander too far from this nearness, she stops and begins again from 'zero': her body-sex organ.

It is therefore useless to trap women into giving an exact definition of what they mean, to make them repeat (them-

*From: Luce Irigaray (1981), 'This sex Which is Not One', in E. Marks and I. de Courtivron (eds), *New French Feminisms*, Brighton: Harvester.

selves) so the meaning will be clear. They are already elsewhere than in this discursive machinery where you claim to take them by surprise. They have turned back within themselves, which does not mean the same thing as 'within yourself.' They do not experience the same interiority that you do and which perhaps you mistakenly presume they share. 'Within themselves' means *in the privacy of this silent, multiple, diffuse tact.* If you ask them insistently what they are thinking about they can only reply: nothing. Everything.

[. . .]

A woman's evolution, however radical it might seek to be, would not suffice then to liberate woman's desire. Neither political theory nor political practice have yet resolved nor sufficiently taken into account this historical problem, although Marxism has announced its importance. But women are not, strictly speaking, a class and their dispersion in several classes makes their political struggle complex and their demands sometimes contradictory.

Their underdeveloped condition stemming from their submission by/to a culture which oppresses them, uses them, cashes in on them, still remains. Women reap no advantage from this situation except that of their quasi-monopoly of masochistic pleasure, housework, and reproduction. The power of slaves? It is considerable since the master is not necessarily well served in matters of pleasure. Therefore, the inversion of the relationship, especially in sexual economy, does not seem to be an enviable objective.

But if women are to preserve their auto-eroticism, their homo-sexuality, and let it flourish, would not the renunciation of heterosexual pleasure simply be another form of this amputation of power that is traditionally associated with women? Would this renunciation not be a new incarceration, a new cloister that women would willingly build? Let women tacitly go on strike, avoid men long enough to learn to defend their desire notably by their speech, let them discover the love of other women protected from that imperious choice of men which puts them in a position of rival goods, let them forge a social status which demands recognition, let them earn their living in order to leave behind their condition of prostitute – These are certainly indispensable steps in their effort to escape their proletarization on the trade market. But, if their goal is to reverse the existing order – even if that were possible – history would simply repeat itself and return to phallocratism, where neither women's sex, their imaginary, nor their language can exist.

EXTRACT

WHEN OUR LIPS SPEAK TOGETHER
[1977]*

Speak just the same. Because your language doesn't follow just one thread, one course, or one pattern, we are in luck. You speak from everywhere at the same time. You touch me whole at the same time. In all senses. Why only one song, one discourse, one text at a time? To seduce, satisfy, fill one of my 'holes'? I don't have any, with you. We are not voids, lacks which wait for sustenance, fulfillment, or plenitude from an other. That our lips make us women does not mean that consuming, consummating, or being filled is what matters to us.

Kiss me. Two lips kiss two lips, and openness is ours again. Our 'world.' Between us, the movement from inside to outside, from outside to inside, knows no limits. It is without end. These are exchanges that no mark, no mouth[1] can ever stop. Between us, the house has no walls, the clearing no enclosure, language no circularity. You kiss me, and the world enlarges until the horizon vanishes. Are we unsatisfied? Yes, if that means that we are never finished. If our pleasure consists of moving and being moved by each other, endlessly. Always in movement, this openness is neither spent nor sated.

They neither taught us nor allowed us to say our multiplicity. That would have been improper speech. Of course, we were allowed – we had to? – display one truth even as we sensed but muffled, stifled another. Truth's other side – its complement? its remainder? – stayed hidden. Secret. Inside and outside, we were not supposed to be the same. That doesn't suit their desires. Veiling and unveiling, isn't that what concerns them, interests them? Always repeating the same operation – each time, on each woman.

*From: Luce Irigaray (1980) 'When Our Lips Speak Together', *Signs*, 6, 1.

You/I then become two to please them. But once we are divided in two – once outside, the other inside – you no longer embrace yourself or me. On the outside, you attempt to conform to an order which is alien to you. Exiled from yourself, you fuse with everything that you encounter. You mime whatever comes near you. You become whatever you touch. In your hunger tǒ find yourself, you move indefinitely far from yourself, from me. Assuming one model after another, one master after another, changing your face, form, and language according to the power that dominates you. Sundered. By letting yourself be abused, you become an impassive travesty. You no longer return as the indifferent one. You return closed and impenetrable.

Speak to me. Can't you? Don't you want to any longer? Do you want to keep to yourself? Remain silent, white, virginal? Preserve the inner self? But it doesn't exist without the other. Don't tear yourself apart with choices that have been imposed on you. *Between us*, there is no rupture between virginal and nonvirginal. No event that makes us women. Long before your birth, you touched yourself, innocently. Your/my body does not acquire a sex by some operation, by the act of some power, function, or organ. You are already a woman; you don't need any special modification or intervention. You don't have to have an 'outside,' since 'the other' already affects you, it is inseparable from you. You have been altered forever, everywhere. This is the crime that you never committed: you disturb their love of property.

How can I tell you that your sexual pleasure is in no way evil, you stranger to goods? There can be no fault until they rob you of your openness and close you up to brand you as their possession; practice their transgressions, infractions, and play other games with the law. When they – and you? speculate with your whiteness. If we play this game, we let ourselves be abused, damaged. We are alienated from ourselves to support the pursuit of their ends. That would be our role. If we submit to their reasoning, we are guilty. Their strategy – deliberate or not – is to make us guilty.

You have come back, divided: 'we' are no more. You are split into red and white, black and white. How can we find each other again? Touch each other? We are cut into pieces, finished: our pleasure is trapped in their system, where 'virgin' means one as yet unmarked by them, for them. Not yet a woman in their terms. Not yet imprinted with their sex, their language. Not yet penetrated or possessed by them. Still inhabiting that candor which is an awaiting, a nothing without them, a void without them. A virgin is but the future for their exchanges, their commerce, and their transports. A kind of reserve for their explorations, consummations, and exploitations – the future coming of their desires. But not ours.

How can I say it? That we are women from the start. That we don't need to be produced by them, named by them, made sacred or profane by them. That this has always already happened, without their labors. And that their history constitutes the locus of our exile. It's not that we have our own territory, but that their nation, family, home, and discourse imprison us in enclosures where we can no longer move – or live as 'we.' Their property is our exile. Their enclosures, the death of our love. Their words, the gag upon our lips.

[. . .]

Don't fret about the 'right' word. There is none. No truth between our lips. Everything has the right to be. Everything is worth exchanging, without privileges or refusals. Exchange? Everything can be exchanged when nothing is bought. Between us, there are no owners and no purchasers, no determinable objects and no prices. Our bodies are enriched by our mutual pleasure. Our abundance is inexhaustible: it knows neither want nor plenty. When we give ourselves 'all,' without holding back or hoarding, our exchanges have no terms. How to say this? The language we know is so limited. . . .

You'll say to me, why talk? We feel the same thing at the same time. Aren't my hands, my eyes, my mouth, my lips, my body enough for you? Isn't what they say to you sufficient? I could say yes, but that would be too easy. It has been said too often to reassure you/us.

If we don't invent a language, if we don't find our body's language, its gestures will be too few to accompany our story. When we become tired of the same ones, we'll keep our desires secret, unrealized. Asleep again, dissatisfied, we will be turned over to the words of men – who have claimed to 'know' for a long time. But *not our body*. Thus seduced, allured, fascinated, ecstatic over our becoming, we will be paralyzed. Deprived of *our movements*. Frozen, although we are made for endless change. Without leaps or falls, and without repetition.

Continue, don't run out of breath. Your body is not the same today as yesterday. Your body remembers. *You* don't need to remember, to store up yesterday like capital in your head. Your memory? Your body reveals yesterday in what it wants today. If you think: yesterday I was, tomorrow I will be, you are thinking: I have died a little. Be what you are becoming, without clinging to what you could have been, might be. Never settle. Let's leave definitiveness to the undecided; we don't need it. Right here and now, our body gives us a very different certainty. Truth is necessary for those who are so distanced from their body that they have forgotten it. But their 'truth' makes us immobile, like statues, if we can't divest ourselves of it. If we don't annul its power by trying to say, here, now, right away, how we are moved.

Notes

1. L. Irigaray plays on *boucle* ('buckle') and *bouche* ('mouth'), to suggest that the female buccal exchanges are endless, their circularity open.

JULIA KRISTEVA 1941–

☐ Julia Kristeva is a practising psychoanalyst and philosopher who teaches linguistics at the Univérsité de Paris VII. Although Kristeva rejects 'feminism' as a term, her writing is primarily concerned with the issue of sexual difference and how this affects the constitution and place of the individual in culture. Kristeva does not identify 'feminine' with a biological woman or 'masculine' with biological man. In an implicitly feminist gesture, Kristeva argues that the place of sexual difference is the semiotic which is the time of mother/child bonding, a moment of body erotics, melodies and maternal rhythms, all of which precede the symbolic – the paternal zone. The meeting point of the semiotic and the symbolic in art and literature is in moments of 'jouissance' or pleasure. In *Desire in Language* (1977) Kristeva suggests that the symbolic represses the maternal drives, the semiotic, but that these erupt into language in the form of puns and verbal slips.

In 'Women's Time' (1979) Kristeva goes further, to describe historical representations of sexual difference. Here the symbolic becomes the 'masculine' time of history which is linear time, and Kristeva equates the 'feminine' with cyclical and monumental time. All language, according to Kristeva, is sexually differentiated. 'Masculinity' retains, and indeed celebrates, logical connections and linearity (the symbolic). This singularity is challenged by the semiotic which contains the 'feminine' drives or voice tones. So that changes to dominant histories, to capitalism and to patriarchy, will depend not only on new political practices (in 'Women's Time' Kristeva discusses terrorist movements) but on new forms of language which revalue the feminine. ☐

COMMENTARY: E. Grosz (1989), *Sexual Subversions*, London: Allen and Unwin.

DESIRE IN LANGUAGE: A SEMIOTIC APPROACH TO LITERATURE AND ART [1977]*

The exclamation marks alternating with three dots even more categorically point to this surge of instinctual drive: a panting, a breathlessness, an acceleration of verbal utterance, concerned not so much with finally reaching a global summing up of the world's meaning, as, to the contrary, with revealing, within the interstices of predication, the rhythm of a drive that remains forever unsatisfied – in the vacancy of judging consciousness and sign – because it could not find an other (an addressee) so as to obtain meaning in this exchange. We must also listen to Céline, Artaud, or Joyce, and read their texts in order to understand that the aim of this practice, which reaches us as a language, is, through the signification of the nevertheless transmitted message, not only to impose a music, a rhythm – that is, a polyphony – but also to wipe out sense through nonsense and laughter. This is a difficult operation that obliges the reader not so much to combine significations as to shatter his own judging consciousness in order to grant passage through it to this rhythmic drive constituted by repression and, once filtered by language and its meaning, experienced as jouissance. Could the resistance against modern literature be evidence of an obsession with meaning, of an unfitness for such jouissance?

[...]

The language of art, too, follows (but differently and more closely) the other aspect of maternal jouissance, the sublimation taking place at the very moment of primal repression within the mother's body, arising perhaps unwittingly

*From: Julia Kristeva (1980), *Desire in Language: A Semiotic Approach to Literature and Art*, Oxford: Blackwell.

out of her marginal position. At the intersection of sign and rhythm, of representation and light, of the symbolic and the semiotic, the artist speaks from a place where she is not, where she knows not. He delineates what, in her, is a body rejoicing [*jouissant*]. The very existence of aesthetic practice makes clear that the Mother as subject is a delusion, just as the negation of the so-called poetic dimension of language leads one to believe in the existence of the Mother, and consequently, of transcendence. Because, through a symbiosis of meaning and nonmeaning, of representation and interplay of differences, the artist lodges into language, and through his identification with the mother (fetishism or incest – we shall return to this problem), his own specific jouissance, thus traversing both sign and object. Thus, before all other speakers, he bears witness to what the unconscious (through the screen of the mother) records of those clashes that occur between the biological and social programs of the species. This means that through and across secondary repression (founding of signs), aesthetic practice touches upon primal repression (founding biological series and the laws of the species). At the place where it obscurely succeeds within the maternal body, every artist tries his hand, but rarely with equal success.

The history of the speaking being (spatially bound precisely because he speaks) is only spatial variation,[1] never shattering the limits of the speaking/forming, but rather displacing it by means of a *praxis* or a *technè*. It is henceforth clear that meaning's closure can never be challenged by another *space*, but only by a different way of *speaking*: another enunciation, another 'literature.' There exists, on the other hand, an epistemological bent toward elucidation that is not, as Husserl postulates, the 'destiny' of the speaking being; rather, it is *one* of its practices, *one* variation of significance not limited to what is 'universally intelligible' – madness and literature are its witnesses. If we remain with this tendency, we must choose between two directions: either we delineate the history of spaces (we practise epistemology), or we investigate what Husserl calls 'human forming.' The second alternative inevitably merges with Freudian preoccupations: the analysis of the 'origins' of forming/speaking follows the path of the Freudian 'error' mentioned above.

Any attentiveness to 'infantile language' (as defined above) seems to be located at that ambiguous point where psychoanalysis opens up the limits of phenomenological meaning by indicating its conditions of production, and where phenomenology encloses the transferential disintegration of meaning – as soon as the latter is being articulated as either demonstrative or simply 'universally intelligible' clauses.

To repeat the question that the infant-analyst puts to maternal attentiveness before any mirror shows him any representation whatsoever, before any language begins to encode his 'idealities': what about the paradoxical *semiosis* of the newborn's body, what about the 'semiotic *chora*,'[2] what about this 'space' prior to the sign, this archaic disposition of primary narcissism that a poet brings to light in order to challenge the closure of meaning ('nothing will have taken place but the place,' certainly, if not 'at heights so far removed that a place fuses with the beyond [. . .] the bewildering successive clash of a whole account in formation . . .' – Mallarmé).

Neither request nor desire, it is an invocation, an anaclisis.[3] Memories of bodily contact, warmth, and nourishment: these underlie the breath of the newborn body as it appeals to a source of support, a fulfillment of care that Spitz properly termed the 'diatrophic mother.' Vocal and muscular contractions, spasms of the glottis and motor system – all make up for the absence of intrauterine life components. Voice is the vehicle of that call for help, directed at a frustrated memory, in order to insure, first through breath and warmth, the survival of an ever premature human being; and this is undoubtedly significant for the acquisition of language, which will soon be articulated along the same vehicle. Every cry is, psychologically and projectively, described as a cry of distress, up to and including the first vocalizations, which seem to constitute distress calls, in short: anaclises. The newborn body experiences three months of such anaclitic 'facilitations' without reaching a stable condition.

Faced with these anaclises, the adult – essentially the mother – offers a disturbed reception, a mobile receptacle, which fashions itself on the invocation, follows its winding course, and eventually accents it with a surge of anguish that the newborn analyzer's body produces in the analysand. From this time on, we must reckon with the mother's desire, beyond which it is hard for her to go, to maintain the newborn child within the invocation: the child as adjunct to the breast, a wealth of her own, may be an analyzer, but it is an analyst lacking any interpretation and who thus locks mother and child within the regression of primary masochism. This is the precise moment for either the 'optimal frustration' that Spitz requires of the mother with regard to the child, or Winnicott's mysterious 'good enough mother': they are intended to break the primary narcissism within which mother and child are wrapped up, from *anaclisis* to *diatrophy*, so that, with the advent of autoeroticism, the door is finally open to a relationship with the object, at the same time as representation and language make their appearance.

Before this step becomes effective, however, and within the subtle drift from primary narcissism to autoeroticism, the 'good enough mother' with her 'optimal frustration' scores a point: laughter.

Notes

1. Is it not true that the only (historical) events today, outside of murder (that is, war) are scientific events: the invention of spaces, from mathematics to astronomy?
2. Cf. 'La Chora sémiotique,' in *La Révolution du language poétique* (Paris: Seuil, 1974), pp. 23–30.
3. R. Spitz, 'Autoeroticism re-examined,' *Psychoanalytical Study of the Child* (1962), 17: 292.

WOMEN'S TIME [1979]*

As for time, female[1] subjectivity would seem to provide a specific measure that essentially retains *repetition* and *eternity* from among the multiple modalities of time known through the history of civilizations. On the one hand, there are cycles, gestation, the eternal recurrence of a biological rhythm which conforms to that of nature and imposes a temporality whose stereotyping may shock, but whose regularity and unison with what is experienced as extrasubjective time, cosmic time, occasion vertiginous visions and unnameable *jouissance*.[2] On the other hand, and perhaps as a consequence, there is the massive presence of a monumental temporality, without cleavage or escape, which has so little to do with linear time (which passes) that the very word 'temporality' hardly fits: All-encompassing and infinite like imaginary space, this temporality reminds one of Kronos in Hesiod's mythology, the incestuous son whose massive presence covered all of Gea in order to separate her from Ouranos, the father.[3] Or one is reminded of the various myths of resurrection which, in all religious beliefs, perpetuate the vestige of an anterior or concomitant maternal cult, right up to its most recent elaboration, Christianity, in which the body of the Virgin Mother does not die but moves from one spatiality to another within the same time via dormition (according to the Orthodox faith) or via assumption (the Catholic faith).[4]

The fact that these two types of temporality (cyclical and monumental) are traditionally linked to female subjectivity insofar as the latter is thought of as necessarily maternal should not make us forget that this repetition and this eternity are found to be the fundamental, if not the sole, conceptions of time in numerous civilizations and experiences,

*From: Julia Kristeva (1982), 'Women's Time', in N.O. Keohane et al. (eds), *Feminist Theory: A Critique of Ideology*, Brighton: Harvester.

particularly mystical ones.[5] The fact that certain currents of modern feminism recognize themselves here does not render them fundamentally incompatible with 'masculine' values.

In return, female subjectivity as it gives itself up to intuition becomes a problem with respect to a certain conception of time: time as project, teleology, linear and prospective unfolding; time as departure, progression, and arrival – in other words, the time of history.[6] It has already been abundantly demonstrated that this kind of temporality is inherent in the logical and ontological values of any given civilization, that this temporality renders explicit a rupture, an expectation, or an anguish which other temporalities work to conceal. It might also be added that this linear time is that of language considered as the enunciation of sentences (noun + verb; topic–comment; beginning–ending), and that this time rests on its own stumbling block, which is also the stumbling block of that enunciation – death. A psychoanalyst would call this 'obsessional time,' recognizing in the mastery of time the true structure of the slave. The hysteric (either male or female) who suffers from reminiscences would, rather, recognize his or her self in the anterior temporal modalities: cyclical or monumental. This antinomy, one perhaps embedded in psychic structures, becomes, nonetheless, within a given civilization, an antinomy among social groups and ideologies in which the radical positions of certain feminists would rejoin the discourse of marginal groups of spiritual or mystical inspiration and, strangely enough, rejoin recent scientific preoccupations. Is it not true that the problematic of a time indissociable from space, of a space–time in infinite expansion, or rhythmed by accidents or catastrophes, preoccupies both space science and genetics? And, at another level, is it not true that the contemporary media revolution, which is manifest in the storage and reproduction of information, implies an idea of time as frozen or exploding according to the vagaries of demand, returning to its source but uncontrollable, utterly bypassing its subject and leaving only two preoccupations to those who approve of it:

Who is to have power over the origin (the programming) and over the end (the use)?

Notes

1. As most readers of recent French theory in translation know, le féminin does not have the same pejorative connotations it has come to have in English. It is a term used to speak about women in general, but, as used most often in this article, it probably comes closest to our 'female' as defined by Elaine Showalter in A Literature of Their Own (Princeton, N.J.: Princeton University Press, 1977). I have therefore used either 'women' or 'female' according to the context (cf. also n. 9 in 'Introduction to Julia Kristeva's "Women's Time" ' [this issue; hereafter cited as 'Introduction']). 'Subjectivity' here refers to the state of being 'a thinking, speaking, acting, doing or writing agent' and never, e.g., as opposed to 'objectivity' (see the glossary in Desire in Language). – AJ.
2. I have retained jouissance – that word for pleasure which defies translation – as it is rapidly becoming a 'believable neologism' in English (see the glossary in Desire in Language). – AJ.
3. This particular mythology has important implications – equal only to those of the oedipal myth – for current French thought. – AJ.
4. See Julia Kristeva, 'Hérétique de l'amour,' Tel quel, no. 74 (1977), pp. 30–49.
5. See H.C. Puech, La Gnose et la temps (Paris: Gallimard, 1977).
6. See 'Introduction.' – AJ.

CAROL GILLIGAN

☐ *In A Different Voice* (1982), by the American writer Carol Gilligan, is a powerful account of gender differences. Gilligan listened to women's stories about abortion decisions (their 'different voices' and the ethics/ morality represented by those voices). She was able to show that Freud's idea that men have a better developed sense of morality than women was nonsense. Women do have a very *different* conception of morality, Gilligan discovered, a morality of responsibility where men have a morality of rights. These differences, Gilligan argues, derive from our different gender formations. Building on Nancy Chodorow's theory that women are encouraged to empathise with, and men to distance themselves from, others, Gilligan argues that gender socialisation produces two different notions of morality. Very early in life, men's individualism and separation from the 'feminine' gives them an ethics of 'justice' while women's affiliation to mothers and others teaches us an ethics of care. Women's morality involves emphasis (stressing the value of), consequence (calculating the effects on others), and context (assessing social circumstances). ☐

COMMENTARY: A. Garry and M. Pearsall (eds) (1989), *Women, Knowledge and Reality*, London: Unwin Hyman.

EXTRACT

IN A DIFFERENT VOICE: PSYCHOLOGICAL THEORY AND WOMEN'S DEVELOPMENT [1982]*

The moral imperative that emerges repeatedly in interviews with women is an injunction to care, a responsibility to discern and alleviate the 'real and recognizable trouble' of this world. For men, the moral imperative appears rather as an injunction to respect the rights of others and thus to protect from interference the rights to life and self-fulfillment. Women's insistence on care is at first self-critical rather than self-protective, while men initially conceive obligation to others negatively in terms of noninterference.

[...]

The abortion study suggests that women impose a distinctive construction on moral problems, seeing moral dilemmas in terms of conflicting responsibilities. This construction was traced through a sequence of three perspectives, each perspective representing a more complex understanding of the relationship between self and other and each transition involving a critical reinterpretation of the conflict between selfishness and responsibility. The sequence of women's moral judgment proceeds from an initial concern with survival to a focus on goodness and finally to a reflective understanding of care as the most adequate guide to the resolution of conflicts in human relationships. The abortion study demonstrates the centrality of the concepts of responsibility and care in women's constructions of the moral domain, the close tie in women's thinking between conceptions of the self and of morality, and ultimately the need for an expanded developmental theory

*From: Carol Gilligan (1982), *In a Different Voice: Psychological Theory and Women's Development*, Cambridge, MA: Harvard University Press.

that includes, rather than rules out from consideration, the differences in the feminine voice. Such an inclusion seems essential, not only for explaining the development of women but also for understanding in both sexes the characteristics and precursors of an adult moral conception.

[. . .]

There seems at present to be only partial agreement between men and women about the adulthood they commonly share. In the absence of mutual understanding, relationships between the sexes continue in varying degrees of constraint, manifesting the 'paradox of egocentrism' which Piaget describes, a mystical respect for rules combined with everyone playing more or less as he pleases and paying no attention to his neighbor (p. 61). For a life-cycle understanding to address the development in adulthood of relationships characterized by cooperation, generosity, and care, that understanding must include the lives of women as well as of men.

Among the most pressing items on the agenda for research on adult development is the need to delineate *in women's own terms* the experience of their adult life. My own work in that direction indicates that the inclusion of women's experience brings to developmental understanding a new perspective on relationships that changes the basic constructs of interpretation. The concept of identity expands to include the experience of interconnection. The moral domain is similarly enlarged by the inclusion of responsibility and care in relationships. And the underlying epistemology correspondingly shifts from the Greek ideal of knowledge as a correspondence between mind and form to the Biblical conception of knowing as a process of human relationship.

Given the evidence of different perspectives in the representation of adulthood by women and men, there is a need for research that elucidates the effects of these differences in marriage, family, and work relationships. My research suggests that men and women may speak different languages that they assume are the same, using similar words to encode disparate experiences of self and social relationships. Because these languages share an overlapping moral vocabulary, they contain a propensity for systematic mistranslation, creating misunderstandings which impede communication and limit the potential for cooperation and care in relationships. At the same time, however, these languages articulate with one another in critical ways. Just as the language of responsibilities provides a weblike imagery of relationships to replace a hierarchical ordering that dissolves with the coming of equality, so the language of rights underlines the importance of including in the network of care not only the other but also the self.

As we have listened for centuries to the voices of men and the theories of development that their experience informs, so we have come more recently to notice not only the silence of women but the difficulty in hearing what they say when they speak. Yet in the different voice of women lies the truth of an ethic of care, the tie between relationship and responsibility, and the origins of aggression in the failure of connection. The failure to see the different reality of women's lives and to hear the differences in their voices stems in part from the assumption that there is a single mode of social experience and interpretation. By positing instead two different modes, we arrive at a more complex rendition of human experience which sees the truth of separation and attachment in the lives of women and men and recognizes how these truths are carried by different modes of language and thought.

To understand how the tension between responsibilities and rights sustains the dialectic of human development is to see the integrity of two disparate modes of experience that are in the end connected. While an ethic of justice proceeds from the premise of equality – that everyone should be treated the same – an ethic of care rests on the premise of nonviolence – that no one should be hurt. In the representation of maturity, both perspectives converge in the realization that just as inequality adversely affects both parties in an unequal relationship, so too violence is destructive for everyone involved. This dialogue between fairness and care not only provides a better understanding of relations between the sexes but also gives rise to a more comprehensive portrayal of adult work and family relationships.

As Freud and Piaget call our attention to the differences in children's feelings and thought, enabling us to respond to children with greater care and respect, so a recognition of the differences in women's experience and understanding expands our vision of maturity and points to the contextual nature of developmental truths. Through this expansion in perspective, we can begin to envision how a marriage between adult development as it is currently portrayed and women's development as it begins to be seen could lead to a changed understanding of human development and a more generative view of human life.

EXTRACT

WOMAN'S PLACE IN MAN'S LIFE CYCLE [1979]*

'It is obvious,' Virginia Woolf said, 'that the values of women differ very often from the values which have been made by the other sex' (1929, p. 76). Yet, she adds, it is the masculine values that prevail. As a result, women come to question the 'normality' of their feelings and to alter their judgments in deference to the opinion of others. In the nineteenth-century novels written by women, Woolf sees at work 'a mind slightly pulled from the straight, altering its clear vision in the anger and confusion of deference to external authority' (1929, p. 77). The same deference that Woolf identifies in nineteenth-century fiction can be seen as well in the judgments of twentieth-century women. Women's reluctance to make moral judgments, the difficulty they experience in finding or speaking publicly in their own voice, emerge repeatedly in the form of qualification and self-doubt, in intimations of a divided judgment, a public and private assessment which are fundamentally at odds (Gilligan, 1977).

Yet the deference and confusion that Woolf criticizes in women derive from the values she sees as their strength. Women's deference is rooted not only in their social circumstances but also in the substance of their moral concern. Sensitivity to the needs of others and the assumption of responsibility for taking care lead women to attend to voices other than their own and to include in their judgment other points of view. Women's moral weakness, manifest in an apparent diffusion and confusion of judgment, is thus inseparable from women's moral strength, an overriding concern with relationships and responsibilities. The reluctance to judge can itself be indicative of the same care

*From: Carol Gilligan (1987), 'Woman's Place in Man's Life Cycle', in S. Harding (ed.), *Feminism and Methodology*, Milton Keynes: Open University Press.

and concern for others that infuses the psychology of women's development and is responsible for what is characteristically seen as problematic in its nature.

Thus women not only define themselves in a context of human relationship but also judge themselves in terms of their ability to care. Woman's place in man's life cycle has been that of nurturer, caretaker, and helpmate, the weaver of those networks of relationships on which she in turn relies. While women have thus taken care of men, however, men have in their theories of psychological development tended either to assume or devalue that care. The focus on individuation and individual achievement that has dominated the description of child and adolescent development has recently been extended to the depiction of adult development as well. Levinson in his study, *The Seasons of a Man's Life* (1978), elaborates a view of adult development in which relationships are portrayed as a means to an end of individual achievement and success. In the critical relationships of early adulthood, the 'Mentor' and the 'Special Woman' are defined by the role they play in facilitating the man's realization of his 'Dream.' Along similar lines Vaillant (1977), in his study of men, considers altruism a defense, characteristic of mature ego functioning and associated with successful 'adaptation to life,' but conceived as derivative rather than primary in contrast to Chodorow's analysis, in which empathy is considered 'built-in' to the woman's primary definition of self.

The discovery now being celebrated by men in mid-life of the importance of intimacy, relationships, and care is something that women have known from the beginning. However, because that knowledge has been considered 'intuitive' or 'instinctive,' a function of anatomy coupled with destiny, psychologists have neglected to describe its development. In my research, I have found that women's moral development centers on the elaboration of that knowledge. Women's moral development thus delineates a critical line of psychological development whose importance for both sexes becomes apparent in the intergenerational framework of a life-cycle perspective. While the subject of moral development provides the final illustration of the reiterative pattern in the observation and assessment of sex differences in the literature on human development, it also indicates more particularly why the nature and significance of women's development has for so long been obscured and considered shrouded in mystery.

[. . .]

Research on moral judgment has shown that when the categories of women's thinking are examined in detail (Gilligan, 1977) the outline of a moral conception different from that described by Freud, Piaget, or Kohlberg begins to emerge and to inform a different description of moral development. In this conception, the moral problem is seen to arise from conflicting responsibilities rather than from competing rights and to require for its resolution a mode of thinking that is contextual and inductive rather than formal and abstract.

This conception of morality as fundamentally concerned with the capacity for understanding and care also develops through a structural progression of increasing differentiation and integration. This progression witnesses the shift from an egocentric through a societal to the universal moral perspective that Kohlberg described in his research on men, but it does so in different terms. The shift in women's judgment from an egocentric to a conventional to a principled ethical understanding is articulated through their use of a distinct moral language, in which the terms 'selfishness' and 'responsibility' define the moral problem as one of care. Moral development then consists of the progressive reconstruction of this understanding toward a more adequate conception of care.

9 ☐ Psychoanalytic feminism

Introduction

☐ Psychoanalytic feminism has one of its sites of origin in Karen Horney's essays on femininity, which challenged Freud with their positive view of the feminine; but also in Helene Deutsch's attention to mothering; in Anna Freud's theories about maternal deprivation and adolescence; and in Melanie Klein's concept of self-integration. Contemporary psychoanalytic feminism begins with Kate Millett's attack on Freud and Phyllis Chesler's work in New York. The rejection of Freudian theory by Millett and early second wave feminists was later challenged by Juliet Mitchell, who focused instead on the differences between psychodynamic and social structures. In response to the Women's Movement, Dorothy Dinnerstein, Jean Baker Miller, Adrienne Rich and Nancy Chodorow created new psychoanalytic theories with reference to heterosexual relations and it is their writings in the period 1970–8 together with Mitchell's which provide the basis of current psychoanalytic feminism. While Dinnerstein and Chodorow (for extract, see below pp. 278–83) focus on the psychosocial relations of mothering, and Miller and Rich describe women's qualities of relatedness and empathy, other theorists, for example Sarah Kofman, examine the positive aspects of 'feminine' instabilities.

More recently psychoanalysis has been plundered by feminist literary critics to show how the 'feminine' is produced and organised in language. For example, Sandra Gilbert and Susan Gubar, in *The Madwoman in the Attic* (1979) draw on object-relations theory to investigate relationships between women writers. In moving towards a more secure, confident feminist psychoanalysis the work of Sarah Kofman and Jean Baker Miller has been especially important because they describe a woman's identity in new and positive terms. Some of the most interesting questions about the relation of psychoanalysis and feminism are about how the feminine can escape and subvert traditional psychoanalytic models, what Kofman terms 'the enigma of woman'. ☐

COMMENTARY: T. Brennan (1989), *Between Feminism and Psychoanalysis*, London: Routledge.

PHYLLIS CHESLER 1940–

☐ The notion that, in contemporary society, female identity is routinely described in motifs of sickness and insanity was the key idea put forward by Phyllis Chesler in *Women and Madness* (1972). In this major empirical study of women in American mental institutions, Chesler came to the conclusion that women's mental illness is a likely result of sex role stereotyping and that when women refuse gender norms consciously or unconsciously, our rebellions are regarded by society as examples of sickness and psychological deviance. Chesler's book is a massive indictment of the way postwar American psychiatry had supported and even encouraged sex role stereotyping. Her view dovetailed with second wave feminism, and its challenge to the social norms of female identity which were current in the 1950s and 1960s, and its faith in alternative meaning makings of feminism, for example consciousness raising. ☐

COMMENTARY: H. Eisenstein (1984), *Contemporary Feminist Thought*, London: Unwin.

EXTRACT

WOMEN AND MADNESS [1972]*

There are very few genuinely (or purely) mad women in our culture. Their madness usually lasts a short time, or is short-circuited by psychiatric intervention altogether. Society generally banishes such experiences from understanding, respect – and from plain view. Madness is shut away from sight, shamed, brutalized, denied and feared. Contemporary men, politics, science – the rational mode itself – does not consult or is not in touch with the irrational, i.e., with the events of the unconscious, or with the meaning of collective history.

Such madness is best understood within a mythological context. For example, mad women in our culture experience certain specific transformations of self, or incorporate the meaning of certain heroines such as Joan of Arc and the Catholic Madonna.[1]

A theoretical proposal

Neither genuinely mad women, nor women who are hospitalized for conditioned female behaviour, are powerful revolutionaries. Their insights and behaviour are as debilitating (for social reasons) as they are profound. Such women act alone, according to rules that make no 'sense' and are contrary to those of our culture. Their behaviour is 'mad' because it represents a socially powerless individual's attempt to unite body and feeling. For example, Valerie Solanas[2] is both 'crazy' and a 'criminal' for acting on what many people are content simply to 'name' and verbally criticize: the existence of misogyny and asexuality in patriarchal culture.

*From: Phyllis Chesler (1972), *Women and Madness*, New York: Doubleday.

What we consider 'madness' whether it appears in women or in men is either the acting-out of the devalued female role or the total or partial rejection of one's sex-role stereotype. Women who fully act out the conditioned female role are clinically viewed as 'neurotic' or 'psychotic'. When and if they are hospitalized, it is for predominantly temale behaviours such as 'depression', 'suicide attempts', 'anxiety neuroses', 'paranoia' or 'promiscuity'. Women who reject or are ambivalent about the female role frighten both themselves and society, so much so that their ostracism and self-destructiveness probably begin very early. Such women are also assured of a psychiatric label and, if they are hospitalized, it is for less 'female' behaviours, such as 'schizophrenia', 'lesbianism' or 'promiscuity'.[3]

[...]

Women whose psychological identities are forged out of concern for their own survival and self-definition, and who withdraw from or avoid any interactions which do not support this formidable endeavour, need not 'give up' their capacity for warmth, emotionality and nurturance. They do not have to forsake the 'wisdom of the heart' and become 'men'. They need only transfer the primary force of their 'supportiveness' to themselves and to each other – and never to the point of self-sacrifice. Women need not stop being tender, compassionate or concerned with the feelings of others. They must start being tender and compassionate with themselves and with other women. Women must begin to 'save' themselves and their daughters before they 'save' their husbands and their sons; before they 'save' the whole world. Women must try to convert the single-minded ruthlessness with which they yearn for, serve and protect a mate or biological child into the 'ruthlessness' of self-preservation and self-development. Perhaps one of the effects of this 'transfer of affections' might be an increase in the male capacity to 'nurture': themselves, each other, children, and hopefully women. Another effect would be the creation of a secure and revolutionary source of emotional and domestic nurturance for women, without which the courage for survival might falter and which, at this point in history, only biological females seem to know how or are willing to provide.

Notes

1. Some women also experience themselves as female Christs or as Dionysus. Dionysus is essentially androgynous but is most often depicted as a male. The male Dionysus is the mirror-image of Persephone's, or the passive Maiden's, sacrifice. Dionysus is killed by women – by women whom he has driven mad. I wonder if Dionysus is not really her mother's female Maiden (or Kore) whose incestual rape drives her mother mad, and often drives her to destroy her real daughter, as she herself was destroyed. Philip E. Slater, in *The Glory of Hera*, sees Dionysus as a male child, forever envied, loved, hated and seduced by his cruelly imprisoned and crippled mother. In understanding Dionysus, he also says that: 'Dionysus' characteristic attribute of boundary-violator is symbolized by the Orphic myth of his serpent birth – a myth whose great antiquity is alleged by Kerenyi (cf. also Euripides: *The Bacchae* . . .).' Demeter is said to have hidden Persephone in a cave in Sicily, guarded by two serpents. While the maiden was engaged in weaving, however, Zeus came to her in the shape of a serpent and copulated with her, Dionysus being the fruit of this union. . . . His ability to shatter cognitive boundaries is thus intrinsic, and does not depend upon any external power. He is in fact born with it – it is the child itself which drives the mother mad by its very existence.
2. The author of *The Scum Manifesto* and the woman who shot Andy Warhol, the film-maker.
3. 'Promiscuity', like 'frigidity', is both a 'female' and a 'non-female' trait: either can mean a flight into or a flight from 'femininity'.

DOROTHY DINNERSTEIN

☐ Dorothy Dinnerstein in *The Mermaid and the Minotaur* (1976) was one of the first American feminists to devise a theory of social psychology which describes the effects of women's mothering and child rearing practices. These practices, Dinnerstein claims, are the central force and shaper of gender identity throughout history. In her account of the pre-Oedipal stage of gender development, Dinnerstein argues that current family arrangements, where women mother, turn women into 'mermaids' and men into 'minotaurs'. Men's absolute dependence on their mothers as infants forces them as adults to seek to control women and, for example, to personify women as natural. Women in turn search for men who appear to control others. These experiences of dependence and fear are locked deep into our unconscious and resurface in men's ambivalent fear of female authority and female flesh and the transference of these fears into social controls over women's public activities. Dinnerstein argues that a solution to this universal dilemma could be achieved only with the end of the sexual division of reproductive labour.   ☐

COMMENTARY J. Flax (1980), *Thinking Fragments: Psychoanalysis, Feminism and Postmodernism in the Contemporary West*, Berkeley, CA: University of California.

THE MERMAID AND THE MINOTAUR [1976]*

The old symbiosis is breaking down – openly where its technological obsoleteness is clearest, and, more subtly, in people's minds, wherever the news that it can in principle become obsolete is grasped. It is breaking down, however, against strong resistance. We have been living with it under proverbial duress; and yet, confronted with the practical possibility of living without it, we tend to lose our nerve. A time-honored bluff has been called – what we have always seen as a set of necessary evils, to be complained about and endured, must now be ended or defended – and we respond with a kind of terror. This terror could be overcome more rapidly if it were more thoroughly understood. In the present study, I address myself to this task of understanding.

To reiterate, then: *it is not my aim here to help spell out what is intolerable in our gender arrangements.* Other writers have for some time been handling that task very well indeed. I shall assume that the reader has assimilated the gist of what they have been saying; I have nothing to add to it. *My aim is to help clarify the reasons why people go on consenting to such arrangements.*

The most central of these reasons, I think, are on the whole unrecognized, both by contemporary opponents and by contemporary advocates of change in our sexual status quo. The former are understandably attracted by the notion that these reasons are too tightly built into the human condition to be budged at all, the latter by the notion that all that is needed to dislodge them is sufficiently vigorous and determined action. Sexual conservatives are accordingly apt to think of people's consent as inborn, as somehow 'natural.' Their tendency (now that describing it as

*From: Dorothy Dinnerstein (1978), *The Rocking of the Cradle and the Ruling of the World* (British title of *The Mermaid and the Minotaur*), London: Souvenir.

'God-ordained' has become intellectually unfashionable) is to overestimate the rigidity of its roots in our species' biology: they see it as less genuinely reversible than it actually is. Champions of change, on the other hand, are apt to think of people's consent as enforced and/or 'learned.' Their tendency is to underestimate the intricacy of its roots in our species' psychopathology: they see it as more directly, externally, mechanically reversible than it actually is.

What at this point most basically enforces our consent, I shall be saying, is something much more deeply mutable than the defenders of the present arrangements, lay and scholarly, would have us think: It is not, most basically, our anatomy, or our hormones. It is not some mysterious genetically determined remnant of the mechanisms that guide the ecologically adaptive relations of male and female gorillas, chimps, and baboons. Neither does it bear any magic and sacred relation to the needs of infants and young children: indeed, it violates some of the most vital of these needs.

At the same time, our consent is far less simple to withdraw than many feminists would like to believe: The law, custom, economic pressure, educational practice, and so on that stand in the way of change – essential as it is to identify and fight each of these on its own level – are the symptoms, not the causes, of the disorder that we must cure. The prevailing symbiosis between men and women is something more than a product of societal coercion. It is part of the neurotic overall posture by means of which humans, male and female, try to cope with massive psychological problems that lie at the heart of our species' situation.

[. . .]

To understand the most basic reasons for our consent we must examine the roots of a peculiarly human pleasure – the pleasure of enterprise, of mastery – through which (as Freud points out) each member of our species tries, while at the same time harboring deep misgivings about the value of the effort, to console itself for a peculiarly human loss – the loss of infant oneness with the world – and to assert itself against a peculiarly human discovery – that the most important features of existence elude control. We must also grasp the importance of the fact that conscious human concern extends peculiarly far into the past and the future, an extension that is made possible (as Solomon Asch points out in his *Social Psychology*) not only by our species' special neural capacities for memory and foresight, but also by its special abilities to pool knowledge and to build social structures based on the interpenetration of subjectivites. It is these cognitive abilities that make possible our singular feelings of vulnerability and loneliness, our singular awareness of mortality, and the singular emotional techniques that we have worked out to make these feelings and this awareness bearable.[1]

Thinking about these matters means surveying certain distinctive properties of human infancy and early childhood; it means taking a real look at the ominous significance of these properties for the development of 'normal' human personality; and it means starting to question a condition of our existence that has till now seemed unquestionable: that the auspices under which human infancy and early childhood are lived out are predominantly female auspices. To examine the full implications of this so far taken for granted condition – to see just what the relationship is between the rocking of the cradle and the ruling of the world – is the first task of this book, the task out of which the rest of the argument grows.

It is senseless, I shall argue, to describe our prevailing male–female arrangements as 'natural.' They are of course a part of nature, but if they should contribute to the extinction of our species, that fact would be part of nature too. Our impulse to change these arrangements is as natural as they are, and more compatible with our survival on earth. To change them, however, we need to understand not only the societal mechanisms by which they are supported, but also *the central psychological 'adjustment' of which they are an expression.* What makes it essential for us to understand this 'adjustment' is that its existence rests on our failure to understand it: It is a massive communal self-deception, designed to allay immediate discomfort and in the long run – a run whose end we are now approaching – suicidal.

[. . .]

The earliest roots of antagonism to women lie in the period before the infant has any clear idea where the self ends and the outside world begins, or any way of knowing that the mother is a separately sentient being. At this stage a woman is the helpless child's main contact with the natural surround, the center of everything the infant wants and feels drawn to, fears losing and feels threatened by. She is the center also of the non-self, an unbounded, still unarticulated region within which the child labors to define itself and to discover the outlines of durable objects, creatures, themes. She is this global, inchoate, all-embracing presence before she is a person, a discrete finite human individual with a subjectivity of her own.

When she does become a person, her person-ness is shot through for the child with these earlier qualities. And when it begins to be clear that this person is a female in a world of males and females, femaleness comes to be the name for, the embodiment of, these global and inchoate and all-embracing qualities, qualities very hard indeed to reconcile with person-ness as one has begun to feel it inside oneself.

[. . .]

So the essential fact that paternal authority, the fact that makes both sexes accept it as a model for the ruling of the world, is that it is under prevailing conditions a sanctuary from maternal authority. It is a sanctuary passionately cherished by the essential part of a person's self that wants to come up (like Andersen's mermaid) out of the drowning sweetness of early childhood into the bright dry light of open day, the light of the adult realm in which human reason and human will – not the boundless and mysterious intentionality, the terrible uncanny omniscience, of the nursery goddess – can be expected, at least ideally, to prevail.

In sum

In sum, the irrevocable thing that has happened – happened to everybody, though not everybody senses it clearly – is this: *The male–female collaboration to keep history mad* that was discussed in Chapter 9 *has become impossible to sustain* in the light of the change in our overall perspective summarized above in 'Overview' – broadly speaking, our changed perspective on 'progress,' on the sources of what we have always thought of as 'evil,' and on the nature of what we are responsible for.

Without that central feature of our symbiotic gender arrangement – central (a) because it bears on the ultimate meaning of our life, the ultimate character of our place in the order of things, and (b) because it is the coordinating matrix for all the other features, the kingpin that has held them together, the fulcrum around which the tensions they generate have been balanced – *the rest of the arrangement crumbles.* So although we (most of us) hate to let it go, we (all of us) have really lost it already. And my effort here has really been an effort to see what it is that we are so sad about: on the one hand what there is in the dying old arrangement that we all have to outgrow or die ourselves; and on the other hand what there is in it that we all legitimately need, that we cannot and should not try to do without, and that we must therefore find other ways of getting.

Note

1. This is a point whose real weight Freud did not appreciate. And Asch, who is eloquent about the relevance of our cognitive abilities to the unique character of our social life, takes no real account of the aspects of our condition to which Freud drew attention.

JULIET MITCHELL 1940–

☐ Following her socialist analysis of production and reproduction, Juliet Mitchell looked to psychoanalytic theory and the utility of Freud's work in order to explain the ways in which the unconscious contributes to our gender identity and hence to women's social oppression. Mitchell was one of the first feminists to make a constructive use of Freud's theories, arguing that Freud's account describes patriarchal society at a particular stage (which still exists) rather than biological universals. Hence Freud's ideas (and Lacan's construction of Freud's concepts) *did* explain the consequences for women of penis envy and the Oedipus complex in a phallic culture, for example masochism and fear of success.

Psychoanalysis and Feminism (1974) gives a general theory of patriarchy. Mitchell follows the structural anthropologist Lévi-Strauss to argue that patriarchy depends on the exchange of women and the incest taboo. Mitchell argues that patriarchy and capitalism are two different but interlocking forces and that while socialism might overthrow capitalism only psychoanalytic change would overthrow patriarchy. ☐

COMMENTARY: E. Wilson (1986), *Hidden Agendas: Theory, Politics and Experience in the Women's Movement*, London: Tavistock.

EXTRACT

PSYCHOANALYSIS AND FEMINISM
[1974]*

The greater part of the feminist movement has identified
Freud as the enemy. It is held that psychoanalysis claims
women are inferior and that they can achieve true femininity only as wives and mothers. Psychoanalysis is seen as
a justification for the status-quo, bourgeois and patriarchal,
and Freud in his own person exemplifies these qualities. I
would agree that popularized Freudianism must answer to
this description; but the argument of this book is that a
rejection of psychoanalysis and of Freud's works is fatal for
feminism. however it may have been used, psychoanalysis
is not a recommendation *for* a patriarchal society, but an
analysis *of* one. If we are interested in understanding and
challenging the oppression of women, we cannot afford to
neglect it.

[. . .]

Symptoms of the unconscious manifest themselves in latent dream-thoughts, slips of pen and memory, etc., and
these are all we can ever know of it in this subjective sense.
But Freud, in systematizing these manifestations, offers objective knowledge. We can see how it works and understand
the need for it to exist to explain what is happening in the
symptom. In one sense, Freud found the unconscious because nothing else would explain what he observed – and he
certainly tried everything anyone could think of first. Once,
after much doubt, he had postulated its existence, he set
out to determine how it worked. This makes the process
sound too sequential: an instance of how it worked, of
course, would also help convince him of its existence. In
other words, unlike the poets and story-tellers to whom he
always gave credit for their recognition of the unconscious,

*From: Juliet Mitchell (1975), *Psychoanalysis and Feminism*, Harmondsworth: Penguin.

Freud could not *believe* in the unconscious, he had to *know* it. To be convinced of his knowledge, we cannot believe it either, but if the laws by which he claimed it operated can be shown to have an internal consistency, then we can give up a faith for a science – imperfect as it may be.

[. . .]

It is within the understanding of the unconscious that all Freud's observations are made – even those that seem not directly to impinge on it. Leaving aside again those questions that relate to his other great discovery, the role of sexuality, what he is therefore saying, for instance, about the nature of femininity, relates to how femininity is lived in the mind.

[. . .]

Freud's analysis of the psychology of women takes place within a concept that it is neither socially nor biologically dualistic. It takes place within an analysis of patriarchy. His theories give us the beginnings of an explanation of the inferiorized and 'alternative' (second sex) psychology of women under patriarchy. Their concern is with how the human animal with a bisexual psychological disposition becomes the sexed social creature – the man or the woman.

In his speculative works on the origins of human culture and man's phylogenesis, in particular in *Totem and Taboo* and *Moses and Monotheism*, Freud shows quite explicitly that the psychoanalytic concept of the unconscious is a concept of mankind's transmission and inheritance of his social (cultural) laws. In each man's unconscious lies all mankind's 'ideas' of his history; a history that cannot start afresh with each individual but must be acquired and contributed to over time. Understanding the laws of the unconscious thus amounts to a start in understanding how ideology functions, how we acquire and live the ideas and laws within which we must exist. A primary aspect of the law is that we live according to our sexed identity, our ever imperfect 'masculinity' or 'femininity'.

[. . .]

Thus *both* sexes repudiate the implications of femininity. Femininity is, therefore, in part a repressed condition that can only be secondarily acquired in a distorted form. It is because it is repressed that femininity is so hard to comprehend both within and without psychoanalytic investigation – it returns in symptoms, such as hysteria. In the body of the hysteric, male and female, lies the feminine protest against the law of the father.[1] But what is repressed is both the representation of the desire and the prohibition against it: there is nothing 'pure' or 'original' about it.

[. . .]

Though, of course, ideology and a given mode of production are interdependent, one cannot be reduced to the other nor can the same laws be found to govern one as govern the other. To put the matter schematically, in analysing contemporary Western society we are (as elsewhere) dealing with two autonomous areas: the economic mode of capitalism and the ideological mode of patriarchy. The interdependence between them is found in the particular expression of patriarchal ideology – in this case the kinship system that defines patriarchy is forced into the straightjacket of the nuclear family. But if we analyse the economic and the ideological situation only at the point of their interpenetration, we shall never see the means to their transformation.

[. . .]

The controlled exchange of women that defines human culture is reproduced in the patriarchal ideology of every form of society. It goes alongside and is interlinked with class conflict, but it is not the same thing. It is not only in the ideology of their roles as mothers and procreators but above all in the very psychology of femininity that women bear witness to the patriarchal definition of human society. But today this patriarchal ideology, while it poses as the ultimate rationalization, is, in fact, in the slow death throes of its own irrationality; in this it is like the capitalist economy itself. But in both cases only a *political* struggle will bring their surcease. Neither can die a natural death; capitalism will, as it is all the time doing, intervene at a political level, to ensure their survival.

Note

1. It is the language or graphology of the body symptomatology, the traces of repressed femininity in hysteria, that the French women's liberation group, *Psychoanalyse et Politique*, is deciphering. It was here in the analysis of the hysterical symptom in his earliest psychoanalytic days that, they consider, Freud stopped short. I am not sure that I would agree with the stress that I understand they put on the father's Oedipal 'rape' of his daughter, as it seems to me that the girl precisely has to learn the arts of seduction, of *winning* love.

JEAN BAKER MILLER

☐ Jean Baker Miller is an American psychologist who examined the psychological effects on women of social oppression and who devised a 'new psychology' of women based on the concepts of 'affiliation' and 'care-taking'. These are the qualities which women develop in order to cope with a lack of social power. Miller suggests, like Nancy Chodorow, that women's capacity for emotional understanding derives from the early symbiotic bond with the mother and that this bond is devalued by the dominant masculine culture.

Toward A New Psychology of Women (1976) acknowledges the political implications of this new women-centred theory. For example Miller claims that women learn important political skills in subordinate roles such as skills in interpersonal relationships. Miller also places this new psychology of women in the realm of the material by arguing that skills of peer support, which women are forced to acquire and men are forced to deny to themselves, can produce new social communities because women learn such skills from useful cultural and social interactions as a defence against the insensitivity of androcentric culture. ☐

COMMENTARY: M.R. Walsh (ed.) (1987), *The Psychology of Women*, New Haven, CT: Yale University Press.

EXTRACT

TOWARD A NEW PSYCHOLOGY OF WOMEN [1976]*

A most basic social advance can emerge through women's outlook, through women putting forward women's concerns. Women have already begun to do so. Here, again, it is not a question of innate biological characteristics. It is a question of the kind of psychological structuring that is encompassed differentially by each sex at this time in our development as a society of human beings – and a question of who can offer the motivation and direction for moving on from here.

The central point here is that women's great desire for affiliation is both a fundamental strength, essential for social advance and at the same time the inevitable source of many of women's current problems. That is, while women have reached for and already found a psychic basis for a more advanced social existence, they are not able to act fully and directly on this value basis in a way that would allow it to flourish. Accordingly, they have not been able to cherish or even recognize this valuable strength. On the contrary, when women act on the basis of this underlying psychological motive, they are usually led into subservience. That is, the only forms of connection that have been available to women are subservient affiliations. In many instances, the search for connection can lead women to a situation that creates serious emotional problems. Many of these are then labeled neuroses and other such names.

[. . .]

Even the very words, the terms in which we conceptualize, reflect the prevailing consciousness – not necessarily the truth about what is happening. This is true in the culture at

---

*From: Jean Baker Miller (1986), *Toward a New Psychology of Women*, Boston: Beacon Press.

large and in psychological theory too. We need a terminology that is not based on inappropriate carryovers from men's situation. Even a word like *autonomy*, which many of us have used and liked, may need revamping for women. It carries the implication – and for women therefore the threat – that one should be able to pay the price of giving up affiliations in order to become a separate and self-directed individual. In reality, when women have struggled through to develop themselves as strong, independent individuals they did, and do, threaten many relationships, relationships in which the other person will not tolerate a self-directed woman. But, when men are autonomous, there is no reason to think that their relationships will be threatened. On the contrary, there is reason to believe that self-development will win them relationships. Others – usually women – will rally to them and support them in their efforts, and other men will respect and admire them. Since women have to face very different consequences, the word *autonomy* seems possibly dangerous; it is a word derived from men's development, not women's.

[. . .]

The issues of power have to be faced; there are conflicting forces among women themselves. Most of all, it is important to sustain the understanding that women do not need to diminish other women; therefore women do not need to take on the destructive attributes which are not necessarily a part of effective power, but were merely a part of maintaining a dominant–subordinate system. Women need the power to advance their own development, but they do not 'need' the power to limit the development of others.

Women start, however, from a position in which they have been dominated. To move out of that position requires a power base from which to make even the first step, that is, to resist attempts to control and limit them. And women need to move on from this first step to more power – the power to make full development possible. This is important to stress. Dominant groups tend to characterize even subordinates' initial small resistance to dominant control as demands for an excessive amount of power! (For example, today, when subordinates take even the first step by refusing to bring the office coffee, they may be treated as if they now had power over the boss.)

There is another way in which power, as we have seen it work so far, has been distorted. It has operated without the special values women can bring to it. Indeed, these womanly qualities have seemed to have no bearing on the 'realities' of power in the world. I am not suggesting that women should soften or ameliorate power – but instead that, by their participation, women can strengthen its appropriate operation. Women can bring more power to power by using it when needed and not using it as a poor substitute for other things – like cooperation. We can then begin to open up closed assumptions.[1] The goal is, eventually, a new integration of the whole area of effective power and womanly strengths as we are seeking to define them.[2]

Notes

1. David C. McClelland, *Power: The Inner Experience* (New York: Irvington, 1979).
2. Elizabeth Janeway, *The Powers of the Weak* (New York: Knopf, 1980).

SARAH KOFMAN 1934–

☐ Sarah Kofman is a French Lacanian theorist whose work has made a major contribution to feminist psychoanalysis and to literary criticism. In *The Enigma of Woman* (1980) she contends that Freud's theory of femininity should not be dismissed as being patriarchal, but can be described as revolutionary paradoxically because Freud *does* portray women so stereotypically. Kofman argues that such stereotyping reveals Freud's fears about the instability, the fluidity of femininity. In Kofman's account these characteristics of the feminine are an indication of female autonomy and 'difference'. If the 'enigma' of women, which Freud could never solve is read positively, Kofman claims, then women's more multiple sexualities and identities could begin to change social relations. ☐

COMMENTARY: T. Moi (1987), *French Feminist Thought*, Oxford: Blackwell.

EXTRACT

THE ENIGMA OF WOMAN: WOMAN IN FREUD'S WRITINGS [1980]*

The Other

To the fear of death is added a supplementary anxiety: the discovery of the radical otherness of woman, which threatens to bring about a thoroughgoing upheaval in psychoanalysis. Freud compares this revolutionary discovery of the *entirely other* to finding the Mycenean civilization behind that of the Greeks: 'Our insight into this early, pre-Oedipus, phase in girls comes to us as a surprise, like the discovery, in another field, of the Minoan–Mycenean civilization behind the civilization of Greece' ('Female Sexuality,' p. 226).

This comparison with the history of civilizations is designed to stress the fact that a great gap separates the two phases of the little girl's libidinal development, since the historians of Freud's day posited a radical break between the fourteenth to twelfth centuries B.C., when Mycenean culture, so close to the Minoan, was flourishing, and the beginnings of archaic Greek culture in the eighth century B.C. Between the two there was thought to have been a dark age, the Hellenic Middle Ages, in which little-known upheavals separated the pre-Hellenic world from the Greek world proper. The Myceneans were thus seen as pre-Hellenes, just as the earliest period of the girl's development was seen as preoedipal; and just as the two peoples, pre-Hellenes and Hellenes, had nothing in common, so a real gulf separates the preoedipal and oedipal periods, and thus the sexual development of little girls and little boys.

[. . .]

*From: Sarah Kofman (1985), *The Enigma of Woman: Woman in Freud's Writings*, Ithaca, New York: Cornell University Press.

Criminal or hysteric

The problem, for me, is this: Why was it unusual for Freud to regard woman as self-sufficient? Why did he seem panic-stricken, unable to bear the sight of his 'double'? Why did he avert his eyes from this inaccessible woman and at the same time turn back from the most powerful advance of his discourse, turn aside from the path that had been leading him toward an entirely different view of woman and the enigma she presents? 'On Narcissism' opened up a possibility that both earlier and later texts neglected: that of conceptualizing the enigma of woman along the lines of the great criminal rather than the hysteric (though for Freud even the hysteric always had something of the criminal about her).

Because it is a matter of ruling out the possibility that woman may one day become man's rival, she whom he basically needs to make his accomplice, Freud fixes and freezes her definitively in a type that corresponds with his 'ideal of femininity.'

Obsessed by his fixed idea, he immobilizes woman, imprisons her in her 'nature' as in a real yoke of iron. It is on that fixity of woman, on the impossibility of her evolving and changing after a certain age – thirty! – as opposed to the flexibility and plasticity of man, who is forever young, never finished, always capable of transforming himself and improving himself, that the lecture ends: *on a death sentence for woman*. Because she has exhausted all her potential in her painful development into femininity, woman finds herself forever fixed in a definitive posture, without hope of undergoing any further development. If psychoanalysis is capable of helping men change, where women are concerned it can only deplore that terrifying state of affairs. Panic-stricken, frozen with horror, the psychoanalyst shrinks back in the face of this zombie he has just manufactured, in the face of this unchangeable rock, the thirty-year-old woman, as if he found himself face to face with Death itself. 'A woman [of about thirty] . . . often frightens [erschreckt] us by her psychical rigidity [Starrheit] and unchangeability' ('Femininity,' pp. 134–5).

After a woman has reached a certain age, psychoanalysis can do nothing but avert its gaze.

Psychoanalysis can never touch woman except to make a dead body of her.

To make a dead body of woman is to try one last time to overcome her enigmatic and ungraspable character, to fix in a definitive and immovable position instability and mobility themselves. 'The seductive flash of gold on the belly of the serpent vita' and 'Vita femina.'[1] For woman's deathlike rigidity serves to keep feminine 'masculinity' in a state of repression. It makes it possible to put an end to the perpetual shifting back and forth between masculinity and femininity which constitutes the whole enigma of 'woman.' That is to say that a woman who has reached maturity, a woman at thirty, cannot be fully a woman except at the price of death – at the price of the triumph of 'femininity' over masculinity within her – the triumph, it would seem, of the death instincts over Eros.

This is a solution to the feminine enigma that is at the very least cheerless, frightening, one that definitively blocks all exits, all paths, all contact.[2]

Notes

1. Friedrich Nietzsche, *The Will to Power*, ed. Walter Kaufmann, trans. W. Kaufmann and R. Hollingdale (New York, 1968), para. 577, p. 310; and 'Die fröhliche Wissenschaft,' in *Nachgelassene Fragmente, Frühjahr 1881 bis Sommer 1882*, ed. Giorgio Colli and Mazzino Montinari (Berlin, 1973), pt. 5, vol. 2, sec. 339 (December 22, 1851), p. 298.

2. The word *frayage*, translated here as 'contact,' comes from the verb *frayer*, which has several meanings: to scrape or rub together (sometimes to the extent of wearing away); to open up or clear a path; to keep company (with someone). In addition, Kofman draws here, after Blanchot, on an association between *frayer* and *effrayer*, to frighten. – *Translator*

10 □ Nature

Introduction

□ Feminist writers point to the ways in which gender differences, and women's subordination which results from gender discriminations, are produced and reproduced in society through a customary association of men with culture and women with nature. Two influential critics, Sherry Ortner and Gayle Rubin, gained attention in a landmark volume of anthropological essays *Woman, Culture and Society* (1974). This book argued a coherent case that in all societies throughout the world women's reproductive routines confine women to the domestic sphere leaving men free to dominate the more prestigious public sphere. At stake within this argument is the relationship of nature and gender difference to the sexual division of labour, to kinship and parenting arrangements and ultimately to power and women's lack of power. □

COMMENTARY: M.Z. Rosaldo and L. Lamphere (eds) (1974), *Woman, Culture and Society*, Stanford: Stanford University Press.

SHERRY ORTNER 1941–

☐ In 'Is Female to Nature as Male is to Culture?', (1972), the American anthropologist Sherry Ortner made a pioneering and much discussed case that, universally, women's reproductive roles are not invested with social status and women are relegated to the private zone because women's concreteness and association with nature is devalued and separated from men's 'abstract' public lives. Ortner's focus is on the universal and symbolic significance for women of this invariable association between women and nature which has generated a particular female personality. Ortner suggests that the deployment of 'nature' by society to devalue women would end only with massive changes in reproduction and child rearing practices combined with dual participation in the work force and politics. ☐

COMMENTARY: R. Tong (1989), *Feminist Thought,* London and Sydney: Unwin Hyman.

EXTRACT

IS FEMALE TO MALE AS NATURE IS TO CULTURE? [1972]*

I translate the problem, in other words, into the following simple question. What could there be in the generalized structure and conditions of existence, common to every culture, that would lead every culture to place a lower value upon women? Specifically, my thesis is that woman is being identified with – or, if you will, seems to be a symbol of – something that every culture devalues, something that every culture defines as being of a lower order of existence than itself. Now it seems that there is only one thing that would fit that description, and that is 'nature' in the most generalized sense. Every culture, or, generically, 'culture', is engaged in the process of generating and sustaining systems of meaningful forms (symbols, artefacts, etc.) by means of which humanity transcends the givens of natural existence, bends them to its purposes, controls them in its interest. We may thus broadly equate culture with the notion of human consciousness, or with the products of human consciousness (i.e., systems of thought and technology), by means of which humanity attempts to assert control over nature.

[. . .]

In any case, my point is simply that every culture implicitly recognizes and asserts a distinction between the operation of nature and the operation of culture (human consciousness and its products); and further, that the distinctiveness of culture rests precisely on the fact that it can under most circumstances transcend natural conditions and turn them to its purpose. Thus culture (i.e. every culture) at some level of awareness asserts itself to be not only distinct from but

*From: Sherry B. Ortner (1982), 'Is Female to Male as Nature Is to Culture', in M. Evans (ed.), *The Woman Question*, London: Fontana.

superior to nature, and that sense of distinctiveness and superiority rests precisely on the ability to transform – to 'socialize' and 'culturalize' – nature.

Returning now to the issue of women, their pan-cultural second-class status could be accounted for, quite simply, by postulating that women are being identified or symbolically associated with nature, as opposed to men, who are identified with culture. Since it is always culture's project to subsume and transcend nature, if women were considered part of nature, then culture would find it 'natural' to subordinate, not to say oppress, them. Yet although this argument can be shown to have considerable force, it seems to oversimplify the case. The formulation I would like to defend and elaborate on in the following section, then, is that women are seen 'merely' as being *closer* to nature than men. That is, culture (still equated relatively unambiguously with men) recognizes that women are active participants in its special processes, but at the same time sees them as being more rooted in, or having more direct affinity with, nature.

[. . .]

Why is woman seen as closer to nature?

It all begins of course with the body and the natural procreative functions specific to women alone. We can sort out for discussion three levels at which this absolute physiological fact has significance: (1) woman's *body and its functions*, more involved more of the time with 'species life', seem to place her closer to nature, in contrast to man's physiology, which frees him more completely to take up the projects of culture; (2) woman's body and its functions place her in *social roles* that in turn are considered to be at a lower order of the cultural process than man's; and (3) woman's traditional social roles, imposed because of her body and its functions, in turn give her a different *psychic structure*, which, like her physiological nature and her social roles, is seen as being closer to nature.

[. . .]

Conclusions

Ultimately, it must be stressed again that the whole scheme is a construct of culture rather than a fact of nature. Woman is not 'in reality' any closer to (or further from) nature than man – both have consciousness, both are mortal. But there are certainly reasons why she appears that way, which is what I have tried to show in this paper. The result is a (sadly) efficient feedback system: various aspects of woman's situation (physical, social, psychological) contribute to her being seen as closer to nature, while the view of her as closer to nature is in turn embodied in institutional forms that reproduce her situation. The implications for social change are similarly circular: a different cultural view can only grow out of a different social actuality; a different social actuality can only grow out of a different cultural view.

It is clear, then, that the situation must be attacked from both sides. Efforts directed solely at changing the social institutions – through setting quotas on hiring, for example, or through passing equal-pay-for-equal-work laws – cannot have far-reaching effects if cultural language and imagery continue to purvey a relatively devalued view of women. But at the same time efforts directed solely at changing cultural assumptions – through male and female consciousness-raising groups, for example, or through revision of educational materials and mass-media imagery – cannot be successful unless the institutional base of the society is changed to support and reinforce the changed cultural view. Ultimately, both men and women can and must be equally involved in projects of creativity and transcendence. Only then will women be seen as aligned with culture, in culture's ongoing dialectic with nature.

GAYLE RUBIN

□ 'The Traffic in Women' (1974) is one of the most influential accounts of the nature/culture opposition on which depends what Rubin calls 'the sex-gender system'. Rubin distinguishes between sex, which she defines as biological genital difference, and gender arguing that biological sex is transformed by culture into gender and into cultural constructs of masculinity and femininity.

By combining psychoanalysis with structural anthropology (specifically Lévi-Strauss's theory of kinship systems) Rubin could argue that it is the reproduction of kinship, or the exchange of women, which reproduces male power and structures gender identity in the family. Women are taught to be feminine products for exchange within a masculine economy. The culmination of this process is the relegation of women to the domestic sphere and to 'natural' functions. Rubin argues that interweaving psychoanalysis with anthropology will help us better understand the psychic impact of the sex-gender system, the opposition between nature/sexuality and culture in the sexual division of labour, as well as historical changes in the family. A transformation of the kinship system, Rubin claims, would bring about changes in individual psyches, changes in the meanings we assign to nature and culture and, inevitably, changes to the sex-gender system itself. □

COMMENTARY: J. Butler (1990), *Gender Trouble: Feminism and the Subversion of Identity*, London: Routledge.

EXTRACT

THE TRAFFIC IN WOMEN: NOTES ON THE 'POLITICAL ECONOMY' OF SEX [1974]*

As a preliminary definition, a 'sex/gender system' is the set of arrangements by which a society transforms biological sexuality into products of human activity, and in which these transformed sexual needs are satisfied.

[. . .]

The realm of human sex, gender, and procreation has been subjected to, and changed by, relentless social activity for millennia. Sex as we know it – gender identity, sexual desire and fantasy, concepts of childhood – is itself a social product. We need to understand the relations of its production, and forget, for awhile, about food, clothing, automobiles, and transistor radios. In most Marxist tradition, and even in Engels' book, the concept of the 'second aspect of material life' has tended to fade into the background, or to be incorporated into the usual notions of material life.' Engels' suggestion has never been followed up and subjected to the refinement which it needs. But he does indicate the existence and importance of the domain of social life which I want to call the sex/gender system.

Other names have been proposed for the sex/gender system. The most common alternatives are 'mode of reproduction' and 'patriarchy.' It may be foolish to quibble about terms, but both of these can lead to confusion. All three proposals have been made in order to introduce a distinction between 'economic' systems and 'sexual' systems, and to indicate that sexual systems have a certain autonomy and cannot always be explained in terms of economic forces. 'Mode of reproduction,' for instance, has been

*From: Gayle Rubin (1974), 'The Traffic in Women: Notes on the "Political Economy" of Sex', in M.Z. Rosaldo and L. Lamphere (eds), Woman, Culture and Society, Stanford: Stanford University Press.

proposed in opposition to the more familiar 'mode of production.' But this terminology links the 'economy' to production, and the sexual system to 'reproduction.' It reduces
the richness of either system, since 'productions' and 'reproductions' take place in both. Every mode of production
involves reproduction – of tools, labor, and social relations.
We cannot relegate all of the multi-faceted aspects of social
reproduction to the sex system. Replacement of machinery
is an example of reproduction in the economy. On the other
hand, we cannot limit the sex system to 'reproduction' in
either the social or biological sense of the term. A sex/
gender system is not simply the reproductive moment of a
'mode of production.' The formation of gender identity is an
example of production in the realm of the sexual system.
And a sex/gender system involves more than the 'relations
of procreation,' reproduction in the biological sense.

[. . .]

A full-bodied analysis of women in a single society, or
throughout history, must take *everything* into account: the
evolution of commodity forms in women, systems of land
tenure, political arrangements, subsistence technology, etc.
Equally important, economic and political analyses are incomplete if they do not consider women, marriage, and sexuality. Traditional concerns of anthropology and social
science – such as the evolution of social stratification and
the origin of the state – must be reworked to include the
implications of matrilateral cross-cousin marriage, surplus
extracted in the form of daughters, the conversion of female
labor into male wealth, the conversion of female lives into
marriage alliances, the contribution of marriage to political
power, and the transformations which all of these varied
aspects of society have undergone in the course of time.

This sort of endeavor is, in the final analysis, exactly
what Engels tried to do in his effort to weave a coherent
analysis of so many of the diverse aspects of social life. He
tried to relate men and women, town and country, kinship
and state, forms of property, systems of land tenure, con-
vertibility of wealth, forms of exchange, the technology of

food production, and forms of trade, to name a few, into a systematic historical account. Eventually, someone will have to write a new version of *The Origin of the Family, Private Property, and the State*, recognizing the mutual interdependence of sexuality, economics, and politics without underestimating the full significance of each in human society.

11☐ Sexuality and reproduction

Introduction

☐ Kate Millett's choice of the two terms 'sexual/politics' for the title of her pioneering book powerfully identified sexuality, not as some simple, 'natural' experience of women and men, but as being socially constructed with political consequences and as being politically constructed with social consequences. One of the most significant achievements of feminist writing over the last two decades has been to make explicit the ways in which sexual practices are articulated by violence, pornography and the economy. The result is that women cannot identify with their own desires. From 1966, when Juliet Mitchell called contraception 'an innovation of world-historic importance', through to Catharine MacKinnon's argument in 'Feminism, Marxism, Method and the State' that sexuality is the linchpin of male power, it is feminist theory which reveals the politics of sexed identities.

It is feminist theory which meshes historical, experiential, economic and social accounts of sexuality within a political frame, and celebrates women's 'different' sexualities. This involves critics in countering operative political assumptions such as the notion of universal heterosexuality; in the assertion of racial and class differences; and in giving women control over reproduction by ensuring our access to contraception and well women health care. In addition, since any notion of sexual transformation requires answers to questions such as, are men and women's sexual desires and needs different or are such differences socially constructed?, it is the task of feminist theory to search for answers to these questions, and to outline a new and positive erotics of women's pleasure. ☐

COMMENTARY: C. S. Vance (1984), *Pleasure and Danger*, London: Routledge.

ANNE KOEDT

☐ Together with Susan Brownmiller and Shulamith Firestone, Anne Koedt was a founder member of the New York Radical feminists. At the very beginning of the Women's Liberation Movement it was Anne Koedt's hugely influential essay 'The Myth of the Vaginal Orgasm' (1970) which gave 'scientific' backing to one of the main arguments of second wave feminism. This is the view that women's oppression stems from men's sexual power over women, which is achieved through actual or threatened physical violence and by psychological inducements such as romance. Koedt built on Masters's and Johnson's laboratory studies of female clitoral orgasms in 1966, to argue that clitoral, not vaginal orgasms (believed by Freud to be 'mature'), are essential to a woman's sexual pleasure. Once the 'myth of the vaginal orgasm' (that women needed penetration by men in order to achieve orgasms) was destroyed then women could be sexually independent of men. ☐

COMMENTARY: H. Eisenstein (1984), *Contemporary Feminist Thought*, London: Unwin.

THE MYTH OF THE VAGINAL ORGASM [1970]*

Whenever female orgasm and frigidity are discussed, a false distinction is made between the vaginal and the clitoral orgasm. Frigidity has generally been defined by men as the failure of women to have vaginal orgasms. Actually the vagina is not a highly sensitive area and is not constructed to achieve orgasm. It is the clitoris which is the center of sexual sensitivity and which is the female equivalent of the penis.

I think this explains a great many things: First of all, the fact that the so-called frigidity rate among women is phenomenally high. Rather than tracing female frigidity to the false assumptions about female anatomy, our 'experts' have declared frigidity a psychological problem of women. Those women who complained about it were recommended psychiatrists, so that they might discover their 'problem' – diagnosed generally as a failure to adjust to their role as women.

The facts of female anatomy and sexual response tell a different story. Although there are many areas for sexual arousal, there is only one area for sexual climax; that area is the clitoris. All orgasms are extensions of sensations from this area. Since the clitoris is not necessarily stimulated sufficiently in the conventional sexual positions, we are left 'frigid.'

Aside from physical stimulation, which is the common cause of orgasm for most people, there is also stimulation through primarily mental processes. Some women, for example, may achieve orgasm through sexual fantasies, or through fetishes. However, while the stimulation may be psychological, the orgasm manifests itself physically. Thus,

*From: Anne Koedt (1973), 'The Myth of the Vaginal Orgasm', in *Radical Feminism*, New York: New York Times Books.

while the cause is psychological, the *effect* is still physical, and the orgasm necessarily takes place in the sexual organ equipped for sexual climax – the clitoris. The orgasm experience may also differ in degree of intensity – some more localized, and some more diffuse and sensitive. But they are all clitoral orgasms.

All this leads to some interesting questions about conventional sex and our role in it. Men have orgasms essentially by friction with the vagina, not the clitoral area, which is external and not able to cause friction the way penetration does. Women have thus been defined sexually in terms of what pleases men; our own biology has not been properly analyzed. Instead, we are fed the myth of the liberated woman and her vaginal orgasm – an orgasm which in fact does not exist.

What we must do is redefine our sexuality. We must discard the 'normal' concepts of sex and create new guidelines which take into account mutual sexual enjoyment. While the idea of mutual enjoyment is liberally applauded in marriage manuals, it is not followed to its logical conclusion. We must begin to demand that if certain sexual positions now defined as 'standard' are not mutually conducive to orgasm, they no longer be defined as standard. New techniques must be used or devised which transform this particular aspect of our current sexual exploitation.

MARY JANE SHERFEY 1933–

□ It was the findings of the American psychologist Mary Sherfey which helped feminists in the early years of the Women's Movement to argue that women's experience of sexuality is very different from society's account of women's sexuality. Sherfey set her description of the female orgasm into an influential critique of male defined sexuality. Like Anne Koedt, Sherfey argued, that if the actual sexual experiences of women were given visible saliency, this would transform notions about female psychology. This was because, as Sherfey discovered, women's orgasmic potency was multiple and potentially capacious. Sherfey added to these arguments the important point that all foetuses are female, not bisexual as Freud had imagined, until some convert to male with the injection of male hormones. Sherfey's attention to ideas of cytogenetics was the basis of later discussions about parthenogenesis (self-reproduction) and the belief of many feminists that heterosexuality is merely one option among others, and that it may not necessarily be a productive option in terms of women's sexual pleasure. □

COMMENTARY: J. Donovan (1985), *Feminist Theory*, New York: Ungar.

EXTRACT

A THEORY ON FEMALE SEXUALITY
[1970]*

No doubt the most far-reaching hypothesis extrapolated from biological data is the existence of the universal and physically normal condition of women's inability ever to reach complete sexual satiation in the presence of the most intense, repetitive orgasmic experiences, no matter how produced. Theoretically, a woman could go on having orgasms indefinitely if physical exhaustion did not intervene.

It is to be understood that repetitive orgasms leading to the satiation-in-insatiation state will be most apt to occur in parous[1] and experienced women during the luteal phase[2] of the menstrual cycle. It is one of the most important ways in which the sexuality of the primate and human female differs from the primate and human male at the physical level; and this difference exists only because of the female's capacity to produce the fulminating pelvic congestion and edema. This capacity is mediated by specific hormonal combinations with high fluid-imbibing action which are found only in certain primates and, probably, a very few other mammalian species.

Historical perspective and cultural dilemma

The nature of female sexuality as here presented makes it clear that, just as the vagina did not evolve for the delivery of big-headed babies, so women's inordinate orgasmic capacity did not evolve for monogamous, sedentary cultures. It is unreasonable to expect that this inordinate sexual capacity could be, even in part, given expression within the

*From: Mary Sherfey (1976), 'A Theory on Female Sexuality', in S. Cox (ed.), *Female Psychology: The Emerging Self*, Chicago: Science Research Associates.

confines of our culture; and it is particularly unreasonable to expect the delayed blooming of the sexuality of many women after the age of thirty or so to find adequate avenues of satisfaction. Less than one hundred years ago, and in many places today, women regularly had their third or fourth child by the time they were eighteen or nineteen, and the life span was no more than thirty-five to forty years. It could well be that the natural synchronization of the peak periods for sexual expression in men and women has been destroyed only in recent years.

These findings give ample proof of the conclusion that neither men nor women, but especially not women, are biologically built for the single-spouse, monogamous marital structure or for the prolonged adolescence which our society can now bestow upon both of them. Generally, men have never accepted strict monogamy except in principle. Women have been forced to accept it; but not, I submit, for the reasons usually given.

Summary

Recent embryological research has demonstrated conclusively that the concept of the initial anatomical bisexuality or equipotentiality of the embryo is erroneous. All mammalian embryos, male and female, are anatomically female during the early stages of fetal life. In humans, the differentiation of the male from the female form by the action of fetal androgen begins about the sixth week of embryonic life and is completed by the end of the third month. Female structures develop autonomously without the necessity of hormonal differentiation. If the fetal gonads are removed from a genetic female before the first six weeks, she will develop into a normal female, even undergoing normal pubertal changes if, in the absence of ovaries, exogenous hormones are supplied. If the fetal gonads are similarly removed from a genetic male, he will develop into a female, also undergoing normal female pubertal changes if exogenous hormones are supplied. The probable relationship of the autonomous female anatomy to the evolution of viviparity is described.

[. . .]

There are many indications from the prehistory studies in the Near East that it took perhaps five thousand years or longer for the subjugation of women to take place. All relevant data from the 12,000 to 8,000 B.C. period indicate that precivilized woman enjoyed full sexual freedom and was often totally incapable of controlling her sexual drive.[3] Therefore, I propose that one of the reasons for the long delay between the earliest development of agriculture (c. 12,000 B.C.) and the rise of urban life and the beginning of recorded knowledge (c. 8,000–5,000 B.C.) was the ungovernable cyclic sexual drive of women. Not until these drives were gradually brought under control by rigidly enforced social codes could family life become the stabilizing and creative crucible from which modern civilized man could emerge.

Although then (and now) couched in superstitious, religious and rationalized terms, behind the subjugation of women's sexuality lay the inexorable economics of cultural evolution which finally forced men to impose it and women to endure it. If that suppression has been, at times, unduly oppressive or cruel, I suggest the reason has been neither man's sadistic, selfish infliction of servitude upon helpless women nor women's weakness or inborn masochism. The strength of the drive determines the force required to suppress it.

Notes

1. 'Parous' describes women who have had at least one child.
2. The luteal phase is the post-ovulatory phase of the menstrual cycle.
3. 'Today it is unfashionable to talk about former more matriarchal orders of society. Nevertheless, there is evidence from many parts of the world that the role of women has weakened since earlier times in several sections of social structure.' The evidence given here lends further support to this statement by J. Hawkes and L. Woolley. See *History of Mankind, Vol. I: Prehistory and the Beginnings of Civilization* (New York: Harper & Row, 1963). However, I must make it clear that the biological data presented

268 □ SEXUALITY AND REPRODUCTION _____

support only the thesis on the intense, insatiable erotism in women. Such erotism could be contained within one or possibly several types of social structures which would have prevailed through most of the Pleistocene period.

I am indebted to Prof. Joseph Mazzeo of Columbia University for calling my attention to the fact that the first study on the existence of a pre-Neolithic matriarchal society was published in 1861: Bachofen's *Das Mutterrecht*. (Basel: B. Schwabe, 1897). Indeed, Bachofen's work remains an unsurpassed, scholarly analysis of the mythologies of the Near East, hypothesizing both a matriarchal society and the inordinate erotism of women. His entire thesis was summarily rejected by twentieth-century anthropologists for lack of objective evidence (and cultural bias). On several scores, the ancient myths have proved more accurate than the modern scientists' theories. I suspect this will be another instance in which the myths prove faithful reflections of former days.

ADRIENNE RICH 1929–

☐ By the 1980s, second wave feminism was revaluing the ties between reproduction and sexuality rather than hoping, as Firestone claimed, that technology would magically undo them. The focus of Adrienne Rich's *Of Woman Born* (1976) is on the ways in which society controls mothering by making the nuclear family the main reproductive institution. Rich describes the erotics of motherhood and argues the case for a clearly confirmed tradition of maternal power. In what has become a classic text of second wave feminism, Rich distinguishes between the social *institution* of motherhood which controls women's reproductive and sexual possibilities, and the experience of motherhood which, either as fact or as potential, gives women great pleasure and great power. This power Rich sets into a huge history of mythological and autobiographical accounts of motherhood. In contradiction to de Beauvoir, Rich does not believe that women's biological and reproductive capacities necessarily cause us to be oppressed, and also that they can be sources of libidinal pleasure.

Of Woman Born interweaves social psychology, biology and history in a new form of feminist scholarship in order to describe the might of matriarchal power. Rich, like Audre Lorde, offers to transform women's eroticism and consciousness through a fresh understanding of women's bodies. ☐

COMMENTARY: C.G. Burke (1986) 'Rethinking the Maternal', in *The Future of Difference*, H. Eisenstein and A. Jardine (eds), Boston, MA: G. K. Hall.

EXTRACT

OF WOMAN BORN: MOTHERHOOD AS EXPERIENCE AND INSTITUTION [1976]*

Throughout this book I try to distinguish between two meanings of motherhood, one superimposed on the other: the *potential relationship* of any woman to her powers of reproduction and to children; and the *institution*, which aims at ensuring that the potential – and all women – shall remain under male control. This institution has been a keystone of the most diverse social and political systems. It has withheld over one-half the human species from the decisions affecting their lives; it exonerates men from fatherhood in any authentic sense; it creates the dangerous schism between 'private' and 'public' life; it calcifies human choices and potentialities. In the most fundamental and bewildering of contradictions, it has alienated women from our bodies by incarcerating us in them. At certain points in history, and in certain cultures, the idea of woman-as-mother has worked to endow all women with respect, even with awe, and to give women some say in the life of a people or a clan. But for most of what we know as the 'mainstream' of recorded history, motherhood as institution has ghettoized and degraded female potentialities.

The power of the mother has two aspects: the biological potential or capacity to bear and nourish human life, and the magical power invested in women by men, whether in the form of Goddess-worship or the fear of being controlled and overwhelmed by women. We do not actually know much about what power may have meant in the hands of strong, prepatriarchal women. We do have guesses, longings, myths, fantasies, analogues. We know far more about how, under patriarchy, female possibility has been literally massacred on the site of motherhood. Most women in

*From: Adrienne Rich (1977), *Of Woman Born: Motherhood as Experience and Institution*, London: Virago.

history have become mothers without choice, and an even greater number have lost their lives bringing life into the world.

[...]

In a living room in 1975, I spent an evening with a group of women poets, some of whom had children. One had brought hers along, and they slept or played in adjoining rooms. We talked of poetry, and also of infanticide, of the case of a local woman, the mother of eight, who had been in severe depression since the birth of her third child, and who had recently murdered and decapitated her two youngest, on her suburban front lawn. Several women in the group, feeling a direct connection with her desperation, had signed a letter to the local newspaper protesting the way her act was perceived by the press and handled by the community mental health system. Every woman in that room who had children, every poet, could identify with her. We spoke of the wells of anger that her story cleft open in us. We spoke of our own moments of murderous anger at our children, because there was no one and nothing else on which to discharge anger. We spoke in the sometimes tentative, sometimes rising, sometimes bitterly witty, unrhetorical tones and language of women who had met together over our common work, poetry, and who found another common ground in an unacceptable, but undeniable anger. The words are being spoken now, are being written down; the taboos are being broken, the masks of motherhood are cracking through.

For centuries no one talked of these feelings. I became a mother in the family-centered, consumer-oriented, Freudian-American world of the 1950s. My husband spoke eagerly of the children we would have; my parents-in-law awaited the birth of their grandchild. I had no idea of what *I* wanted, what *I* could or could not choose. I only knew that to have a child was to assume adult womanhood to the full, to prove myself, to be 'like other women.'

[...]

At the core of patriarchy is the individual family unit which originated with the idea of property and the desire to see one's property transmitted to one's biological descendants. Simone de Beauvoir connects this desire with the longing for immortality – in a profound sense, she says, 'the owner transfers, alienates, his existence into his property; he cares more for it than for his very life; it overflows the narrow limits of his mortal lifetime, and continues to exist beyond the body's dissolution – the earthly and material incorporation of the immortal soul. But this survival can only come about if the property remains in the hands of its owner; it can be his beyond death only if it belongs to individuals in whom he sees himself projected, who are *his*.'[1] A crucial moment in human consciousness, then, arrives when man discovers that it is he himself, not the moon or the spring rains or the spirits of the dead, who impregnates the woman; that the child she carries and gives birth to is *his* child, who can make *him* immortal, both mystically, by propitiating the gods with prayers and sacrifices when he is dead, and concretely, by receiving the patrimony from him. At this crossroads of sexual possession, property ownership, and the desire to transcend death, developed the institution we know: the present-day patriarchal family with its supernaturalizing of the penis, its division of labor by gender, its emotional, physical, and material possessiveness, its ideal of monogamous marriage until death (and its severe penalties for adultery by the wife), the 'illegitimacy' of a child born outside wedlock, the economic dependency of women, the unpaid domestic services of the wife, the obedience of women and children to male authority, the imprinting and continuation of heterosexual roles.

Again: some combination or aspect of patriarchal values prevails, whether in an Orthodox Jewish family where the wife mediates with the outer world and earns a living to enable the husband to study Torah; or for the upper-class European or Oriental couple, both professionals, who employ servants for domestic work and a governess for the children. They prevail even where women are the nominal 'heads of households.' For, much as she may act as the coequal provider or so-called matriarch within her own family, every mother must deliver her children over within a few years of their birth to the patriarchal system of education, of law, of religion, of sexual codes; she is, in fact, *expected* to prepare them to enter that system without rebelliousness or 'maladjustment' and to perpetuate it in their own adult lives. Patriarchy depends on the mother to act as a conservative influence, imprinting future adults with patriarchal values even in those early years when the mother–child relationship might seem most individual and private; it has also assured through ritual and tradition that the mother shall cease, at a certain point, to hold the child – in particular the son – in her orbit. Certainly it has created images of the archetypal Mother which reinforce the conservatism of motherhood and convert it to an energy for the renewal of male power.

[. . .]

Childbirth is (or may be) one aspect of the entire process of a woman's life, beginning with her own expulsion from her mother's body, her own sensual suckling or being held by a woman, through her earliest sensations of clitoral eroticism and of the vulva as a source of pleasure, her growing sense of her own body and its strengths, her masturbation, her menses, her physical relationship to nature and to other human beings, her first and subsequent orgasmic experiences with another's body, her conception, pregnancy, to the moment of first holding her child. But that moment is still only a point in the process if we conceive it not according to patriarchal ideas of childbirth as a kind of production, but as part of female experience.

[. . .]

Beyond birth comes nursing and physical relationship with an infant, and these are enmeshed with sexuality, with the ebb and flow of ovulation and menses, of sexual desire. During pregnancy the entire pelvic area increases in its vascularity (the production of arteries and veins) thus increasing the capacity for sexual tension and greatly increasing the frequency and intensity of the orgasm.[2] During pregnancy, the system is flooded with hormones which not only induce the growth of new blood vessels but increase clitoral responsiveness and strengthen the muscles effective in orgasm. A woman who has given birth has a biologically increased capacity for genital pleasure, unless her pelvic organs have been damaged obstetrically, as frequently happens. Many women experience orgasm for the first time after childbirth, or become erotically aroused while nursing. Frieda Fromm-Reichmann, Niles Newton, Masters and Johnson, and others have documented the erotic sensations experienced by women in actually giving birth. Since there are strong cultural forces which desexualize women as mothers, the orgasmic sensations felt in childbirth or while suckling infants have probably until recently been denied even by the women feeling them, or have evoked feelings of guilt. Yet, as Newton reminds us, 'Women . . . have a more varied heritage of sexual enjoyment than men';[3] and the sociologist Alice Rossi observes,

> I suspect that the more male dominance characterizes a Western society, the greater is the dissociation between sexuality and maternalism. It is to men's sexual advantage to restrict women's sexual gratification to heterosexual coitus, though the price for the woman and a child may be a less psychologically and physically rewarding relationship.[4]

The divisions of labor and allocations of power in patriarchy demand not merely a suffering Mother, but one divested of sexuality: the Virgin Mary, *virgo intacta*, perfectly chaste. Women are permitted to be sexual only at a certain time of life, and the sensuality of mature – and certainly of aging – women has been perceived as grotesque, threatening, and inappropriate.

If motherhood and sexuality were not wedged resolutely apart by male culture, if we could *choose* both the forms of our sexuality and the terms of our motherhood or non-motherhood freely, women might achieve genuine sexual autonomy (as opposed to 'sexual liberation').

[. . .]

This cathexis between mother and daughter – essential, distorted, misused – is the great unwritten story. Probably there is nothing in human nature more resonant with charges than the flow of energy between two biologically alike bodies, one of which has lain in amniotic bliss inside the other, one of which has labored to give birth to the other. The materials are here for the deepest mutuality and the most painful estrangement. Margaret Mead offers the possibility of 'deep biochemical affinities between the mother and the female child, and contrasts between the mother and the male child, of which we now know nothing.'[5] Yet this relationship has been minimized and trivialized in the annals of patriarchy. Whether in theological doctrine or art or sociology or psychoanalytic theory, it is the mother and son who appear as the external, determinative dyad. Small wonder, since theology, art, and social theory have been produced by sons. Like intense relationships between women in general, the relationship between mother and daughter has been profoundly threatening to men.

[. . .]

We are, none of us, 'either' mothers or daughters; to our amazement, confusion, and greater complexity, we are both. Women, mothers or not, who feel committed to other women, are increasingly giving each other a quality of caring filled with the diffuse kinds of identification that exist between actual mothers and daughters. Into the mere notion of 'mothering' we may carry, as daughters, negative echoes of our own mothers' martyrdom, the burden of their valiant, necessarily limited efforts on our behalf, the confusion of their double messages. But it is a timidity of the imagination which urges that we can be 'daughters' – therefore free spirits – rather than 'mothers' – defined as eternal givers. Mothering and nonmothering have been such charged concepts for us, precisely because *whichever we did has been turned against us.*

To accept and integrate and strengthen both the mother and the daughter in ourselves is no easy matter, because patriarchal attitudes have encouraged us to split, to polarize, these images, and to project all unwanted guilt, anger, shame, power, freedom, onto the 'other' woman. But any radical vision of sisterhood demands that we integrate them.

[. . .]

The repossession by women of our bodies will bring far more essential change to human society than the seizing of the means of production by workers. The female body has been both territory and machine, virgin wilderness to be exploited and assembly-line turning out life. We need to imagine a world in which every woman is the presiding genius of her own body. In such a world women will truly create new life, bringing forth not only children (if and as we choose) but the visions, and the thinking, necessary to sustain, console, and alter human existence – a new relationship to the universe. Sexuality, politics, intelligence, power, motherhood, work, community, intimacy will develop new meanings; thinking itself will be transformed.

This is where we have to begin.

Notes

1. Simone de Beauvoir, *The Second Sex*, trans. H.M. Parshley (New York: Knopf, 1953), p. 82.
2. Mary Jane Sherfey, *The Nature and Evolution of Female Sexuality* (New York: Vintage, 1973), pp. 100–1.
3. Niles Newton, 'The Trebly Sensuous Woman,' *Psychology Today*, issue on 'The Female Experience,' 1973.
4. Alice Rossi, 'Maternalism, Sexuality and the New Femininism,' in *Contemporary Sexual Behavior: Critical Issues in the 1970's*, ed. J. Zubin and J. Money (Baltimore: Johns Hopkins University Press, 1973), pp. 145–71.
5. Margaret Mead, *Male and Female* (New York: Morrow, 1975), p. 61.

NANCY CHODOROW 1944–

☐ Nancy Chodorow trained initially as a sociologist, but in *The Repro-duction of Mothering* (1978) became one of the most influential feminist psychoanalytic theorists of sexual difference. Like contemporary French feminists, Chodorow argues that the mother is the central element in differential identity formation. What Chodorow's term 'reproduction of mothering' describes is how the sexual division of labour encourages mainly women to 'mother' and how this in turn has different effects on the psychological development of girls and boys. Given female parenting, girls develop relational capacities by internalising the role of caring and 'reproducing' their mothers; while boys learn to reject the female aspects of themselves such as nurturing and empathy in order to adopt a mas-culine gender identity (to be not the mother). In brief, women as adults carry with them the ability to experience other people's needs and feel-ings while men develop a defensive desire for autonomy based on the abstract model of the absent father.

Chodorow focuses on the mother and on the pre-Oedipal period in reaction to Freud's focus on the father and on the Oedipus complex. *The Reproduction of Mothering* is a significant revision of Freudian theory with its major premise that it is mothering relations, not the Oedipus complex, which structure gender differences. The systematic psychic differences between women and men enter culture which encourages men to further deny femininity and to be emotionally distant from women and from each other. The social consequence is that men domi-nate women. Sexual inequality, not simply gender socialisation, is the result. ☐

COMMENTARY: E. Spelman (1988), *Inessential Woman*, London: Women's Press; and N. Chodorow et al. (1981) 'On the Reproduction of Mothering: A Methodological Debate', *Signs*, 6 (Spring): 482–514.

EXTRACT

THE REPRODUCTION OF MOTHERING: PSYCHOANALYSIS AND THE SOCIOLOGY OF GENDER [1978]*

This book is a contribution to the feminist effort. It analyzes the reproduction of mothering as a central and constituting element in the social organization and reproduction of gender. In what follows, I argue that the contemporary reproduction of mothering occurs through social structurally induced psychological processes. It is neither a product of biology nor of intentional role-training. I draw on the psychoanalytic account of female and male personality development to demonstrate that women's mothering reproduces itself cyclically. Women, as mothers, produce daughters with mothering capacities and the desire to mother. These capacities and needs are built into and grow out of the mother-daughter relationship itself. By contrast, women as mothers (and men as non-mothers) produce sons whose nurturant capacities and needs have been systematically curtailed and repressed. This prepares men for their less effective later family role, and for primary participation in the impersonal extrafamilial world of work and public life. The sexual and familial division of labor in which women mother and are more involved in interpersonal, affective relationships than men produces in daughters and sons a division of psychological capacities which leads them to reproduce this sexual and familial division of labor.

I attempt to provide a theoretical account of what has unquestionably been true – that women have had primary responsibility for child care in families and outside of them; that women by and large want to mother, and get gratification from their mothering; and finally, that, with all the conflicts and contradictions, women have succeeded at mothering.

[...]

*From: Nancy Chodorow (1978), *The Reproduction of Mothering: Psychoanalysis and the Sociology of Gender*, Berkeley, CA: University of California Press.

Post-Oedipal gender personality: a recapitulation

Children of both sexes are originally matrisexual, though, as many accounts suggest, they have different kinds of relationships to their mother and later their father. Girls, for many overdetermined reasons, do develop penis envy and may repress knowledge of their vagina because they cannot otherwise win their heterosexual mother; because of exhibitionistic desires; because the penis symbolizes independence from the (internalized) powerful mother; as a defense against fantasies of acting on sexual desires for their father and anxiety at the possible consequence of this; because they have received either conscious or unconscious communication from their parents that penises (or being male) are better, or sensed maternal conflict about the mother's own genitals; and because the penis symbolizes the social privileges of their father and men. The only psychoanalytic account of the origin of penis envy that seems inconceivable is Freud's original claim that a girl 'makes her judgment and her decision in a flash' – that as soon as she learns about genitals different from hers, she wants a penis. Yet there is little to suggest either that penis envy completely permeates women's lives, or that the envy, jealousy, vanity, and pettiness that supposedly result from penis envy are characteristic of women. Similarly, most contemporary analysts agree that passivity, masochism, and narcissism are psychological defenses found in both women and men, and have the same object-relational origins in each, in the early mother–infant relationship. To the extent that these are (or were) more characteristically women's solutions to anxiety or guilt, this is not because of female biology but because the particular generating mother–child pattern is more characteristic of women's than men's early experience.[1]

The oedipus complex, according to the psychoanalytic paradigm, is a time of major developmental differentiation in personality and of a relative fixing of personality structure for girls and boys. For the traditional psychoanalyst, the major developmental outcomes of the oedipus complex are erotic heterosexuality and superego formation, masculinity and femininity. Even within this traditional account, however, with its teleological formulation of conscious parental and social goals arising from their own assumptions about appropriate gender roles, and unconscious goals arising from unconscious parental attitudes to gender and sexuality and their own oedipal stance, it is clear that what is being negotiated and what needs explaining is different for boys and girls as a result of the asymmetrical structure of parenting. For boys, gender identifications are more the issue; for girls, psychosexual development. Because both are originally involved with their mother, the attainment of heterosexuality – achieved with the feminine change of object – is the major traditional oedipal goal for girls. For boys the major goal is the achievement of personal masculine identification with their father and sense of secure masculine self, achieved through superego formation and disparagement of women. Superego formation and further identification with their mother also happen for girls, and giving up the original attachment to their mother is also an issue for boys. Yet the ways these happen, the conflicts and defenses involved, and typical gender differences between them are not elaborated in the psychoanalytic account. (These differences include varying forms of superego operation; differences in what identification with the parent of the same gender means; differences in what doubt about femininity and doubt about masculinity consist in; the particular ways in which each does and does not give up the mother as a love object; and implications for asymmetries in modes of libidinal relationship and heterosexual love.)

My account suggests that these gender-related issues may be influenced during the period of the oedipus complex, but they are not its only focus or outcome. The negotiation of these issues occurs in the context of broader object-relational and ego processes. These broader processes have equal influence on psychic structure formation, and psychic life and relational modes in men and women. They account for differing modes of identification and orientation to heterosexual objects, for the more asymmetrical oedipal issues psychoanalysts describe. These outcomes, like more traditional oedipal outcomes, arise from the asymmetrical organization of parenting, with the mother's role as primary parent and the father's typically greater remoteness and his investment in socialization especially in areas concerned with gender-typing.

The oedipal period is a nodal time of the creation of psychic reality in a child and of important internalizations of objects in relation to the ego. The main importance of the oedipus complex, I argue, is not primarily in the development of gender identity and socially appropriate heterosexual genitality, but in the constitution of different forms of 'relational potential' in people of different genders.[2] The oedipus complex is the form in which the internal interpersonal world will later be imposed on and help to create the external. Post-oedipal (and, in the girl, postpubertal) personality is the relatively stable foundation upon which other forms of relational development will build.

A girl continues a preoedipal relationship to her mother for a long time. Freud is concerned that it takes the girl so long to develop an oedipal attachment to her father and the 'feminine' sexual modes that go with this attachment. The stress is on the girl's attachment as *pre*oedipal rather than on the attachment itself.

It is important to stress the other side of this process. Mothers tend to experience their daughters as more like, and continuous with, themselves. Correspondingly, girls tend to remain part of the dyadic primary mother–child relationship itself. This means that a girl continues to experience herself as involved in issues of merging and separation, and in an attachment characterized by primary identification and the fusion of identification and object choice. By contrast, mothers experience their sons as a male opposite. Boys are more likely to have been pushed out of the preoedipal relationship, and to have had to curtail their primary love and sense of empathic tie with their mother. A boy has engaged, and been required to engage, in a more emphatic individuation and a more defensive firming of experienced ego boundaries. Issues of differentiation have become intertwined with sexual issues. This does not mean that women have 'weaker' ego boundaries than men or are more prone to psychosis. Disturbances in the early relation to a caretaker have equally profound effects on each, but these effects differ according to gender. The earliest mode of individuation, the primary construction of the ego and its inner object-world, the earliest conflicts and the earliest unconscious definitions of self, the earliest threats to individuation, and the earliest anxieties which call up defenses, all differ for boys and girls because of differences in the character of the early mother–child relationship for each.

Girls emerge from this period with a basis for 'empathy' built into their primary definition of self in a way that boys do not. Girls emerge with a stronger basis for experiencing another's needs or feelings as one's own (or of thinking that one is so experiencing another's needs and feelings). Furthermore, girls do not define themselves in terms of the denial of preoedipal relational modes to the same extent as do boys. Therefore, regression to these modes tends not to feel as much a basic threat to their ego. From very early, then, because they are parented by a person of the same gender (a person who has already internalized a set of unconscious meanings, fantasies, and self-images about this gender and brings to her experience her own internalized early relationship to her own mother), girls come to experience themselves as less differentiated than boys, as more continuous with and related to the external object-world and as differently oriented to their inner object-world as well.

[. . .]

Women's mothering, then, produces asymmetries in the relational experiences of girls and boys as they grow up, which account for crucial differences in feminine and masculine personality, and the relational capacities and modes which these entail. Women and men grow up with personalities affected by different boundary experiences and differently constructed and experienced inner object-worlds, and are preoccupied with different relational issues. Feminine personality comes to be based less on repression of inner objects, and fixed and firm splits in the ego, and more on retention and continuity of external relationships. From the retention of preoedipal attachments to their mother, growing girls come to define and experience themselves as continuous with others; their experience of self contains more flexible or permeable ego boundaries. Boys come to define themselves as more separate and distinct, with a greater sense of rigid ego boundaries and differentiation. The basic feminine sense of self is connected to the world, the basic masculine sense of self is separate.

Notes

1. Moore, Burness E., 1976, 'Freud and Female Sexuality: A Current View,' *International Journal of Psycho-Analysis*, 57, no. 3, pp. 287–300.
2. Dicks, Henry V., 1967, *Marital Tensions*, New York, Basic Books.

AUDRE LORDE 1934–

☐ The most controversial debates in Anglo-American feminist theory in the last decade have been about the value of different sexualities. Audre Lorde, the Afro-American lesbian poet, makes very clear that there can be no *one* experience and no *one* language of female sexuality. Lorde argues that definitions of sexuality currently rest upon problematic and culturally specific oppositions, for example intellect/passions. In addition, Western representations offer inappropriate images for the experiences of black women.

In her influential essay 'Uses of the Erotic' (1978), Lorde examines the links between sexuality and power. Lorde revivifies the original meaning of the Greek term Eros, which incorporates the idea of self-trust, and she opposes the erotic to violent pornography and later, to sado-masochism. Lorde argues that the erotic is a life-giving force which can be a source of power, change and creativity. Because the erotic is a space of exploration and pleasure it can create dialogue between people of different races and sexualities since it is our silences which immobilise us not our differences. Lorde turns her writing into a form of therapy in order to return our repressed pleasures to us and to help us reject the compartmentalisation of the erotic from rational thought and everyday life. What Lord systematically explodes are the social and sexual stereotypes of black women which were so prevalent in the 1950s and 1960s. ☐

COMMENTARY: J. Braxton and A. McLaughlin (1990), *Wild Women in the Whirlwind*, London: Serpent's Tail.

EXTRACT

USES OF THE EROTIC: THE EROTIC AS POWER [1978]*

There are many kinds of power, used and unused, acknowledged or otherwise. The erotic is a resource within each of us that lies in a deeply female and spiritual plane, firmly rooted in the power of our unexpressed or unrecognized feeling. In order to perpetuate itself, every oppression must corrupt or distort those various sources of power within the culture of the oppressed that can provide energy for change. For women, this has meant a suppression of the erotic as a considered source of power and information within our lives.

We have been taught to suspect this resource, vilified, abused, and devalued within western society. On the one hand, the superficially erotic has been encouraged as a sign of female inferiority; on the other hand, women have been made to suffer and to feel both contemptible and suspect by virtue of its existence.

It is a short step from there to the false belief that only by the suppression of the erotic within our lives and consciousness can women be truly strong. But that strength is illusory, for it is fashioned within the context of male models of power.

[...]

The dichotomy between the spiritual and the political is also false, resulting from an incomplete attention to our erotic knowledge. For the bridge which connects them is formed by the erotic – the sensual – those physical, emotional, and psychic expressions of what is deepest and strongest and richest within each of us, being shared: the passions of love, in its deepest meanings.

*From: Audre Lorde (1984), *Sister Outsider*, Trumansburg, New York: The Crossing Press.

Beyond the superficial, the considered phrase, 'It feels right to me,' acknowledges the strength of the erotic into a true knowledge, for what that means is the first and most powerful guiding light toward any understanding. And understanding is a handmaiden which can only wait upon, or clarify, that knowledge, deeply born. The erotic is the nurturer or nursemaid of all our deepest knowledge.

[. . .]

Only now, I find more and more women-identified women brave enough to risk sharing the erotic's electrical charge without having to look away, and without distorting the enormously powerful and creative nature of that exchange. Recognizing the power of the erotic within our lives can give us the energy to pursue genuine change within our world, rather than merely settling for a shift of characters in the same weary drama.

For not only do we touch our most profoundly creative source, but we do that which is female and self-affirming in the face of a racist, patriarchal, and anti-erotic society.

GAYLE RUBIN

□ Not surprisingly, black 're-visions' of sexuality challenge white feminist theory. Gayle Rubin in 'Thinking Sex' (1984) describes her own reassessment in these terms. 'I am now arguing that it is essential to separate gender and sexuality analytically to more accurately reflect their separate social existence'. Rubin's separate models enable her to speak more freely of 'transgressive' variations in sexuality. She contests the boundaries between physical experiences and the means of speaking about such bodily pleasures. For example lesbian sado-masochistic friendships, which Rubin argues disrupt conventional patterns of pleasure, can also represent new images of consent and dialogue. When feminist theory demands autonomy for women from socially conditioned sexual choices, this does not have to connote individual, isolated forms of sexuality, Rubin claims, but can enable women to share choices and collective pleasures. □

COMMENTARY: J. Flax (1990), *Thinking Fragments: Psychoanalysis, Feminism and Postmodernism in the Contemporary West*, Berkeley, CA: University of California.

EXTRACT

THINKING SEX: NOTES FOR A RADICAL THEORY OF THE POLITICS OF SEXUALITY [1984]*

In contrast to my perspective in 'The Traffic in Women,' I am now arguing that it is essential to separate gender and sexuality analytically to more accurately reflect their separate social existence. This goes against the grain of much contemporary feminist thought, which treats sexuality as a derivation of gender. For instance, lesbian feminist ideology has mostly analyzed the oppression of lesbians in terms of the oppression of women. However, lesbians are also oppressed as queers and perverts, by the operation of sexual, not gender, stratification. Although it pains many lesbians to think about it, the fact is that lesbians have shared many of the sociological features and suffered from many of the same social penalties as have gay men, sadomasochists, transvestites, and prostitutes.

Catherine MacKinnon has made the most explicit theoretical attempt to subsume sexuality under feminist thought. According to MacKinnon, 'Sexuality is to feminism what work is to marxism . . . the molding, direction, and expression of sexuality organizes society into two sexes, women and men.'[1] This analytic strategy in turn rests on a decision to 'use sex and gender relatively interchangeably.'[2] It is this definitional fusion that I want to challenge.

There is an instructive analogy in the history of the differentiation of contemporary feminist thought from Marxism. Marxism is probably the most supple and powerful conceptual system extant for analyzing social inequality. But attempts to make Marxism the sole explanatory system

*From: Gayle Rubin (1984), 'Thinking Sex: Notes for a Radical Theory of the Politics of Sexuality', in C.S. Vance (ed.), Pleasure and Danger: Exploring Female Sexuality, London: Routledge.

for all social inequalities have been dismal exercises. Marxism is most successful in the areas of social life for which it was originally developed – class relations under capitalism.

In the early days of the contemporary women's movement, a theoretical conflict took place over the applicability of Marxism to gender stratification. Since Marxist theory is relatively powerful, it does in fact detect important and interesting aspects of gender oppression. It works best for those issues of gender most closely related to issues of class and the organization of labor. The issues more specific to the social structure of gender were not amenable to Marxist analysis.

The relationship between feminism and a radical theory of sexual oppression is similar. Feminist conceptual tools were developed to detect and analyze gender-based hierarchies. To the extent that these overlap with erotic stratifications, feminist theory has some explanatory power. But as issues become less those of gender and more those of sexuality, feminist analysis becomes irrelevant and often misleading. Feminist thought simply lacks angles of vision which can encompass the social organization of sexuality. The criteria of relevance in feminist thought do not allow it to see or assess critical power relations in the area of sexuality.

In the long run, feminism's critique of gender hierarchy must be incorporated into a radical theory of sex, and the critique of sexual oppression should enrich feminism. But an autonomous theory and politics specific to sexuality must be developed.

It is a mistake to substitute feminism for Marxism as the last word in social theory. Feminism is no more capable than Marxism of being the ultimate and complete account of all social inequality. Nor is feminism the residual theory which can take care of everything to which Marx did not attend. These critical tools were fashioned to handle very specific areas of social activity. Other areas of social life, their forms of power, and their characteristic modes of oppression, need their own conceptual implements. In this essay, I have argued for theoretical as well as sexual pluralism.

Notes

1. Catherine MacKinnon, 'Feminism, Marxism, Method and the State: An Agenda for Theory', *Signs*, vol. 7, no. 3, spring 1982, pp. 515–16.
2. Catherine MacKinnon, 'Feminism, Marxism, Method, and the State: Toward Feminist Jurisprudence', *Signs*, vol. 8, no. 4, summer 1983, p. 635.

ROSALIND PETCHESKY 1942–

□ By the 1990s feminist theory turned from debates about women's right to unconstrained sexuality to other sexual issues including pornography, abortion, genetic engineering, and the medical and legal parameters of reproduction. The new reproductive technologies have become the focus of investigation and much debate in feminist theory, for example in Renate D. Klein's *Infertility* (1989) and Michelle Stanworth's (ed.) *Reproductive Technologies* (1987).

In her pioneering book *Abortion* (1985), Rosalind Petchesky defines abortion as a potential need that some women will have, but not as an inalienable right of all women. From a socialist feminist perspective, Petchesky points out that abortions take place as part of a much larger political struggle about the meanings of sexuality, the family and motherhood. Therefore a woman's claim to reproductive rights *per se* could not adequately challenge all these social meanings. Petchesky takes up this conviction in a full historical sociology of reproduction. A future sexuality for and of women, she argues, would include women's economic and social independence and women's emotional and erotic empowerment in relation to the different needs of class, race and sexual preferences. □

COMMENTARY: R. Gatlin (1987), *American Women Since 1945*, Basingstoke and London: Macmillan.

EXTRACT

ABORTION AND WOMAN'S CHOICE: THE STATE, SEXUALITY, AND REPRODUCTIVE FREEDOM [1985]*

As in the United States, such barriers to access fall most heavily on women with the fewest resources and the greatest need: poor women, women of color, immigrants, the very young.

This contradictory reality brings home with particular force the inadequacy of bourgeois 'rights' ('personal choice') as a basis for women's reproductive freedom. Indeed, abortion presents the paradigm case of a 'privacy right' that is empty without social content. Challenging economic and social impediments to abortion access – or to the material necessities for *having* children when they are wanted – means confronting fundamental class and race divisions in health care, work, incomes, child care, and basic social services. A feminist language and consciousness about reproduction begins to encompass this basic structural challenge when it moves beyond defending 'privacy' as some abstract good to enunciate a discourse of *public* morality, one that acknowledges abortion access as a *social right* of women if they are to function as full persons in the public domain.

At the same time, a critical stance toward liberal formulations of individual rights does not mean *abandoning* 'rights' discourse but rather pushing it to its logical conclusions. It is important to be very clear about this in order to differentiate the socialist-feminist position on 'a woman's right to choose' from bourgeois notions of 'privacy'.[1] A socialist-feminist politics of reproductive freedom must acknowledge the subversive, radically democratic traditions embedded in the idea of individual choice; we have not simply 'inherited' this discourse but have helped to shape

*From: Rosalind Petchesky (1986), *Abortion and Woman's Choice: The State, Sexuality, and Reproductive Freedom*, London: Verso.

its complex meanings. While the idea of individual rights is one that originated in the same historical tradition that gave us private property and the market as ultimate locus of freedom, from its early modern beginnings its meanings have differed depending on the contexts in which it was raised and the social identities of the voices raising it. It meant something altogether different in 17th century England when John Locke argued for the 'natural right to life, liberty, and the pursuit of property' and when the Levellers, earlier, asserted 'a selfe propriety' given 'to every individual in nature.'2 And it means something altogether different today when the U.S. Supreme Court authorizes the 'private choice' of abortion for those who can pay the market price, and when a young Native American woman writes: 'Personally legal abortion allowed me the choice as a teenager living on a very poor Indian Reservation to finish growing up and make something of my life.'3

Two distinct elements permeate this radical notion of rights. The first, which is the core of the concept of social rights, demands that rights, to be meaningful, must carry the necessary enabling conditions that will make them *concretely realizable* and *universally available*. This is just another way of saying that certain social conditions – decent health care, education, housing, nutrition, etc. – are so fundamental to individual moral agency and citizenship that the society must provide them to everyone. Extended to abortion, such a concept of social rights implies, first, embedding abortion itself in the full range of social services – health care, prenatal care, child care, safe and reliable contraception, sex education, protection from sexual and sterilization abuse – that make up authentic reproductive choice; and, second, standing in solidarity with all women, however young or poor, to make sure they have access to those services.

The second element of rights discourse descending from radical traditions, and particularly inherent in feminism, is one that privileges the body, the person. The idea that 'my body belongs to me' (originally a Leveller idea) expresses the value of self-determination, but it transcends the negative, exclusionary connotation of bourgeois individualism which often associates it with property rights. It asserts that people's need for personal autonomy in the decisions that affect their bodies, their persons, is an indispensable condition of their full participation in society. This is the underlying principle of a feminist morality of abortion. It protests the deep contradiction in 'pro-life' ideology – and Christian patriarchy – which treats women's bodies as passive vessels yet holds women morally responsible for what becomes of fetuses, and children.

[...]

The value of these feminist theories of reproduction is that they begin to see reproduction as a distinct realm of activity that not only structures the lives of women but is culturally, consciously shaped by them. A problem they leave – one that a number of feminist theorists are currently trying to solve[4] – is to demonstrate that the connection between women's reproductive activities and their social and political situation is historical, not 'biological' (i.e., 'natural' and unchanging). This book attempts to reconnect, in a way that is sensitive to historical and cultural variations, the body of its gender-specific processes; the 'social mediations' of the body; the larger systems – the capitalist patriarchal state and political economy – from which those mediations arise; and women's consciousness. Because the analytical framework is mostly limited to the United States (with some reference in Chapter 1 to the history of fertility control in Western Europe), the cross-cultural dimension is regrettably weak. But the principle of historical, class, and cultural particularity figures prominently in the book. And so does the role of women as conscious agents of reproductive processes.

I start from the premise that reproduction generally, and fertility control in particular, must be understood as a historically determined, socially organized activity (separate from the activity of mothering), encompassing decisions about whether, when, under what conditions, and with whom to bear or avoid bearing children; the material/technological conditions of contraception, abortion, and children; and the network of social and sexual relations in which those decisions and conditions exist. These relations include those between 'providers' (doctors, family planners, population controllers) and 'consumers' (women), between women and their male sexual and procreative partners, and between parents and children. It is out of these relations, which are dynamic and historically changing, that women's consciousness develops and acts upon reproductive life.

Feminist theory requires this social perspective in order to explain the great differences – of class, culture, occupation, locale, and history – in women's reproductive experience. We need it to free us and our theory from the oppressive persistence of the 'body eternal.' A theory and analysis of the social relations of reproduction is necessary to make concrete the idea of reproduction as a domain that constructs women as a gender and women's own consciousness. This is a difficult and complex task to achieve in theory. In practice, feminists of many varieties and in many countries, by fighting for abortion rights, birth control, maternity and child care, and free sexual expression, have implied their agreement that '. . . *the way in which the biology of human reproduction is integrated into social relations is not a biological question: it is a political issue.*'⁵

Notes

1. M. Barrett and M. McIntosh (1982) *The Anti-Social Family*, London: Verso, quoting Denise Riley, pp. 136–37.
2. John Locke, *Two Treatises of Government*, ed. P. Laslett (New York: Cambridge, 1963); and C. B. MacPherson, *The Political Theory of Possessive Individualism* (London: Oxford, 1962), p. 140.
3. *Thornburgh et al. v. ACOG, Brief of the National Abortion Rights Action League*, p. 29. The young woman speaking probably received public funds, now extremely limited at the federal level and available in only a handful of states, to pay for her abortion.
4. For example, Michele Barrett, *Women's Oppression Today* (London: Verso, 1980); Mary O'Brien, *The Politics of Reproduction* (London: Routledge and Kegan Paul, 1981); Beechey; Janet Sayers, *Biological Politics: Feminist and Anti-Feminist Perspectives* (London: Tavistock, 1982); and Zillah Eisenstein, *Feminism and Sexual Equality: The Crisis of Liberal America* (New York: Monthly Review, forthcoming).
5. Barrett, p. 76; emphasis added.

12 □ Peace

Introduction

□ One of the great achievements of second wave feminism since the 1980s has been the success of peace activism. Feminist theory widens the meaning of peace to encompass both arguments against the direct violence of war, and arguments against indirect violence, for example the impact of militarism on the Third World or of industrialism on the planet as a whole. A feminist peace perspective can include theories about domestic violence, for example about battered women, about rape and genital mutilation and about the indirect violence women experience in everyday life caused by sexual harassment, authority and hierarchy. Feminist theory argues that all forms of violence are gendered including social values and practices. That is to say they stem from, and reinforce, traditional gender roles. These roles are institutionalised in militarism and in the ethos of scientific and military research.

Many first wave pacifist women, for example Charlotte Perkins Gilman and the British Women's Cooperative Guild and the WILPF advanced similar feminist claims, but it was the founding of the women's peace camp at Greenham Common in 1981, followed by other peace camps and environmental movements in Svevo, Italy, India and elsewhere, which created new spiritual and social models of environmental action. These models draw on rituals and imagery from women-centred culture, for example webs and spinning, to symbolise an alternative and feminist pacifist knowledge, one often identified with maternalism.   □

COMMENTARY: B. Brock-Utne (1985), *Educating for Peace*, Oxford: Pergamon.

SARA RUDDICK 1935–

☐ Sara Ruddick believes that feminist theory should be active not contemplative, and that feminist theory should transform human life; in short, that feminist theory could create a peaceful world. Ruddick takes maternal understanding to be the centre of women's pacifist ethics and epistemology. Ruddick's article 'Maternal Thinking' (1980) inspired much debate in second wave feminism because it argued that the values and knowledge derived from women's mothering capacities could adequately provide an ethical alternative to masculine aggression. Ruddick, like Adrienne Rich, does not limit 'mothering' only to biological mothers, but argues that maternal thinking is a form of cognition available to all women. Maternal thinking visible in the techniques mothers have to acquire of reconciliation and 'letting go', refuses to separate means from ends and it teaches us skills of reconciliation, empathy and respect for others, and (Ruddick's major term) 'preservative love'. These skills, Ruddick argues, are at this moment specifically female but if they were enacted publicly they might transform all human life by promoting a politics of peace and ecology. ☐

COMMENTARY: J. Trebilcot (ed.) (1984), *Mothering: Essays in Feminist Theory*, Totowa, New Jersey: Rowman and Allenheld.

PRESERVATIVE LOVE AND MILITARY DESTRUCTION: SOME REFLECTIONS ON MOTHERING AND PEACE [1984]*

Women historically have played a dominant role in pacifist movements. Because of their courage and effectiveness as pacifists in a society where women had little voice, these women publicized a pacifism that was self-consciously maternal. But while women pacifists struggled against war and male dominance, other women prepared for war.[1] Both militarists and pacifists have justified their choices in maternal terms. Some mothers wanted their sons freed forever from the threat of war; others wanted them to fight with the best guns and ships their state could produce. 'Earlier I buttered bread for him, now I paint grenades and think "this is for him." '[2]

Even if we could believe in the peacefulness of mothers, it is not clear that we would want to. If feminism has empowered women, it has often done so by attacking the identification of women with maternity. Conversely, emphasizing the maternity of women has proved an effective strategy of male supremacists. Dr. Caldicott herself, in her celebration of female bodies, slips into a romanticism that is both silly and dangerous. To confine mothers in domestic work and nurturant bodies, and then to praise them for peacefulness, disparages both the woman and the virtue she is said to possess. Mothers rightly resent a sentimentality which obscures the complex power and real, limited abilities of maternal work. Men and women doubt the effectiveness of a virtue acquired in conditions of powerlessness and confined to the home.

Hopes and doubts about traditional female work and virtues are part of a dialog in which feminists are now engaged,

*From: Sara Ruddick (1984), 'Preservative Love and Military Destruction: Some Reflections of Mothering and Peace', in J. Trebilcot (ed.), *Mothering: Essays in Feminist Theory*, Totowa, New Jersey: Rowman & Allenheld.

a dialog many of us carry on in our heads. As I write in America, in the winter of 1982, the dangers of connecting being female with being a mother seem stark. Once again, women are being forced and are forcing each other into accepting unchosen maternity and into leading powerless, if idealized, maternal lives. Yet at the same time, we are living in a militarized state, armed with insanely destructive and self-destructive weapons, plagued by violences not only against individuals and nations, but against classes and races. 'Enemies' abound, self-righteous hatred seems a virtue, murder is legitimate. In these circumstances, any resource of peacefulness should be made politically effective.

Despite the risk and because of the dangers we find ourselves in, I stop the dialog in my head and respond to Dr. Caldicott's call. I believe mothers do have a tradition of peacefulness that can be strengthened and mobilized for the public good. Attending to this female virtue seems justified by the horrors of military and domestic violence. Moreover, on reflection, feminist politics and maternal peacefulness are not at odds. Indeed, I argue later that if domestic pacifism is to become a public good, it must be transformed by feminism. It is true that appeals to womanly maternity have a reactionary sound, if not effect. But finally the dangers of reaction seem outweighed by the possibility that mothers and other women have a distinctive contribution to make to the cause of peace.

Were I a leader and persuader, I would attempt to rally mothers and other women to a mother-identified politics of protest. What I will do here, instead, is to explore some of the connections that justify such a politics: connections between mothers and other women, between maternal thinking and pacifism, between maternal pacifism and feminism. Briefly my claim is this: the conventional and symbolic association between women and peace has a real basis in maternal practice. Out of maternal practice a distinctive kind of thinking arises that is incompatible with military strategy but consonant with pacifist commitment to nonviolence. The peacefulness of mothers, however, is not now

a reliable source for peace. In order for motherly peacefulness to be publicly significant, maternal practice must respect and extend its pacifism. For this to happen, maternal
thinking would have to be transformed by a feminist
politics.

[. . .]

Pacifism and maternal practice

The pacifist renounces those strategies which the militarist
accepts – strategies which, at the very least put at risk, at
the worse set out to destroy, the lives which mothers preserve. Pacifist renunciation seems closely linked to preservative love, especially for those religious and (occasionally)
secular pacifists who make the 'sanctity of life' a basis for
their commitment. Preservative love, however, does not
play the defining role in pacifist theory that it does in maternal thinking. Pacifism is *defined* by its theory of conflict,
with its two components of reconciliation and nonviolent
resistance. Explicit beliefs about the preservation of life
may, but also may not, underlie the theory. Maternal practice, on the other hand, takes as its defining aim, first, the
preservation of life and then maintenance of conditions in
which psychological and moral growth take place. Mothers
would be happy if conflict were so rare that no theory of
conflict were necessary. In fact, conflict is a part of maternal daily life. A mother finds herself embattled with her
children, with an outside world at odds with her or their
interests, with a man or other adults in her home, with her
children's enemies. She is spectator and arbiter of her children's battles with each other and their companions. It is
not surprising, then, that maternal thinking has articulated
a theory of conflict consonant with the aims of maternal
practice. This theory in several ways is congruent with
pacifism.

Both in their homes and outside them, mothers typically
experience themselves as powerless. They cannot control

the vagaries of fate, visited upon them most painfully in the form of accidents and disease that befall their children and people their children depend upon. They are powerless as mothers, unable to determine the wills, friendships, and ambitions of their children. They are usually powerless socially – objects rather than agents of wars, economic plans, and political policies. Most mothers are directly dependent upon the good favor of individual men and publicly effective people – teachers, doctors, welfare workers, dentists, park supervisors, clinic directors, restaurant keepers, movie house owners, selective service administrators, and all those others who decide under what conditions children will be provided with services from the 'outside' world.

Like other powerless combatants, mothers often resort to nonviolent strategies because they have no weapons to damage – neither guns, nor legal effectiveness, nor economic clout. Mothers know that officials – teachers, welfare workers, landlords, doctors, and the like – can retaliate against their children as well as against themselves at the hint of maternal violence, perhaps even of anger. Instead of force, then, mothers engage in nonviolent techniques: prayer, persuasion, appeasement, self-suffering, psychological manipulation, negotiation, and bribery. Each of these techniques has its place in public nonviolent coercion.

A striking fact about mothers is that they remain peaceful in situations in which they are powerful, namely in battles with their own and other children. Dorothy Dinnerstein has written eloquently about the power of mothers perceived from the infant-child's point of view.[3] A mother is our first audience, jailor, trainer, protector – a being upon whose favor we depend for our happiness, even survival. The more isolated she is, the greater her power is, since it is shared among other adults and a wider caretaking community. We have learned that at least in our society, we are intensely ambivalent about our early pleasurable and fearful dependency on mothers and other women.

Little has been written about this same maternal power from a mother's point of view. A young, typically powerless woman confronts her children. Hassled if not harassed by the officials of an outside world and, usually, by her own employers, she is nonetheless powerful, the more so precisely the more alone she is. Such a young woman finds herself embattled with weak creatures whose wills are unpredictable and resistant, whose bodies she could quite literally destroy, whose psyches are at her mercy. I can think of no other situation in which someone with the resentments of social powerlessness, under enormous pressures of time and anger, faces a recalcitrant but helpless combatant with so much restraint. It is clear that violence – techniques of struggle that *damage* – is by definition inimical to the interests of maternal work. Indeed, maternal thinking would count as violent just those actions which deliberately or predictably risk the child's life, health, psychological strength, or moral well-being. It is also clear that physical and psychological violence is a temptation of maternal practice and a fairly common occurrence. What is remarkable is that in a daily way mothers make so much peace instead of fighting, and then, when peace fails, conduct so many battles without resorting to violence.

I do not claim that maternal pacifist commitment is a product of deliberation or virtue. There are heavy social penalties for maternal violence, even for the appearance of violence. Moreover, there is a sense in which non-violence comes naturally to many mothers. Young women who have internalized maternal thinking take as their own the demands of preservation, growth, and acceptability from which a commitment to non-violence follows. Renunciation of certain techniques of struggle may come too early, bringing in its wake cheery denial, passivity, inauthenticity, and obedience – forms of *self* renunciation which are the defining vices of maternal practice. I do not want to trumpet a virtue but to point to a fact: that non-violence is a constitutive principle of maternal thinking, and that mothers honor it not in the breach, but in their daily practice, despite objective temptations to violence.

Notes

1. See especially Barbara J. Steinson, 'The Mother Half of Humanity': American Women in the Peace and Preparedness Movements in World War I,' in *Women, War and Revolution*, edited by Carol R. Berkin and Clara M. Lovett (New York: Holmes & Meier, 1980); and Jean Bethke Elshtain, 'Women as Mirror and Other: Towards a Theory of Women, War and Feminism' (unpublished manuscript).
2. A Nazi mother cited in Leila J. Rupp, *Mobilizing Women for War* (Princeton: Princeton University Press, 1978).
3. Dorothy Dinnerstein, *The Mermaid and the Minotaur* (New York: Harper & Row, 1976).

13 □ Philosophy and the sciences

Introduction

□ The compatibility between masculinity and traditional forms of science and philosophy was the startling finding of a new and now influential feminist philosophy of science in the 1980s. By examining the sexist practices in which science operates, in particular its control over women's bodies through medical and reproductive technology, feminist theorists are able to show how science, like any other institution, discriminates against women. All feminist theory is dedicated to finding a perspective, a way of knowing the world that is a truer 'standpoint' than existing paradigms. Evelyn Fox Keller, Sandra Harding, Dorothy Smith are among the feminist writers often labelled feminist standpoint theorists. A consequence of their far-reaching inquiry into the nature of scientific thought is a challenge to the traditional ideology and institutions of science.

Feminist theory confronts and contests the notion that science is dedicated to an objective pursuit of truth. It suggests that, from the seventeenth century to the present, science has worked with a limited notion of rationality – one which is biased against women and the natural world which scientists frequently equate imagistically. Feminist writers recall the invasive exploration of the natural world undertaken by Francis Bacon which continues in the bifurcation scientists make today between their emotions and their exploitations of natural resources. The current model of science is one appropriate to a masculine world because it creates knowledge about reproductive technology which is detrimental to women's interests and it services militarism. One result of feminist research is that feminist scholars have recovered the work of hitherto disparaged women scientists, for example reminding us that it was Rosalind Franklin who discovered DNA. □

COMMENTARY: S. Harding (1986), *The Science Question in Feminism*, Ithaca, New York: Cornell University Press.

DOROTHY SMITH 1926–

☐ Feminist attacks on the abstract masculinity which dominates our scientific language are clearly an important deconstructive force in contemporary philosophical thought. The Canadian sociologist Dorothy Smith claims that science traditionally devalues women's experience and our way of thinking about our experience, for example women's contextualism, because science devalues the specific subjectivities of any person whom it observes. In a series of influential essays, Smith set out to show how feminist theory can help to create a better social science. Science could evolve less biased methods and representations, Smith claims, if it recognised that all thinking is interdependent with emotion and if science comes to grips with the subjectivity of the thinker as a gendered social being. In addition, science should explore women's experiences of oppression. Smith outlined a 'sociology for women', in which women's experience of the 'everyday world' will help us construct alternative ways of knowing to those taught in academic institutions.

The strength of Smith's critique lies in her insight that the *process* of knowledge construction is as significant as the *content* of knowledge. Feminism must subvert any simple notion of objectivity by directly confronting science with more plural, multiple realities. If it concerned itself with women's biographies then social science could return knowledge to women. ☐

COMMENTARY: M. Belenky, B. Clinchy, N. Goldberger and J. Tarule (1986), *Women's Ways of Knowing*, New York: Basic Books.

EXTRACT

WOMEN'S PERSPECTIVE AS A RADICAL CRITIQUE OF SOCIOLOGY [1974]*

5. Women sociologists stand at the center of a contradiction in the relation of our discipline to our experience of the world. Transcending that contradiction means setting up a different kind of relation than that which we discover in the routine practice of our worlds.

The theories, concepts and methods of our discipline claim to account for, or to be capable of accounting for and analyzing the same world as that which we experience directly. But these theories, concepts, and methods have been organized around and built up out of a way of knowing the world which takes for granted the boundaries of an experience in the same medium in which it is constituted. It therefore takes for granted and subsumes without examining the conditions of its existence. It is not capable of analyzing its own relation to its conditions because the sociologist as actual person in an actual concrete setting has been cancelled in the procedures which objectify and separate him from his knowledge. Thus the linkage which points back to its conditions is lacking.

For women those conditions are central as a direct practical matter, to be somehow solved in the decision to take up a sociological career. The relation between ourselves as practicing sociologists and ourselves as working women is continually visible to us, a central feature of experience of the world, so that the bifurcation of consciousness becomes for us a daily chasm which is to be crossed, on the one side of which is this special conceptual activity of thought, research, teaching, administration, and on the other the world of concrete practical activities in keeping things clean,

*From: Dorothy Smith (1987), 'Women's Perspective as a Radical Critique of Sociology', in S. Harding (ed.), *Feminism and Methodology: Social Science Issues*, Milton Keynes: Open University Press.

managing somehow the house and household and the children, a world in which the particularities of persons in their full organic immediacy (cleaning up the vomit, changing the diapers, as well as feeding) are inescapable. Even if we don't have that as a direct contingency in our lives, we are aware of that as something that our becoming may be inserted into as a possible predicate.

It is also present for us to discover that the discipline is not one which we enter and occupy on the same terms as men enter and occupy it. We do not fully appropriate its authority, i.e., the right to author and authorize the acts and knowing and thinking which are the acts and knowing and thinking of the discipline as it is thought. We cannot therefore command the inner principles of our action. That remains lodged outside us. The frames of reference which order the terms upon which inquiry and discussion are conducted originate with men. The subjects of sociological sentences (if they have a subject) are male. The sociologist is 'he.' And even before we become conscious of our sex as the basis of an exclusion (they are not talking about us), we nonetheless do not fully enter ourselves as the subjects of its statements, since we must suspend our sex, and suspend our knowledge of who we are as well as who it is that in fact is speaking and of whom. Therefore we do not fully participate in the declarations and formulations of its mode of consciousness. The externalization of sociology as a profession which I have described above becomes for women a double estrangement.

There is then for women a basic organization of their experience which displays for them the structure of the bifurcated consciousness. At the same time it attenuates their commitment to a sociology which aims at an externalized body of knowledge based on an organization of experience which excludes theirs and excludes them except in a subordinate relation.

6. An alternative approach must somehow transcend this contradiction without reentering Bierstedt's 'transcendental realm' (1966). Women's perspective, as I have analyzed it

here, discredits sociology's claim to constitute an objective knowledge independent of the sociologist's situation. Its conceptual procedures, methods, and relevances are seen to organize its subject matter from a determinate position in society. This critical disclosure becomes, then, the basis for an alternative way of thinking sociology. If sociology cannot avoid being situated, then sociology should take that as its beginning and build it into its methodological and theoretical strategies. As it is now, these separate a sociologically constructed world from that which is known in direct experience and it is precisely that separation which must be undone.

I am not proposing an immediate and radical transformation of the subject matter and methods of the discipline nor the junking of everything that has gone before. What I am suggesting is more in the nature of a re-organization which changes the relation of the sociologist to the object of her knowledge and changes also her problematic. This reorganization involves first placing the sociologist where she is actually situated, namely at the beginning of those acts by which she knows or will come to know; and second, making her direct experience of the everyday world the primary ground of her knowledge.

We would reject, it seems to me, a sociology aimed primarily at itself. We would not be interested in contributing to a body of knowledge the uses of which are not ours and the knowers of whom are who knows whom, but generally male – particularly when it is not at all clear what it is that is constituted as knowledge in that relation. The professional sociologist's practice of thinking it as it is thought would have to be discarded. She would be constrained by the actualities of how it happens in her direct experience. Sociology would aim at offering to anyone a knowledge of the social organization and determinations of the properties and events of their directly experienced world. Its analyses would become part of our ordinary interpretations of the experienced world, just as our experience of the sun's sinking below the horizon is transformed by our knowledge that the world turns. (Yet from where we are it seems to sink and that must be accounted for.)

The only way of knowing a socially constructed world is knowing it from within. We can never stand outside it. A relation in which sociological phenomena are objectified and presented as external to and independent of the observer is itself a special social practice also known from within. The relation of observer and object of observation, of sociologist to 'subject,' is a specialized social relationship. Even to be a stranger is to enter a world constituted from within as strange. The strangeness itself is the mode in which it is experienced.

When Jean Briggs (1970) made her ethnographic study of the ways in which an Eskimo people structure and express emotion, what she learned and observed emerged for her in the context of the actual developing relations between her and the family with whom she lived and other members of the group. Her account situates her knowledge in the context of those relationships. Affections, tensions, and quarrels were the living texture in which she learnt what she describes. She makes it clear how this context structured her learning and how what she learnt and can speak of became observable to her. Briggs tells us what is normally discarded in the anthropological or sociological telling. Although sociological inquiry is necessarily a social relation, we have learned to disattend our own part in it. We recover only the object of its knowledge as if that stood all by itself and of itself. Sociology does not provide for seeing that there are always two terms to this relation. An alternative sociology must be reflexive (Gouldner, 1971), i.e., one that preserves in it the presence, concerns, and experience of the sociologist as knower and discoverer.

To begin from direct experience and to return to it as a constraint or 'test' of the adequacy of a systematic knowledge is to begin from where we are located bodily. The actualities of our everyday world are already socially organized. Settings, equipment, 'environment,' schedules, occasions, etc., as well as the enterprises and routines of actors are socially produced and concretely and symbolically organized prior to our practice. By beginning from her original and immediate knowledge of her world, sociology offers a way of making its socially organized properties first observable and then problematic.

Let me make it clear that when I speak of 'experience' I do not use the term as a synonym for 'perspective.' Nor in proposing a sociology grounded in the sociologist's actual experience, am I recommending the self-indulgence of inner exploration or any other enterprise with self as sole focus and object. Such subjectivist interpretations of 'experience' are themselves an aspect of that organization of consciousness which bifurcates it and transports us into mind country while stashing away the concrete conditions and practices upon which it depends. We can never escape the circles of our own heads if we accept that as our territory. Rather the sociologist's investigation of our directly experienced world as a problem is a mode of discovering or rediscovering the society from within. She begins from her own original but tacit knowledge and from within the acts by which she brings it into her grasp in making it observable and in understanding how it works. She aims not at a reiteration of what she already (tacitly) knows, but at an exploration through that of what passes beyond it and is deeply implicated in how it it.

EVELYN FOX KELLER 1936–

☐ Compared to the growth of feminist theory in the humanities and social sciences, feminist critiques of science were slow to start due to the inadequate representation of women in science and due too to the dominant 'value free' scientific ideology of the academy. Following the work of Jessie Bernard, Evelyn Fox Keller's 'Gender and Science' (1978) made a pioneering account of how science could be labelled masculinist both historically and in terms of its current techniques. Building on Nancy Chodorow's theory that masculinity is predicated on a separation from a mothering environment, Fox Keller argues that science has traditionally been a masculine enterprise because it has a marked sexual division of labour and because it perceives and pursues nature as if nature was a female object. Science is based on binaries between mind (masculine) and nature (feminine). Keller's essay interweaves history, psychology and philosophy to reveal how the objectification of nature is not necessarily the practice of all scientists (for example physics attends to the process of knowledge construction as much as to scientific products) but that such a view informs science's paradigms, world view and choices of research.

One of Fox Keller's central arguments is that while much of science might be multiple and collective the dominant *ideology* of science is intensely individualistic and masculine. Her solution is to replace this dominant view by increasing the representation of women in science as well as by encouraging scientists to create plural realities, a feeling for organic nature and an abandonment of the masculinist either/or approach all of which, she claims, would transform science into 'a quiet conversation with Nature'. ☐

COMMENTARY: J. Donovan (1985), *Feminist Theory*, New York: Ungar.

EXTRACT

FEMINISM AND SCIENCE [1982]*

But the possibility of extending the feminist critique into the foundations of scientific thought is created by recent developments in the history and philosophy of science itself.[1] As long as the course of scientific thought was judged to be exclusively determined by its own logical and empirical necessities, there could be no place for any signature, male or otherwise, in that system of knowledge. Furthermore, any suggestion of gender differences in our thinking about the world could argue only too readily for the further exclusion of women from science. But as the philosophical and historical inadequacies of the classical conception of science have become more evident, and as historians and sociologists have begun to identify the ways in which the development of scientific knowledge has been shaped by its particular social and political context, our understanding of science as a social process has grown. This understanding is a necessary prerequisite, both politically and intellectually, for a feminist theoretic in science.

Joining feminist thought to other social studies of science brings the promise of radically new insights, but it also adds to the existing intellectual danger a political threat. The intellectual danger resides in viewing science as pure social product; science then dissolves into ideology and objectivity loses all intrinsic meaning. In the resulting cultural relativism, any emancipatory function of modern science is negated, and the arbitration of truth recedes into the political domain.[2] Against this background, the temptation arises for feminists to abandon their claim for representation in scientific culture and, in its place, to invite a return to a purely 'female' subjectivity, leaving rationality and objectivity in the male domain, dismissed as products of a purely male consciousness.[3]

*From: Evelyn Fox Keller (1982), 'Feminism and Science', in N.O. Keohane *et al.* (eds), *Feminist Theory: A Critique of Ideology*, Brighton: Harvester.

Many authors have addressed the problems raised by total relativism;[4] here I wish merely to mention some of the special problems added by its feminist variant. They are several. In important respects, feminist relativism is just the kind of radical move that transforms the political spectrum into a circle. By rejecting objectivity as a masculine ideal, it simultaneously lends its voice to an enemy chorus and dooms women to residing outside of the realpolitik modern culture; it exacerbates the very problem it wishes to solve. It also nullifies the radical potential of feminist criticism for our understanding of science. As I see it, the task of a feminist theoretic in science is twofold: to distinguish that which is parochial from that which is universal in the scientific impulse, reclaiming for women what has historically been denied to them; and to legitimate those elements of scientific culture that have been denied precisely because they are defined as female.

It is important to recognize that the framework inviting what might be called the nihilist retreat is in fact provided by the very ideology of objectivity we wish to escape. This is the ideology that asserts an opposition between (male) objectivity and (female) subjectivity and denies the possibility of mediation between the two. A first step, therefore, in extending the feminist critique to the foundations of scientific thought is to reconceptualize objectivity as a dialectical process so as to allow for the possibility of distinguishing the objective effort from the objectivist illusion. As Piaget reminds us:

> Objectivity consists in so fully realizing the countless intrusions of the self in everyday thought and the countless illusions which result – illusions of sense, language, point of view, value, etc. – that the preliminary step to every judgement is the effort to exclude the intrusive self. Realism, on the contrary, consists in ignoring the existence of self and thence regarding one's own perspective as immediately objective and absolute. Realism is thus anthropocentric illusion, finality – in short, all those illusions which teem in the history of science. So long as thought has not become conscious of self, it is a prey to perpetual confusions between objective and subjective, between the real and the ostensible.[5]

In short, rather than abandon the quintessentially human effort to understand the world in rational terms, we need to refine that effort. To do this, we need to add to the familiar methods of rational and empirical inquiry the additional process of critical self-reflection. Following Piaget's injunction, we need to 'become conscious of self.' In this way, we can become conscious of the features of the scientific project that belie its claim to universality.

The ideological ingredients of particular concern to feminists are found where objectivity is linked with autonomy and masculinity, and in turn, the goals of science with power and domination. The linking of objectivity with social and political autonomy has been examined by many authors and shown to serve a variety of important political functions.[6] The implications of joining objectivity with masculinity are less well understood. This conjunction also serves critical political functions. But an understanding of the sociopolitical meaning of the entire constellation requires an examination of the psychological process through which these connections become internalized and perpetuated. Here psychoanalysis offers us an invaluable perspective, and it is to the exploitation of that perspective that much of my own work has been directed. In an earlier paper, I tried to show how psychoanalytic theories of development illuminate the structure and meaning of an interacting system of associations linking objectivity (a cognitive trait) with autonomy (an effective trait) and masculinity (a gender trait).[7] Here, after a brief summary of my earlier argument, I want to explore the relation of this system to power and domination.

Along with Nancy Chodorow and Dorothy Dinnerstein, I have found that branch of psychoanalytic theory known as object relations theory to be especially useful.[8]

[. . .]

I suggest that the impulse toward domination does find expression in the goals (and even in the theories and practice) of modern science, and argue that where it finds such expression the impulse needs to be acknowledged as projection. In short, I argue that not only in the denial of interaction between subject and other but also in the access of domination to the goals of scientific knowledge, one finds the intrusion of a self we begin to recognize as partaking in the cultural construct of masculinity.

The value of consciousness is that it enables us to make choices – both as individuals and as scientists. Control and domination are in fact intrinsic neither to selfhood (i.e., autonomy) nor to scientific knowledge. I want to suggest, rather, that the particular emphasis Western science has placed on these functions of knowledge is twin to the objectivist ideal. Knowledge in general, and scientific knowledge in particular, serves two gods: power and transcendence. It aspires alternately to mastery over and union with nature.[9] Sexuality serves the same two gods, aspiring to domination and ecstatic communion – in short, aggression and eros. And it is hardly a new insight to say that power, control, and domination are fueled largely by aggression, while union satisfies a more purely erotic impulse.

To see the emphasis on power and control so prevalent in the rhetoric of Western science as projection of a specifically male consciousness requires no great leap of the imagination. Indeed, that perception has become a commonplace. Above all, it is invited by the rhetoric that conjoins the domination of nature with the insistent image of nature as female, nowhere more familiar than in the writings of Francis Bacon. For Bacon, knowledge and power are one, and the promise of science is expressed as 'leading to you Nature with all her children to bind her to your service and make her your slave,'[10] by means that do not 'merely exert a gentle guidance over nature's course; they have the power to conquer and subdue her, to shake her to her foundations.'[11] In the context of the Baconian vision, Bruno Bettelheim's conclusion appears inescapable: 'Only with phallic psychology did aggressive manipulation of nature become possible.'[12]

The view of science as an oedipal project is also familiar from the writings of Herbert Marcuse and Norman O. Brown.[13] But Brown's preoccupation, as well as Marcuse's, is with what Brown calls a 'morbid' science. Accordingly, for both authors the quest for a nonmorbid science, an 'erotic' science, remains a romantic one. This is so because their picture of science is incomplete: it omits from consideration the crucial, albeit less visible, erotic components already present in the scientific tradition. Our own quest, if it is to be realistic rather than romantic, must be based on a richer understanding of the scientific tradition, in all its dimensions, and on an understanding of the ways in which this complex, dialectical tradition becomes transformed into a monolithic rhetoric. Neither the oedipal child nor modern science has in fact managed to rid itself of its pre-oedipal and fundamentally bisexual yearnings. It is with this recognition that the quest for a different science, a science undistorted by masculinist bias, must begin.

Notes

1. The work of Russell Hanson and Thomas S. Kuhn was of pivotal importance in opening up our understanding of scientific thought to a consideration of social, psychological, and political influences.
2. See, e.g., Paul Feyerabend, *Against Method* (London: New Left Books, 1975); and *Science in a Free Society* (London: New Left Books, 1978).
3. This notion is expressed most strongly by some of the new French feminists (see Elaine Marks and Isabelle de Courtivron, eds., *New French Feminisms: An Anthology* [Amherst: University of Massachusetts Press, 1980]), and is currently surfacing in the writings of some American feminists. See, e.g., Susan Griffin, *Woman and Nature: The Roaring Inside Her* (New York: Harper & Row, 1978).
4. See, e.g., Steven Rose and Hilary Rose, 'Radical Science and Its Enemies,' *Socialist Register 1979*, ed. Ralph Miliband and John Saville (Atlantic Highlands, N.J.: Humanities Press, 1979), pp. 317–35. A number of the points made here have also been made by Elizabeth Fee in 'Is Feminism a Threat to Objectivity?' (paper presented at the American Association for the Advancement of Science meeting. Toronto, January 4, 1981).
5. Jean Piaget, *The Child's Conception of the World* (Totowa, N.J.: Littlefield, Adams & Co., 1972).
6. Jerome R. Ravetz, *Scientific Knowledge and Its Social Problems* (London: Oxford University Press, 1971); and Hilary Rose and Steven Rose, *Science and Society* (London: Allen Lane, 1969).
7. Evelyn Fox Keller, 'Gender and Science,' *Psychoanalysis and Contemporary Thought* 1 (1978): 409–33.
8. Nancy Chodorow, *The Reproduction of Mothering: Psychoanalysis and the Sociology of Gender* (Berkeley: University of California Press, 1978);

and Dorothy Dinnerstein, *The Mermaid and the Minotaur: Sexual Arrangements and Human Malaise* (New York: Harper & Row, 1976).

9. For a discussion of the different roles these two impulses play in Platonic and in Baconian images of knowledge, see Evelyn Fox Keller, 'Nature as "Her" ' (paper delivered at the Second Sex Conference, New York Institute for the Humanities, September (1979).

10. B. Farrington, '*Temporis Partus Masculus*: An Untranslated Writing of Francis Bacon,' *Centaurus* 1 (1951): 193–205, esp. 197.

11. Francis Bacon, 'Description of the Intellectual Globe,' in *The Philosophical Works of Francis Bacon*, ed. J.H. Robertson (London: Routledge & Sons, 1905), p. 506.

12. Quoted in Norman O. Brown, *Life against Death* (New York: Random House, 1959), p. 280.

13. Brown; and Herbert Marcuse, *One-Dimensional Man* (Boston: Beacon Press, 1964).

SANDRA HARDING 1935–

☐ Sandra Harding, the American philosopher, provided a wide-ranging feminist taxonomy appropriate to our rapidly changing technological and scientific world which she calls the feminist standpoint theory. Standpoint theorists reject the notion that there are universal truths or universal answers to social questions by pointing out that gender, class and race will always shape any individual understanding of the world.

Harding suggests that women's experience of marginality combined with our material activities of reproduction, labour and our refusal of dualisms such as culture/nature, mind/body, provide us with an understanding of social life which is distinct from, and perhaps superior to, that of men. This feminist challenge to the very frameworks of Western rationalism, argues that if philosophic and scientific traditions and cultures are distorted by abstraction and a separatism from the world then genuine social understanding can only develop from relational capacities, from moral and political commitment and from an ethic of care rather than one of exploitation. ☐

COMMENTARY: H. Rose (1985), 'Hand, Brain and Heart: A Feminist Epistemology for the Natural Sciences', *Signs*, 9(1) (Autumn): 73–90.

EXTRACT

CONCLUSION: EPISTEMOLOGICAL QUESTIONS [1987]*

A second set of epistemological issues has arisen between the feminist empiricists and standpoint theorists, on the one hand, and the feminist critics of Enlightenment assumptions – the feminist postmodernists – on the other hand. The empiricists and standpoint theorists are both attempting to ground accounts of the social world which are less partial and distorted than the prevailing ones. In this sense, they are attempting to produce a feminist science – one that better reflects the world around us than the incomplete and distorting accounts provided by traditional social science. This science would not substitute one gender-loyalty for the others, but, instead, advance the objectivity of science. The feminist postmodernists raise questions about this epistemological project. Can there be a feminist science, or is any *science* doomed to replicate undesirable – and perhaps even androcentric – ways of being in the world?

There appear to be two at least somewhat distinct origins of skepticism about the kind of epistemological project in which both the feminist empiricists and the standpoint theorists are engaged. One emerges from feminists who participate in the agendas of such otherwise disparate discourses as those of semiotics, deconstruction, and psychoanalysis. The other has appeared in the writings of women of color.

The discourses mentioned are all deeply skeptical of universalizing claims for reason, science, language, progress, and the subject/self. Thus both of the feminist epistemological strategies we examined are legitimate targets of such skepticism, since they assume that through reason, observation, and progressive politics, the more

*From: Sandra Harding (1987), 'Conclusion: Epistemological Questions', in S. Harding (ed.), *Feminism and Methodology: Social Science Issues*, Milton Keynes: Open University Press.

authentic 'self' produced by feminist struggles can tell 'one true story' about 'the world': there can be a kind of feminist author of a new 'master story,' a narrative about social life which feminist inquiry will produce. The critics respond, but 'perhaps "reality" can have "a" structure only from the falsely universalizing perspective of the master. That is, only to the extent that one person or group can dominate the whole, can "reality" appear to be governed by one set of rules or be constituted by one privileged set of social relations.'[1]

This kind of criticism points to the way science constructs the fiction of the human mind as a glassy mirror which can reflect a world that is out there and ready-made for reflecting.[2] In contrast, we can detect ('in reality'?) that at any moment in history there are many 'subjugated knowledges' that conflict with, and are never reflected in, the dominant stories a culture tells about social life. Moreover, some argue that women are a primary location of these subjugated knowledges – in fact, that the female subject is a 'site of differences.'[3] From this perspective, there can never be *a* feminist science, sociology, anthropology, or epistemology, but only many stories that different women tell about the different knowledge they have.

A second source of criticism of a unitary feminist perspective implied by the two epistemological strategies emerges from women of color. For instance, Bell Hooks insists that what makes feminism possible is not that women share certain kinds of experiences, for women's experiences of patriarchal oppression differ by race, class, and culture. Instead, feminism names the fact that women can federate around their common resistance to all the different forms of male domination.[4] Thus there could not be 'a' feminist standpoint as the generator of true stories about social life. There could, presumably, only be feminist oppositions, and criticisms of false stories. There could not be feminist science, because feminism's opposition to domination stories locates feminism in an antagonistic position towards any attempts to do science – androcentric or not. These strains of postmodernism are richer and more complex than these few paragraphs can reveal. But one can already sense the troubles they create for other feminist epistemologies.

Should feminists be willing to give up the political benefits which can accrue from believing that we are producing a new, less biased, more accurate, social science? Social scientists might well want to respond to the postmodernist critics that we do need to federate our feminisms in opposition to all of the ways in which domination is enacted and institutionalized. But it is premature for women to be willing to give up what they have never had. Should women – no matter what their race, class, or culture – find it reasonable to give up the desire to know and understand the world from the standpoint of their experiences *for the first time*? As several feminist literary critics have suggested, perhaps only those who have had access to the benefits of the Enlightenment can 'give up' those benefits.[5]

There are good reasons to find valuable the tension between these two epistemological positions. We need to think critically about the fundamental impulses of knowledge-seeking, and especially of science, even as we transform them to feminists' (plural!) ends.

One can easily see that the new feminist analyses unsettle traditional assumptions about knowledge as they challenge familiar beliefs about women, men, and social life. How could it have been otherwise when our ways of knowing are such an important part of our ways of participating in the social world?

Notes

1. Jane Flax, 'Gender as a Social Problem: In and For Feminist Theory,' *American Studies/Amerika Studien*, Journal of the German Association for American Studies (1986): 17. It is interesting that one of the theorists responsible for contributing to the development of the standpoint epistemology here voices skepticism toward it. I think that postmodernist skepticisms of the sort indicated can be found in all of the feminist standpoint theorists – another good reason to see both as transitional epistemologies.

2. Richard Rorty's *Philosophy and the Mirror of Nature* (Princeton: Princeton University Press, 1979) provides a powerful criticism of the philosophical groundings of these assumptions.
3. Teresa de Lauretis's phrase, in *Feminist Studies/Critical Studies*, ed. T. de Lauretis (Bloomington: Indiana University Press, 1986), p. 14.
4. Bell Hooks, *Feminist Theory From Margin to Center* (Boston: South End Press, 1983).
5. See Nancy K. Miller, 'Changing the Subject: Authorship, Writing, and the Reader,' and Biddy Martin and Chandra Talpade Mohanty, 'Feminist Politics: What's Home Got to Do with It?,' in *Feminist Studies/Critical Studies*, ed. T. de Lauretis.

14 □ History

Introduction

□ As Joan Kelly Gadol points out, feminism has restored women to history and restored history to women. Feminist historians began by attacking historiography (the methods of history) for ignoring gender in historical representations. By producing detailed accounts of the experiences of women who were unacknowledged in traditional histories (what Gerda Lerner calls 'compensatory scholarship') feminists went on to challenge the masculine assumptions which shape historical models. This particular assault sees itself involved in creating new historical categories to match the new content – of reproductive histories, the history of women's sexuality and sexual constraints. The third area of overlapping concern is the attempt to redefine the discipline of history itself. This involves a challenge to boundaries between public and private which obscure women's experience, for example by describing the connections between a woman's role in the family and her role in work. A fourth concern is to document the careers of the powerful women of history which entails redefining the categories of political history to include women's community groups and informal trade associations, for example Sheila Rowbotham's *Hidden From History*.

Currently one of the most important aims of feminist historians is to make visible all the contradictions of race, gender sexuality and history as for example in Angela Davis's account of the educative and procreative power of black slave women (*Women, Race and Class*, 1981). If the androcentric framework of past history minimised the importance of gender, illiteracy and race then feminist history, with its attention to anthropology and to other disciplines, can restore complexity and variation. □

COMMENTARY: J. Newton, M. Ryan and J. Walhowitz, (eds) (1983), *Sex and Class in Women's History*, New York and London: Routledge & Kegan Paul.

GERDA LERNER 1920–

☐ Gerda Lerner was one of the first American historians to insist that all women, in every class, race and economic group, had made an active contribution to history and therefore must be included in any category of historical analysis. Arguing that women were the *majority* and not the minority of history, Lerner's scholarship prepared the ground for feminist research in the 1970s into childbirth practices; for feminist attacks on the methods of family history; and for a feminist reinterpretation of women's roles throughout history.

Lerner believes that women's culture is better examined bottom up through anecdotal sources as well as through statistical data. Lerner calls this women's 'contribution' history, or compensatory history. She also believes that historians must study women on their own terms adopting a women-centred analysis, rather than assessing women's activities only in relation to well documented institutions such as political parties. But Lerner's most important contribution to women's history as well as to feminist theory is to argue that racial differences as well as differences of education and class must be considered in any historical account. Her collection *Black Women in White America* (1972) acknowledges that complexity. ☐

COMMENTARY: C. Kramarae and D. Spender (1991), *The Knowledge Explosion: Feminism and the Academic Disciplines*, Oxford: Pergamon.

EXTRACT

THE MAJORITY FINDS ITS PAST:
PLACING WOMEN IN HISTORY [1979]*

In the brief span of five years in which American historians have begun to develop women's history as an independent field, they have sought to find a conceptual framework and a methodology appropriate to the task.

The first level at which historians, trained in traditional history, approach women's history is by writing the history of 'women worthies' or 'compensatory history.'[1] Who are the women missing from history? Who are the women of achievement and what did they achieve? The resulting history of 'notable women' does not tell us much about those activities in which most women engaged, nor does it tell us about the significance of women's activities to society as a whole. The history of notable women is the history of exceptional, even deviant women, and does not describe the experience and history of the mass of women. This insight is a refinement of an awareness of class differences in history: Women of different classes have different historical experiences. To comprehend the full complexity of society at a given stage of its development, it is essential to take account of such differences.

Women also have a different experience with respect to consciousness, depending on whether their work, their expression, their activity is male-defined or woman-oriented. Women, like men, are indoctrinated in a male-defined value system and conduct their lives accordingly. Thus, colonial and early 19th-century female reformers directed their activities into channels which were merely an extension of their domestic concerns and traditional roles. They taught school, cared for the poor, the sick, the aged. As their consciousness developed, they turned their attention toward

*From: Gerda Lerner (1979), *The Majority Finds Its Past: Placing Women in History*, New York: Oxford University Press.

the needs of women. Becoming woman-oriented, they began to 'uplift' prostitutes, organize women for abolition or temperance, and sought to upgrade female education, but only in order to equip women better for their traditional roles. Only at a later stage, growing out of the recognition of the separate interests of women as a group, and of their subordinate place in society, did their consciousness become woman-defined. Feminist thought starts at this level and encompasses the active assertion of the rights and grievances of women. These various stages of female consciousness need to be considered in historical analysis.

The next level of conceptualizing women's history has been 'contribution history': describing women's contribution to, their status in, and their oppression by male-defined society. Under this category we find a variety of questions being asked: What have women contributed to abolition, to reform, to the Progressive movement, to the labor movement, to the New Deal? The movement in question stands in the foreground of inquiry; women made a 'contribution' to it; the contribution is judged first of all with respect to its effect on that movement and secondly by standards appropriate to men.

The ways in which women were aided and affected by the work of these 'great women,' the ways in which they themselves grew into feminist awareness, are ignored. Jane Addams' enormous contribution in creating a female support network and new structures for living are subordinated to her role as a Progressive, or to an interpretation which regards her as merely representative of a group of frustrated college-trained women with no place to go. In other words, a deviant from male-defined norms. Margaret Sanger is seen merely as the founder of the birth-control movement, not as a woman raising a revolutionary challenge to the centuries-old practice by which the bodies and lives of women are dominated and ruled by man-made laws. In the labor movement, women are described as 'also there' or as problems. Their essential role on behalf of themselves and of other women is seldom considered a central theme in writing their history. Women are the outgroup, Simone de Beauvoir's 'Other.'

Another set of questions concerns oppression and its opposite, the struggle for woman's rights. Who oppressed women and how were they oppressed? How did they respond to such oppression?

Such questions have yielded detailed and very valuable accounts of economic or social oppression, and of the various organizational, political ways in which women as a group have fought such oppression. Judging from the results, it is clear that to ask the question – why and how were women victimized – has it usefulness. We learn what society or individuals or classes of people have done to women, and we learn how women themselves have reacted to conditions imposed upon them. While inferior status and oppressive restraints were no doubt aspects of women's historical experience, and should be so recorded, the limitation of this approach is that it makes it appear either that women were largely passive or that, at the most, they reacted to male pressures or to the restraints of patriarchal society. Such inquiry fails to elicit the positive and essential way in which women have functioned in history. Mary Beard was the first to point out that the ongoing and continuing contribution of women to the development of human culture cannot be found by treating them only as victims of oppression.[2] It is far more useful to deal with this question as one aspect of women's history, but never to regard it as the *central* aspect of women's history. Essentially, treating women as victims of oppression once again places them in a male-defined conceptual framework: oppressed, victimized by standards and values established by men. The true history of women is the history of their ongoing functioning in that male-defined world *on their own terms*. The question of oppression does not elicit that story, and is therefore a tool of limited usefulness to the historian.

A major focus of women's history has been on women's rights struggles, especially the winning of suffrage, on organizational and institutional history of the women's movement, and on its leaders. This, again, is an important aspect of women's history, but it cannot and should not be its central concern.

[...]

Women's history presents a challenge to the periodization of traditional history. The periods in which basic changes occur in society and which historians have commonly regarded as turning points for all historical development, are not necessarily the same for men as for women. This is not surprising when we consider that the traditional time frame in history has been derived from political history. Women have been the one group in history longest excluded from political power and they have, by and large, been excluded from military decision-making. Thus the irrelevance of periodization based on military and political developments to their historical experience should have been predictable.

Women are and always have been at least half of humankind, and most of the time have been the majority. Their culturally determined and psychologically internalized marginality seems to be what makes their historical experience essentially different from that of men. But men have defined their experience as history and have left women out. At this time, as during earlier periods of feminist activity, women are urged to fit into the empty spaces, assuming their traditional marginal, 'subgroup' status. But the truth is that history, as written and perceived up to now, is the history of a minority, who may well turn out to be the 'subgroup.' In order to write a new history worthy of the name, we will have to recognize that no single methodology and conceptual framework can fit the complexities of the historical experience of all women.

The first stage of 'transitional history' may be to add some new categories to the general categories by which historians organize their material: Sexuality, reproduction, the link between child-bearing and child-rearing; role indoctrination; sexual values and myths: female consciousness. Further, all of these need to be analyzed, taking factors of race, class, ethnicity, and, possibly, religion into consideration. What we have here is not a single framework for dealing with women in history, but new questions to all of history.

The next stage may be to explore the possibility that what we call women's history may actually be the study of a separate women's culture. Such a culture would include not only the separate occupations, status, experiences, and rituals of women but also their consciousness, which internalizes patriarchal assumptions. In some cases, it would include the tensions created in the culture between the prescribed patriarchal assumptions and women's efforts to attain autonomy and emancipation.

The questions asked about the past of women may demand interdisciplinary approaches. They also may demand broadly conceived group research projects that end up giving functional answers; answers that deal not with slices of a given time or society or period, but which instead deal with a functioning organism, a functioning whole, the society in which both men and women live.

A following stage may develop a synthesis: a history of the dialectic, the tensions between the two cultures, male and female. Such a synthesis could be based on close comparative study of given periods in which the historical experience of men is compared with that of women, their tensions and interactions being as much the subject of study as their differences. Only after a series of such detailed studies can we hope to find the parameters by which to define the new universal history. My guess is that no one conceptual framework will fit so complex a subject.

Methods are tools for analysis – some of us will stick with one tool, some of us will reach for different tools as we need them. For women, the problem really is that we must acquire not only the confidence needed for using tools, but for making new ones to fit our needs. We should do so relying on our learned skills and our rational skepticism of handed-down doctrine. The recognition that we had been denied our history came to many of us as a staggering flash of insight, which altered our consciousness irretrievably. We have come a long way since then. The next step is to face, once and for all and with all its complex consequences, that women are the majority of humankind and have been essential to the making of history. Thus, all history as we now know it, is, for women, merely prehistory.

Notes

1. For the term 'women worthies,' I am indebted to Natalie Zemon Davis, Stanford University. For the terms 'compensatory history' and 'contribution history' I am indebted to Mari Jo Buhle, Ann G. Gordon, and Nancy Schrom, 'Women in American Society: An Historical Contribution,' *Radical America*, Vol. 5, No. 4 (July–Aug. 1971), 3–66.
2. Mary R. Beard, *Woman as Force* (New York, 1946). See also a further discussion of this question in Chapter 1 of this book.

JOAN KELLY-GADOL 1928–82

☐ There are acute differences between the findings of feminist historians and the traditional organisation of historical knowledge. The American feminist Joan Kelly-Gadol was one of the first historians to question the authority of 'history', with her evidence that history is generally arranged into periods shaped by wars and revolutions and that periods which carry connotations of progress, for example the Renaissance, are misnamed because these were times when women actually *lost* power and status.

In her influential essay 'The Social Relation of the Sexes' (1976), Kelly-Gadol argues from a Marxist perspective, that in order to understand the full and complex relations of sexuality, class and social organisations over time, historians must examine and describe in an ethnographic manner the way property, or the lack of it, determines women's roles in public and private. In other words, in order to describe historical experiences accurately we must focus on gender and social systems not as *separate* areas of analysis but as having an interactive and predictive impact on each other. ☐

COMMENTARY: E. Abel and E.K. Abel (1983), 'Introduction', *The Signs Reader*, Chicago: University of Chicago.

EXTRACT

THE SOCIAL RELATION OF THE SEXES: METHODOLOGICAL IMPLICATIONS OF WOMEN'S HISTORY [1976]*

Women's history has a dual goal: to restore women to history and to restore our history to women. In the past few years, it has stimulated a remarkable amount of research as well as a number of conferences and courses on the activities, status, and views of and about women. The interdisciplinary character of our concern with women has also newly enriched this vital historical work. But there is another 'aspect of women's history that needs to be considered: its theoretical significance, its implications for historical study in general.[1] In seeking to add women to the fund of historical knowledge, women's history has revitalized theory, for it has shaken the conceptual foundations of historical study. It has done this by making problematical three of the basic concerns of historical thought: (1) periodization, (2) the categories of social analysis, and (3) theories of social change.

[. . .]

Regardless of how these periods have been assessed, they have been assessed from the vantage point of men. Liberal historiography in particular, which considers all three periods as stages in the progressive realization of an individualistic social and cultural order, expressly maintains – albeit without considering the evidence – that women shared these advances with men. In Renaissance scholarship, for example, almost all historians have been content to situate women exactly where Jacob Burckhardt placed them in 1890: 'on a footing of perfect equality with men.'

*From: Joan Kelly-Gadol (1983), 'The Social Relation of the Sexes: Methodological Implications of Women's History' in E. Abel and E.K. Abel (eds), *The Signs Reader: Women, Gender and Scholarship*, Chicago: University of Chicago Press.

For a period that rejected the hierarchy of social class and the hierarchy of religious values in its restoration of a classical, secular culture, there was also, they claim, 'no question of "woman's rights" or female emancipation, simply because the thing itself was a matter of course.'[2] Now while it is true that a couple of dozen women can be assimilated to the humanistic standard of culture which the Renaissance imposed upon itself, what is remarkable is that *only* a couple of dozen women can. To pursue this problem is to become aware of the fact that there was no 'renaissance' for women – at least not during the Renaissance. There was, on the contrary, a marked restriction of the scope and powers of women. Moreover, this restriction is a consequence of the very developments for which the age is noted.[3]

[. . .]

On the other hand, although women may adopt the interests and ideology of men of their class, women as a group cut through male class systems. Although I would quarrel with the notion that women of all classes, in all cultures, and at all times are accorded secondary status, there is certainly sufficient evidence that this is generally, if not universally, the case. From the advent of civilization, and hence of history proper as distinct from prehistorical societies, the social order has been patriarchal. Does that then make women a caste, a hereditary inferior order? This notion has its uses, too, as does the related one drawn chiefly from American black experience, which regards women as a minority group.[4] The sense of 'otherness' which both these ideas convey is essential to our historical awareness of women as an oppressed social group. They help us appreciate the social formation of 'femininity' as an internalization of ascribed inferiority which serves, at the same time, to manipulate those who have the authority women lack. As explanatory concepts, however, notions of caste and minority group are not productive when applied to women. *Why* should this majority be a minority? And why is it that the members of this particular caste, unlike all other castes, are not of the same rank throughout society? Clearly the minority psychology of women, like their caste status and quasi-class oppression, has to be traced to the universally distinguishing feature of all women, namely their sex. Any effort to understand women in terms of social categories that obscure this fundamental fact has to fail, only to make more appropriate concepts available. As Gerda Lerner put it, laying all such attempts to rest: 'All analogies – class, minority group, caste – approximate the position of women, but fail to define it adequately. Women are a category unto themselves: an adequate analysis of their position in society demands new conceptual tools.[5] In short, women have to be defined as women. We are the social opposite, not of a class, a caste, or of a majority, since we are a majority, but of a sex: men. We are a sex, and categorization by gender no longer implies a mothering role and subordination to men, except as social role and relation recognized as such, as socially constructed and socially imposed.

[. . .]

Theories of social change

If the relationship of the sexes is as necessary to an understanding of human history as the social relationship of classes, what now needs to be worked out are the connections between changes in class and sex relations.[6] For this task, I suggest that we consider significant changes in the respective roles of men and women in the light of fundamental changes in the mode of production. I am not here proposing a simple socioeconomic scheme. A theory of social change that incorporates the relation of the sexes has to consider how general changes in production affect and shape production in the family and, thereby, the respective roles of men and women. And it has to consider, as well, the flow in the other direction: the impact of family life and the relation of the sexes upon psychic and social formations.

Notes

1. The central theme of this paper emerged from regular group discussions, from which I have benefited so much, with Marilyn Arthur, Blanche Cook, Pamela Farley, Mary Feldblum, Alice Kessler-Harris, Amy Swerdlow, and Carole Turbin. Many of the ideas were sharpened in talks with Gerda Lerner, Renate Bridenthal, Dick Vann, and Marilyn Arthur, with whom I served on several panels on women's history and its theoretical implications. My City College students in Marxism/feminism and in fear of women, witchcraft, and the family have stimulated my interests and enriched my understanding of many of the issues presented here. To Martin Fleisher and Nancy Miller I am indebted for valuable suggestions for improving an earlier version of this paper, which I delivered at the Barnard College Conference on the Scholar and the Feminist II: Toward New Criteria of Relevance, April 12, 1975.
2. *The Civilization of the Renaissance in Italy* (London: Phaidon Press, 1950), p. 241. With the exception of Ruth Kelso, *Doctrine for the lady of the Renaissance* (Urbana: University of Illinois Press, 1956), this view is shared by every work I know of on Renaissance women except for contemporary feminist historians. Even Simone de Beauvoir, and of course Mary Beard, regard the Renaissance as advancing the condition of women, although Burckhardt himself pointed out that the women of whom he wrote 'had no thought of the public; their function was to influence distinguished men, and to moderate male impulse and caprice.'
3. See the several contemporary studies recently or soon to be published on Renaissance women: Susan Bell, 'Christine de Pizan,' *Feminist Studies* (Winter 1975/760: Joan Kelly-Gadol, 'Notes on Women in the Renaissance and Renaissance Historiography,' in *Conceptual Frameworks in Women's History* (n. 2 above); Margaret Leah King, 'The Religious Retreat of Isotta Nogarola, 1418–66,' *Signs* (in press); an article on women in the Renaissance by Kathleen Casey in *Liberating Women's History*, Berenice Carroll, ed. (Urbana: University of Illinois Press, 1976); Joan Kelly-Gadol, 'Did Women Have a Renaissance?' in *Becoming Visible*, ed. R. Bridenthal and C. Koonz (Boston: Houghton Mifflin Co., 1976).
4. Helen Mayer Hacker did interesting work along these lines in the 1950s, 'Women as a Minority Group,' *Social Forces* 30 (October 1951–May 1952): 60–69, and subsequently, 'Women as a Minority Group: Twenty Years Later' (Pittsburgh: Know, Inc., 1972). Degler has recently taken up these classifications and also finds he must reject them (see n. 2 above).
5. 'The Feminists: A Second Look,' *Columbia Forum* 13 (Fall 1970): 24–30.
6. M. Arthur, R. Bridenthal, J. Kelly-Gadol, *Conceptual Frameworks in Women's History* (Bronxville, NY: Sarah Lawrence Publications, 1976).

CARROLL SMITH-ROSENBERG

☐ Where Joan Kelly-Gadol focuses on the interaction between gender and historical categories, Carroll Smith-Rosenberg examines the very different cultural worlds of men and women in the nineteenth century. The essay reprinted here opened the first issue of the American feminist journal *Signs*. It marked the emergence of historical writing from a resolute attention to the public zone.

Smith-Rosenberg's argument is that the sensual, emotional and private relationships of nineteenth-century women created a women's culture which was every bit as dynamic as public politics. Smith-Rosenberg's analysis of nineteenth-century diaries and autobiographies inspired feminists in other disciplines, for example the literary critic Lillian Faderman who examined the careers of women-affiliated-women writers. Smith-Rosenberg's study of historical entities such as diaries combined with statistical data involved her in exploring new concepts for women's history. For example she adopts the term 'domestic feminism' to describe the ways in which women's friendships provided them with more diffuse and contingent identities than those created by their family environments. ☐

COMMENTARY: D. Riley (1989), 'Feminism and the Consolidations of "Women" in History', in E. Weed (ed.), *Coming to Terms*, London: Routledge.

EXTRACT

THE FEMALE WORLD OF LOVE AND RITUAL: RELATIONS BETWEEN WOMEN IN NINETEENTH-CENTURY AMERICA [1975]*

The female friendship of the nineteenth century, the long-lived, intimate, loving friendship between two women, is an excellent example of the type of historical phenomena which most historians know something about, which few have thought much about, and which virtually no one has written about.[1] It is one aspect of the female experience which consciously or unconsciously we have chosen to ignore. Yet an abundance of manuscript evidence suggests that eighteenth- and nineteenth-century women routinely formed emotional ties with other women. Such deeply felt, same-sex friendships were casually accepted in American society. Indeed, from at least the late eighteenth through the mid-nineteenth century, a female world of varied and yet highly structured relationships appears to have been an essential aspect of American society. These relationships ranged from the supportive love of sisters, through the enthusiasms of adolescent girls, to sensual avowals of love by mature women. It was a world in which men made but a shadowy appearance.[2]

Defining and analyzing same-sex relationships involves the historian in deeply problematical questions of method and interpretation. This is especially true since historians, influenced by Freud's libidinal theory, have discussed these relationships almost exclusively within the context of individual psychosexual developments or, to be more explicit, psychopathology.[3] Seeing same-sex relationships in terms of a dichotomy between normal and abnormal, they have

*From: Carroll Smith-Rosenberg (1983), 'The Female World of Love and Ritual: Relations between Women in Nineteenth-century America', in E. Abel and E.K. Abel (eds), *The Signs Reader: Women, Gender and Scholarship*, Chicago: University of Chicago Press.

sought the origins of such apparent deviance in childhood or adolescent trauma and detected the symptoms of 'latent' homosexuality in the lives of both those who later became 'overtly' homosexual and those who did not. Yet theories concerning the nature and origins of same-sex relationships are frequently contradictory or based on questionable or arbitrary data. In recent years such hypotheses have been subjected to criticism both from within and without the psychological professions. Historians who seek to work within a psychological framework, therefore, are faced with two hard questions: Do sound psychodynamic theories concerning the nature and origins of same-sex relationships exist? If so, does the historical datum exist which would permit the use of such dynamic models?

I would like to suggest an alternative approach to female friendships – one which would view them within a cultural and social setting rather than from an exclusively individual psychosexual perspective. Only by thus altering our approach will we be in the position to evaluate the appropriateness of particular dynamic interpretations. Intimate friendships between men and men and women and women existed in a larger world of social relations and social values. To interpret such friendships more fully they must be related to the structure of the American family and to the nature of sex-role divisions and of male–female relations both within the family and in society generally. The female friendship must not be seen in isolation; it must be analyzed as one aspect of women's overall relations with one another. The ties between mothers and daughters, sisters, female cousins and friends, at all stages of the female life cycle constitute the most suggestive framework for the historian to begin an analysis of intimacy and affection between women. Such an analysis would not only emphasize general cultural patterns rather than the internal dynamics of a particular family or childhood; it would shift the focus of the study from a concern with deviance to that of defining configurations of legitimate behavioral norms and options.[4]

Of perhaps equal significance are the implications we can garner from this framework for the understanding of heterosexual marriages in the nineteenth century. If men and women grew up as they did in relatively homogeneous and segregated sexual groups, then marriage represented a major problem in adjustment. From this perspective we could interpret much of the emotional stiffness and distance that we associate with Victorian marriage as a structural consequence of contemporary sex-role differentiation and gender-role socialization. With marriage both women and men had to adjust to life with a person who was, in essence, a member of an alien group.

I have thus far substituted a cultural or psychosocial for a psychosexual interpretation of women's emotional bonding. But there are psychosexual implications in this model which I think it only fair to make more explicit. Despite Sigmund Freud's insistence on the bisexuality of us all or the recent American Psychiatric Association decision on homosexuality, many psychiatrists today tend explicitly or implicitly to view homosexuality as a totally alien or pathological behavior – as totally unlike heterosexuality. I suspect that in essence they may have adopted an explanatory model similar to the one used in discussing schizophrenia. As a psychiatrist can speak of schizophrenia and of a borderline schizophrenic personality as both ultimately and fundamentally different from a normal or neurotic personality, so they also think of both homosexuality and latent homosexuality as states totally different from heterosexuality. With this rapidly dichotomous model of assumption, 'latent homosexuality' becomes the indication of a disease in progress – seeds of a pathology which belie the reality of an individual's heterosexuality.

Yet at the same time we are well aware that cultural values can affect choices in the gender of a person's sexual partner. We, for instance, do not necessarily consider homosexual-object choice among men in prison, on shipboard or in boarding schools a necessary indication of pathology. I would urge that we expand this relativistic model and hypothesize that a number of cultures might well tolerate or even encourage diversity in sexual and nonsexual relations. Based on my research into this nineteenth-century world of female intimacy, I would further suggest that rather than seeing a gulf between the normal and the abnormal we view sexual and emotional impulses as part of a continuum or spectrum of affect gradations strongly affected by cultural norms and arrangements, a continuum influenced in part by observed and thus learned behavior. At one end of the continuum lies committed heterosexuality, at the other uncompromising homosexuality; between, a wide latitude of emotions and sexual feelings. Certain cultures and environments permit individuals a great deal of freedom in moving across this spectrum. I would like to suggest that the nineteenth century was such a cultural environment. That is, the supposedly repressive and destructive Victorian sexual ethos, may have been more flexible and responsive to the needs of particular individuals than those of mid-twentieth century.

Notes

1. The most notable exception to this rule is now eleven years old: William R. Taylor and Christopher Lasch, 'Two "Kindred Spirits"': Sorority and Family in New England, 1839–1846,' New England Quarterly 36 (1963): 25–41. Taylor has made a valuable contribution to the history of women and the history of the family with his concept of 'sororial' relations. I do not, however, accept the Taylor–Lasch thesis that female friendships developed in the mid-nineteenth century because of geographic mobility and the breakup of the colonial family. I have found these friendships as frequently in the eighteenth century as in the nineteenth and would hypothesize that the geographic mobility of the mid-nineteenth century eroded them as it did so many other traditional social institutions. Helen Vendler (Review of Notable American Women, 1607–1950, ed. Edward James and Janet James, New York Times) [November 5, 1972]: sec. 7 points out the significance of these friendships.

2. I do not wish to deny the importance of women's relations with particular men. Obviously, women were close to brothers, husbands, fathers, and sons. However, there is evidence that despite such closeness relationships between men and women differed in both emotional texture and frequency from those between women. Women's relations with each other, although they played a central role in the American family and American society, have been so seldom examined either by general social historians or by historians of the family that I wish in this article simply to examine their nature and analyze their implications for our understanding of social relations and social structure. I have discussed some aspects of male-female relationships in two articles: 'Puberty to Menopause: The Cycle of Femininity in Nineteenth-Century America,' Feminist Studies 1 (1973):

58–72, and, with Charles Rosenberg, 'The Female Animal: Medical and Biological Views of Women in 19th Century America,' *Journal of American History* 59 (1973): 331–56.

3. See Freud's classic paper on homosexuality, 'Three Essays on the Theory of Sexuality,' in *The Standard Edition of the Complete Psychological Works of Sigmund Freud*, trans. James Strachey (London: Hogarth Press, 1953), 7:135–72. The essays originally appeared in 1905. Prof. Roy Shafer, Department of Psychiatry, Yale University, has pointed out that Freud's view of sexual behavior was strongly influenced by nineteenth-century evolutionary thought. Within Freud's schema, genital heterosexuality marked the height of human development (Schafer, 'Problems in Freud's Psychology of Women,' *Journal of the American Psychoanalytic Association* 22 [1974]: 459–85).

4. For a novel and most important exposition of one theory of behavioral norms and options and its application to the study of human sexuality, see Charles Rosenberg, 'Sexuality, Class and Role,' *American Quarterly* 25 (1973): 131–53.

SHEILA ROWBOTHAM 1943–

□ British feminist history grew out of the flourishing branch of socialist historiography associated with the trade union college Ruskin College and which has its politics of location in the *History Workshop Journal*. So that while, like Kelly-Gadol, Rowbotham examines the gap between public accounts of historical periods and women's actual experiences in such periods, the grand sweep of *Hidden From History* (1973) is devoted to working-class women. In *Dreams and Dilemmas* (1983) Rowbotham was careful to show how class divisions could disrupt women's politics as for example in the Suffrage campaign. The separation of class from economic institutions and gender in many histories, is precisely what feminist historians challenge with their vivid accounts of new political groupings, for example the British Miners' Wives Movement. In *Woman's Consciousness, Man's World* (1973), Rowbotham gives an extensive account of women's resistance to, and alternatives to, male power and this led her to refuse the term 'patriarchy' since its ahistoricity failed to convey a sense of movement.   □

COMMENTARY: C. Ramazanoglu (1989), *Feminism and the Contradictions of Oppression*, London: Routledge.

EXTRACT

SEARCH AND SUBJECT, THREADING CIRCUMSTANCE [1974]*

History which includes women will mean that we study the role of women in movements which are usually described from the point of view of men, for example, the part women have played in revolutions, in political organisations, in trade unions, as well as women's own movements for suffrage or for peace. Similarly, we need to know how periods of change and upheaval have affected women, war, revolution, the growth of capitalism, imperialism. But more than this, we have to go outside the scope of what history usually is. We need to look at folk beliefs, at magic, at the means by which people sought control over sexuality, fertility and birth. The personal testimony of any woman who can remember – not just women who have witnessed major political events – is a source for this history. It is also a source which can enlarge our concept of what we're looking for. Our definition of women's work will include not only production paid in wages, but the unpaid labour of women in the home which makes work outside possible. We have to understand the relationship in different historical periods between procreation, the production of new life which will make existence possible in the future, housework, the labour in the home which enables workers to go out and continue to labour in the wages system in capitalism, child rearing, making the survival of the future makers of new life possible, and women's work outside the home for wages, which in modern capitalism is becoming more and more general. We can only understand women's part in production when we can trace changes and grasp the interactions between these various aspects of women's labour.

*From: Sheila Rowbotham (1983), 'Search and Subject, Threading Circumstance' in *Dreams and Dilemmas*, London: Virago.

Women's history, though, is not just about production in a material sense, for human beings create and re-create themselves in the effort to control, to bring the material world within the grasp of consciousness. Here too we inherit what we seek to go beyond and what defines our limits. We are the daughters of the tales our mother told us and drop easily back into the same way of seeing and telling even if the tales are changed by our transformed circumstances. We learn how to relate through our families and with children who themselves come from families. These relationships affect us not as external ideas but from the innermost self – feelings in our bones. They are nonetheless part of the movement of society. Our views about love between men and women, women and women, men and men, parents and children are historically shaped as much as our views about government, poverty, the organisation of production. Moreover, not just our conscious ideas of love but our unconscious experience of loving relationships, the manner in which we express sensual feelings, are also socially learned and as such are the proper if buried subject matter of history.

Much of this is such an uncharted province that to ignore any maps and compasses which exist, however imperfect, would be feckless. My own suggestions of how to begin are necessarily bounded by my own ignorance, the contours of my own history: the writing of earlier feminists, Marx's theories about history and class consciousness, anthropological studies of production and reproduction in pre-capitalist societies, new work in social history which seeks to uncover the everyday perceptions of the poor, demographic history, oral history. It is one thing to announce that all these could be useful. However, it is quite another thing to *use* them, and beyond my present knowledge. The writing of our history is not just an individual venture but a continuing social communication. Our history strengthens us in the present by connecting us to the lives of countless women. Threads and strands of long-lost experience weave into the present. In rediscovering the dimensions of female social existence lost in the tangled half memories of myth and dream, we are uncovering and articulating a cultural sense of what it is to be a woman in a world defined by men. We are tracing the boundaries of oppression and the perpetual assertion of self against their confines, the erosion and encirclement, the shifts and tremors of new forms of resistance. We are heaving ourselves into history, clumsy with the newness of creation, stubborn and persistent in pursuit of our lost selves, fortunate to be living in such transforming times.

15 □ Culture

Introduction

□ The idea that woman is positioned as the 'Other' or object of man's attention in all mainstream and popular culture is one of the major arguments of feminist cultural criticism. The intervening years since Kate Millett's analysis of the misogyny of male writers in *Sexual Politics* have witnessed feminists deploying various cultural models, including those of psychoanalysis, semiotics and aesthetics, in order to counter the stereotyping of women in popular culture and high art.

Instead of a feminist poetics, what we have is a 'problematics' of feminism which contests the prevailing view that art and culture are apolitical and universally humanising because 'human' so often excludes women. For example feminists have revised our understanding of periods such as modernism by adding accounts of modernist women like Gertrude Stein to the former male canon. Feminist critics have redefined traditional aesthetic categories by creating a new aesthetics which pays attention to women's 'invisible' arts such as quilting and cooking. A crucial contribution to feminist criticism is the invocation of maternal cultures by Afro-American women and women of colour, for example, Alice Walker lovingly evokes her mother's aesthetic skills as a gardener in *In Search of Our Mothers' Gardens*.

The paradox of feminism is: how to create a feminist art from a position of marginality when all we have available, as Audre Lorde so resonately phrases it, are the 'Master's tools'? One answer is to turn to female mythology, for example Mary Daly's *Gyn/Ecology*; another is to turn to images of women's reproductive power, for example Judy Chicago's *Birth Project*; another is to write autobiographically about women's hitherto invisible culture, for example Adrienne Rich's *Of Woman Born*.   □

COMMENTARY: S. Sheridan (ed.) (1988), *Crafts: Feminist Cultural Criticism*, London: Verso.

LAURA MULVEY

☐ Laura Mulvey's essay 'Visual Pleasure and Narrative Cinema' (1975) is generally regarded as the first major essay of feminist film theory. It inspired contemporary critics and film makers to challenge the conventions of classic Hollywood cinema. Mulvey's focus is on gender. Her insight, derived from her study of the relationship between film techniques, spectators and viewing pleasure, is that structures of looking, which films deliberately create, are masculine. It is the 'gaze', Mulvey argues, which is the main mechanism of control. According to Mulvey cinema, particularly Hollywood cinema, relies on the scopophilic instinct (a term Freud chose for the activity of looking at another as an erotic object). Mulvey concluded that this 'gaze' was male and that cinema relies on three kinds of gaze: the camera often looking at women as passive objects and usually operated by a man; the look of male actors within the film which is structured to make their gaze powerful; and the gaze of the spectator who is presumed to be male identifying with the camera and voyeuristically watching women acting often in stereotypical ways.

The essay also inspired feminists in other disciplines such as literary criticism, for example Sandra Gilbert and Susan Gubar's *No Man's Land*, and the journal *Screen*, in which the essay first appeared, became the foremost journal of British film theory. Together with Peter Wollen, Mulvey made the films *Riddle of the Sphinx* and *Amy!* which, by drawing attention to their own filmic processes, attempted new forms of film making. Mulvey has subsequently refined her theory. In 'Changes: Thoughts on Myth, Narrative and Historical Experience' (1985), she argues against adopting an overly negative stance to Hollywood film. Instead Mulvey proposes that political and historical 'changes' continually rework relationships between women viewers and cinema.   ☐

COMMENTARY: C. Penley (1989), *The Future of an Illusion*, London: Routledge.

EXTRACT

VISUAL PLEASURE AND NARRATIVE CINEMA [1975]*

Introduction

A. *A Political Use of Psychoanalysis.* This paper intends to use psychoanalysis to discover where and how the fascination of film is reinforced by pre-existing patterns of fascination already at work within the individual subject and the social formations that have moulded him. It takes as starting point the way film reflects, reveals and even plays on the straight, socially established interpretation of sexual difference which controls images, erotic ways of looking and spectacle. It is helpful to understand what the cinema has been, how its magic has worked in the past, while attempting a theory and a practice which will challenge this cinema of the past. Psychoanalytic theory is thus appropriated here as a political weapon, demonstrating the way the unconscious of patriarchal society has structured film form.

[. . .]

Woman as image, man as bearer of the look

A. In a world ordered by sexual imbalance, pleasure in looking has been split between active/male and passive/female. The determining male gaze projects its phantasy on to the female figure which is styled accordingly. In their traditional exhibitionist role women are simultaneously looked at and displayed, with their appearance coded for strong visual and erotic impact so that they can be said to connote *to-be-looked-at-ness.* Woman displayed as sexual object is the leit-motif of erotic spectacle: from pin-ups to strip-tease,

*From: Laura Mulvey (1975), 'Visual Pleasure and Narrative Cinema', *Screen*, 16:3.

from Ziegfeld to Busby Berkeley, she holds the look, plays to and signifies male desire. Mainstream film neatly combined spectacle and narrative. (Note however, how in the musical, song-and-dance numbers break the flow of the diegesis.) The presence of woman is an indispensable element of spectacle in normal narrative film, yet her visual presence tends to work against the development of a story line, to freeze the flow of action in moments of erotic contemplation. This alien presence then has to be integrated into cohesion with the narrative. As Budd Boetticher has put it:

> What counts is what the heroine provokes, or rather what she represents. She is the one, or rather the love or fear she inspires in the hero, or else the concern he feels for her, who makes him act the way he does. In herself the woman has not the slightest importance.

(A recent tendency in narrative film has been to dispense with this problem altogether, hence the development of what Molly Haskell has called the 'buddy movie', in which the active homosexual eroticism of the central male figures can carry the story without distraction.) Traditionally, the woman displayed has functioned on two levels: as erotic object for the characters within the screen story, and as erotic object for the spectator within the auditorium, with a shifting tension between the looks on either side of the screen. For instance, the device of the show-girl allows the two looks to be unified technically without any apparent break in the diegesis. A woman performs within the narrative, the gaze of the spectator and that of the male characters in the film are neatly combined without breaking narrative verisimilitude. For a moment the sexual impact of the performing woman takes the film into a no-man's-land outside its own time and space. Thus Marilyn Monroe's first appearance in *The River of No Return* and Lauren Bacall's songs in *To Have or Have Not*. Similarly, conventional close-ups of legs (Dietrich, for instance) or a face (Garbo) integrate into the narrative a different mode of eroticism. One part of a fragmented body destroys the Renaissance space, the illusion of depth demanded by the narrative, it gives flatness, the quality of a cut-out or icon rather than verisimilitude to the screen.

B. An active/passive heterosexual division of labour has similarly controlled narrative structure. According to the principles of the ruling ideology and the physical structures that back it up, the male figure cannot bear the burden of sexual objectification. Man is reluctant to gaze at his exhibitionist like. Hence the split between spectacle and narrative supports the man's role as the active one of forwarding the story, making things happen. The man controls the film phantasy and also emerges as the representative of power in a further sense: as the bearer of the look of the spectator, transferring it behind the screen to neutralise the extra-diegetic tendencies represented by woman as spectacle. This is made possible through the processes set in motion by structuring the film around a main controlling figure with whom the spectator can identify. As the spectator identifies with the main male[1] protagonist, he projects his look on to that of his like, his screen surrogate, so that the power of the male protagonist as he controls events coincides with the active power of the erotic look, both giving a satisfying sense of omnipotence. A male movie star's glamorous characteristics are thus not those of the erotic object of the gaze, but those of the more perfect, more complete, more powerful ideal ego conceived in the original moment of recognition in front of the mirror. The character in the story can make things happen and control events better than the subject/spectator, just as the image in the mirror was more in control of motor coordination. In contrast to woman as icon, the active male figure (the ego ideal of the identification process) demands a three-dimensional space corresponding to that of the mirror-recognition in which the alienated subject internalised his own representation of this imaginary existence. He is a figure in a landscape. Here the function of film is to reproduce as accurately as possible the so-called natural conditions of human perception. Camera technology (as exemplified by deep focus in particular) and camera movements (determined by the action of the protagonist), combined with invisible editing (demanded by realism) all tend to blur the limits of screen space. The male protagonist is free to command the stage, a stage of spatial illusion in which he articulates the look and creates the action.

Summary

The psychoanalytic background that has been discussed in this article is relevant to the pleasure and unpleasure offered by traditional narrative film. The scopophilic instinct (pleasure in looking at another person as an erotic object), and, in contradistinction, ego libido (forming identification processes) act as formations, mechanisms, which this cinema has played on. The image of woman as (passive) raw material for the (active) gaze of man takes the argument a step further into the structure of representation, adding a further layer demanded by the ideology of the patriarchal order as it is worked out in its favourite cinematic form – illusionistic narrative film. The argument returns again to the psychoanalytic background in that woman as representation signifies castration, inducing voyeuristic or fetishistic mechanisms to circumvent her threat. None of these interacting layers is intrinsic to film, but it is only in the film form that they can reach a perfect and beautiful contradiction, thanks to the possibility in the cinema of shifting the emphasis of the look. It is the place of the look that defines cinema, the possibility of varying it and exposing it. This is what makes cinema quite different in its voyeuristic potential from, say, strip-tease, theatre, shows, etc. Going far beyond highlighting a woman's to-be-looked-at-ness, cinema builds the way she is to be looked at into the spectacle itself. Playing on the tension between film as controlling the dimension of time (editing, narrative) and film as controlling the dimension of space (changes in distance, editing), cinematic codes create a gaze, a world, and an object, thereby producing an illusion cut to the measure of desire. it is these cinematic codes and their relationship to formative external structures that must be broken down before mainstream film and the pleasure it provides can be challenged.

To begin with (as an ending), the voyeuristic-scopophilic look that is a crucial part of traditional filmic pleasure can itself be broken down. There are three different looks associated with cinema: that of the camera as it records the pro-filmic event, that of the audience as it watches the final product, and that of the characters at each other within the screen illusion. The conventions of narrative film deny the first two and subordinate them to the third, the conscious aim being always to eliminate intrusive camera presence and prevent a distancing awareness in the audience. Without these two absences (the material existence of the re-cording process, the critical reading of the spectator), fictional drama cannot achieve reality, obviousness and truth. Nevertheless, as this article has argued, the structure of looking in narrative fiction film contains a contradiction in its own premises: the female image as a castration threat constantly endangers the unity of the diegesis and bursts through the world of illusion as an intrusive, static, one-dimensional fetish. Thus the two looks materially present in time and space are obsessively subordinated to the neu-rotic needs of the male ego. The camera becomes the mech-anism for producing an illusion of Renaissance space, flowing movements compatible with the human eye, an ideology of representation that revolves around the percep-tion of the subject; the camera's look is disavowed in order to create a convincing world in which the spectator's surro-gate can perform with verisimilitude. Simultaneously, the look of the audience is denied an intrinsic force: as soon as fetishistic representation of the female image threatens to break the spell of illusion, and the erotic image on the screen appears directly (without mediation) to the specta-tor, the fact of fetishisation, concealing as it does castration fear, freezes the look, fixates the spectator and prevents him from achieving any distance from the image in front of him.

This complex interaction of looks is specific to film. The first blow against the monolithic accumulation of traditional film conventions (already undertaken by radical film-makers) is to free the look of the camera into its materiality in time and space and the look of the audience into dialectics, passionate detachment. There is no doubt that this destroys the satisfaction, pleasure and privilege of the 'invisible guest', and highlights how film has depended on voyeuristic active/passive mechanisms. Women, whose image has continually been stolen and used for this end, cannot view the decline of the traditional film form with anything much more than sentimental regret.[2]

Notes

1. There are films with a woman as main protagonist, of course. To analyse this phenomenon seriously here would take me too far afield. Pam Cook and Claire Johnston's study of *The Revolt of Mamie Stover* in Phil Hardy, ed: *Raoul Walsh*, Edinburgh 1974, shows in a striking case how the strength of this female protagonist is more apparent than real.
2. This article is a reworked version of a paper given in the French Department of the University of Wisconsin, Madison, in the Spring of 1973.

TERESA DE LAURETIS 1938–

☐ In *Alice Doesn't* (1984), *Technologies of Gender* (1987), and her other writing, Teresa de Lauretis sets out her theories of film. In these she interweaves semiotics with feminism to argue that gender ideologies shape the products of cinema (the films) and shape the process (the technology) of cinema's representation. Teresa de Lauretis's central claim is that our gendered subjectivity is constructed by our languages and our cultural practices and that it is only through these that the world has significance to us. The media in particular, de Lauretis argues, has become a battleground where universal beliefs about the objectivity of art are continually contested because people look at cultural objects and at themselves with the biases of class, race and gender. Building on Laura Mulvey's psychoanalytic theories, de Lauretis argues that spectators can 'remake' films through parody and by bringing their social needs and historical understanding to any viewing experience. All of these combine to undermine ideas of universality. By being aware of this complexity, de Lauretis argues, we can imagine real alternatives to the gendered messages of cinema.   ☐

COMMENTARY: A. Kaplan (1990), *Psychoanalysis and Cinema*, London: Routledge.

EXTRACT

ALICE DOESN'T: FEMINISM, SEMIOTICS, CINEMA [1984]*

As social beings, women are constructed through effects of language and representation. Just as the spectator, the term of the moving series of filmic images, is taken up and moved along successive positions of meaning, a woman (or a man) is not an undivided identity, a stable unity of 'consciousness,' but the term of a shifting series of ideological positions. Put another way, the social being is constructed day by day as the point of articulation of ideological formations, an always provisional encounter of subject and codes at the historical (therefore changing) intersection of social formations and her or his personal history. While codes and social formations define positions of meaning, the individual reworks those positions into a personal, subjective construction. A social technology – cinema, for example – is the semiotic apparatus in which the encounter takes place and the individual is addressed as subject. Cinema is at once a material apparatus and a signifying practice in which the subject is implicated, constructed, but not exhausted. Obviously, women are addressed by cinema and by film, as are men. Yet what distinguishes the forms of that address is far from obvious (and to articulate the different modes of address, to describe their functioning as ideological effects in subject construction, is perhaps the main critical task confronting cinematic and semiotic theory).

Whether we think of cinema as the sum of one's experiences as spectator in the socially determined situations of viewing, or as a series of relations linking the economics of film production to ideological and institutional reproduction, the dominant cinema specifies woman in a particular social and natural order, sets her up in certain positions of

*From: Teresa de Lauretis (1984), *Alice Doesn't: Feminism, Semiotics, Cinema*, London: Macmillan.

meaning, fixes her in a certain identification. Represented as the negative term of sexual differentiation, spectacle-fetish or specular image, in any case ob-scene, woman is constituted as the ground of representation, the looking-glass held up to man. But, as historical individual, the female viewer is also positioned in the films of classical cinema as spectator–subject; she is thus doubly bound to that very representation which calls on her directly, engages her desire, elicits her pleasure, frames her identification, and makes her complicit in the production of (her) woman-ness. On this crucial relation of woman as constituted in representation to women as historical subjects depend at once the development of a feminist critique and the possibility of a materialist, semiotic theory of culture. For the feminist critique is a critique of culture at once from within and from without, in the same way in which women are both *in* the cinema as representation and *outside* the cinema as subjects of practices. It is therefore not simple numerical evidence (women hold up half of the sky) that forces any theoretical speculation on culture to hear the questions of women, but their direct critical incidence on its conditions of possibility.

[. . .]

This is where the specificity of a feminist theory may be sought: not in femininity as a privileged nearness to nature, the body, or the unconscious, an essence which inheres in women but to which males too now lay a claim; not in a female tradition simply understood as private, marginal and yet intact, outside of history but fully there to be discovered or recovered; not, finally, in the chinks and cracks of masculinity, the fissures of male identity or the repressed of phallic discourse; but rather in that political, theoretical, self-analyzing practice by which the relations of the subject in social reality can be rearticulated from the historical experience of women. Much, very much, is still to be done, therefore. 'Post-feminism,' the *dernier cri* making its way across the Atlantic into feminist studies and the critical establishment, 'is not an idea whose time has come,' Mary

Russo remarks, and then goes on to show how indeed 'it is not an idea at all.'[1]

From a city built to represent woman, but where no women live, we have come to the gravel path of the academic campus. We have learned that one becomes a woman in the very practice of signs by which we live, write, speak, see. . . . This is neither an illusion nor a paradox. It is a real contradiction – women continue to become woman. The essays collected here have attempted to work through and with the subtle, shifting, duplicitous terms of that contradiction, but not to reconcile them. For it seems to me that only by knowingly enacting and re-presenting them, by knowing us to be both woman and women, does a woman today become a subject. In this 1984, it is the signifier who plays and wins before Alice does, even when she's aware of it. But to what end, if Alice doesn't?

Note

1. Mary Russo, 'Notes on "Post-Feminism",' in *The Politics of Theory*, ed. Francis Barker *et al.* (Colchester: University of Essex, 1983), p. 27. Russo is discussing the recent work of Julia Kristeva and Maria Antonietta Macciocchi, the two intellectual figures principally associated with this latest 'ism,' and their attempts to bring feminism in line with antihumanist philosophy.

GISELA ECKER

☐ Gisela Ecker edited the first collection in English of European, specifically German, feminist aesthetics and cultural criticism *Feminist Aesthetics* (1985). Two distinguishing features of European feminist theory are: its concern with *all* forms of art including literature, film, architecture, music, theatre, and the visual arts; and its interest in *ideas*, in philosophical speculations as much as in artistic techniques.

The collection aims, like much other contemporary feminist criticism, to show how traditionally the strategies of art are an implicit part of the misogynist politics of art. Ecker does not privilege either theory or artistic practice, but rather shows how feminist art is frequently and self-consciously theoretical. All the contributors to the volume make clear that, for these feminists, there can be no *formal* aesthetic criteria for defining feminist art and culture and isolating a feminist praxis, caught, as feminist artists are, between the demands of feminism for positive images of women and the technical demands of any artistic medium in itself. A feminist theory of culture, they argue, is one in which women are represented in art as social subjects not simply as images, and women artists are able to produce and reproduce an art which can transform sexist values. ☐

COMMENTARY: T. de Lauretis (1987), *Technologies of Gender*, London: Macmillan.

EXTRACT

FEMINIST AESTHETICS [1985]*

For all the reasons given above, I am convinced that it is important to pursue not a 'feminine' but a 'feminist' aesthetics. The second demands reflecting on the first. It takes the complications of subjectivity into account, and feminist investigations of aesthetic theory necessarily aim at a critique of traditional assumptions. We have to be aware of the paradox that there cannot be any certainty about what is feminine in art but that we have to go on looking out for it. 'Feminist' would indicate a commitment which is relative to the historical moment with its specific necessities. The articles in this book demonstrate that each field of art has to confront its own problems. For example, in music, more than in writing, it is still very important to continue analysing the various reasons for exclusion from composing or from directing. In architecture there are so many pragmatic problems to solve and topics to discuss – like violence in the streets or the ideology of the nuclear family – that the question of aesthetic forms is put into a secondary [but still important] position. The institutions by which each art form is organised, and the artistic language which is used, lead to a range of different questions from those which are normally discussed in relation to writing. In any case, this diversity emphasises that externally there is still a lot to be done in addition to the necessary reflections on the internal site of struggle within the female subject-in-process.

As long as this myth of a *general* art, literature, etc. persists in the way it has done up to now, feminist aesthetic theory must insist that all investigations into art have to be *thoroughly genderised*. When I think of the women artists I have met, I know that this will be a highly unpopular suggestion, for one of the most urgent demands expressed by many of them is that they wish gender to be treated as

*From: Gisela Ecker (1985), *Feminist Aesthetics*, London: The Women's Press.

irrelevant or at least marginal: for centuries women artists have been confronted with apparently gender-neutral, but what is in fact male, 'Art', and their work has been set aside as 'women's art', a status which contained massive stereotypes about women. Why should they now, they ask, when institutions seem to have become more 'tolerant' and open to them, deliberately show that they are painting, writing, composing, constructing and filming *as women*? Although I can see that this has to be taken seriously as an effect of the ideologies which go along with the notion 'women's art', something must be profoundly wrong if any artist (or critic) feels she has to suppress her gender.

A truly genderised perspective would mean that the sex – male *or* female – of both the artist and the critic is taken into account. This also implies their relation to gender-values in the institutions and within the theories they apply. It cannot be stressed enough that it is impossible to deconstruct this myth of gender-neutrality in art if, at the same time, male artists and critics do not develop a consciousness of their own gender. If they do not, we'll have to make it transparent to them that what they term 'natural' or 'general' norms are questionable. Otherwise women artists will still be forced either to bang on the doors of 'Art' for admittance or establish secluded spheres of women-only art, if they are not to be silenced altogether. The same applies to women critics, of course. As soon as we analyse *as women*, with our specific concerns and our skills (developed in our historical position), the apparently gender-neutral and disinterested institution university reacts as if frightfully offended. It employs its own intricate web of trivialisations and nice little sanctioning gestures which nevertheless often end in exclusion. Gisela Breitling's appeal for a radically changed concept of universality in art points, I believe, to a future stage which cannot be achieved without going through the equally radical introduction of gender into hitherto 'unaffected' fields.

GRISELDA POLLOCK 1949–

☐ Together with Rozsika Parker, Griselda Pollock has made an eloquent British feminist response to traditional art history. Parker and Pollock have been part of the British feminist art movement for over two decades, as teachers, authors and members of the Women's Art History Collective. *Old Mistresses: Women, Art and Ideology* (1981) was an extensive catalogue of the misogyny of art institutions, art practices and male artists. The book made a pioneering evaluation and upgrading of women's popular and domestic arts such as quilt making and weaving.

In this later essay, part of which is reprinted here, Pollock argues that, whatever modernism's artistic and social ideals were at its inception, its claims to universalism, and its view of the artist as an individual genius, are gender specific. Historians of modernism operated in tight boundaries which excluded women artists. In addition, Pollock went on to argue, art institutions have a solid alliance with social power, and art forms are historically and culturally determined by patriarchy because both institutions and forms reflect and sustain the sexual divisions which structure society.   ☐

COMMENTARY: J. Wolff (1981), *The Social Production of Art*, London: Macmillan.

EXTRACT

FEMINISM AND MODERNISM [1987]*

There have to date been several attempts to map out the field of feminist artistic practice.[1] All disdain the idea of answering the question 'What is feminist art?'. There is no such entity; no homogeneous movement defined by characteristic style, favoured media or typical subject-matter. There are instead feminist artistic practices which cannot be comprehended by the standard procedures and protocols of modernist art history and criticism which depend upon isolating aesthetic considerations such as style or media. The somewhat clumsy phrase 'feminist artistic practices' is employed to shift our attention from the conventional ways we consume works of art as *objects* and stress the conditions of production of art as a matter of texts, events, representations whose effects and meanings depend upon their conditions of reception – where, by whom, against the background of what inherited conventions and expectations. In a paper given at the Art and Politics Conference in London in 1977 (see Section IV, 10), Mary Kelly introduced yet another term: the 'feminist problematic in art'. A problematic, borrowed from developments in Marxist philosophy, defines the underlying theoretical or ideological field which structures the forming of concepts and the making of statements.

Thus, for instance, the concept 'feminist art' is the product of a bourgeois problematic in which 'art' is assumed to be a discrete and self-evident entity in which a knowing, conscious individual expresses herself in terms of an object which contains – acts as a repository for – a recognisable content called a feminist point of view or feminist ideology. Kelly uses the notion of 'the ideological' developed in structuralist marxism to counter this: 'the ideological is the

*From: Griselda Pollock (1987), 'Feminism and Modernism', in R. Parker and G. Pollock (eds), *Framing Feminism: Art and the Women's Movement 1970–85*, London: Pandora.

non-unitary complex of social practices and systems of representation which have political consequences'. Thus feminist artistic practice has initially to begin to define a problematic in relation to an understanding of the ways in which it can be effective – not by expressing some singular and personal set of ideas or experiences but by calculated interventions (often utilising or addressing explicitly women's experiences ignored or obliterated in our culture). Therefore the study of feminist cultural practices leads to a series of tactical activities and strategically developed practices of representation which represent the world for a radically different order of knowledge of it. These interventions occur in the context of established institutions and discourses which circulate the dominant definitions and accepted limits of what is ratified as art and how it should be consumed.

Feminist activities of representation have drawn upon an increasingly complex range of theories which enable women to understand how institutions operate, how ideology works, how images produce meanings for their viewers and thereby construct those viewers. There has been, in addition, a necessary investigation of those areas and modes of practice – video, photo-text, scripto-visual work, performance, street theatre, postal art etc., which offer the maximum flexibility and potential for both a dislocation of existing and dominant regimes of power and knowledge, and a construction of a new multiplicity of powers and knowledges for the diverse communities of the oppressed – women are not a homogeneous group but are fractured by class, race, age. How to undertake this has generated considerable debate in a diversified field of practices, positions and priorities. This essay is intended to cover a selected range of both debates and practices which focus primarily on the historic exchange between feminism and Modernism.

[. . .]

Cultural interventions by women can be understood to refer to those activities which lead to greater numbers of women being involved in culture – more women film makers, more women artists in public exhibitions etc. This expansion is certainly a feminist project, or it is inspired by the Women's Movement. But simply more women in a particular field is not the main or even central aim of the Women's Movement. In addition encouraging women to voice or represent their particular and 'personal' experience – speaking with a gendered voice – is also an aspect of feminism. But feminism in culture cannot be reduced to substituting *women's* for men's subjectivities in an otherwise unchanged notion of art as self-expression. It is not, therefore, the fact that activities or representations are undertaken by *women* which renders them feminist. Their feminism is crucially a matter of *effect*. To be feminist at all work must be conceived within the framework of a structural, economic, political and ideological critique of the power relations of society and with a commitment to collective action for their radical transformation. An art work is not feminist because it registers the ideas, politics or obsessions of its feminist maker. It has a political effect as a feminist intervention according to the way the work acts upon, makes demands of, and produces positions for its viewers. It is feminist because of the way it works as a text within a specific social space in relation to dominant codes and conventions of art and to dominant ideologies of femininity. It is feminist when it subverts the normal ways in which we view art and are usually seduced into a complicity with the meanings of the dominant and oppressive culture.

[. . .]

Feminism occupies a particular place, therefore, in the challenge to Modernism in an order of sense, as the hegemonic culture of patriarchal capitalist societies. Unlike the limited rebellions against Modernism which remain locked into the system, feminist practices are founded in a political movement. Feminism's relation to Modernism and therefore its force as a potential emergent cultural formation is a result of its relation to a movement of women for

their total emancipation. Feminism's struggle is therefore
not a campaign to raise quotas of women in exhibitions or
to find spaces for the expression of women's experiences,
although these are parts of the tactical activity of the movement. It is a struggle about meanings, a fight against dominant and established systems of meaning and the positions
and identities which they attempt to secure. To sustain a
genuine intervention which can unsettle the dominant 'regime of truth' oppositional practices must articulate with
alternative, contrary sets of meanings and social practices,
ideologies which are being constructed in terms of historically relevant social struggles. Feminism is the expression
of a political movement which is attempting through diverse practices to disarticulate the meanings of the dominant
social order and to articulate new meanings for the dominated gender within the subordinated classes and races.
This does not imply the simple invention of meanings released suddenly, already formed from the repressed subcultures. It will occur and has occurred in the knowing
exploitation of the implicated but radical position of
women within the institutions and ideologies of society. It
necessitates the negotiation of those forms and practices
within the dominant ideologies of art such as Modernism
which, shaped within the real and contradictory conditions
of modern social relations may none the less provide means
of representation adequate to the complexity of those social
relations. For it is with these conditions feminist practices
contend at the level of the text, of the institution and of the
social organisation of revolution.

Feminist artistic practices cannot pretend to a greater
effectivity in political change than the relative position socially designated for such activities by the society as a
whole. But equally they cannot be denied a strategic necessity within a broad spectrum of contemporary political activities. Not all feminist practices contend with these
dominant discourses and institutions in the manner discussed in this section. But those which do operate upon this
terrain will gain in political effectivity through the recognition and understanding of their procedures by the women's

movement which is their necessary base. At the same time, however, it is important to assert the historically central place of feminist opposition to Modernism, not for any heroic purpose, but because of the way in which the structural sexism of cultural institutions in the present conservative climate actively denies the feminist tradition.

Note

1. In this anthology we include essays by Mary Kelly (Section IV, 10), Rozsika Parker (Section III, 22), Judith Barry and Sandy Flitterman (Section IV, 11). Other studies include: Alexis Hunter, 'Feminist Perceptions', *Artscribe*, 1980 no. 25; Griselda Pollock; 'A Politics of Art or an Aesthetics for Women?', *Feminist Art News (FAN)*, 1981 no. 5; Laura Mulvey 'Interview' in *Wedge* (GB), 1978 no. 2; Lisa Tickner, 'Feminism, Femininity and Women's Art', *LIP* (Australia), 1984 vol. 8.

16 ☐ Language and writing

Introduction

☐ Second wave feminism is deeply concerned about the material and political effects on women of the everyday sexism we encounter in social language and cultural productions. Current feminist accounts of language uses follow on from Kate Millett's analysis of literary stereotypes in *Sexual Politics* and Dale Spender's influential account of the politics of naming in *Manmade Language*.

Feminist debates about forms of sexism in language and about whether women can use language in an 'uncontaminated' way cover a number of issues. These issues range from assessing how English usage discriminates against women when 'man' purportedly stands for both male and female; proposing a non-sexist vocabulary such as 'chairperson'; examining literary representations of women and men; and investigating how gender ideology is produced and reproduced in popular culture. The term 'women's language' was used by Robin Lakoff in her pioneering essay 'Language and Woman's Place' (1975) which argued that language did have gendered features (or 'genderlects').

It is in language that femininity and masculinity disclose themselves. Gender rules define the limits of our experiences and hence of our subjectivities and our writing worlds. As we have seen, French feminists assert that there *are* gender differences in language and these writers have developed a specifically 'feminine' and revolutionary language. Black feminist criticism makes a radical challenge to literary institutions and white literary values by developing a black poetics which draws on black women's creative writing and community culture. ☐

COMMENTARY: M. Humm (1986), *Feminist Criticism: Women as Contemporary Critics*, Brighton: Harvester.

367

ADRIENNE RICH 1929–

☐ Adrienne Rich is one of the foremost feminist poets and theorists writing in America today but, in 1971 when Rich wrote 'When We Dead Awaken' for a forum of the Commission on the Status of Women in the Professions, arguably a feminist aesthetic did not exist. In this and her subsequent essays, Rich examines the relation between cultural repro- ductions and women's difference(s). Rich creates a feminist poetics based on the idea that feminist writing can provide historical and mythical accounts of women's lives which will help to counter the violence of patriarchy. This preoccupation emerges in Rich's vivid use of auto- biography and in the way in which she introduces her readers to an inter- national range of emblematic women heroines.

Adrienne Rich took the term 're-vision' from the American poet Robert Duncan who first uses it in *The Artist's View* in 1953. But where Duncan's 'revision' involves him only in uncovering or 're-vising', his own 'dead' past poetry, Rich's 're-vision' is part of an intrinsically open and unresolvd discussion with her women readers. Rich defines 're- vision' as: first an historical activity, then a cultural activity but also a psychic event – an analysis of our deepest assumptions. The activity of re-vision will, Rich hopes, be part of a feminist culture which will be organised around women's friendships and backed by the critical force of feminist traditions. ☐

COMMENTARY: C.R. Stimpson (1988), *Where the Meanings Are*, London: Routledge.

EXTRACT

WHEN WE DEAD AWAKEN: WRITING AS RE-VISION [1971]*

Re-vision – the act of looking back, of seeing with fresh eyes, of entering an old text from a new critical direction – is for women more than a chapter in cultural history: it is an act of survival. Until we can understand the assumptions in which we are drenched we cannot know ourselves. And this drive to self-knowledge, for women, is more than a search for identity: it is part of our refusal of the self-destructiveness of male-dominated society. A radical critique of literature, feminist in its impulse, would take the work first of all as a clue to how we live, how we have been living, how we have been led to imagine ourselves, how our language has trapped as well as liberated us, how the very act of naming has been till now a male prerogative, and how we can begin to see and name – and therefore live – afresh. A change in the concept of sexual identity is essential if we are not going to see the old political order reassert itself in every new revolution. We need to know the writing of the past, and know it differently than we have ever known it; not to pass on a tradition but to break its hold over us.

[. . .]

In those years formalism was part of the strategy – like asbestos gloves, it allowed me to handle materials I couldn't pick up barehanded.

[. . .]

In closing I want to tell you about a dream I had last summer. I dreamed I was asked to read my poetry at a mass women's meeting, but when I began to read, what came out were the lyrics of a blues song. I share this dream with you

*From: Adrienne Rich (1980), 'When We Dead Awaken: Writing as Re-Vision', in *On Lies, Secrets, and Silence: Selected Prose 1966–1978*, London: Virago.

because it seemed to me to say something about the problems and the future of the woman writer, and probably of women in general. The awakening of consciousness is not like the crossing of a frontier – one step and you are in another country. Much of woman's poetry has been of the nature of the blues song: a cry of pain, of victimization, or a lyric of seduction.[1] And today, much poetry by women – and prose for that matter – is charged with anger. I think we need to go through that anger, and we will betray our own reality if we try, as Virginia Woolf was trying, for an objectivity, a detachment, that would make us sound more like Jane Austen or Shakespeare. We know more than Jane Austen or Shakespeare knew: more than Jane Austen because our lives are more complex, more than Shakespeare because we know more about the lives of women – Jane Austen and Virginia Woolf included.

Both the victimization and the anger experienced by women are real, and have real sources, everywhere in the environment, built into society, language, the structures of thought. They will go on being tapped and explored by poets, among others. We can neither deny them, nor will we rest there. A new generation of women poets is already working out of the psychic energy released when women begin to move out towards what the feminist philosopher Mary Daly has described as the 'new space' on the boundaries of patriarchy.[2] Women are speaking to and of women in these poems, out of a newly released courage to name, to love each other, to share risk and grief and celebration.

To the eye of a feminist, the work of Western male poets now writing reveals a deep, fatalistic pessimism as to the possibilities of change, whether societal or personal, along with a familiar and threadbare use of women (and nature) as redemptive on the one hand, threatening on the other; and a new tide of phallocentric sadism and overt woman-hating which matches the sexual brutality of recent films. 'Political' poetry by men remains stranded amid the struggles for power among male groups; in condemning U.S. imperialism or the Chilean junta the poet can claim to speak for the oppressed while remaining, as male, part of a system of sexual oppression. The enemy is always outside the self, the struggle somewhere else. The mood of isolation, self-pity, and self-imitation that pervades 'nonpolitical' poetry suggests that a profound change in masculine conscious-ness will have to precede any new male poetic – or other – inspiration. The creative energy of patriarchy is fast run-ning out; what remains is its self-generating energy for de-struction. As women, we have our work cut out for us.

Notes

1. A.R., 1978: When I dreamed that dream, was I wholly ignorant of the tradition of Bessie Smith and other women's blues lyrics which tran-scended victimization to sing of resistance and independence?
2. Mary Daly, *Beyond God the Father: Towards a Philosophy of Women's Liberation* (Boston: Beacon, 1973).

BARBARA SMITH 1946–

☐ Barbara Smith is a black, lesbian feminist critic who co-founded Kitchen Table Press and is the editor of major collections of writing by black women: *Conditions: The Black Women's Issue* (1979), *All The Women Are White, All the Blacks Are Men, But Some of Us Are Brave: Black Women's Studies* (1982), and *Home Girls* (1983).

Black and lesbian critics ask resonating and polemical questions about writing and reproduction in terms of fundamental marginalities and misrepresentations. Barbara Smith's *Toward a Black Feminist Criticism* (1977) is a pathbreaking statement about black culture. In this much anthologised piece, Smith sets out the contours of black women's writing and proposes an original black feminist aesthetic. In the following extract, Smith refuses to efface the black woman author from her reading. Indeed Smith exposes the major displacement of the black woman in criticism written by black men, in white feminist criticism and the total exclusion of black lesbians in all literary criticism. In reading Toni Morrison's *Sula* as a black lesbian novel, Smith makes an ideologically inspired account of writing differences, brilliantly answering performatively Ros Coward's call for politically informed feminist criticism. ☐

COMMENTARY: D.E. McDowell (1980), 'New Directions for Black Feminist Criticism', *Black America Literary Forum*, 14.

EXTRACT

TOWARD A BLACK FEMINIST CRITICISM [1977]*

I do not know where to begin. Long before I tried to write this I realized that I was attempting something unprecedented, something dangerous, merely by writing about Black lesbian writers from any perspective at all. These things have not been done. Not by white male critics, expectedly. Not by Black male critics. Not by white women critics who think of themselves as feminists. And most crucially not by Black women critics who, although they pay the most attention to Black women writers as a group, seldom use a consistent feminist analysis or write about Black lesbian literature. All segments of the literary world – whether establishment, progressive, Black, female, or lesbian – do not know, or at least act as if they do not know, that Black women writers and Black lesbian writers exist.

For whites, this specialized lack of knowledge is inextricably connected to their not knowing in any concrete or politically transforming way that Black women of any description dwell in this place. Black women's existence, experience, and culture and the brutally complex systems of oppression which shape these are in the 'real world' of white and/or male consciousness beneath consideration, invisible, unknown.

[. . .]

Before suggesting how a Black feminist approach might be used to examine a specific work, I will outline some of the principles that I think a Black feminist critic could use. Beginning with a primary commitment to exploring how both sexual and racial politics and Black and female identity are inextricable elements in Black women's writing, she

*From: Barbara Smith (1980), *Toward a Black Feminist Criticism*, Trumansburg, New York: The Crossing Press.

would also work from the assumption that Black women writers constitute an identifiable literary tradition. The breadth of her familiarity with these writers would have shown her that not only is theirs a verifiable historical tradition that parallels in time the tradition of Black men and white women writing in this country, but that thematically, stylistically, aesthetically and conceptually Black women writers manifest common approaches to the act of creating literature as a direct result of the specific political, social and economic experience they have been obliged to share. The way, for example, that Zora Neale Hurston, Margaret Walker, Toni Morrison, and Alice Walker incorporate the traditional Black female activities of rootworking, herbal medicine, conjure and midwifery into the fabric of their stories is not mere coincidence, nor is their use of specifically Black female language to express their own and their characters' thoughts accidental. The use of Black women's language and cultural experience in books by Black women *about* Black women results in a miraculously rich coalescing of form and content and also takes their writing far beyond the confines of white/male literary structures. The Black feminist critic would find innumerable commonalities in works by Black women.

Another principle which grows out of the concept of a tradition and which would also help to strengthen this tradition would be for the critic to look first for precedents and insights in interpretation within the works of other Black women. In other words she would think and write out of her own identity and not try to graft the ideas or methodology of white/male literary thought upon precious materials of Black women's art. Black feminist criticism would by definition be highly innovative, embodying the daring spirit of the works themselves. The Black feminist critic would be constantly aware of the political implications of her work and would assert the connections between it and the political situation of all Black women. Logically developed, Black feminist criticism would owe its existence to a Black feminist movement while at the same time contributing ideas that women in the movement could use.

Black feminist criticism applied to a particular work can overturn previous assumptions about it and expose for the first time its actual dimensions. At the 'Lesbians and Literature' discussion at the 1976 Modern Language Association convention, Bertha Harris suggested that if in a woman writer's work a sentence refuses to do what it is supposed to do, if there are strong images of women, and if there is a refusal to be linear, the result is innately lesbian literature. As usual, I wanted to see if these ideas might be applied to the Black women writers that I know and quickly realized that many of their works were, in Harris' sense, lesbian. Not because women are 'lovers,' but because they are the central figures, are positively portrayed and have pivotal relationships with one another. The form and language of these works is also nothing like what white patriarchal culture requires or expects.

ROS COWARD

☐ Ros Coward is a British, cultural critic who eloquently argues that the reproduction of 'languages' of femininity and masculinity in film, television and literature construct gender hierarchies and marginalise women. Coward argues that the application of psychoanalytic theory to these reproductions can explain how our viewing desires and pleasures are gendered.

No writing or cultural reproduction is 'safe' from ideology, she argues. Hence writing by women largely for women, for example romance novels or soap operas, is not more 'authentically' feminist just by virtue of its authorship or readership.

This is the argument of Coward's challenging essay 'Are Women's Novels Feminist Novels?' (1980) which was written as a response to Rebecca O'Rourke's account of women's novels, such as Marilyn French's *The Women's Room*, also published in *Feminist Review*. Coward argues that what we should value as feminist criticism and writing is not some idealist belief in authorship or devotion to women's experience but an engagement with political ideas. ☐

COMMENTARY: L.J. Nicholson (ed.) (1990), *Feminism/Postmodernism*, London: Routledge.

EXTRACT

'THIS NOVEL CHANGES LIVES': ARE WOMEN'S NOVELS FEMINIST NOVELS? [1980]*

Over recent years we have been witness to a strange phenomenon, the emergence of what we may loosely call the 'feminist novel'. This phenomenon has involved the immense commercial success and popular appeal of some novels which claim explicit allegiance to the women's liberation movement. Some of these novels, like Marilyn French's *The Women's Room* and Sara Davison's *Loose Change*, even use the practice of 'consciousness-raising' as framing devices. These novels have been published alike by feminist publishing groups and commercial publishers yet the number printed of such novels is far in excess of the number printed of other forms of feminist writing: magazines, journals and political tracts. Accompanying the appearance of novels like these has been a practice, initiated by feminist publishing groups, of reprinting novels written by women who have fallen into relative oblivion. All these novels are read with pleasure and interest by feminists; they are frequently discussed informally. It seems as though, unlike many other contemporary political movements, feminism is accompanied by the development of a 'feminist culture' – something which is not confined to literature but is also evidenced by the proliferation of feminist theatre and film groups.

Yet in the informal networks in which the phenomena like the 'feminist novel' are discussed, responses are rarely unambiguous. No one is quite sure about the political validity of the admixture of conventional entertainment with a serious political message. Many are suspicious of the commercial success of 'the novel that changes lives' and are

*From: Ros Coward (1980), ' "This Novel Changes Lives": Are Women's Novels Feminist Novels? A Response to Rebecca O'Rourke's Article "Summer Reading" ', *Feminist Review*, 5.

eager to demonstrate how these novels are ultimately 'not feminist'. This has been the fate of Erica Jong's *Fear of Flying*. Others question the nature of the popular appeal of these novels, when other aspects of feminist political involvement are so readily ridiculed in the media through designations like 'bra-burners' or 'women's libbers'. Is it that these novels are carrying out subversive politicization, drawing women into structures of consciousness-raising without their knowing it? Or is it that the accounts of women's experiences which they offer in fact correspond more closely to popular sentiment than they do to feminist aspirations? These are not insignificant questions. They relate to debates over what effective feminist politics are; whether ideological practices like literature, theatre or film can be political; and finally, whether it is the centrality which these novels attribute to women's experience which would justify their designation as 'feminist'.

Women-centred writing

It is just not possible to say that women-centred writings have any necessary relationship to feminism. Women-centred novels are by no means a new phenomenon. The Mills and Boon romantic novels are written by, read by, marketed for and are all about women. Yet nothing could be further from the aims of feminism than these fantasies based on the sexual, racial and class submission which so frequently characterise these novels. The plots and elements of these novels are frequently so predictable that cynics have suggested that Mills and Boon's treasured authors might well be computers. Yet the extraordinary rigidity of the formula of the novels, where the heroine invariably finds material success through sexual submission and marriage, does not prevent these publishers having larger sales than Pan and Penguin. The average print run for each novel is 115,000. While Mills and Boon may have a highly individual market, their formulae are not so radically different from romance fiction in general. Such im-

mensely popular writers as Mary Stewart and Georgette
Heyer invariably have the experience of the heroine at the
centre, and concentrate on the vagaries of her emotions as
the principal substance of the novel. In the cinema, the
equivalent of the romantic novel is melodrama, and melodrama is often promoted as 'women's pictures', suggesting
that they are directed towards women as well as being
about women. Indeed it would not be stretching credibility
too far to suggest that the consciousness of the individual
heroine has been a principal narrative device of the English
novel in the last century, a fact which may well have contributed to the relative presence of women writers in this
field.

While this all shows how misguided it would be to mark
a book of interest to feminism because of the centrality it
attributes to women's experiences, it could be argued that
what we loosely call feminist novels are qualitatively different. But to make such a claim it would be necessary to
specify in what way 'women-centred' writing, allying itself
with feminist politics, did mark itself out as different. Some
of the so-called feminist novels like *The Women's Room*
and *A Piece of the Night* do make explicit their allegiance
to the women's liberation movement. However, many of
the others in roughly the same genre do not. *Fear of Flying*,
Kinflicks and *Loose Change* all fall into this category. Yet
the encounter with the milieu and aspirations of feminism
often forms a central element in the narrative of these novels. And, the practice of consciousness raising – the reconstruction of personal histories within a group of women –
sometimes forms the structure of the novel. Then there is a
further category. Here we find novels like Kate Millett's
Sita whose feminist commitment is guaranteed not so
much by the content of the book as by the other theoretical
and political writings of the author. And finally there is a
whole host of novels which are adopted as honorary 'feminist novels', taking in such different writers as Doris Less-
ing, Fay Weldon and Alison Lurie. Their writings deal not
so much with the milieu of contemporary feminism as with
charting the experience of women's oppression.

Now, there is a certain convention within all these novels which does clearly mark them off from the romance genre for example. One striking feature is the frequency with which we meet with the quasi-autobiographical structure. *The Women's Room, Fear of Flying, Kinflicks, Sita* all foreground the writer, struggling to turn her experience into literature, even if this figure loiters in the background in god-like omnipotence as in *The Women's Room*. Moreover the 'voice' of the central protagonist, if not presenting itself directly as the author's voice, frequently offers itself as 'representative' of women in general, firstly claiming sexual experience as a vital terrain of all women's experience, sometimes also making generalities as to the oppressive nature of that experience. The distinctiveness of the genre has attracted attention; a *Sunday Times* colour supplement heading shows one response to the self-consciously 'representative' nature of these novels:

> Liberating the Libido. Getting sex straight was an essential first step along the noisy road to liberation; writing about it could be the next leap forward. Books by women surveying sex, and novels by women whose heroines savour sex are selling like hotdogs in America – beating men into second place and turning the authoresses into millionairesses at the drop of a hard sell dust-jacket.

I have raised this here in order to show that we do not have a recognizable group of novels whose roots are, in a variety of ways, in the women's liberation movement but that their relation to feminism is not the necessary outcome of taking women's experience as central. But other questions arise in relation to this statement, questions as to whether the 'representativeness' which these novels claim is simply a reflection of 'feminist consciousness', or a propaganda device towards such a consciousness, or whether we have to be more cautious in analysing their structure and effects.

ELAINE SHOWALTER 1941–

☐ Elaine Showalter has been a professor of English at Rutgers and Princeton and her influential accounts of women's writing gave feminist criticism a vivid literary history. When Showalter wrote *A Literature of Their Own* in 1977, feminist critics were concerned to create an alternative canon of writing by women. Under the banner of 'gynocriticism' Showalter described that full history of women writers – their literary careers, their favoured genres and their techniques. She arranged this history into three phases: 'feminine' (1840 to 1880), when women writers imitated men; 'feminist' (1880 to the 1920s), when writers made political protests part of their writing; and 'female' (1920 to the present), when women's writing involves itself in self transformation.

Showalter argued that gynocriticism could help to create, not only an alternative canon of women's writing, but also a more appropriate criticism for feminism if it drew on anthropology and women's subcultures. Showalter suggests that women's writing has four foci – biological, linguistic, psychological and cultural – to which she matches two kinds of response – a feminist critique (which is concerned with women readers) and gynocritics (a concern with women writers). Showalter puts feminist criticism to the task of counteracting women's marginality with a complex inquiry into women's language and its possibilities. ☐

COMMENTARY: C. Belsey and J. Moore (1989), *The Feminist Reader: Essays in the Politics of Literary Criticism*, London: Macmillan.

EXTRACT

TOWARDS A FEMINIST POETICS [1979]*

Feminist criticism can be divided into two distinct varieties. The first type is concerned with *woman as reader* –
with woman as the consumer of male-produced literature,
and with the way in which the hypothesis of a female reader changes our apprehension of a given text, awakening us
to the significance of its sexual codes. I shall call this kind
of analysis the *feminist critique,* and like other kinds of
critique it is a historically grounded inquiry which probes
the ideological assumptions of literary phenomena. Its subjects include the images and stereotypes of women in literature, the omissions and misconceptions about women in
criticism, and the fissures in male-constructed literary history. It is also concerned with the exploitation and manipulation of the female audience, especially in popular
culture and film; and with the analysis of woman-as-sign in
semiotic systems. The second type of feminist criticism is
concerned with *woman as writer* – with woman as the producer of textual meaning, with the history, themes, genres
and structures of literature by women. Its subjects include
the psychodynamics of female creativity; linguistics and
the problem of a female language; the trajectory of the individual or collective female literary career; literary history;
and, of course, studies of particular writers and works. No
term exists in English for such a specialised discourse, and
so I have adapted the French term *la gynocritique:*
'gynocritics' (although the significance of the male
pseudonym in the history of women's writing also suggested the term 'georgics').

---

*From: Elaine Showalter (1979), 'Towards a Feminist Poetics', in M. Jacobus (ed.),
Women Writing and Writing about Women, London: Croom Helm.

Gynocritics and female culture

In contrast to this angry or loving fixation on male literature, the programme of gynocritics is to construct a female
framework for the analysis of women's literature, to develop new models based on the study of female experience,
rather than to adapt male models and theories. Gynocritics
begins at the point when we free ourselves from the linear
absolutes of male literary history, stop trying to fit women
between the lines of the male tradition, and focus instead
on the newly visible world of female culture. This is comparable to the ethnographer's effort to render the experience
of the 'muted' female half of a society, which is described in
Shirley Ardener's collection, *Perceiving Women*.[1] Gynocritics is related to feminist research in history, anthropology,
psychology and sociology, all of which have developed hypotheses of a female subculture including not only the ascribed status, and the internalised constructs of femininity,
but also the occupations, interactions and consciousness of
women. Anthropologists study the female subculture in the
relationships between women, as mothers, daughters, sisters and friends; in sexuality, reproduction and ideas about
the body; and in rites of initiation and passage, purification
ceremonies, myths and taboos. Michelle Rosaldo writes in
Woman, Culture, and Society.

> the very symbolic and social conceptions that appear to set
> women apart and to circumscribe their activities may be
> used by women as a basis for female solidarity and worth.
> When men live apart from women, they in fact cannot con-
> trol them, and unwittingly they may provide them with the
> symbols and social resources on which to build a society of
> their own.[2]

Thus in some women's literature, feminine values penetrate and undermine the masculine systems which contain
them; and women have imaginatively engaged the myths of
the Amazons, and the fantasies of a separate female society,
in genres from Victorian poetry to contemporary science
fiction.

In the past two years, pioneering work by four young American feminist scholars has given us some new ways to interpret the culture of nineteenth-century American women, and the literature which was its primary expressive form. Carroll Smith-Rosenberg's essay. 'The Female World of Love and Ritual' examines several archives of letters between women, and outlines the homosocial emotional world of the nineteenth century. Nancy Cott's *The Bonds of Womanhood: Woman's Sphere in New England 1780–1835* explores the paradox of a cultural bondage, a legacy of pain and submission, which none the less generates a sisterly solidarity, a bond of shared experience, loyalty and compassion. Ann Douglas's ambitious book, *The Feminization of American Culture*, boldly locates the genesis of American mass culture in the sentimental literature of women and clergymen, two allied and 'disestablished' post-industrial groups. These three are social historians; but Nina Auerbach's *Communities of Women: An Idea in Fiction* seeks the bonds of womanhood in women's literature, ranging from the matriarchal households of Louisa May Alcott and Mrs Gaskell to the women's schools and colleges of Dorothy Sayers, Sylvia Plath and Muriel Spark. Historical and literary studies like these, based on English women, are badly needed; and the manuscript and archival sources for them are both abundant and untouched.[3]

Notes

1. Shirley Ardener (ed.), *Perceiving Women* (London, 1975).
2. 'Women, Culture, and Society: A Theoretical Overview' in Louise Lamphere and Michelle Rosaldo (eds), *Women, Culture and Society* (Stanford, 1974), p. 39.
3. Carroll Smith-Rosenberg, 'The Female World of Love and Ritual: Relations Between Women in Nineteenth-Century America', *Signs: Journal of Women in Culture and Society*, vol. i (Autumn 1975), pp. 1–30; Nancy Cott, *The Bonds of Womanhood* (New Haven, 1977); Ann Douglas, *The Feminization of American Culture* (New York, 1977); Nina Auerbach, *Communities of Women* (Cambridge, Mass., 1978).

RACHEL BLAU DUPLESSIS 1941–

☐ During the 1970s and 1980s, feminist criticism continually attacked the gender bias of a literary history constructed largely from texts written by men (the canon). Not surprisingly, this feminist challenge to traditional aesthetic choices has coincided with a challenge to the form of critical writing itself.

DuPlessis's essay was first published in *The Future of Difference* (1980) and is a stunning encounter between autobiography, literary criticism, and feminist theory. She wrote the essay collectively with her students, but DuPlessis has since continually and self-reflexively rewritten the piece using feminist techniques which highlight the writing process and fluid sentences to skewer any 'pure' notion of literary criticism.

The essay juxtaposes entries from her diary together with literary criticism about Virginia Woolf and memories of her graduate life, extracts from Freud and a summary of Etruscan history. The Etruscans stand as a grand metaphor for the exclusion of women's meanings from the canon. The Etruscan script, like women's writing, is *known* in the sense that its vocabulary has been translated, but we lack knowledge about the social and emotional *context* in which it was spoken and written. DuPlessis creates a powerful feminist aesthetic – a fluid, collective mixing of literary genres. ☐

COMMENTARY: E. Showalter (1985), 'Introduction: The Feminist Critical Revolution', in E. Showalter (ed.), *The New Feminist Criticism*, New York: Pantheon.

FOR THE ETRUSCANS [1980]*

Thinking smugly, 'She shouldn't be working on Woolf.'
1964. 'Doesn't she know that she'd better not work on a
woman?' Why was I lucky to know this. What was the
threat? Dickinson? Marginality? Nin? I bought Nin's book,
I threw it out. What! Didn't want it, might confront

> The great difficulties in understanding the language . . . not
> . . . from an ability to read the script, every letter of which is
> now clearly understood. It is as if books were discovered,
> printed in our own Roman letters, so that one could articu-
> late the words without trouble, but written in an unknown
> language with no known parallels.[1]

myself. 1979. The general feeling (of the dream) was that I
was free of the testers. However, I was entirely obligated to
take and pass their test. My relationship to the testers is – ?
1965. My big ambition, my hemmed and nervous space.
Her uncompromising, oracular poems. Her fluid, decisive
writing. Her dream life, surfacing. Not even to read this? to
read with contempt? 'This is a Blossom of the Brain –/A
small – italic Seed' (Dickinson, no. 945).

What is going on here? 1968. Is the female aesthetic
simply an (1978) enabling myth? Fish on one foot, hook on
the other, angling for ourselves. Woolf: catching 'something
about the body.'[2] Crash. MOM! WHAT! 'You never buy
what I like! Only what YOU like!' (Fig Newtons.)

A golden bough. The torch is passed on. His son clutches
his hand, his crippled father clings to his back, three male

*From: Rachel Blau DuPlessis (1990), 'For the Etruscans', from *The Pink Guitar: Writing as Feminist Practice*, London: Routledge.

generations leave the burning city.The wife, lost. Got lost in burning. No one knows what happened to her, when they became the Romans.

She became the Etruscans?

> Even so, there is nothing to prevent those with a special aptitude for cryptography from tackling Etruscan, which is the last of the important languages to require translating.[3]

Sheepish, I am sheepish and embarrassed to mention this

that for me it was always the herding. The herding, the bonding the way you can speak their language but also have a different language or different needs so hard to say this. Always: I have heard this story from many sources – they bond and clump outside your door and never 'ask you to lunch' or they talk and be wonderful, lambent, but when you walk up 'they turn away' or 'they turn on you, teasing, making sexual jokes'

all headed in the same direction, herding and glistening, of course some don't. But it has been difficult for these to separate from the rest. Probably the reward system?

To translate ourselves from our disguises. The enthralled sexuality, the knife-edge brilliance, the intellectual dowdiness, evasions, embarrassments, imprecisions, deferments; smug primness with which there is no dialogue. Combativeness straight into malice. Invisibility, visibility, crossing the legs, uncrossing them. Knights in shining armour. Daddy to the rescue. 'Imposing' sex on the situation. 'Not imposing' 'sex' on the 'situation.' 'Doesn't she know she'd better not work on a woman?' She'd better now work on a woman. 'I bid you take a wisp from the wool of their precious fleece.'[4] The golden fleece. The golden bough. The female quest?

Frankly, it was *The Golden Notebook* (1966). Which pierced my heart with its two-headed arrow.

How to be? How to be-have? I remember one preceptor who brought her little white dog to school and trotted it up and down the fourth floor of Hamilton Hall. What delightful, charming, adorable girls! The temptation of Eve was fruit, of Mary, lambs. Thinking that they followed *you* to school.

Notes

'For the Etruscans' is a shortened and revised version of what was said at Workshop 9, Barnard College, Scholar and Feminist Conference in 1979, and what was published in *The Future of Difference: The Scholar and the Feminist*, ed. Hester Eisenstein and Alice Jardine (Boston: G.K. Hall, 1980). For this text, I have also drawn on the version written for delivery at SUNY-Buffalo early in 1980. I have avoided the anachronistic temptation to alter opinions or to respond to commentary on the work, though I have updated some of the notes.

With special thanks to Carol Ascher, Frances Jaffer, Sara Lennox, Jo Ann McNamara, Lou Roberts, Mira Schor, and Louise Yelin for their own letters and notes on Workshop 9, not all of which are retained in this version of the essay.

My source of inspiration for this kind of writing was Robert Duncan's *H. D. Book* (chapters scattered in little magazines through the past decades), Virginia Woolf's essays, and my own letters. But (and) many people have reinvented the essay.

1. Ellen Macnamara, *Everyday Life of the Etruscans* (London: B.T. Batsford, 1973), p. 181.
2. Virginia Woolf, 'Professions for Women,' *The Death of the Moth and Other Essays* (1942); reprint ed., New York: Harcourt Brace Jovanovich, 1974), p. 240.
3. James Wellard, *The Search for the Etruscans* (New York: Saturday Review Press, 1973), p. 192.
4. The second task of Psyche. See Erich Neumann, *Amor and Psyche: The Psychic Development of the Feminine: A Commentary on the Tale by Apuleius*, trans. Ralph Manheim (1952; reprint ed., Princeton, N.J.: Princeton University Press, 1971). See also Rachel Blau DuPlessis, 'Psyche, or Wholeness,' *Massachusetts Review* 20 (Spring 1979): 77–96.

17 □ Feminism and education

Introduction

□ A main aim of second wave feminism is to make visible the omission of women from most organised forms of knowledge, such as the academic disciplines. This created a surge of interest in the politics of knowledge. In Britain educational institutions must not contravene the Sex Discrimination Act (1975) but not one complaint of sex discrimination was upheld in the first fifteen years of the Act's history, although boys are clearly given greater attention, greater scope and encouraged to reach higher levels of education than are girls. So that the rise of feminist socialisation theory, which focuses on the sociopsychological processes boys and girls go through in the home, in curriculum choices, and through the sexual division of labour in schools, has direct political consequences. Feminist research in education brought the issue of discrimination explosively into the foreground by mapping the impact of misogynist institutions and educational policies on women and on men.

In the now classic account of women's education – *A Vindication of the Rights of Woman* – Mary Wollstonecraft argued that a woman's proper use of reason was an important means of her citizenship. In *Three Guineas* Virginia Woolf described the value of a separatist women's college. In the academy, women's studies is the place where the sexist and racist structures of society are critically examined and where new ways of thinking and new forms of social action can be explored. In women's studies feminists, alongside academic feminists in other disciplines, created new scholarship about gender and new models of teaching and learning *with* women. Today feminists agree that because educational hierarchies are systems of power, only collective work which focuses on women's experiences and needs is likely to produce useful knowledge. Currently the multiplicity of feminist learning in settings outside formal institutions, for example in women's arts and video centres, black women's centres, health centres, and adult education, as well as in the academy, makes possible a vital and autonomous women's education. □

COMMENTARY: M.J. Boxer (1982), 'For and About Women: The Theory and Practice of Women's Studies in the United States', in N.O. Keohane *et al.* (eds) *Feminist Theory*, Brighton: Harvester.

ADRIENNE RICH 1929–

☐ Adrienne Rich's 'Toward a Woman-Centered University' powerfully argues the case, first described by Virginia Woolf in *Three Guineas*, that the knowledge creation, content and processes of education must focus on women. Rich describes a model institution where hierarchies will give way to collective work, shared by secretaries and cleaners as well as by academics; where research oriented to and controlled by government, industry and defence will give way to health and community concerns, and where the border between the academy and the outside world will cease to exist. The catalyst for change will be women's studies because women's studies can create new constituencies of learners and become the womb for feminist research. Rich attacks the ways in which education is used as a weapon of colonialisation. Only feminist pedagogy, Rich claims, can legitimate personal experience and begin to change the reproduction of knowledge in academic institutions and the content and priorities of research.

Rich takes feminism to mean, depending on its direction, two very different things. On the one hand, feminism is something very affective, an emotional sisterhood. On the other it is the cognate celebration of women's history, achievements and language. Feminist education, therefore, includes not just the study of women's topics but an acknowledgement of that relationship suppressed by the academy – of women-affiliated-women. ☐

COMMENTARY: M. Humm (1986), *Feminist Criticism: Women as Contemporary Critics*, Brighton: Harvester.

EXTRACT

TOWARD A WOMAN-CENTERED UNIVERSITY [1973]*

The hidden assumptions on which the university is built comprise more than simply a class system. In a curious and insidious way the 'work' of a few men – especially in the more scholarly and prestigious institutions – becomes a sacred value in whose name emotional and economic exploitation of women is taken for granted. The distinguished professor may understandably like comfort and even luxury and his ego requires not merely a wife and secretary but an au pair girl, teaching assistant, programmer, and student mistress; but the justification for all this service is the almost religious concept of 'his work.' (Those few women who rise to the top of their professions seem in general to get along with less, to get their work done along with the cooking, personal laundry, and mending without the support of a retinue.) In other words, the structure of the man-centered university constantly reaffirms *the use of women as means* to the end of male 'work' – meaning male careers and professional success. Professors of Kantian ethics or Marxist criticism are no more exempt from this exploitation of women than are professors of military science or behavioral psychology. In its very structure, then, the university encourages women to continue perceiving themselves as means and not as ends – as indeed their whole socialization has done.

[. . .]

I have described the kinds of ad hoc teaching that might take place under university auspices. As a research institution, it should organize its resources around problems specific to its community; for example, adult literacy; public

*From: Adrienne Rich (1980), 'Toward a Woman-Centered University', in *On Lies, Secrets, Silence: Selected Prose 1966–1978*, London: Virago.

health; safer, cheaper, and simpler birth control; drug addiction; community action; geriatrics and the sociology and psychology of aging and death; the history and problems of women and those of people in nonwhite, non-middle-class cultures; urban (or rural) adolescence; public architecture; child development and pediatrics; urban engineering with the advice and consent of the engineered; folk medicine; the psychology, architecture, economics, and diet of prisons; union history; the economics of the small farmer – the possibilities would vary from place to place. The 'community' is probably a misleading term. In fact, most large urban universities have many communities. The 'community' around Columbia University, for example, is not simply black and Puerto Rican, but white middle-class, poor and aged, Jewish, Japanese, Cuban, etc. A sympathetic and concerned relationship with all these groups would involve members of the university in an extremely rich cluster of problems. And the nature of much research (and its usefulness) might be improved if it were conceived as research *for*, rather than *on*, human beings.

[. . .]

It is likely that in the immediate future various alternatives will be explored. Women's studies programs, where they are staffed by feminists, will serve as a focus for feminist values even in a patriarchal context. Even where staffed largely by tokenists, their very existence will make possible some rising consciousness in students. Already, alternate feminist institutes are arising to challenge the curriculum of established institutions.[1] Feminists may use the man-centered university as a base and resource while doing research and writing books and articles whose influence will be felt far beyond the academy. Consciously woman-centered universities – in which women shape the philosophy and the decision making though men may choose to study and teach there – may evolve from existing institutions. Whatever the forms it may take, the process of women's repossession of ourselves is irreversible. Within and without academe, the rise in women's expectations has gone far beyond the middle class and has released an incalculable new energy – not merely for changing institutions but for human redefinition; not merely for equal rights but for a kind of being.

Note

1. A. R. 1978. For example, the Feminist Studio Workshop in Los Angeles, the Sagaris Institute, the Maiden Rock Institute in Minnesota, the projected Feminist Art Institute in New York.

MARCIA WESTKOTT 1943–

☐ From the first British Women's Studies course run by Juliet Mitchell at the Anti-University in 1968–9 and the first American courses at San Diego State University and the Free University of Chicago, Anglo-American women's studies has grown to over 30,000 courses. The 1970s and 1980s have seen an equally rapid growth in new forms of research, and new teaching methods many of which adopted consciousness-raising techniques from the Women's Movement. The American sociologist Marcia Westkott was one of the first critics to indicate how feminism might revolutionise the disciplines. She argues that a feminist perspective of education is not simply an academic view but an educational strategy for social change.

Westkott describes how the methods, content and aims of traditional social sciences marginalise women. She focuses on the contradictory position of feminist scholarship which is both 'inside' and 'outside' disciplines. Westkott argues that feminist research is *for* women rather than about women. She describes forms of thinking and research which derive from affinities between people, between subject and object, between past and future and, most importantly, between theory and practice. Westkott calls this 'intersubjectivity' which will oppose the traditional binary divisions in the sciences. Westkott calls for action research and 'conscious subjectivity' so that women's studies can be a feminist powerhouse, creating a symbiosis between women's studies and the women's liberation movement. ☐

COMMENTARY: F. Maher (1983), 'Classroom Pedagogy and the New Scholarship on Women', in M. Culley and C. Portuges (eds), *Gendered Subjects: The Dynamics of Feminist Teaching*, London: Routledge.

WOMEN'S STUDIES AS A STRATEGY FOR CHANGE: BETWEEN CRITICISM AND VISION [1983]*

The development of this feminist critical approach to knowledge begins with an awareness of our relationship to the historical contexts in which we live. Those who teach Women's Studies courses are familiar with the process of developing this awareness. It begins with the fact that in Women's Studies courses women students are no longer studying material that is totally outside themselves, but are learning about the ways in which their social contexts have shaped them as women. In this process social knowledge and self-knowledge become mutually informing. Not only can students illuminate knowledge of themselves through understanding their social contexts, but also they can test interpretations of their social contexts from the perspectives of their own experience. For them the personal becomes intellectual, and the intellectual, personal.[1]

The great possibility of such courses where knowledge of the social world becomes personalized is the chance of connecting psyche and history. These are the moments when we discover that buried parts of ourselves are held in common with others. These 'experiences of consciousness-in-history' are exciting not only because they reveal to us knowledge of ourselves that we have buried and 'forgotten,' but also because they link us to others through the experiences that we hold in common. To study the history of women, especially as it is recorded through the consciousness of women themselves, is to set the opportunity for discovering how one's life experiences are connected to those of other women. Psyche and history are thus joined in

*From: Marcia Westkott (1983) 'Women's Studies as a strategy for change: between criticism and vision', in G.B. Bowles and R. Duelli-Klein (eds), *Theories of Women's Studies*, London: Routledge.

the discovery of the ways that one's personal life has been shaped by being born a woman.

[...]

We know from our classes in Women's Studies the importance of pushing our criticism past itself to the visions that the criticism suggests. Unless we do that, we offer no hope for directing the anger that is often generated by the critical awareness, and we are left with paralyzing fury or hopeless resignation ('Is this another moan course?', a Women's Studies major asked on the first day of class). To push beyond criticism, however, is not to relinquish it, but to hold it in tension with vision. The criticism indicates to us an absence or a problem which our imagination can transcend. This transcendence is a visionary transformation of the conditions which we oppose, a new world view rather than a mere extension or rearrangement of present structures. Feminist vision is thus, not a feasibility study, but an imaginative leap that stands opposed to sexist society. As negations of the conditions that we criticize, visions both reflect those conditions and oppose them. In the words of Josephine Donovan, 'The feminist critic is thus on the cutting edge of the dialectic. She must, in a sense, be Janus-headed: engaged in negations that yield transcendences' (1975, p. 80).

By engaging in 'negations that yield transcendence' our Women's Studies classes are 'educational strategies' for change. First, by articulating that which we oppose and by envisioning alternative futures, we identify the goals and strategies for action; that is, we clarify what it is we want to move *away from* as well as what it is we want to move *toward*. Change is thus informed by purpose and goal. Second, through the classroom process itself we create changes in the forms of learning: in student-teacher relationship, in the personal-intellectual mediation, in the dialogue and negotiations from which critical perspectives and transcending visions emerge. In the processes of creating these changes in the classroom itself, we not only produce models for other contexts, but also learn about processes for creating feminist change. We learn, for example, that criticism and vision are not static ideations but are related in a continuing mediation in which they themselves are changed. Hence, the very processes of creating alternative possibilities changes the way in which we understand the problems we criticize; and to the extent that we realize our visions, the problems themselves will be transformed.

[. . .]

And yet, criticizing this compromise taken by some academic women does not remove the underlying dilemma that women in the academy face. To have a woman-centered university (Rich, 1979) requires at the very least having women in the university, and beyond that, having women in positions of power to make changes for women. To criticize the culture, history, and procedures that undergird the institution through whose ranks we seek to advance, and to expect that our criticism will be accepted as a valid means to that advancement, is to face a tough problem, indeed. How we personally mediate the various contradictions inherent in this problem cannot be prescribed, but emerges from our own commitments and needs as well as the conditions that we face.[2] Whatever the specific risks and compromises that we may choose, whether we leave the academy or attempt to advance or survive within it, the goal of creating change *for* women guides us in our struggle.

Notes

1. See, for example, Rutenberg, 'Learning Women's Studies,' this volume Chapter 5.
2. A collective strategy is no less complex, but it does create power in union that may be lacking in individual rank. For an excellent analysis of an example of successful campus organizing, see Karen Childers, Phillis Rackin, Cynthia Secor, and Carol Tracy, 'A Network of One's Own,' unpublished paper.

GLORIA HULL (1944–) and BARBARA SMITH (1946–)

☐ Although Alice Walker taught the first American course on black women at Wellesley College twenty years ago in 1972, white feminist academics, as much as the traditional academy, often ignore black and lesbian experiences and politics. *But Some of Us* (1982) is the first feminist collection to give full attention to black women in education. As the pioneers of black women's studies Gloria Hull and Barbara Smith, who are poets and literary critics, argue that it is possible to move feminist theory out of the academy and into the larger world of social praxis. The book provides that space between the centre and the margins by including accounts by many black women students, teachers, writers, and community workers which challenge the monolithic academy. Hull and Smith argue that a black women's studies curriculum offers a way out of the power hierarchies of traditional education because it addresses a wide variety of issues in black experience: black women's intellectual traditions, black women's special relationship with the community, maternal histories, and issues of naming and health. Black feminists know that they must first place the subjectivities of black women into education before they can contest the black female stereotypes, created by traditional teaching. A primary goal of black women's studies then is to construct a black women's intellectual tradition and to fight the sexist and racist erasure of black female ideas and political struggles.

Black women's studies offer all women a 'different' view of themselves and their world from that put forward by the dominant culture, because, uniquely, it teaches women to think differently about the social construction of gender when women know about the racial as well as sexist biases which shape that construction. In coalitions, both academic and activist, feminist studies can develop new models of social change. ☐

COMMENTARY: P.H. Collins (1990), *Black Feminist Thought*, London: Unwin Hyman.

EXTRACT

THE POLITICS OF BLACK WOMEN'S STUDIES [1982]*

Merely to use the term 'Black women's studies' is an act charged with political significance. At the very least, the combining of these words to name a discipline means taking the stance that Black women exist – and exist positively – a stance that is in direct opposition to most of what passes for culture and thought on the North American continent. To use the term and to act on it in a white-male world is an act of political courage.

Like any politically disenfranchised group, Black women could not exist consciously until we began to name ourselves. The growth of Black women's studies is an essential aspect of that process of naming. The very fact that Black women's studies describes something that is really happening, a burgeoning field of study, indicates that there are political changes afoot which have made possible that growth. To examine the politics of Black women's studies means to consider not only what it is but why it is and what it can be. Politics is used here in its widest sense to mean any situation/relationship of differential power between groups or individuals.

[. . .]

Only a Black *and* feminist analysis can sufficiently comprehend the materials of Black women's studies; and only a creative Black feminist perspective will enable the field to expand. A viable Black feminist movement will also lend its political strength to the development of Black women's studies courses, programs, and research, and to the funding they require. Black feminism's total commitment to the liberation of Black women and its recognition of Black

*From: Gloria T. Hull and Barbara Smith (1982), 'The Politics of Black Women's Studies', in G.T. Hull, P. Bell Scott and B. Smith (eds) *All the Women Are White, All the Blacks Are Men, But Some of Us Are Brave: Black Women's Studies*, New York: Feminist Press.

women as valuable and complex human beings will provide the analysis and spirit for the most incisive work on Black women. Only a feminist, pro-woman perspective that acknowledges the reality of sexual oppression in the lives of Black women, as well as the oppression of race and class, will make Black women's studies the transformer of consciousness it needs to be.

Women's studies began as a radical response to feminists' realization that knowledge of ourselves has been deliberately kept from us by institutions of patriarchal 'learning.' Unfortunately, as women's studies has become both more institutionalized and at the same time more precarious within traditional academic structures, the radical life-changing vision of what women's studies can accomplish has constantly been diminished in exchange for acceptance, respectability, and the career advancement of individuals. This trend in women's studies is a trap that Black women's studies cannot afford to fall into. Because we are so oppressed as Black women, every aspect of our fight for freedom, including teaching and writing about ourselves, must in some way further our liberation. Because of the particular history of Black feminism in relation to Black women's studies, especially the fact that the two movements are still new and have evolved nearly simultaneously, much of the current teaching, research, and writing about Black women is not feminist, is not radical, and unfortunately is not always even analytical. Naming and describing our experience are important initial steps, but not alone sufficient to get us where we need to go. A descriptive approach to the lives of Black women, a 'great Black women' in history or literature approach, or any traditional male-identified approach will not result in intellectually groundbreaking or politically transforming work. We cannot change our lives by teaching solely about 'exceptions' to the ravages of white-male oppression. Only through exploring the experience of supposedly 'ordinary' Black women whose 'unexceptional' actions enabled us and the race to survive, will we be able to begin to develop an overview and an analytical framework for understanding the lives of Afro-American women.

Courses that focus on issues which concretely and materially affect Black women are ideally what Black women's studies/feminist studies should be about. Courses should examine such topics as the sexual violence we suffer in our own communities; the development of Black feminist economic analysis that will reveal for the first time Black women's relationship to American capitalism; the situation of Black women in prison and the connection between their incarceration and our own; the social history of Black women's domestic work; and the investigation of Black women's mental and physical health in a society whose 'final solution' for us and our children is death.

[...]

To do the work involved in creating Black women's studies requires not only intellectual intensity, but the deepest courage. Ideally, this is passionate and committed research, writing, and teaching whose purpose is to question everything. Coldly 'objective' scholarship that changes nothing is not what we strive for. 'Objectivity' is itself an example of the reification of white-male thought. What could be less objective than the totally white-male studies which are still considered 'knowledge'? Everything that human beings participate in is ultimately subjective and biased, and there is nothing inherently wrong with that. The bias that Black women's studies must consider as primary is the knowledge that will save Black women's lives.

In conclusion

☐ Feminist research comes from the need of feminists for information about discrimination, their need for techniques they can acquire to catalogue women's social discrimination, and their need to create policies to help eradicate that discrimination. Feminist researchers have created new terms for social issues hitherto ignored or 'misnamed'. Verbal and physical hostility towards women is now identified as 'sexual harassment'. The all too casual stereotyping of gay men and women is now identified as 'homophobia'. The economic disadvantages experienced by women ghettoised in the workplace, receiving inadequate pay for more than equal work is now called 'the sexual division of labour', and the imbalance between male and female earnings is now called the 'gender gap'. Just as the economic disadvantages experienced by women home workers and carers, by women late returners and underskilled women can now be explained by theories of 'reserve armies'. These terms and concepts and the knowledge and thinking which lies behind their invention owes much to feminism(s).

In addition the idea that a collective sharing of experiences – of histories and activities, linked to the community concerns (whether of battered women or street safety) which caused women to meet collectively – can be called research is also feminism(s).

The development of Afro-centric feminist thought and the distinctive standpoints which lesbians, black and white, have created all extend our histories and agencies. Asian and Afro-centric women's politics reveal fresh insights about multiple oppressions and the dynamics which oppose these, for example the long tradition of sisterhood in non-white communities. Lesbian thinkers describe the 'lesbian continuum' of women's friendships long extant historically. Both have identified further terms to describe and combat this greater range of discriminations, for example 'neither/nor', 'womanism', 'creative coalitions'.

The notion that any Reader should have a single summary or conclusion to make about the forms of feminist knowledge and the processes which create that knowledge is clearly impossible. The title *Feminisms* itself is ambiguous. It can refer to either the ideas of self-declared feminists or be a collective noun describing the processes available to any woman when coming to understand and to contest her gendered identity and situation. My reasoning was that ambiguity matters less than refusing to flag a single body of ideas or dogma. Recognising diversity necessarily involves ambiguity. The title is deliberately 'either/or'. However, *Feminisms* does suggest an important focus on the *politics* of women's ideas and practices. Historically people and movements have been called feminist when they recognised the connections between social inequalities, deprivations and oppressions and gender differences. Currently feminists are pursuing questions about the consequences for women and for men when gender oppressions intersect with other forms of oppression – with homophobia, classism, ageism, disability and racism.

Feminisms are the thoughts, practices, critical moments and writings in which feminists engage in their attempts to confront these consequences and to change them. The multiplicity of the term is needed to help us challenge the multi/duplicity of sexist assumptions and sexist constructions which surround us everywhere. *Feminisms* is an ongoing and continuously significant area of thinking here partially, but I hope happily, caught for a moment between two book covers, in order that we can study the ideas of a huge variety of very gifted women.   □

Glossary

☐ **Abolitionist feminism**: One of the main theories of nineteenth-century feminism. It took the view that woman's oppression and emancipation paralleled the struggle for black liberation from slavery.

Affirmative action: Affirmative action dates from the programme introduced by President Lyndon Johnson in 1964 prohibiting employment discrimination. The programme requires contractors to establish measurable integration goals and timetables in order to achieve equal opportunity regardless of race, colour, religion, sex or national origin.

Anarchist feminism: A theory that female subordination is determined as much by a system of sexual and familial relationships as by state controls, and that legal change cannot in itself provide equality without full psychological independence.

Androcentrism: Male centredness, which is the value set of our dominant culture based on male norms.

Androgyny: Greek word from andro (male) and gyn (female) which means a psychological and psychic mixture of traditional masculine and feminine virtues. The first feminist theories of androgyny described a hybrid model. For example Elizabeth Cady Stanton in *The Women's Bible* (1895 and 1898) describes the Heavenly Being as androgynous.

Biological determinism: The concept that physiological differences between men and women determine social roles. This concept is the basis of discriminatory legislation which prohibits women from full expression of their potential.

Black feminism: The theory of black-defined women's struggles. Black feminists argue that all feminist theory must understand imperialism and challenge it.

Canon: A term for the list of literary *master*pieces in traditional literary studies. The canon is an informal institution of literature whose specific inclusions and exclusions, deletions and exceptions are nowhere codified.

Capitalist patriarchy: An historically specific form of patriarchy in which patriarchy operates through class and productive relations. The subordination of women is shaped by specific modes of production.

Chicana theory: The culture of women of Mexican ancestry.

Christian feminism: Feminist theories of Christianity fall into three categories: those that challenge the theological view of women and the androcentricity of traditional theology; those that challenge the theological laws that bar women from ordination; those that evaluate the church as an institution and aim to upgrade the professional status of women in the church.

Class: People of the same social and economic level. Existing concepts of class, whether they are formations in history or categories of occupation and social groupings, are inappropriate for feminism. Socialist feminists argue that a full social analysis must accommodate both class and gender. They claim that the category of female interacts in a complex way with class but never overlaps it completely.

Compulsory heterosexuality: A term in radical and lesbian theory for the enforcement of heterosexuality. It includes the ideological and political control of women's sexuality.

Consciousness raising (CR): A form of verbal self examination taking place with the support and collaboration of other women in small groups.

Cultural feminism: Feminist theory which is dedicated to creating a separate and radical women's culture.

Culture: The symbolic realm of the arts. Feminist theory extends the definition to include all symbolic products of society. This frees women from being defined by the expression 'subculture'. Feminist historians use the term culture to refer to the broad-based commonality of values, institutions and relationships focusing on the domesticity and morality of late eighteenth-century and nineteenth-century women.

Difference: A necessary polarity between women and men and between women. Feminists define difference politically not simply in terms of sexual categories.
Defining difference has been the single greatest contribution of second wave feminism to theory. Difference has two senses in feminism. A primary meaning is that women have a different voice, a different psychology and a different experience of love, work and the family from men. Difference also means a negative category which includes the exclusion and subordination of women.

Discipline: A field of study. Feminist research examines the sets of assumptions around which the academic disciplines ask questions and form conclusions and the way each discipline has its own language and way of ordering the world.

Discourse: The relation between language and social reality.

Division of labour: An exploitative relation in society and in economic production.

Domestic labour: The way in which women regenerate labour power for capitalism by servicing the home and socialising their families.

Double consciousness: The way women inhabit the world – in and of society but in important ways not 'of' it. Women see and think in terms of culture yet have always consciousness, another potential language.

Écriture Féminine: The term for women's writing in French feminist theory. 'Feminine' linguistics are characterised by simultaneity, plurality and mobility. By stressing the *metaphors* of sexual desire, *écriture féminine* is not a question of physical biology, but is instead a fundamental epistemological *and* historical form.

Epistemology: The theory of knowledge.

Essentialism: The belief in a unique female nature.

Ethnicity: In anthropology ethnicity characterises the culture of a distinctive, sometimes racially distinct, group. Feminist anthropologists are concerned about the arbitrariness of race categories and that, whatever the system of classification, women often remain a 'muted' group.

Eurocentric or ethnocentric: A way of thinking which is unable to see difference and which universalises all values and ideas from the subject's experience of her own white ethnic group. Eurocentricity creates models which leave no room for validating the actual struggles and experiences of black and Third World women.

Family wage: Men's income, paid on the assumption that men are the only or major economic support of families.

Female: This is a term reserved in feminist theory for the purely biological aspect of sexual difference with 'feminine' as the term for the social construction of women. This avoids the deliberate confusion of these terms by patriarchy which constructs female as the binary opposite of male.

Feminine: French theorists argue that the term feminine is an arbitrary category given to women's appearance or behaviour by patriarchy.

Feminism: The definition incorporates both a doctrine of equal rights for women (the organised movement to attain women's rights) and an ideology of social transformation aiming to create a world for women beyond simple social equality.

First wave: Sometimes known as 'old wave', the term usually refers to the mobilisation of the Suffrage movement in America and England between 1890 and 1920, although an organised 'feminist' movement for women's suffrage had existed for forty years earlier.

Functionalism: The theory that every social institution or practice has a function in maintaining the social process.

Gender: A culturally shaped group of attributes and behaviours given to the female or to the male. Contemporary feminist theory is careful to distinguish between sex and gender.

Gynocentric: The sharing of certain kinds of women-centred beliefs and women-centred social organisations.

Heterosexism: This term refers to the unconscious or explicit assumption that heterosexuality is the only 'normal' mode of sexual and social relations. Feminist theorists agree that heterosexuality, as an institution and as an ideology, is a cornerstone of patriarchy.

Hispanic: Cherrie Moraga calls Hispanic theory a 'rite of passage' because it comes to terms with community, racism and internal colonialisation.

Ideology: A feminist ideology is a body of ideas which describes the sexism of any particular society and describes a future society in which sexist contradictions would be eradicated.

Identity: Feminist theories of identity have moved from neo-Freudian psychoanalysis and current poststructuralist theory. Feminists argue that identity is not the goal but rather the point of departure of any process of self-consciousness. They suggest that women's understanding of identity is multiple and even self-contradictory.

Imaginary: A concept in French feminist theory which stands for female strength and identity.

Inequality: A social model of female inequality has been outlined by Michelle Rosaldo. She defines inequality as a state where women are universally subordinate to men; where men are dominant due to their participation in public life and their relegation of women to the domestic sphere. The differential participation of men and women in public life gives rise not only to universal male authority over women but to a higher valuation of male over female roles.

Knowledge: The traditional organisation of ideas which is attacked by feminists in all disciplines. Feminist theory pays attention to women's different ideas especially the way in which feminist knowledge is constructed through the interaction of the self and the natural world. Within feminism social knowledge and self-knowledge become mutually informing and Marcia Westkott suggests that feminist knowledge begins with an awareness of our relationship to the historical context in which we live.

Lesbian feminism: A belief that women-identified women, committed together for political, sexual and economic support, provide an alternative model to male–female relations which lesbians see as oppressive.

Liberal feminism: The theory of individual freedom for women. Liberal feminism is one of the main streams of feminist political and social theory and has the most long-term history.

Liberation: The liberation of women is the chief goal of feminist theory. Contemporary women's liberation, or feminist action, is consciously revolutionary. It breaks with reformism, it is internationalist; and it simultaneously attacks the state, cultural ideology and the economy.

Marxist feminism: The aims of Marxist feminism are: to describe the material basis of women's subjugation, and the relationship between the modes of production and women's status; and to apply theories of women and class to the role of the family.

Matriarchy: A form of society in which mothers are leaders and operate a women's descent line. Ideologically matriarchy assumes that the power of maternal energy and mother love is a socially cohesive force.

Metaphysical feminism: Feminist theory which believes that one woman's experience can be all women's experience. Metaphysical feminism takes an extreme woman-centred perspective and encourages women to make spiritual journeys rather than political ones.

Nature: Since the exploitation of nature is a major feature of patriarchal capitalism, defining a feminist concept of nature is a central task for feminism. Feminists argue that a new definition of nature will provide the rationale and impetus for social or political strategies and goals.

Nonaligned feminism: A term coined by Charlotte Bunch to describe the perspective of *Quest* contributors and what she thinks should be the aim of the women's movement. Nonaligned feminism involves a genuine commitment to cross-cultural, and cross-political analysis.

Objectification: Sexual objectification is the primary form of the subjection of women, Catharine MacKinnon argues, which she calls the male epistemological stance. There is no distinction, for women, between objectification and alienation.

Pacifism: There are several concepts of nonviolence and ideas about the relation of militarism and gender in contemporary feminism. For example, feminism both campaigns for a demilitarised world and argues that military practices depend on degraded definitions of womanhood – definitions based on women's second-class citizenship and sexual exploitation.

Paradigm: A term for scientific perspective coined by Thomas Khun in *The Structure of Scientific Revolutions* (1962). Scientific revolutions, according to Kuhn, involve shifts in paradigms. The goal of radical feminist analysis is to change consciousness through paradigm shifts which redescribe reality.

Patriarchy: A system of male authority which oppresses women through its social, political and economic institutions. In any of the historical forms that patriarchal society takes, whether it is feudal, capitalist or socialist, a sex/gender system and a system of economic discrimination operate simultaneously. Patriarchy has power from men's greater access to, and mediation of, the resources and rewards of authority structures inside and outside the home.

Phallocentric: A term in feminist theory used to describe the way society regards the phallus or penis as a symbol of power, and believes that attributes of masculinity are the norm for cultural definitions. The phallocentric fallacy in disciplines is the assumption that 'person' stands for male and therefore that women's experience has made no contribution to disciplinary methods or content.

Positive discrimination: Positive discrimination (and its successors affirmative action and comparable worth) is defined by governments in terms of social and legal provision designed to eradicate areas of sexual inequality.

Praxis: Feminist theologians define praxis as the struggle to unite theory and practice in action and reflection upon the world in order to transform it for women.

Radical feminism: Radical feminism argues that women's oppression comes from being categorised as an inferior class to the class 'men' on the basis of gender. Radical feminism aims to destroy this sex class system. What makes this feminism radical is that it focuses on the roots of male domination and claims that all forms of oppression are extensions of male supremacy. Radical feminism argues that patriarchy is the defining characteristic of our society.

Representation: Feminism, alongside semiology and Marxism, has made a complex appraisal of representation, or the construction of images. The term 'representation' or 'signification' includes *processes* by which meanings are produced. Feminists argue that representation continually creates, endorses, or alters ideas of gender identity.

Reproduction: There are two meanings of reproduction in feminist theory: the processes of intergenerational reproduction and the reproduction of daily life in the maintenance and socialisation activities of the home; and, second, the socially mediated processes of biological reproduction and sexuality.

Second wave: A term coined by Marsha Weinman Lear to refer to the formation of women's liberation groups in America, Britain and Germany in the late 1960s. The term 'second wave' implies that 'first wave' feminism ended in the 1920.

Separatism: The belief that women will only develop their own strengths if separated from male-dominated institutions. There are two main uses of the term 'separatism' in feminist theory which can be summed up in the difference between the socialist feminist concept of alternative institutions and the radical feminist concept of a womanculture.

Sexual identity: A sense of one's own sexuality. Feminist theory argues that this identity is culturally rather than biologically determined, for example that it represents only the public presentation of sexual aims and objectives as integrated into the personality.

Sex difference: With the re-emergence of feminism in the 1960s, feminist psychology developed theories about sexual inequality and difference. The term refers to a body of research which covers a broad spectrum, beginning with differences between the sexes in attitudes and abilities and research finding the origins of these in terms of sex role socialisation.

Sexual politics: The political character of sexuality which is based on the unequal power of sexual relations. A major premise of feminist theory is that sexual politics supports patriarchy in its politicisation of the personal life.

Socialist feminism: One of the main theories of Western feminism, socialist feminism believes that women are second-class citizens in patriarchal capitalism which depends for its survival on the exploitation of working people, and on the special exploitation of women.

Spiritual feminism: Sometimes called myth feminism, this is a growing area of feminist theory. The ecology of myth described by critics such as Carol Christ, Mary Daly and Charlene Spretnak involves the construction of cultural archetypes of power useful to women and psychological tools which can enable women to articulate desire through symbols and rituals.

Symbolic: In French feminist theory symbolic means the language system of patriarchy. Using techniques drawn from linguistics and psychoanalysis writers such as Hélène Cixous and Luce Irigaray argue that the symbolic represents not only a form of language but a way of thinking and ordering the world to the benefit of men. Opposed to the symbolic is the feminine semiotic or the representation of mother–child relations.

Woman-centredness: The term defines that branch in feminist theory which is based on a notion of women's difference and which argues for the creation of a holistic world culture. Woman-centredness argues that female experience ought to be a prime topic of study and a source of values for culture as a whole.

Womanism: The term now implies black feminism.

Women's liberation: The name of the contemporary women's movement which was adopted by feminists in the 1960s, in a conscious effort to avoid earlier connotations of 'the woman question'.

Acknowledgements

The editor and publishers acknowledge with thanks permission granted to reproduce in this volume the following material previously published elsewhere. Every effort has been made to trace copyright holders, but if any have been inadvertently overlooked the publishers will be pleased to make the necessary arrangement at the first opportunity.

From *Sociological Inquiry*, 44 (1) © 1974; excerpts from 'Women's Perspective as a Radical Critique', by Dorothy Smith. By permission of the University of Texas Press. Gilligan, Carol, 'Woman's Place in Man's Life Cycle', *Harvard Educational Review*, 49 (4): 431–46. Copyright © 1979 by the President and Fellows of Harvard College. All rights reserved. From Joyce Ladner, *Tomorrow's Tomorrow*. Copyright © Doubleday a division of Bantam, Doubleday, Dell Publishing Group, Inc. From Amina Mama 'Black Women, the Economic Crisis and the British State', *Feminist Review* (1984) 17: 23–5. From Amina Mama, 'Violence Against Black Women: Gender, Race and State Response', *Feminist Review* (1989) 32: 31–48. From Carol Gilligan, *In A Different Voice*, (1982), by permission of Harvard University Press. From *Abortion and Woman's Choice: The State, Sexuality, and Reproductive Freedom* by Rosalind Pollack Petchesky, Copyright © 1984 by Rosalind Pollack Petchesky. Reprinted with the permission of North Eastern University Press. From *The Radical Future of Liberal Feminism* by Zillah R. Eisenstein. Copyright © 1981 by Zillah R. Eisenstein. Reprinted with the permission of North Eastern University Press. From Sarah Kofman, *The Enigma of Woman* (1985). By permission of Cornell University Press. From Audre Lorde, *Sister Outsider*. Copyright © 1984 by Audre Lorde. Printed with the permission of the Charlotte Sheady Literary Agency, Inc. From Barbara Smith, *Toward a Black Feminist Criticism*. Copyright © 1977 by Barbara Smith. Printed with the permission of the Crossing Press, Freedom, CA, USA. From Betty Friedan, *The Feminine Mystique* (1963). Printed with the permission of W.W. Norton and Co. From Michèle Barrett, *Women's Oppression Today* (1981) by permission of Verso. From *Feminist Aesthetics*, Gisela Ecker (editor) published by the Women's Press, London, 1985. From Andrea Dworkin, *Pornography*, published by the Women's Press, London, 1981. By permission of the Women's Press. From Julia Kristeva, *Desire in Language*. Copyright © 1982 Columbia University Press. Used by permission. From Gloria Anzaldúa 'La Prieta' Mitsuye Yamada 'Asian Pacific American Women', Rosario Morales 'I Am What I Am', Combahee River Collective 'What We Believe'. From *This Bridge Called My Back* (eds) C. Moraga and G. Anzaldúa (1981, 1983). Used by permission of Kitchen Table: Women of Color Press, P.O. Box 908, Latham, NY 12110. Excerpts from *Sexual Politics* by Kate Millett, Copyright © 1969, 1970 by Kate Millett. Used by permission of Doubleday, a division of Bantam, Doubleday, Dell Publishing Group, Inc. and by permission of Virago Press. From Sheila Rowbotham, *Dreams and Dilemmas* (1983). By permission of Virago Press. From Vera Brittain and Winifred Holtby, *Testament of a Generation* (1985), by permission of Virago Press. From Ray Strachey, *The Cause* (1979), by permission of Virago Press. From Jane Marcus, *The Young Rebecca* (1983), by permission of Virago Press. From Olive Schreiner, *Woman and Labour* (1978), by permission of Virago Press. From Adrienne Rich, *On Lies, Secrets and Silence* (1980), by permission of Virago Press. From Adrienne Rich, *Of Woman Born* (1977), by permission of Virago Press. From *Women and Madness*, Harcourt Brace Jovanovich NY/Calif. with amendments 1989. By kind permission of the author Phyllis Chesler. From Teresa de Lauretis, *Alice Doesn't: Feminism, Semiotics, Cinema* (1984). By permission of Macmillan Press. From Laura Mulvey, *Visual and Other Pleasures* (1989), by permission of Macmillan Press. By kind permission of the author. By permission of *Screen*, John Logie Baird Centre. From Alice Walker, *In Search of Our Mothers' Gardens*, Harcourt, Brace Jovanovich (1983). By permission of the Wendy Weil Agency Inc. From *Psychoanalysis and Feminism*, by Juliet Mitchell. Copyright © 1974 by Juliet Mitchell. Reprinted by permission of Pantheon Books, a Division of Random House Inc. and Penguin Books Ltd. From *The Nature and Evolution of Female Sexuality*, by Mary Jane Sherfey, M.D. Copyright © 1966, 1972 by Mary Jane Sherfey. Reprinted by permission of Random House, Inc. From *Women, Race and Class*, by Angela Davis. Copyright © 1981 by Angela Davis. Reprinted by permission of Random House Inc. Excerpt from *The Mermaid and the Minotaur* by Dorothy Dinnerstein. Copyright © 1976 by Dorothy Dinnerstein. Reprinted by permission of Harper & Row, Publishers, Inc. From C. Vance (ed.) *Pleasure and Danger* (1984). By permission of Routledge & Kegan Paul. Excerpt from Marcia Westkott, 'Women's Studies as a Strategy for Change: Between Criticism and Vision', in G. Bowles and R. Duelli Klein, *Theories of Women's Studies* (1983). By permission of Routledge & Kegan Paul. From R. Coward 'Are Women's Novels Feminist Novels?', *Feminist Review*, N5 (1980). By permission of Routledge. From M. Jacobus (ed.) *Women Writing and Writing About Women* (1979). By permission of Routledge. From G. Pollock, 'Feminism and Modernism', from R. Parker and G. Pollock, *Framing Feminism* (1987). By permission of Unwin Hyman Ltd. From Nancy Chodorow, *Reproduction of Mothering: Psychoanalysis and the Sociology of Gender*. Copyright © 1978 The Regents of the University of California. By permission of the University of California Press. From Virginia Woolf, *A Room of One's Own* (1929). By permission of the Executors of the Virginia Woolf Estate and the Hogarth Press. From Virginia Woolf, *Three Guineas* (1938). By permission of the Executors of the Virginia Woolf Estate and the Hogarth Press. From 'The Myth of the Vaginal Orgasm'. Copyright © 1970 by Anne Koedt. The article is the introductory part of a longer article of the same title. It appeared in the publication *Notes from the Second Year: Women's Liberation*, (1970) and in *Radical Feminism* (1973) New York Times Books edited by Anne Koedt, Ellen Levine and Anita Rapone. Permission and copyright line were given by author. From Shulamith Firestone, *The Dialectic of Sex* (1970) Jonathan Cape and William Morrow Co., Inc. By permission of Laurence Pollinger Ltd. From *Toward A New Psychology of Women* by Jean Baker Miller. Copyright © 1976 by Jean Baker Miller. Reprinted by permission of Beacon Press and by kind permission of the author. From 'For the Etruscans'. Copyright © 1984 by Rachel Blau DuPlessis. Reprinted by kind permission of the author. Essay in full, in *The Pink Guitar: Writing as Feminist*

Practice (Routledge). From Mary Daly, *Gyn/Ecology: The Metaethics of Radical Feminism* (1978) Beacon Press. By kind permission of the author. From *Women, Culture and Society*, edited by Michelle Zimbalist Rosaldo and Louise Lamphere. With the permission of the publishers, Stanford University Press © 1974 by the Board of Trustees of the Leland Stanford Junior University. From *All the Women Are White, All the Men Are Black, but Some of Us Are Brave* (eds) Gloria T. Hull, Patricia Bell Scott and Barbara Smith. Copyright © 1982 by Barbara Smith and Gloria T. Hull. By kind permission of the authors. From Juliet Mitchell 'Women the Longest Revolution', *New Left Review*, N40 (1966). By permission *New Left Review*. 'Not by Degrees: Feminist Theory and Education' from *Learning Our Way* (pp. 249 and 250). Copyright © Charlotte Bunch 1983. By kind permission of the author. From *Against Our Will* by Susan Brownmiller. Copyright ©, 1975, Martin Seeker and Warburg. Reprinted by permission of Martin Secker and Warburg. From *Toward an Anthropology of Women*. Copyright © 1975 by Rayna R. Reiter. Reprinted by permission of Monthly Review Foundation. From Simone de Beauvoir, *The Second Sex*, Copyright © 1953 Jonathan Cape Ltd. By permission of publishers. From Susan Griffin *Woman and Nature* Harper & Row and *Pornography and Silence*. The Women's Press Copyright © 1975 and 1981 Susan Griffin. By kind permission of the author, Women's Press Ltd and Artillus Ltd. From *Woman's Consciousness, Man's World* by Sheila Rowbotham (Penguin Books 1973) Copyright © Sheila Rowbotham, 1973 by permission of the publishers. From Heidi Hartmann 'The Unhappy Marriage of Marxism and Feminism, from *Women and Revolution* (ed.) P. Sargent, South End Press. Copyright © 1981. Free use by kind permission of author. From Heidi Hartmann, 'Capitalism, Patriarchy and Job Segregation by Sex' from *The Signs Reader* (eds) E. Abel and E.K. Abel. Copyright © 1976 by the University of Chicago. By permission of publisher and kind permission of the author. From Catharine MacKinnon 'Feminism, Marxism, Method and the State'. Copyright © 1983 by the University of Chicago. By permission of publisher and kind permission of the author. From Joan Kelly-Gadol, 'The Social Relations of the Sexes: Methodological Implications of Women's History', from *The Signs Reader* (eds) E. Abel and E.K. Abel. Copyright © 1976 by the University of Chicago. By permission of publisher. From Carroll Smith-Rosenberg, 'The Female World of Love and Ritual: Relations Between Women in Nineteenth-Century America', from *The Signs Reader* (eds) E. Abel and E.K. Abel. Copyright © 1976 by the University of Chicago. By permission of publisher. From Hélène Cixous, 'The Laugh of the Medusa', from *The Signs Reader*, (eds) E. Abel and E.K. Abel, University of Chicago, copyright © 1976 by Hélène Cixous. By permission of publisher and kind permission of translators K. Cohen and P. Cohen. From Julia Kristeva, 'Women's Time' from *Feminist Theory: A Critique of Ideology* (eds) N.O. Keohane *et al.*, University of Chicago Copyright © 1981 by Julia Kristeva. By permission of publisher, and kind permission of author and translator Alice Jardine. From Zillah Eisenstein, 'The Sexual Politics of the New Right', from *Feminist Theory: A Critique of Ideology*, (eds) N.O. Keohane *et al.*, University of Chicago. Copyright © 1982 by the University of Chicago. By permission of publisher and by kind permission of author. From Evelyn Fox Keller, 'Feminism and Science', from *Feminist Theory: A Critique of Ideology*, (eds) N.O. Keohane *et al.* University of Chicago. Copyright © 1982 by the University of Chicago. By permission of the publisher, and kind permission of the author. From Luce Irigaray, 'When Our Lips Speak Together', *Signs*, (6)1 (1980). Copyright © 1980 by the University of Chicago. By permission of publisher. From Luce Irigaray

'This Sex Which Is Not One', *New French Feminisms* (eds) E. Marks and I. de Courtivron, Schocken Books Inc. Copyright © 1977 by Editions de Minuit. By kind permission of the translator editors. Extract from S. Ruddick: 'Preservative Love' in J. Treblicot (ed.), *Mothering: Essays in Feminist Theory*, Rowman and Attenheld. By permission of Rowman & Littlefield.

☐ Index